Gothic Sports

ANIKE HAGE

1

HAMBURG // LONDON // LOS ANGELES // TOKYO

CONTENTS

CHAPTER 1: STARTING SIGNAL   7
CHAPTER 2: THE BET   35
CHAPTER 3: BENCHWARMERS   63
CHAPTER 4: FORMATION   91
CHAPTER 5: UNIFORMS   119
CHAPTER 6: WARM-UP   147

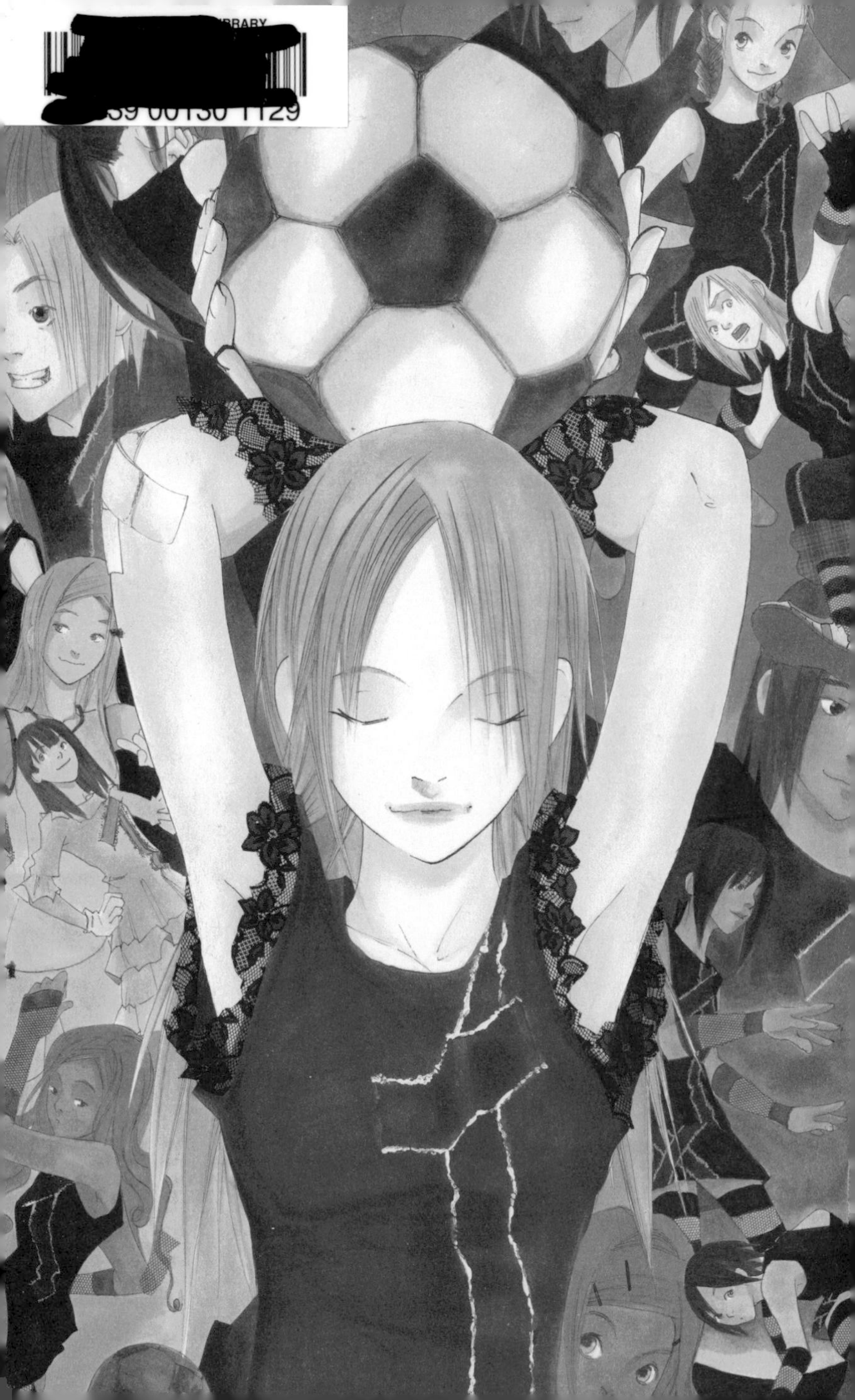

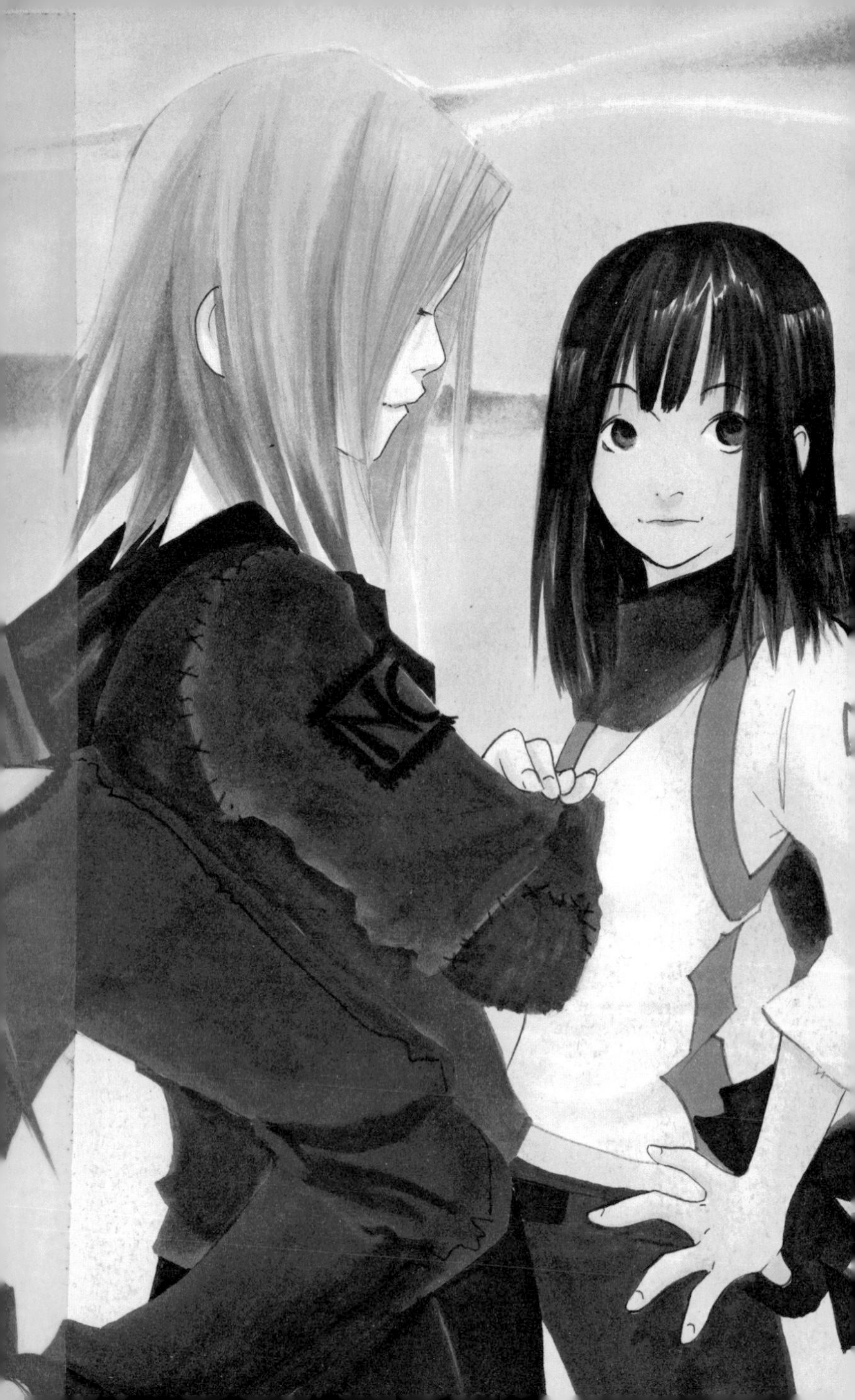

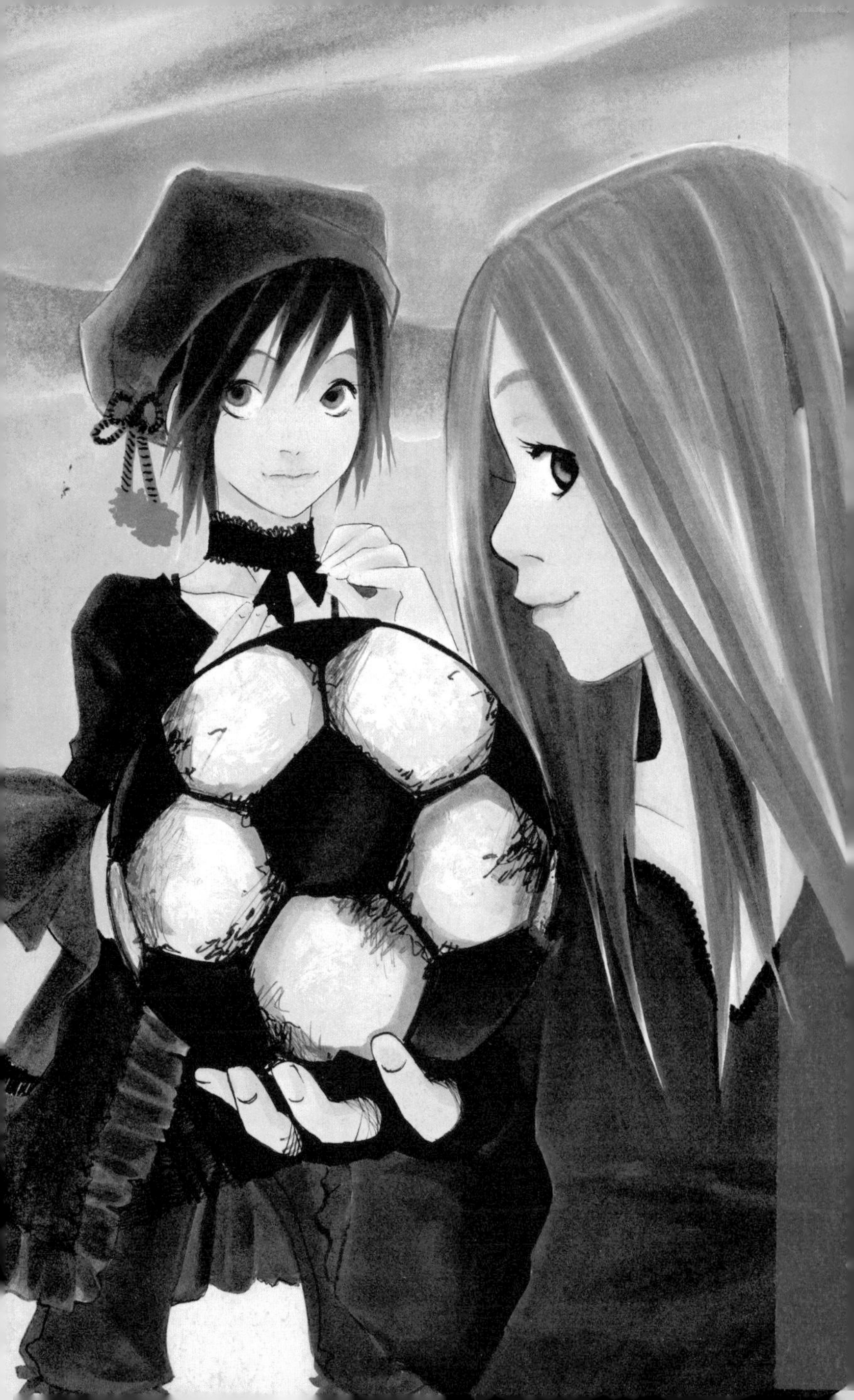

Gothic Sports Vol. 1
Created by Anike Hage

Translation - Annika Romero
English Adaptation - Erin M. Blakemore
Retouch and Lettering - Star Print Brokers
Production Artist - Mike Estacio
Cover Design - Jose Macasocol, Jr.

Editor - Carol Fox
Digital Imaging Manager - Chris Buford
Pre-Production Supervisor - Erika Terriquez
Art Director - Anne Marie Horne
Production Manager - Elisabeth Brizzi
Managing Editor - Vy Nguyen
VP of Production - Ron Klamert
Editor-in-Chief - Rob Tokar
Publisher - Mike Kiley
President and C.O.O. - John Parker
C.E.O. and Chief Creative Officer - Stuart Levy

A  Manga

TOKYOPOP Inc.
5900 Wilshire Blvd. Suite 2000
Los Angeles, CA 90036

E-mail: info@TOKYOPOP.com
Come visit us online at www.TOKYOPOP.com

ISBN: 978-1-59816-992-8

First TOKYOPOP printing: May 2007

10 9 8 7 6 5 4 3

Printed in the USA

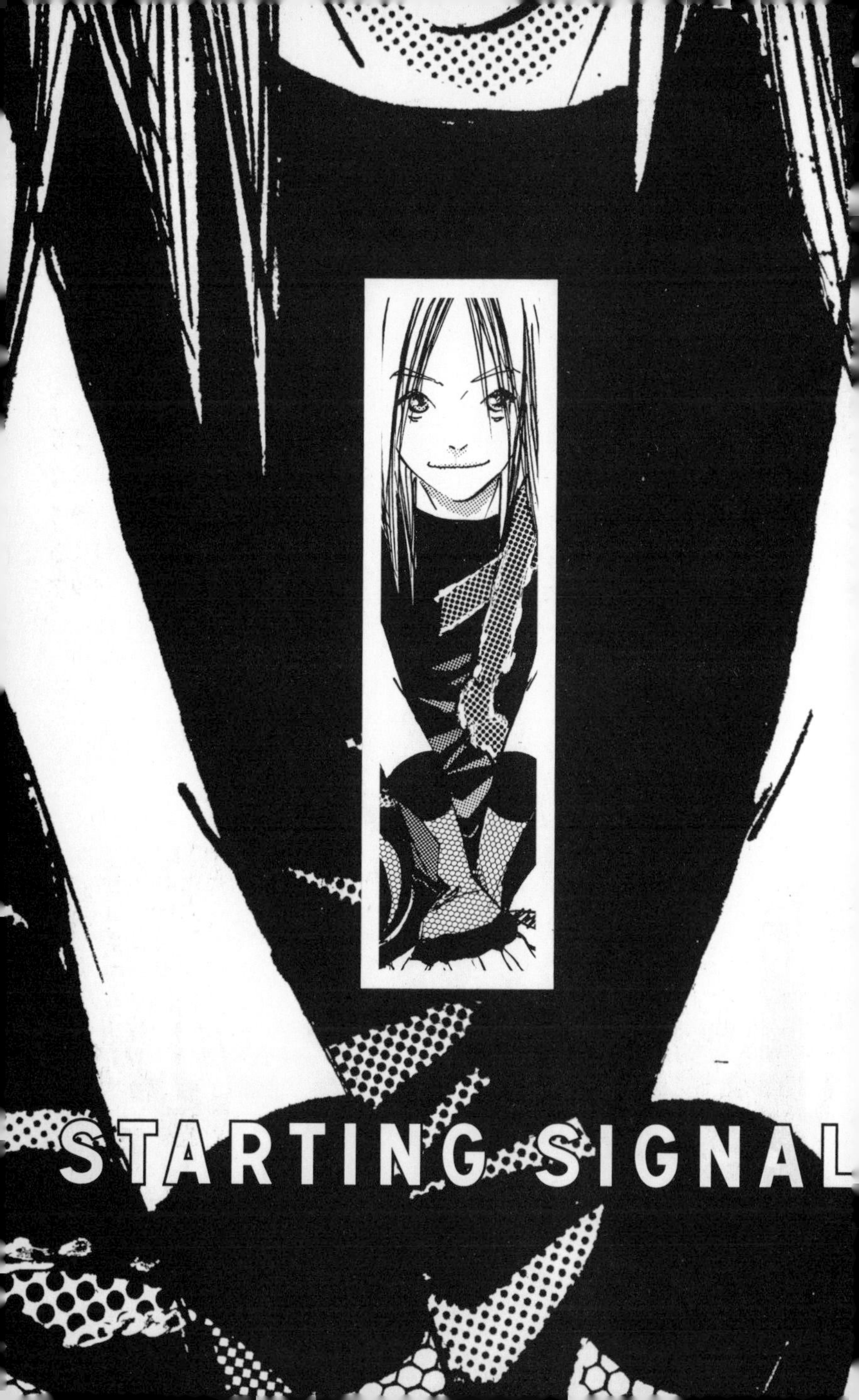
STARTING SIGNAL

ANYA

AGE: 16
HEIGHT: 1.5 M (4'11")
WEIGHT: 45 KILOS (99 LBS)
SIGN: ARIES
LIKES: APPROVAL, SPAGHETTI, SPORTS JERSEYS, BERLIN
DISLIKES: BEING WRITTEN OFF
HOBBIES: KARAOKE, SPORTS

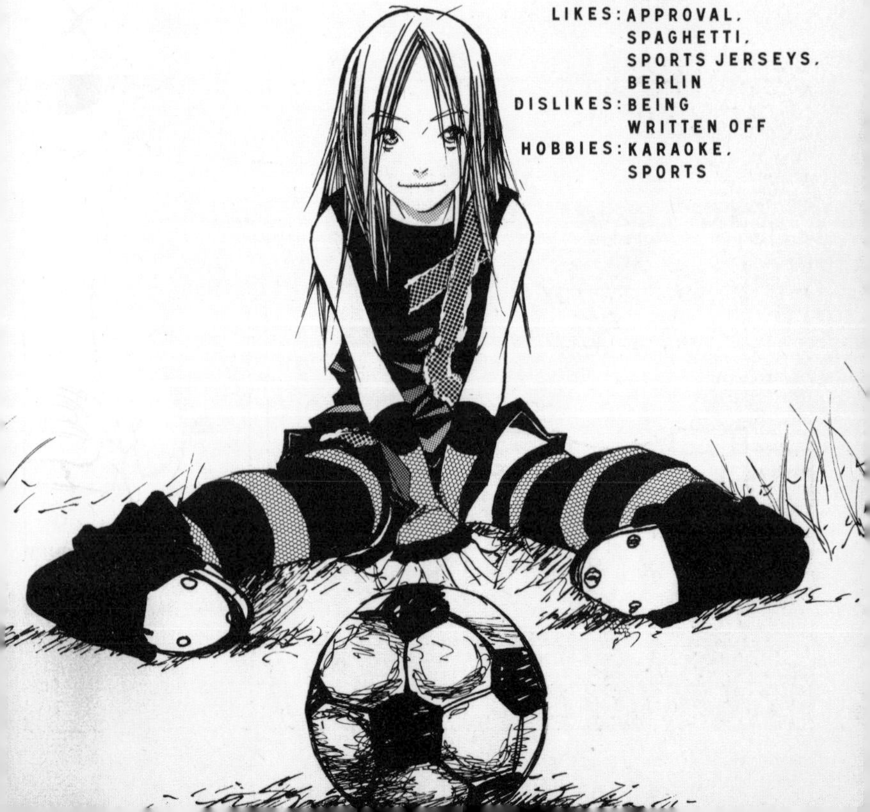

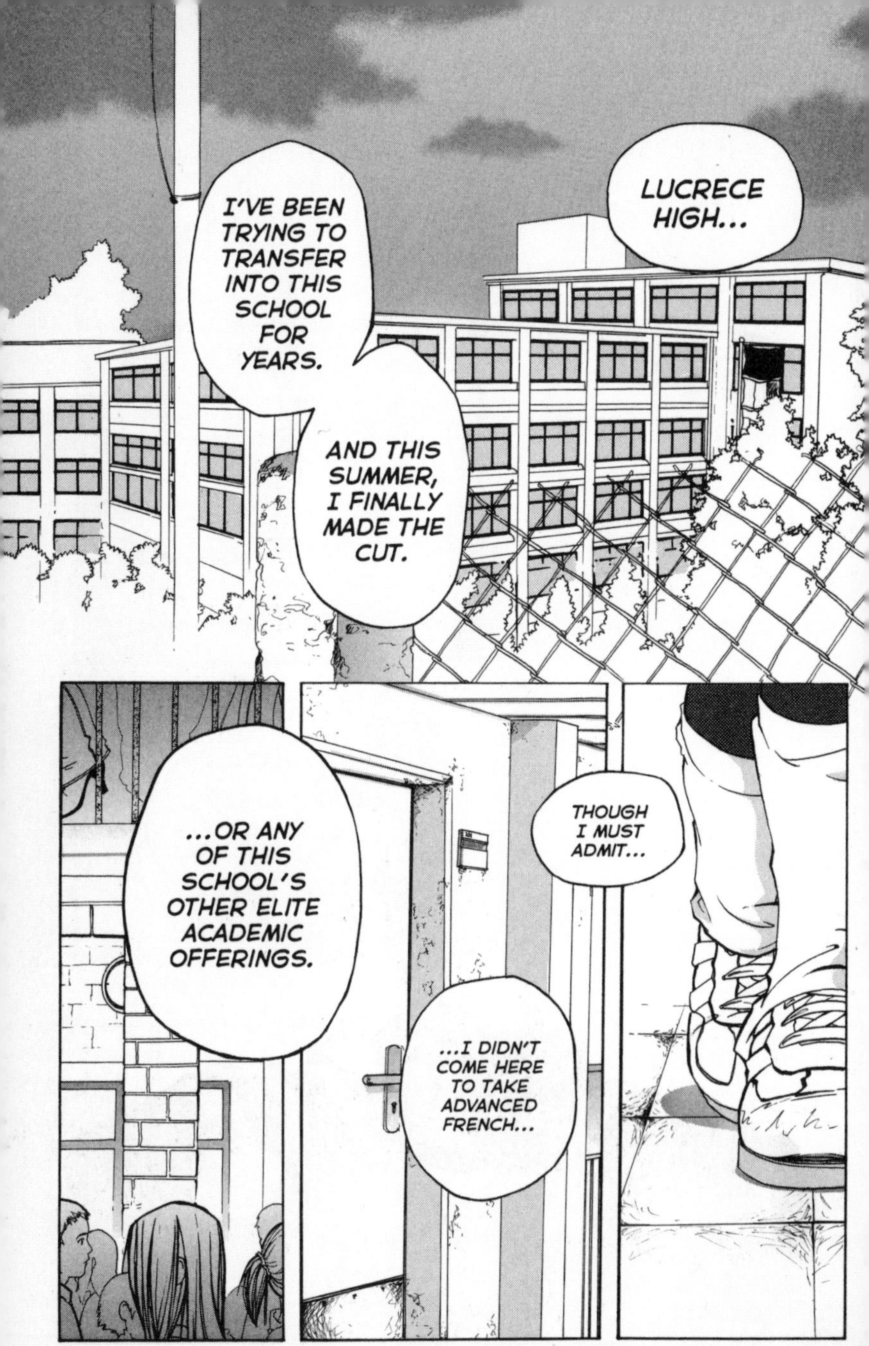
LUCRECE HIGH...
I'VE BEEN TRYING TO TRANSFER INTO THIS SCHOOL FOR YEARS.
AND THIS SUMMER, I FINALLY MADE THE CUT.
THOUGH I MUST ADMIT...
...I DIDN'T COME HERE TO TAKE ADVANCED FRENCH...
...OR ANY OF THIS SCHOOL'S OTHER ELITE ACADEMIC OFFERINGS.

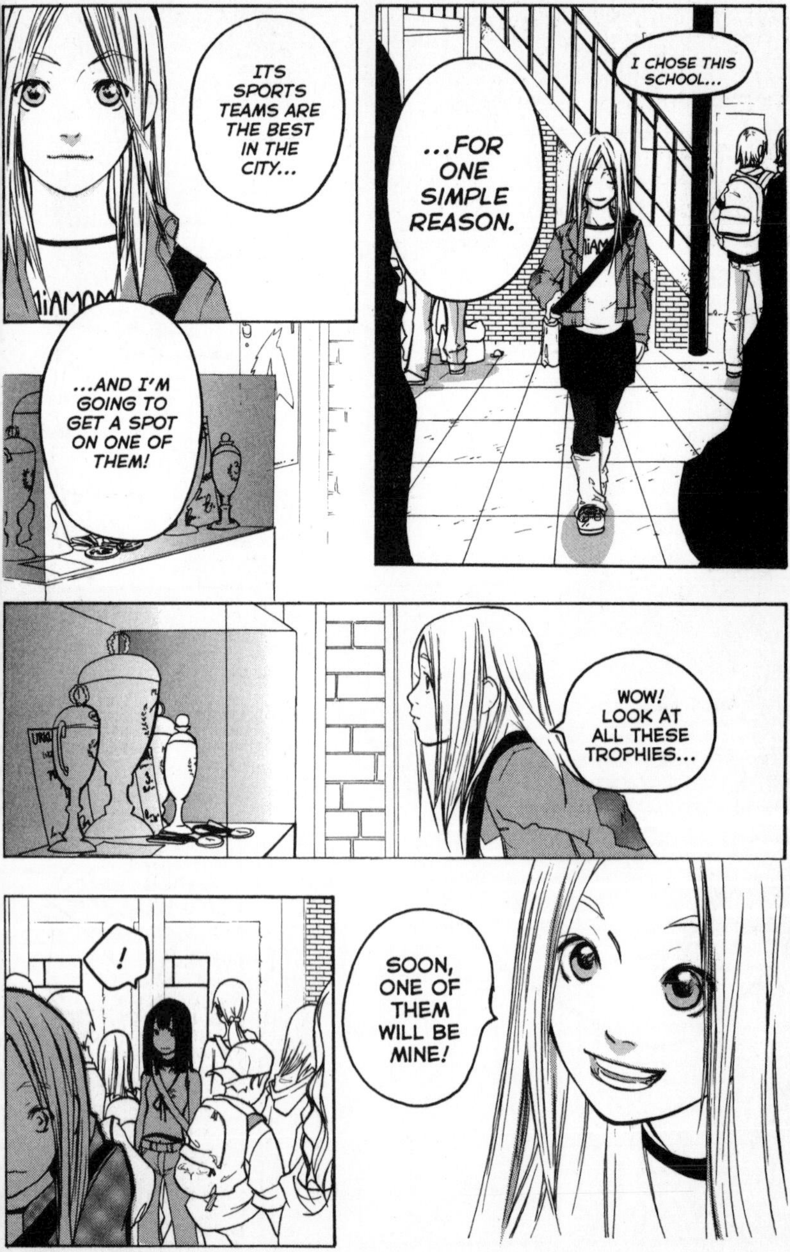
I CHOSE THIS SCHOOL...
...FOR ONE SIMPLE REASON.
ITS SPORTS TEAMS ARE THE BEST IN THE CITY...
...AND I'M GOING TO GET A SPOT ON ONE OF THEM!
WOW! LOOK AT ALL THESE TROPHIES...
SOON, ONE OF THEM WILL BE MINE!
!

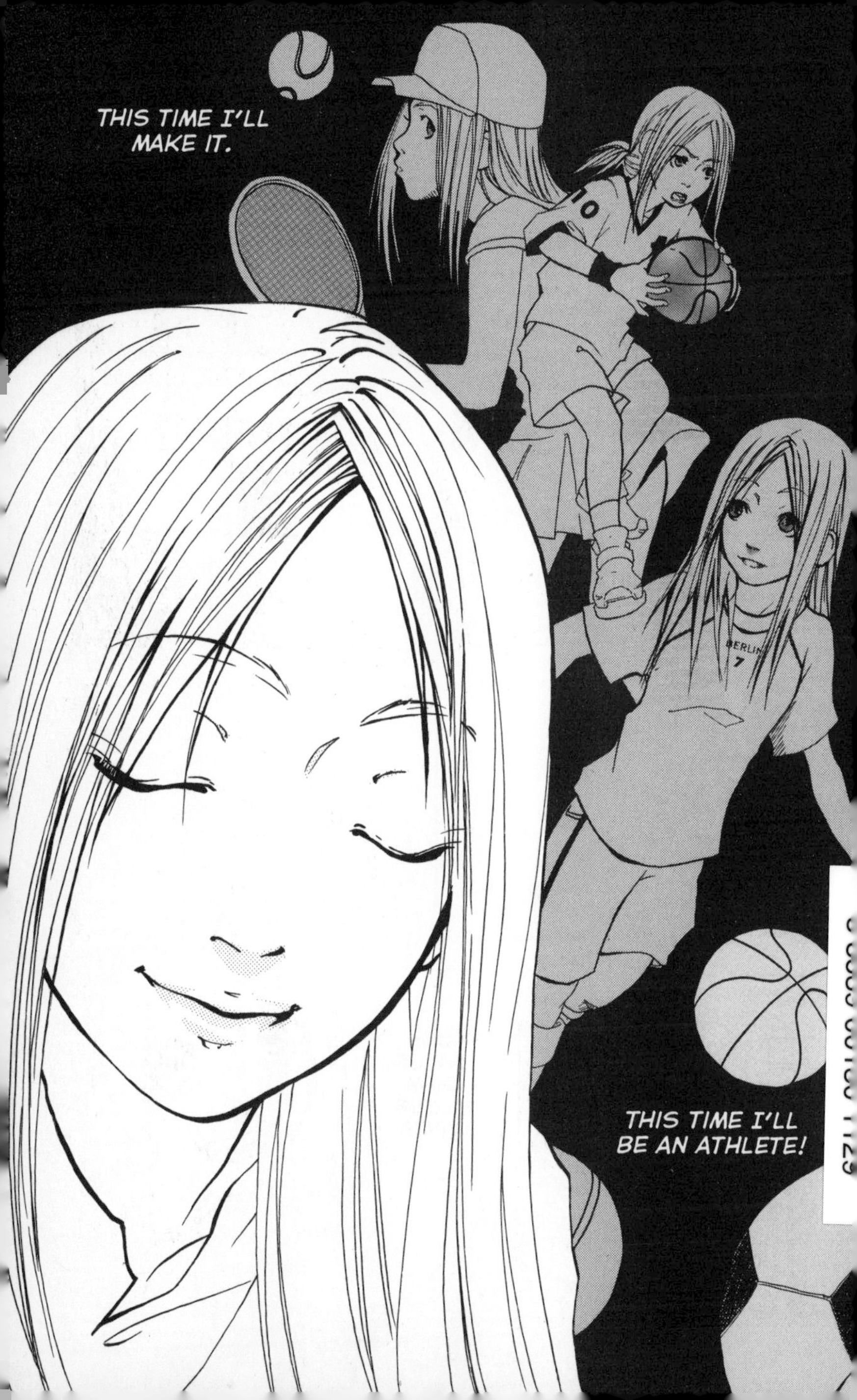
THIS TIME I'LL MAKE IT.
THIS TIME I'LL BE AN ATHLETE!

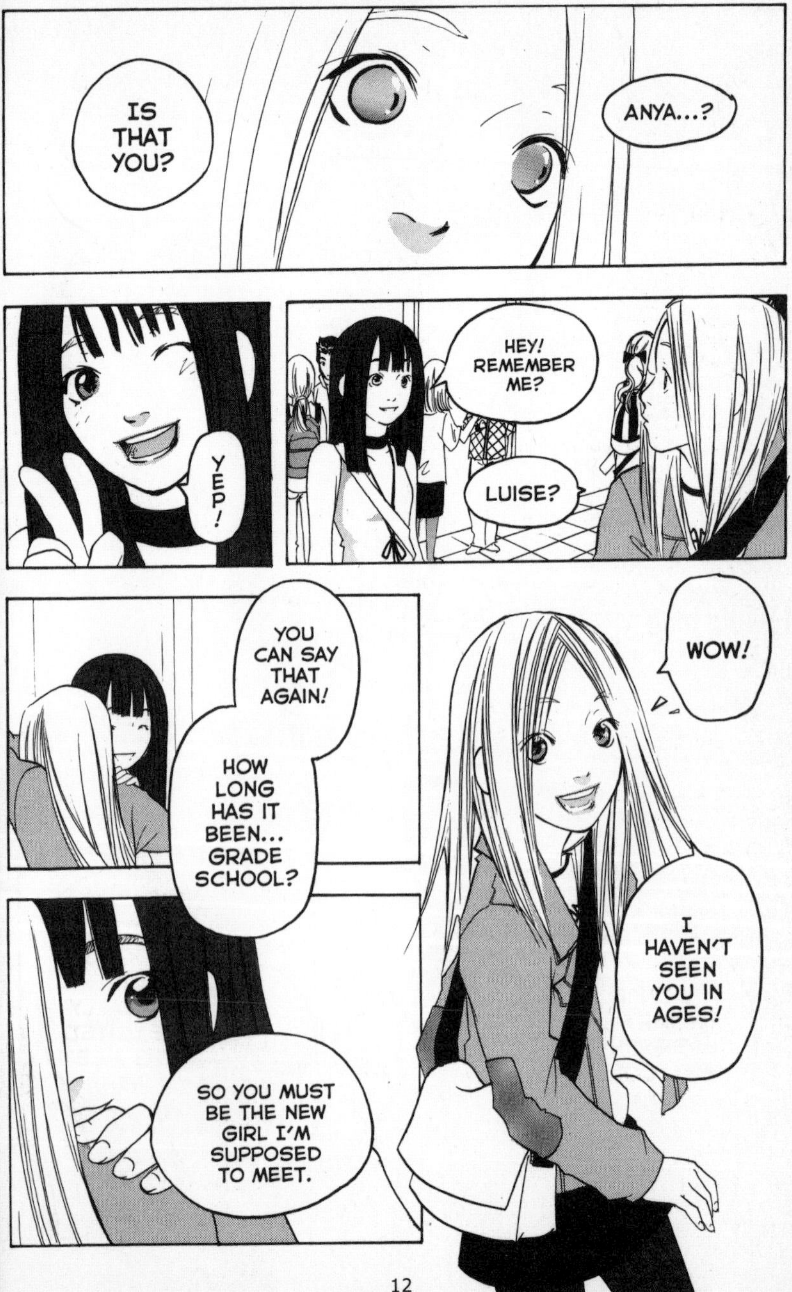
ANYA...?
IS THAT YOU?
HEY! REMEMBER ME?
LUISE?
YEP!
WOW!
I HAVEN'T SEEN YOU IN AGES!
YOU CAN SAY THAT AGAIN!
HOW LONG HAS IT BEEN... GRADE SCHOOL?
SO YOU MUST BE THE NEW GIRL I'M SUPPOSED TO MEET.

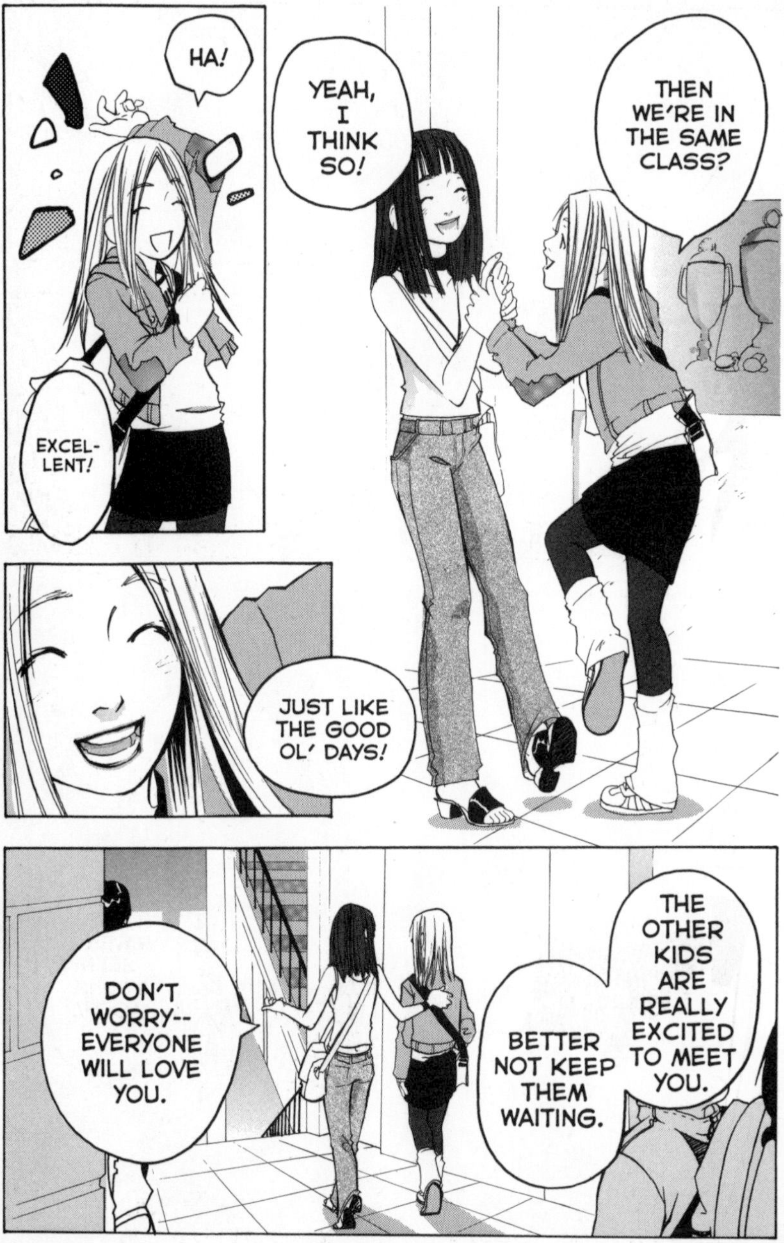
THEN WE'RE IN THE SAME CLASS?
YEAH, I THINK SO!
HA!
EXCEL-LENT!
JUST LIKE THE GOOD OL' DAYS!
THE OTHER KIDS ARE REALLY EXCITED TO MEET YOU.
BETTER NOT KEEP THEM WAITING.
DON'T WORRY-- EVERYONE WILL LOVE YOU.

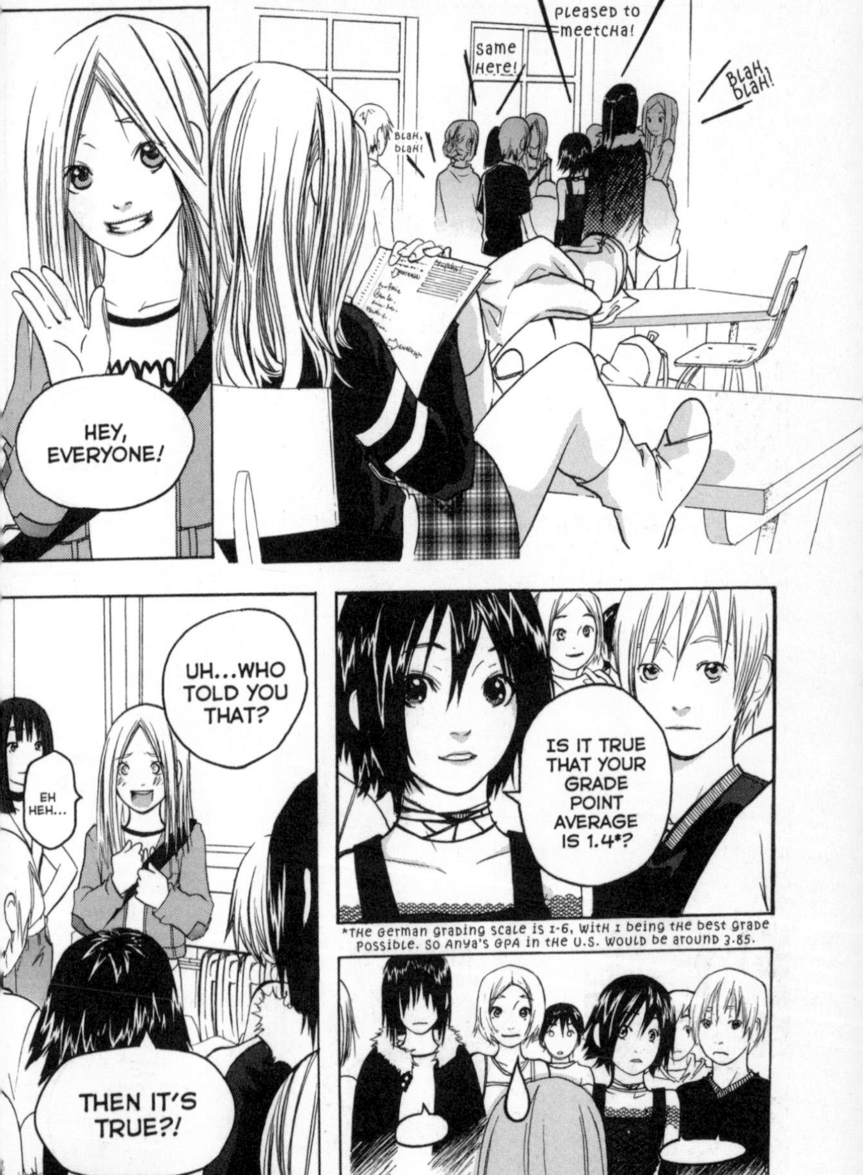
Blah blah!
Pleased to meetcha!
Same here!
Blah, blah!
HEY, EVERYONE!
IS IT TRUE THAT YOUR GRADE POINT AVERAGE IS 1.4*?
UH...WHO TOLD YOU THAT?
EH HEH...
THEN IT'S TRUE?!

*The German grading scale is 1-6, with 1 being the best grade possible. So Anya's GPA in the U.S. would be around 3.85.

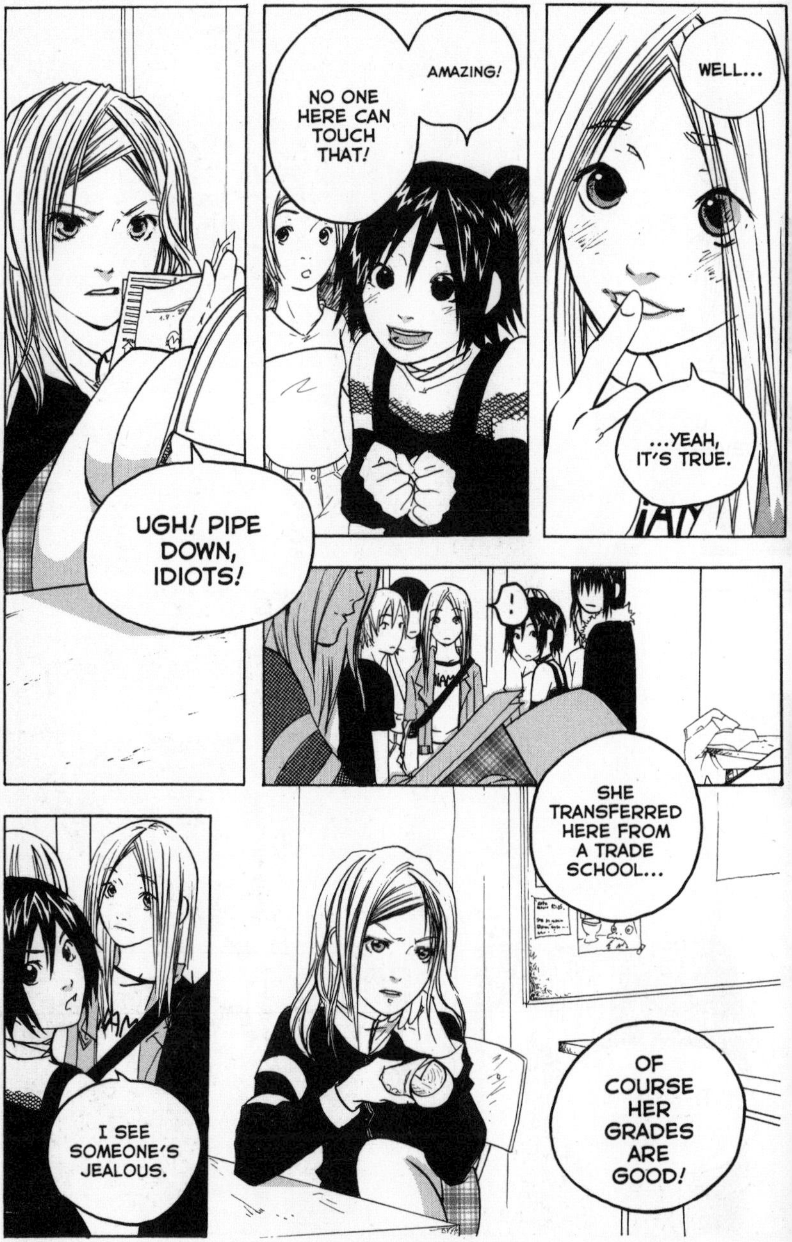
WELL...
...YEAH, IT'S TRUE.
AMAZING!
NO ONE HERE CAN TOUCH THAT!
UGH! PIPE DOWN, IDIOTS!
!
SHE TRANSFERRED HERE FROM A TRADE SCHOOL...
OF COURSE HER GRADES ARE GOOD!
I SEE SOMEONE'S JEALOUS.

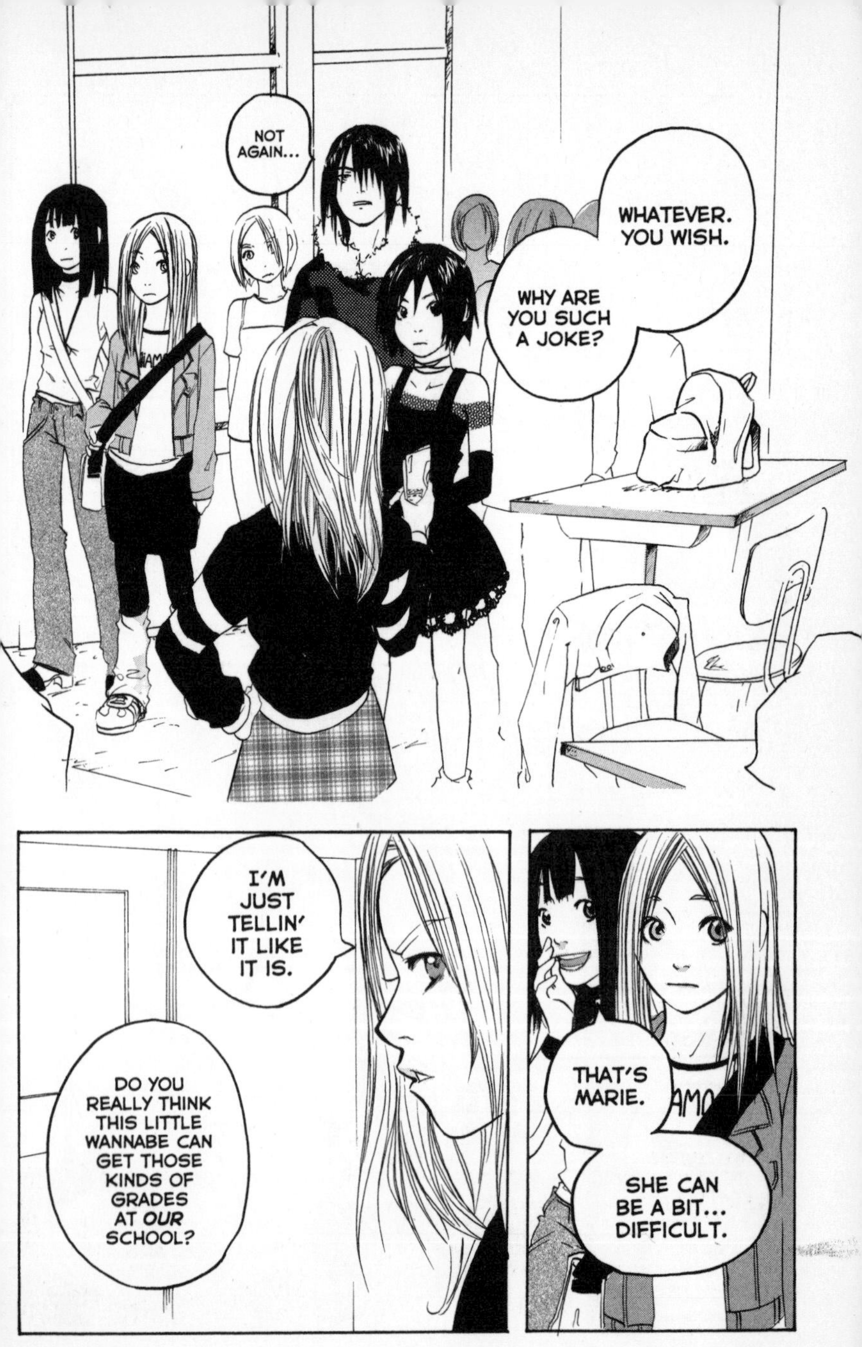
WHATEVER. YOU WISH.
WHY ARE YOU SUCH A JOKE?
NOT AGAIN...
THAT'S MARIE.
SHE CAN BE A BIT... DIFFICULT.
I'M JUST TELLIN' IT LIKE IT IS.
DO YOU REALLY THINK THIS LITTLE WANNABE CAN GET THOSE KINDS OF GRADES AT *OUR* SCHOOL?

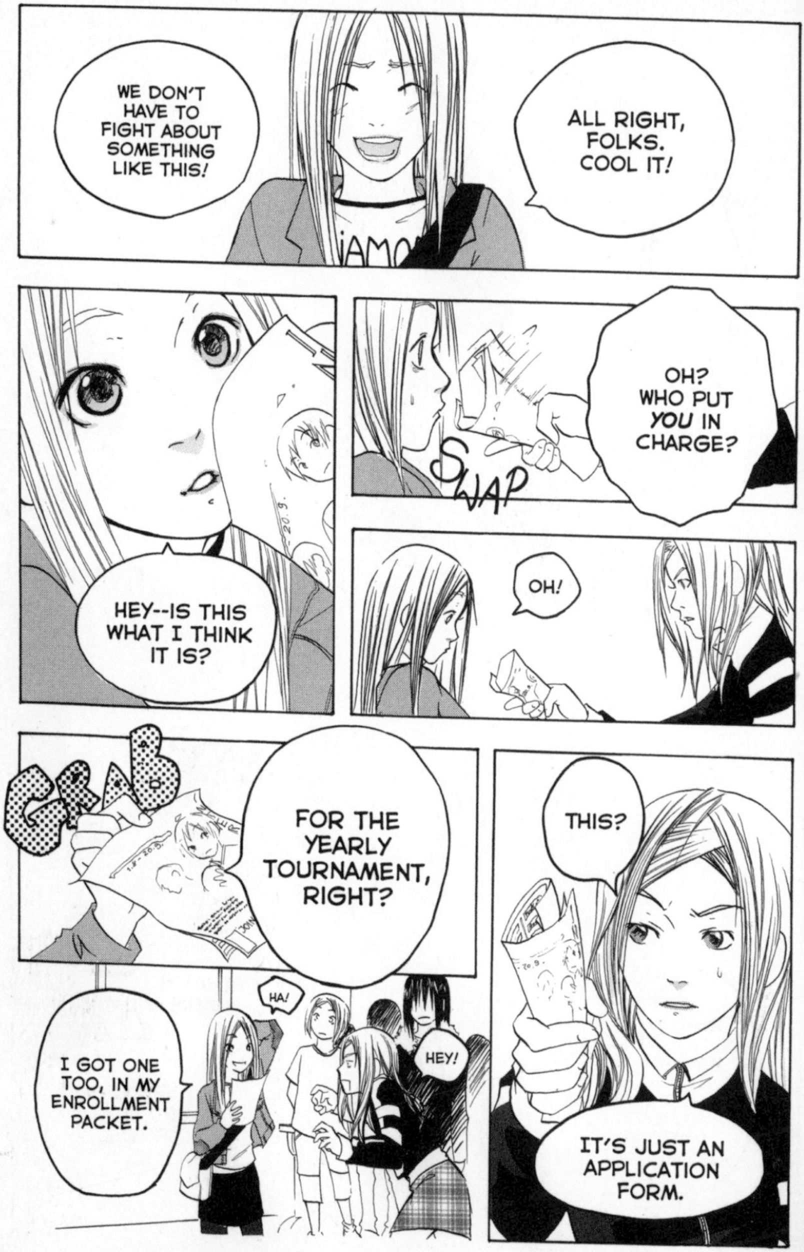
ALL RIGHT, FOLKS. COOL IT!
WE DON'T HAVE TO FIGHT ABOUT SOMETHING LIKE THIS!
OH? WHO PUT *YOU* IN CHARGE?
SWAP
OH!
HEY--IS THIS WHAT I THINK IT IS?
THIS?
IT'S JUST AN APPLICATION FORM.
GRAB
FOR THE YEARLY TOURNAMENT, RIGHT?
HA!
HEY!
I GOT ONE TOO, IN MY ENROLLMENT PACKET.

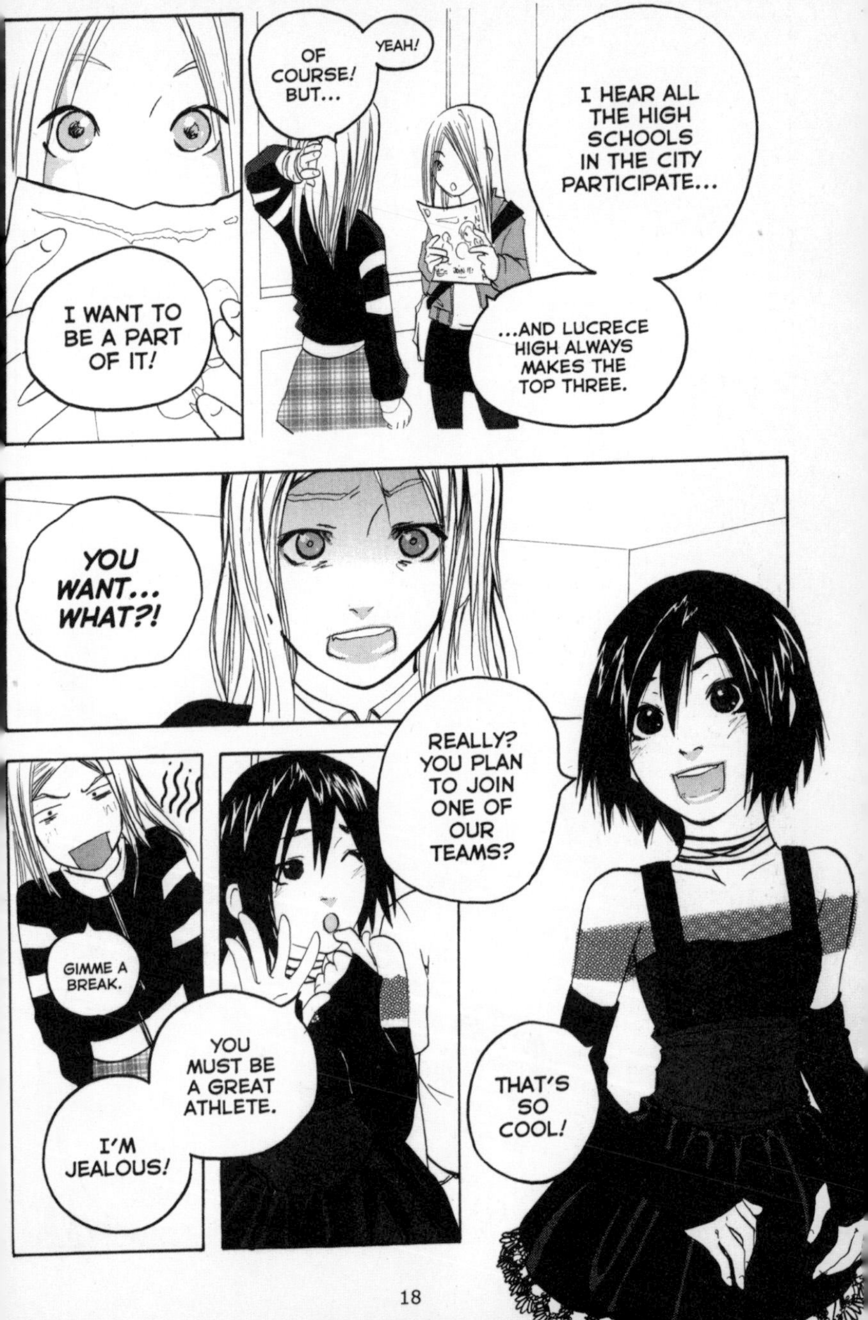
I HEAR ALL THE HIGH SCHOOLS IN THE CITY PARTICIPATE...
...AND LUCRECE HIGH ALWAYS MAKES THE TOP THREE.
YEAH!
OF COURSE! BUT...
I WANT TO BE A PART OF IT!
YOU WANT... WHAT?!
REALLY? YOU PLAN TO JOIN ONE OF OUR TEAMS?
THAT'S SO COOL!
YOU MUST BE A GREAT ATHLETE.
I'M JEALOUS!
GIMME A BREAK.

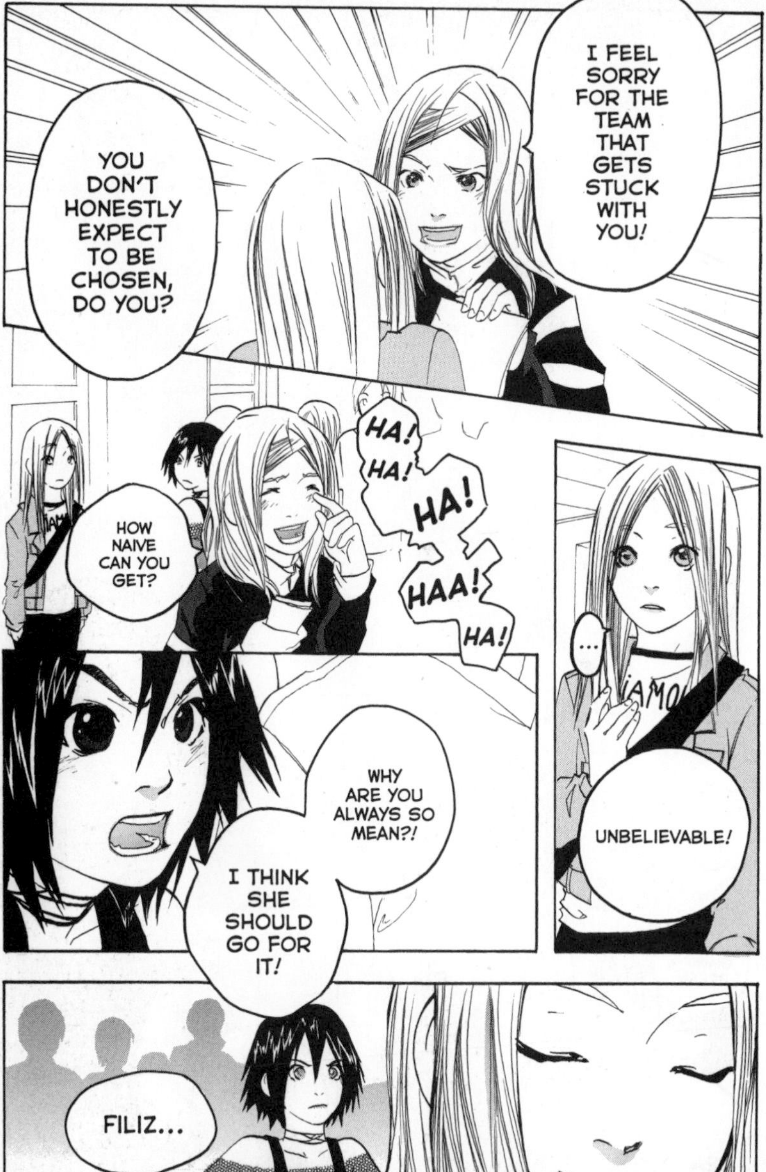
YOU DON'T HONESTLY EXPECT TO BE CHOSEN, DO YOU?
I FEEL SORRY FOR THE TEAM THAT GETS STUCK WITH YOU!
HOW NAIVE CAN YOU GET?
HA! HA! HA! HAA! HA!
...
UNBELIEVABLE!
WHY ARE YOU ALWAYS SO MEAN?!
I THINK SHE SHOULD GO FOR IT!
FILIZ...

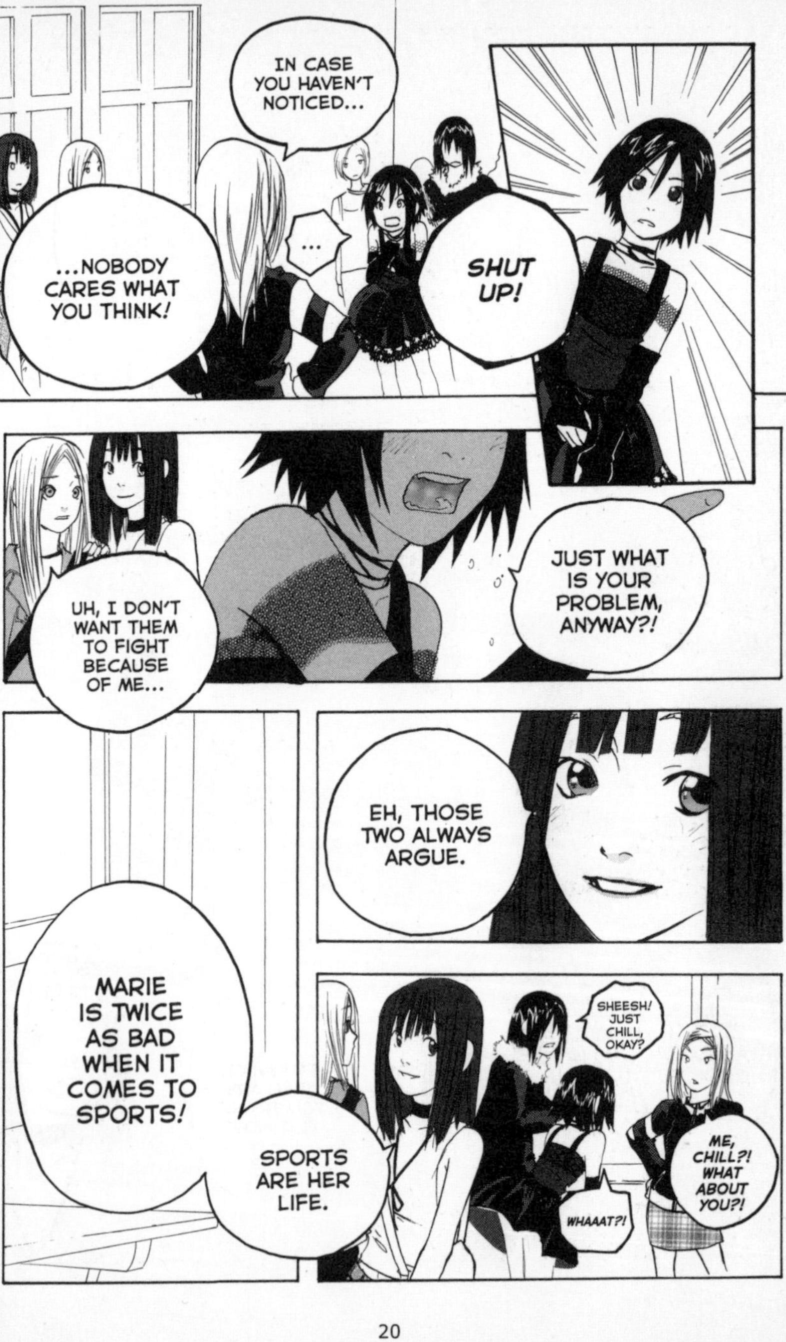
SHUT UP!
IN CASE YOU HAVEN'T NOTICED...
...NOBODY CARES WHAT YOU THINK!
...
JUST WHAT IS YOUR PROBLEM, ANYWAY?!
UH, I DON'T WANT THEM TO FIGHT BECAUSE OF ME...
EH, THOSE TWO ALWAYS ARGUE.
MARIE IS TWICE AS BAD WHEN IT COMES TO SPORTS!
SPORTS ARE HER LIFE.
SHEESH! JUST CHILL, OKAY?
ME, CHILL?! WHAT ABOUT YOU?!
WHAAAT?!

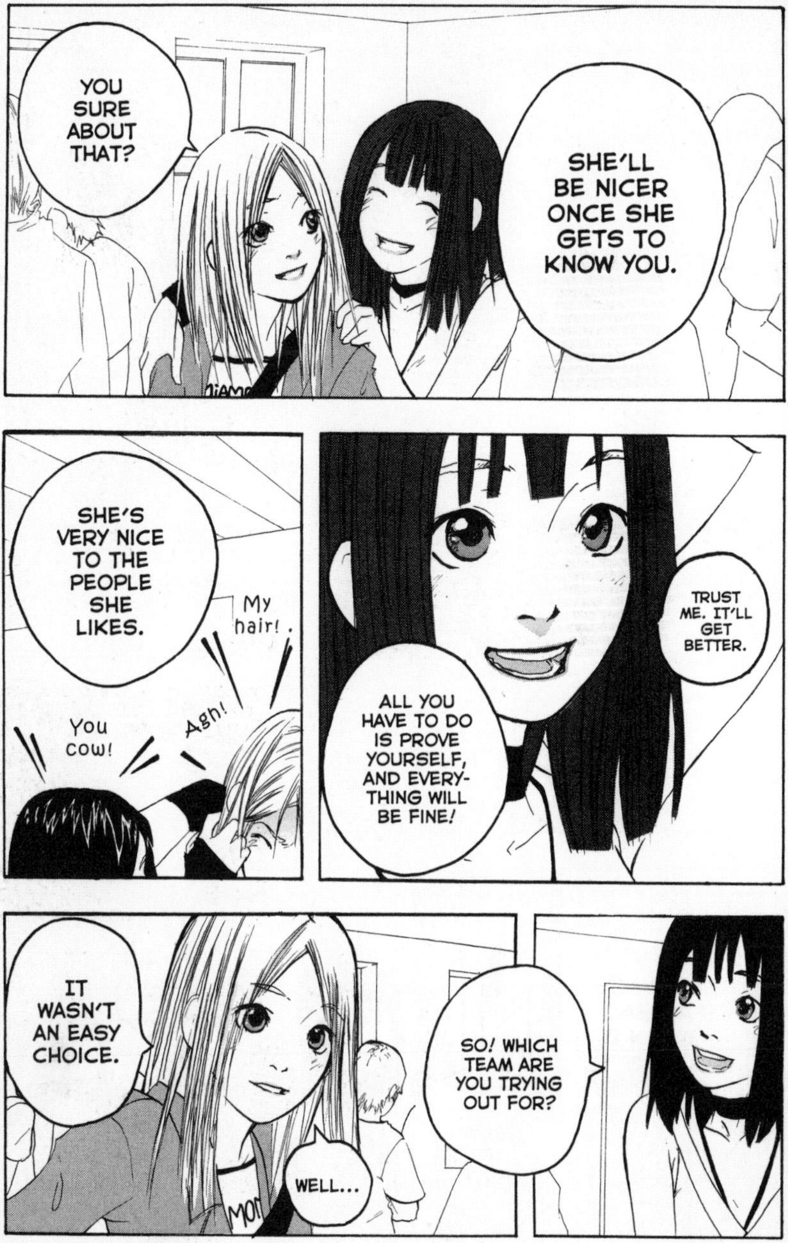
SHE'LL BE NICER ONCE SHE GETS TO KNOW YOU.
YOU SURE ABOUT THAT?
TRUST ME. IT'LL GET BETTER.
ALL YOU HAVE TO DO IS PROVE YOURSELF, AND EVERY-THING WILL BE FINE!
SHE'S VERY NICE TO THE PEOPLE SHE LIKES.
My hair!
Agh!
You cow!
SO! WHICH TEAM ARE YOU TRYING OUT FOR?
WELL...
IT WASN'T AN EASY CHOICE.

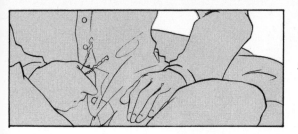

I STAYED UP ALL NIGHT THINKING ABOUT IT.

SOCCER OR BASKETBALL...

I'M NOT MUCH BETTER AT ONE THAN THE OTHER...

BASKETBALL!

...SO I DECIDED BY DRAWING LOTS!

WHAT? WHAT'S THE MATTER?

URK!

ER...

YUP!

BASKET-BALL?!

22

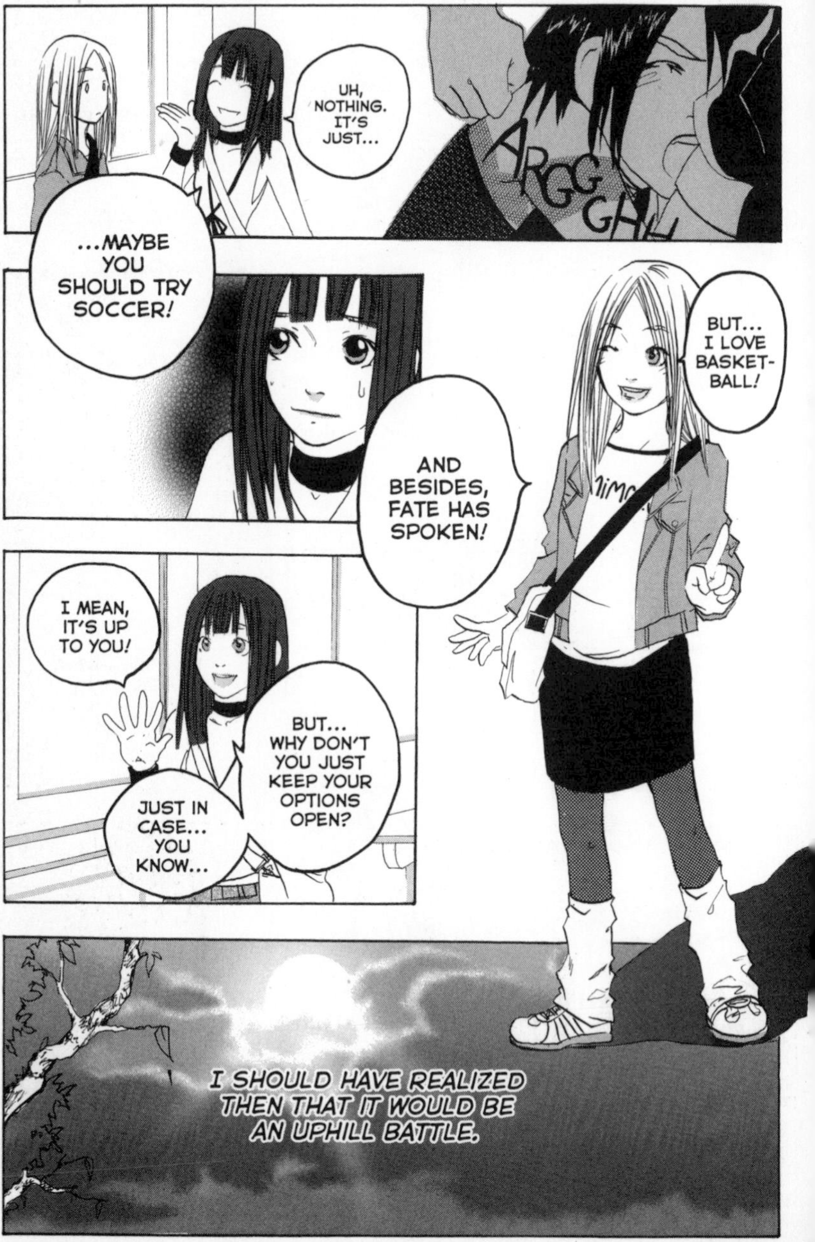
ARGGGHH
UH, NOTHING. IT'S JUST...
...MAYBE YOU SHOULD TRY SOCCER!
BUT... I LOVE BASKET-BALL!
AND BESIDES, FATE HAS SPOKEN!
I MEAN, IT'S UP TO YOU!
BUT... WHY DON'T YOU JUST KEEP YOUR OPTIONS OPEN?
JUST IN CASE... YOU KNOW...
I SHOULD HAVE REALIZED THEN THAT IT WOULD BE AN UPHILL BATTLE.

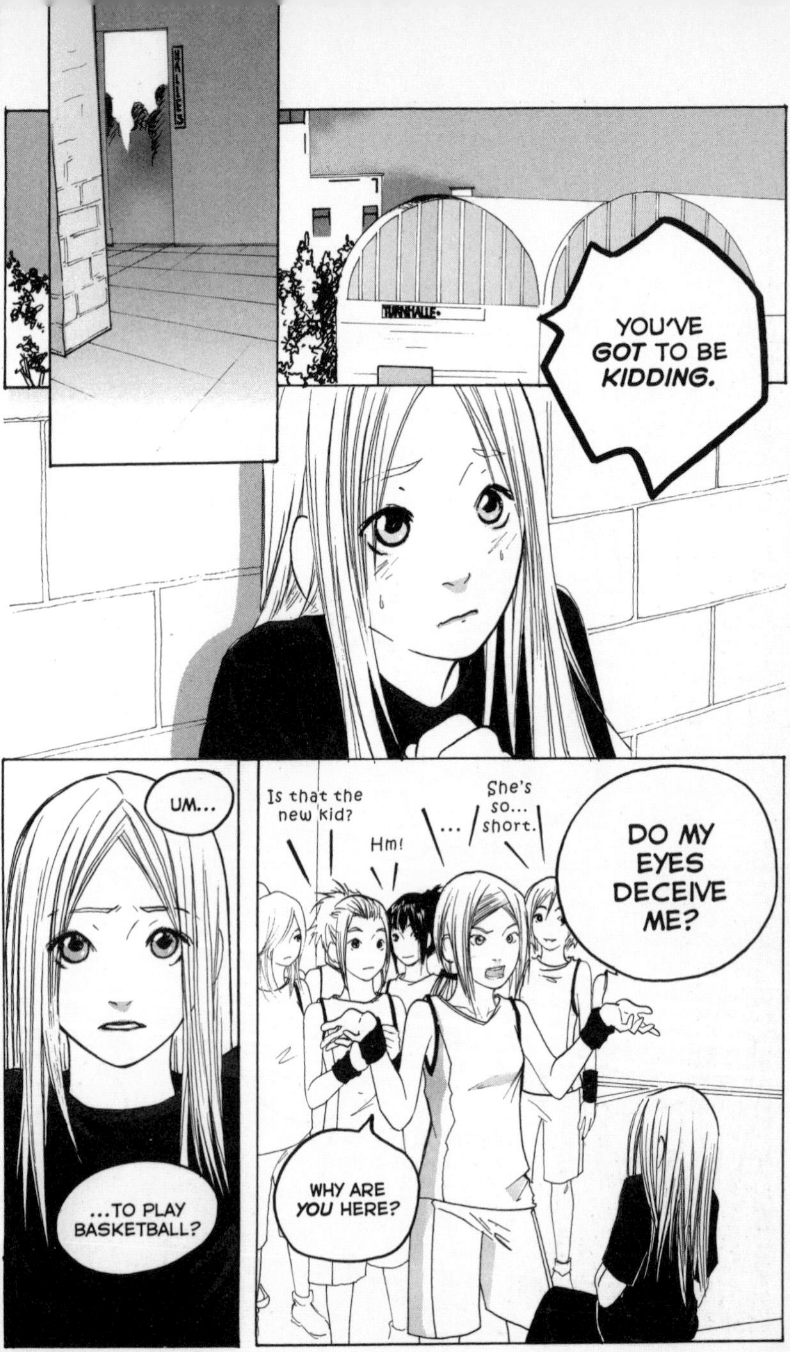

TURNHALLE
YOU'VE GOT TO BE KIDDING.
DO MY EYES DECEIVE ME?
She's so... short.
...
Hm!
Is that the new kid?
WHY ARE YOU HERE?
UM...
...TO PLAY BASKETBALL?

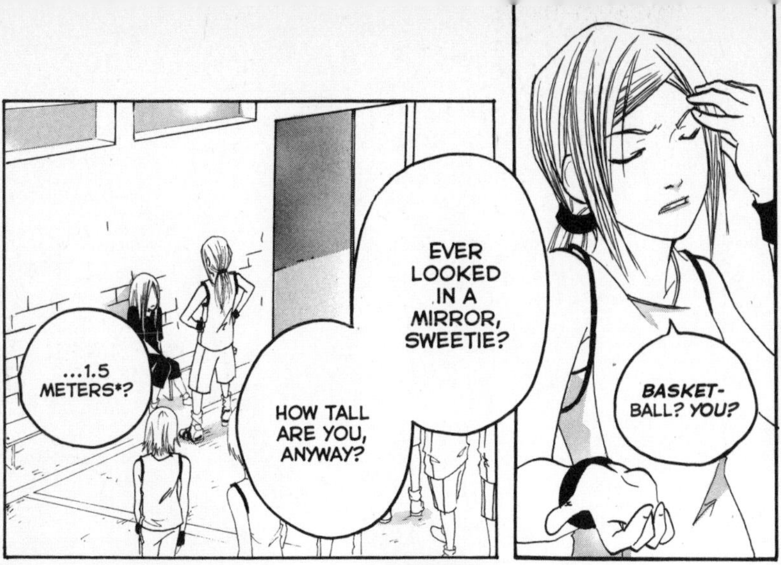
BASKET-BALL? YOU?
EVER LOOKED IN A MIRROR, SWEETIE?
HOW TALL ARE YOU, ANYWAY?
...1.5 METERS*?

*Four feet, eleven inches!

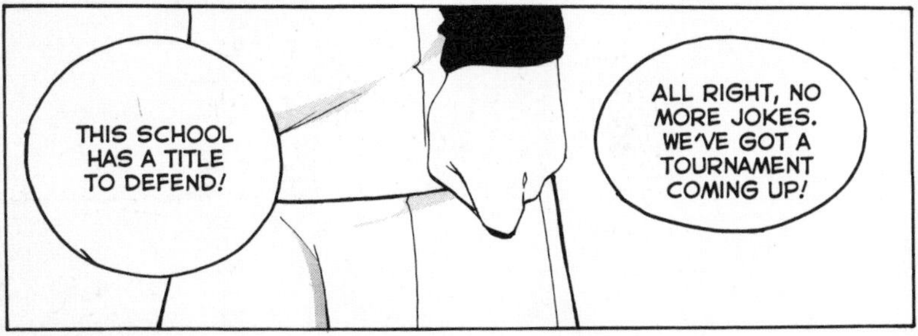
ALL RIGHT, NO MORE JOKES. WE'VE GOT A TOURNAMENT COMING UP!
THIS SCHOOL HAS A TITLE TO DEFEND!

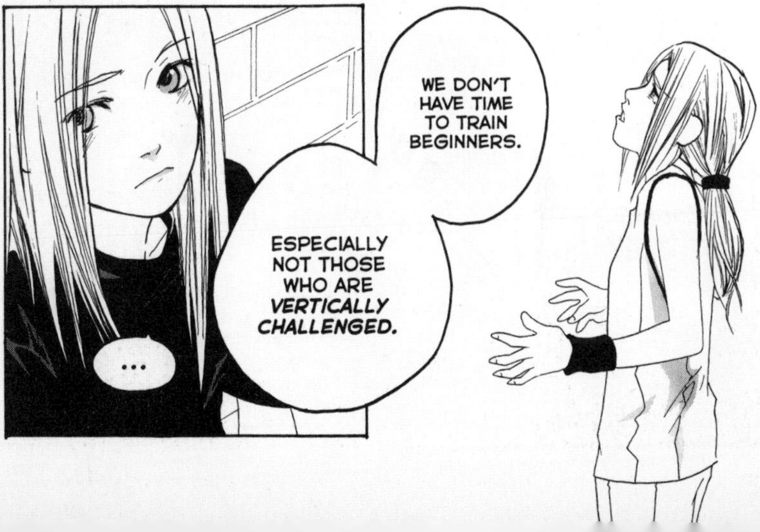
WE DON'T HAVE TIME TO TRAIN BEGINNERS.
ESPECIALLY NOT THOSE WHO ARE *VERTICALLY CHALLENGED.*
...

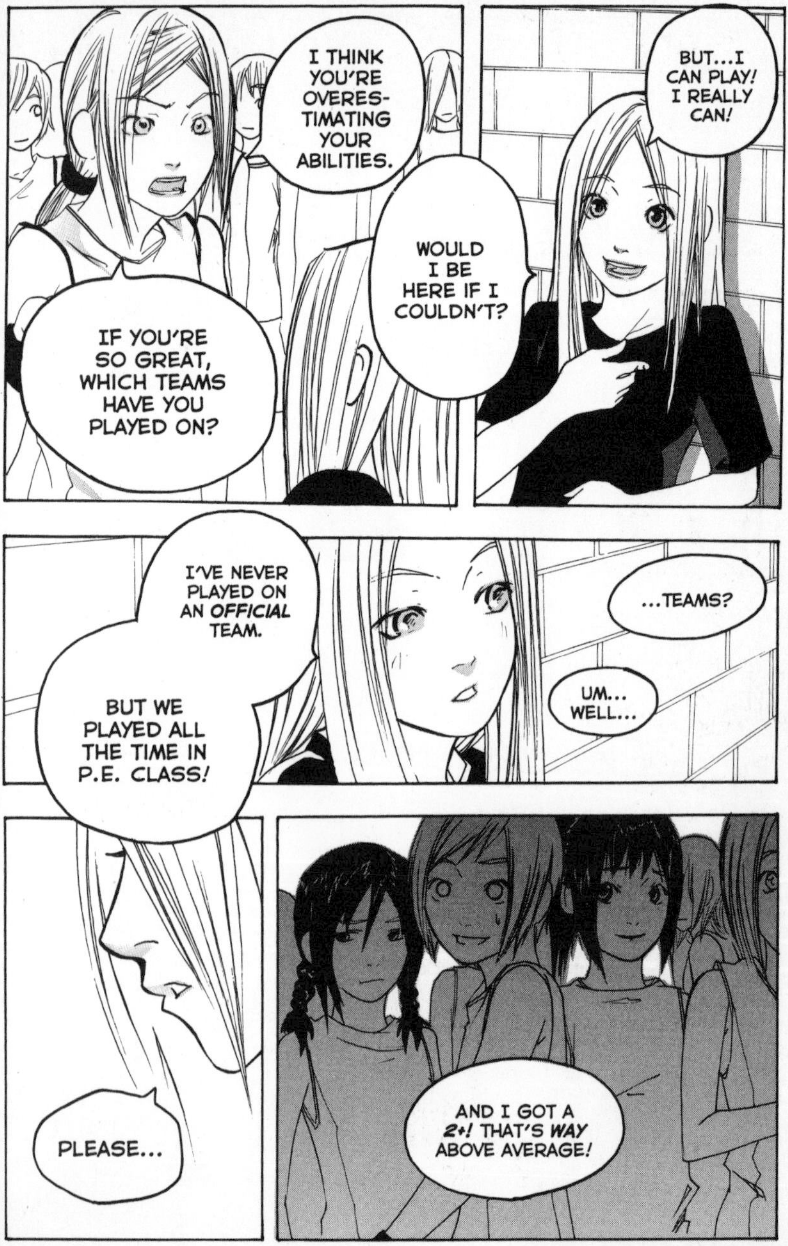
BUT...I CAN PLAY! I REALLY CAN!
WOULD I BE HERE IF I COULDN'T?
I THINK YOU'RE OVERES-TIMATING YOUR ABILITIES.
IF YOU'RE SO GREAT, WHICH TEAMS HAVE YOU PLAYED ON?
...TEAMS?
UM... WELL...
I'VE NEVER PLAYED ON AN *OFFICIAL* TEAM.
BUT WE PLAYED ALL THE TIME IN P.E. CLASS!
AND I GOT A *2+!* THAT'S *WAY* ABOVE AVERAGE!
PLEASE...

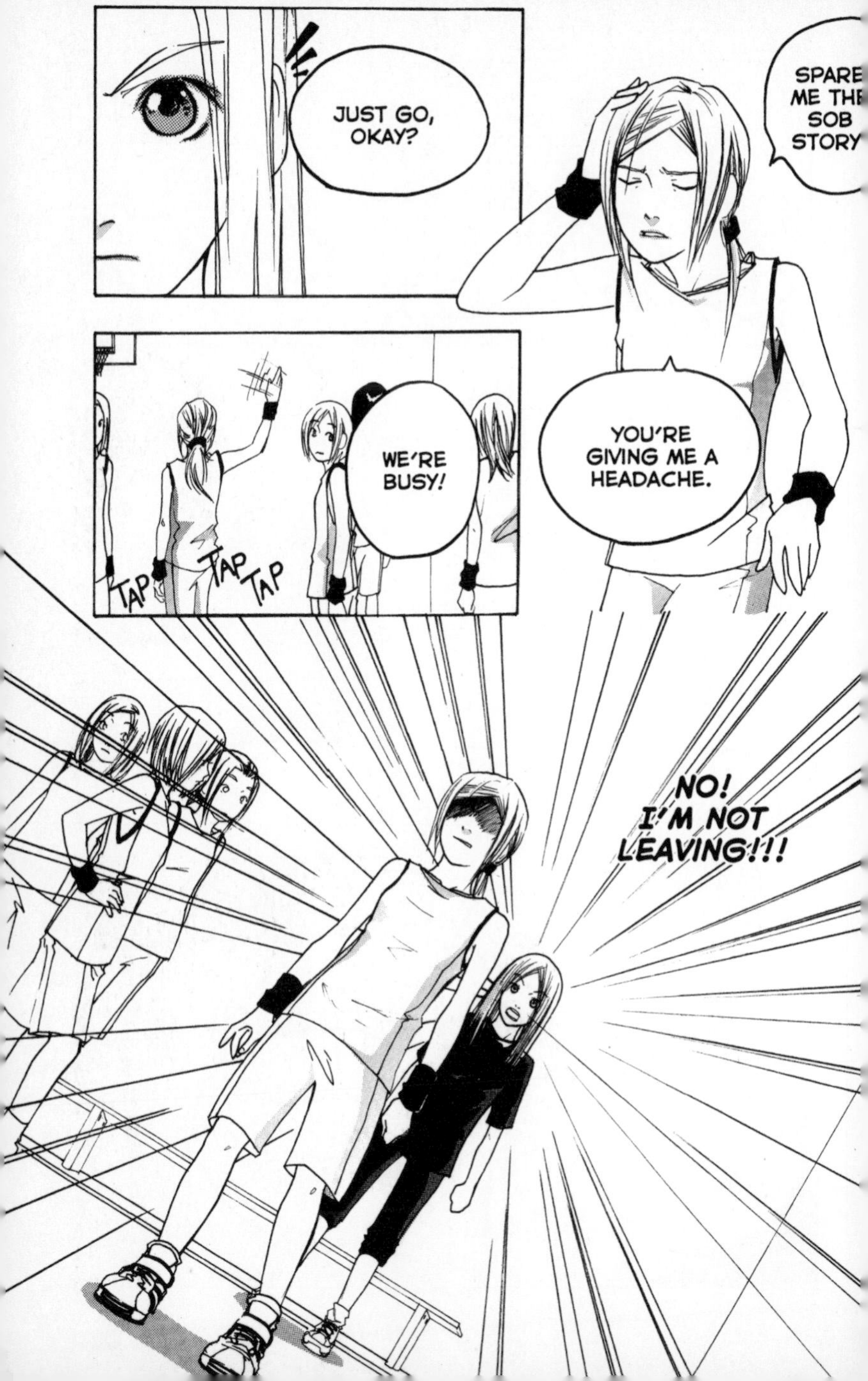
SPARE ME THE SOB STORY
YOU'RE GIVING ME A HEADACHE.
JUST GO, OKAY?
WE'RE BUSY!
TAP TAP TAP
NO! I'M NOT LEAVING!!!

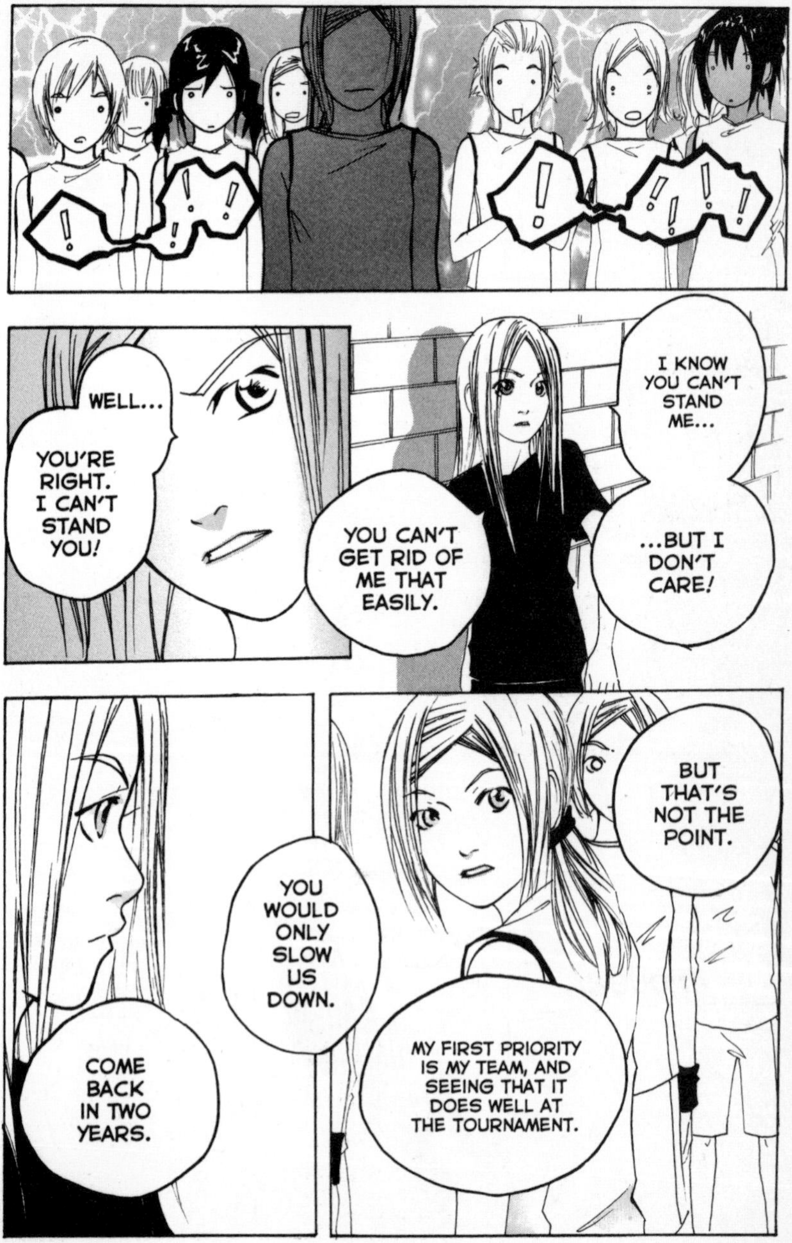

! ! ! !
!
! ! !
!
I KNOW YOU CAN'T STAND ME...
...BUT I DON'T CARE!
YOU CAN'T GET RID OF ME THAT EASILY.
WELL...
YOU'RE RIGHT. I CAN'T STAND YOU!
BUT THAT'S NOT THE POINT.
MY FIRST PRIORITY IS MY TEAM, AND SEEING THAT IT DOES WELL AT THE TOURNAMENT.
YOU WOULD ONLY SLOW US DOWN.
COME BACK IN TWO YEARS.

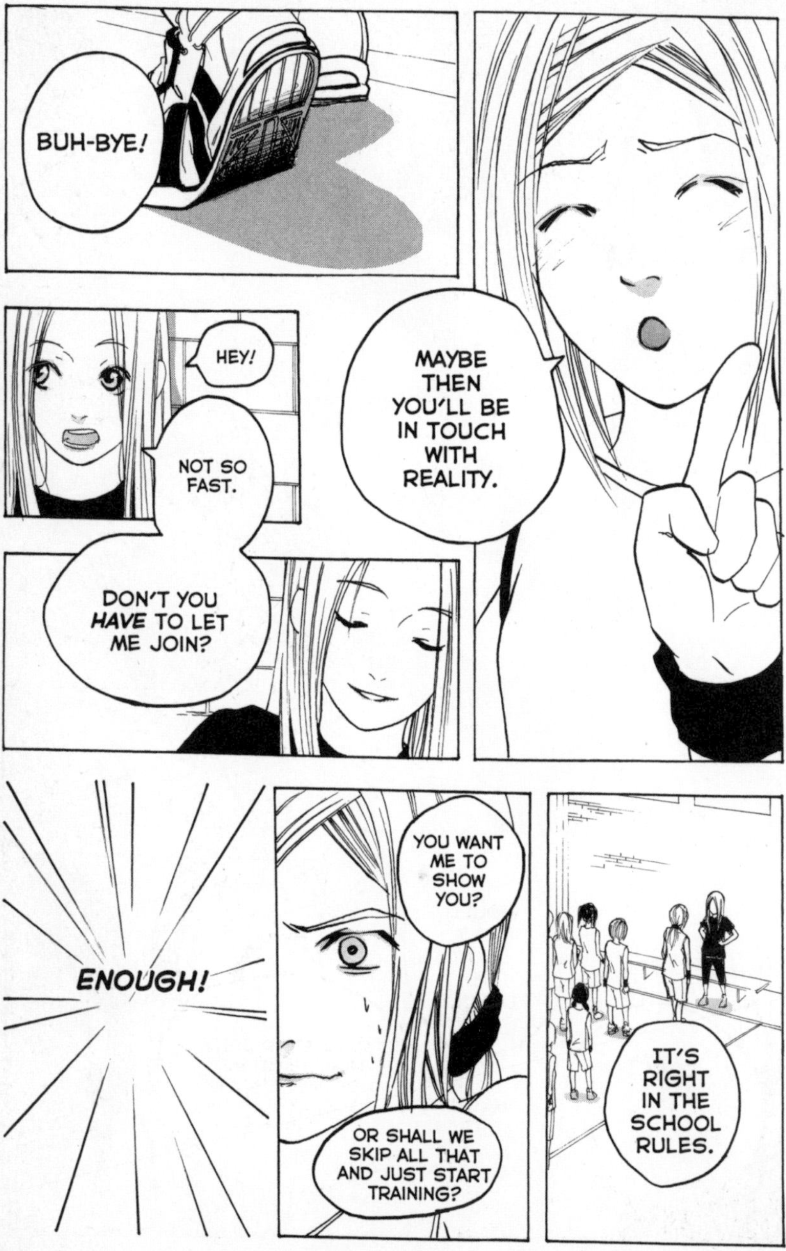
MAYBE THEN YOU'LL BE IN TOUCH WITH REALITY.
BUH-BYE!
HEY!
NOT SO FAST.
DON'T YOU *HAVE* TO LET ME JOIN?
IT'S RIGHT IN THE SCHOOL RULES.
YOU WANT ME TO SHOW YOU?
OR SHALL WE SKIP ALL THAT AND JUST START TRAINING?
ENOUGH!

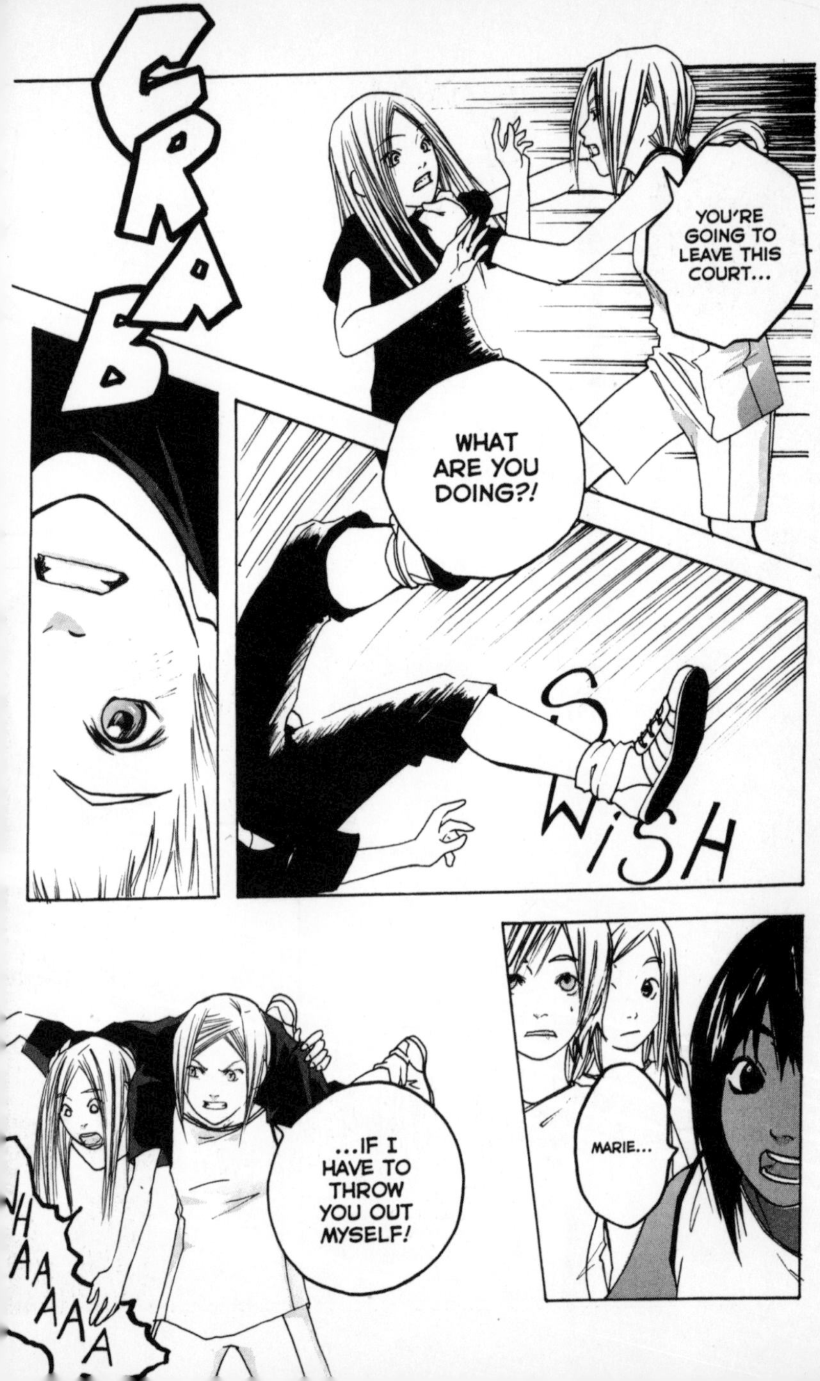
YOU'RE GOING TO LEAVE THIS COURT...
GRAB
WHAT ARE YOU DOING?!
SWISH
MARIE...
...IF I HAVE TO THROW YOU OUT MYSELF!
HAAAAAA

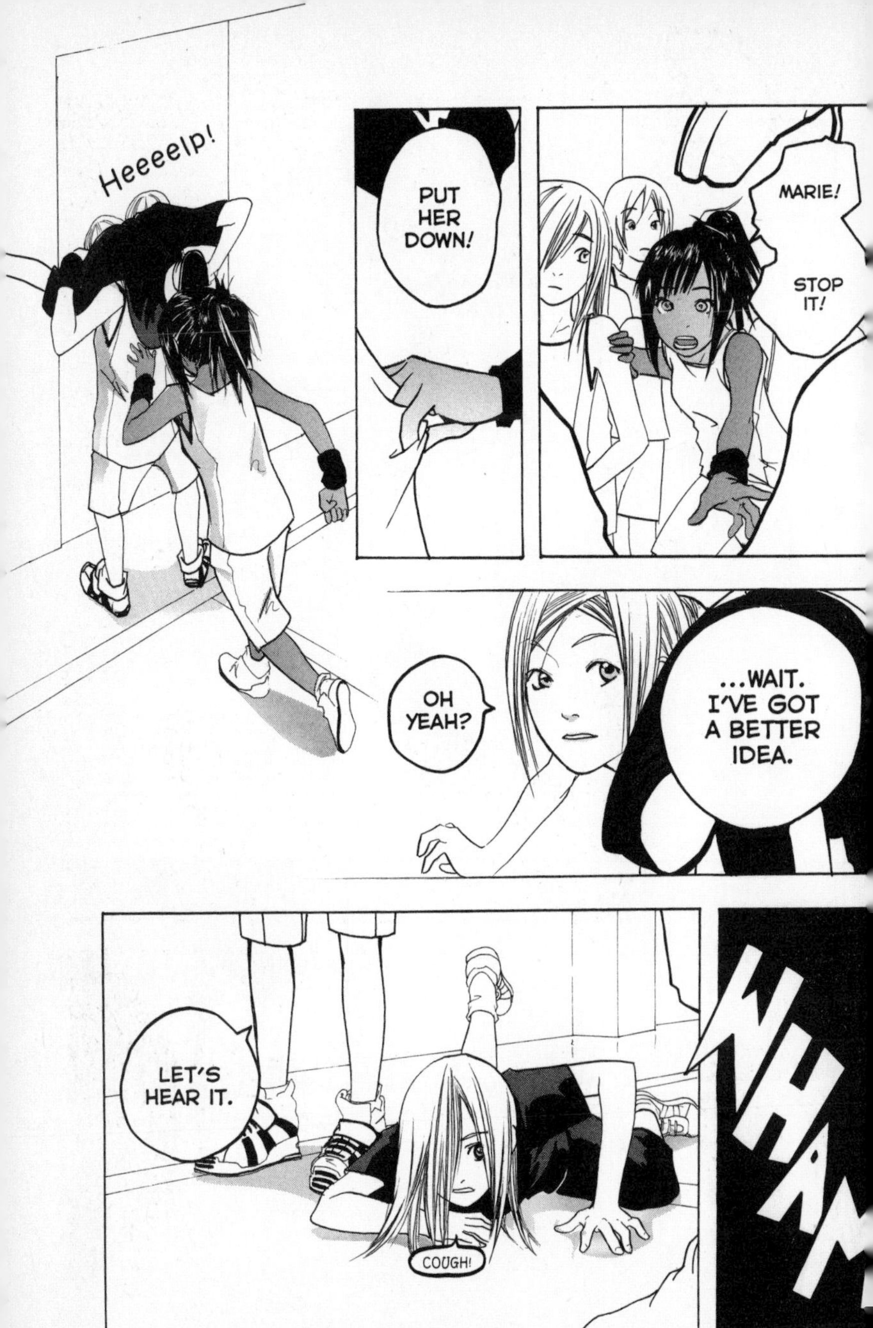
MARIE!
STOP IT!
PUT HER DOWN!
...WAIT. I'VE GOT A BETTER IDEA.
OH YEAH?
Heeeelp!
WHAM
LET'S HEAR IT.
COUGH!

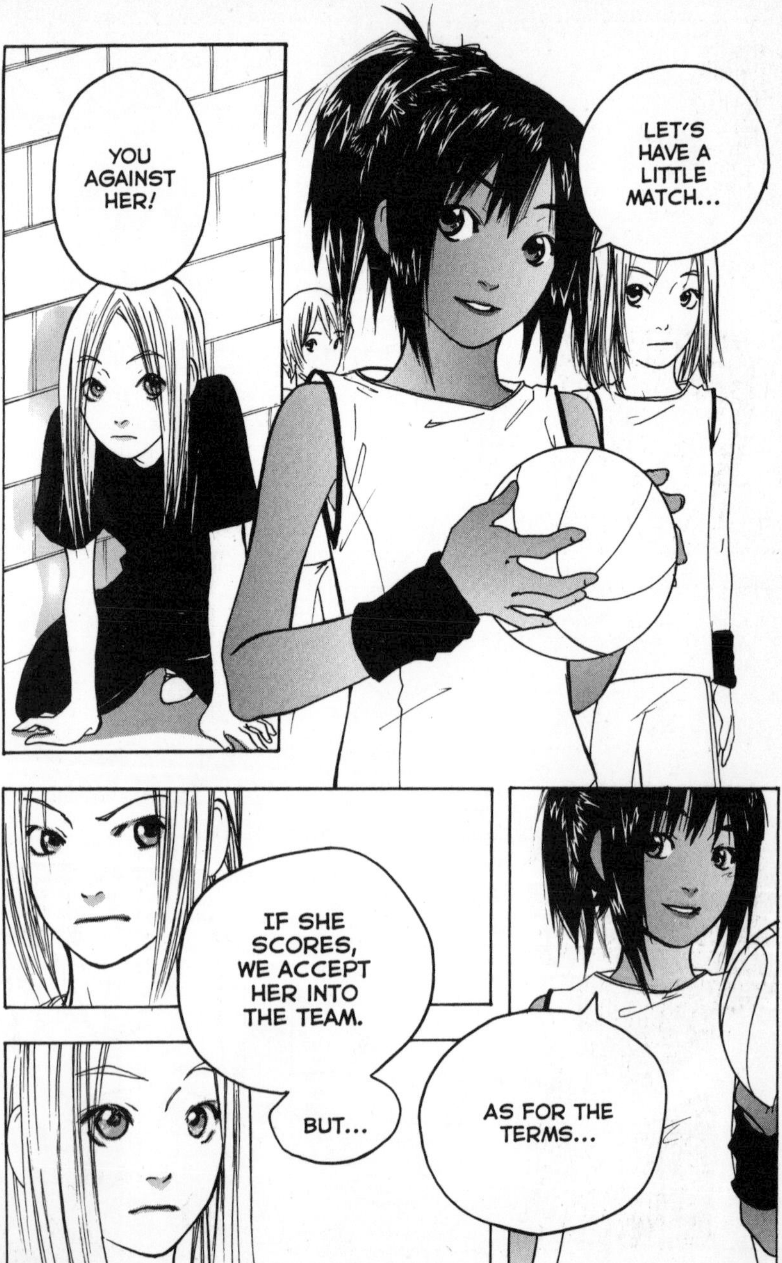
LET'S HAVE A LITTLE MATCH...
YOU AGAINST HER!
IF SHE SCORES, WE ACCEPT HER INTO THE TEAM.
BUT...
AS FOR THE TERMS...

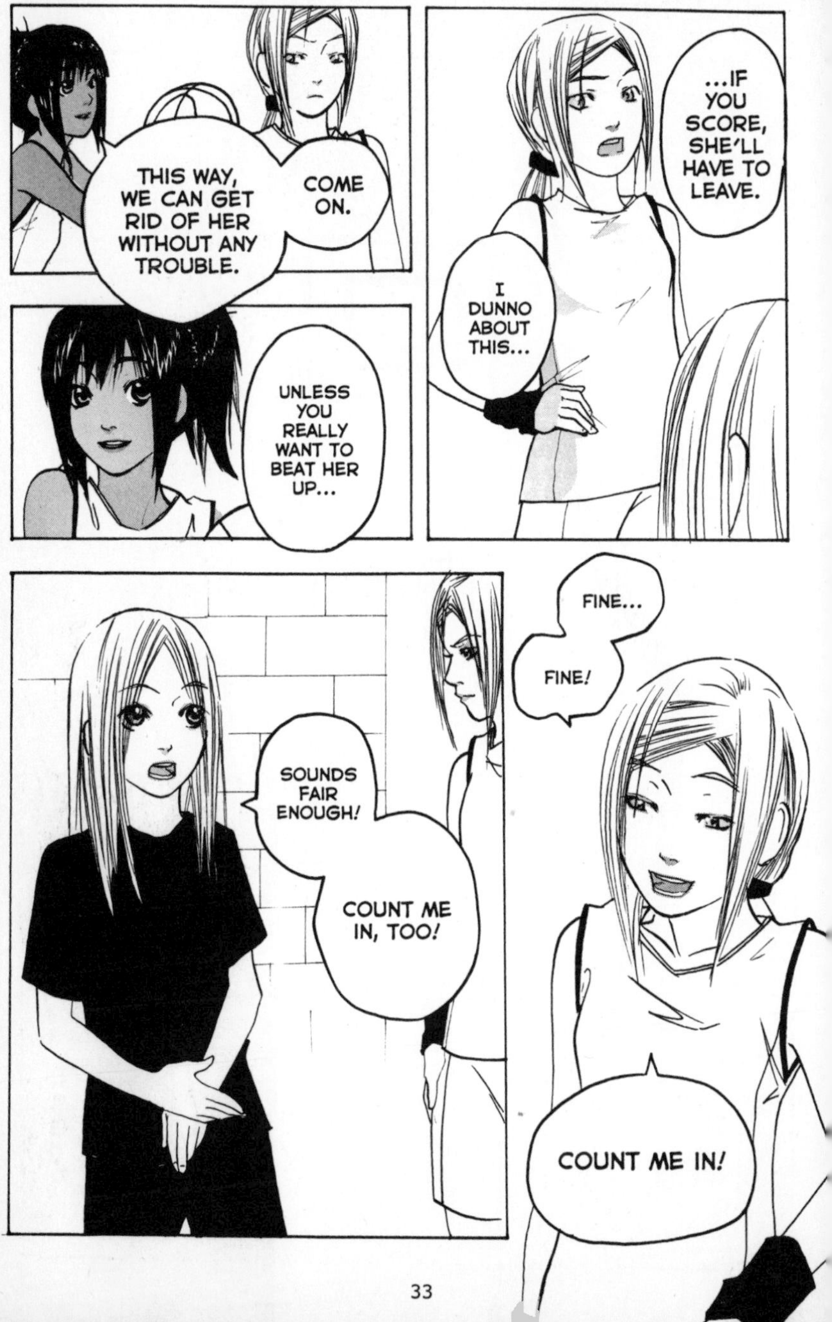
...IF YOU SCORE, SHE'LL HAVE TO LEAVE.
I DUNNO ABOUT THIS...
COME ON.
THIS WAY, WE CAN GET RID OF HER WITHOUT ANY TROUBLE.
UNLESS YOU REALLY WANT TO BEAT HER UP...
FINE...
FINE!
COUNT ME IN!
SOUNDS FAIR ENOUGH!
COUNT ME IN, TOO!

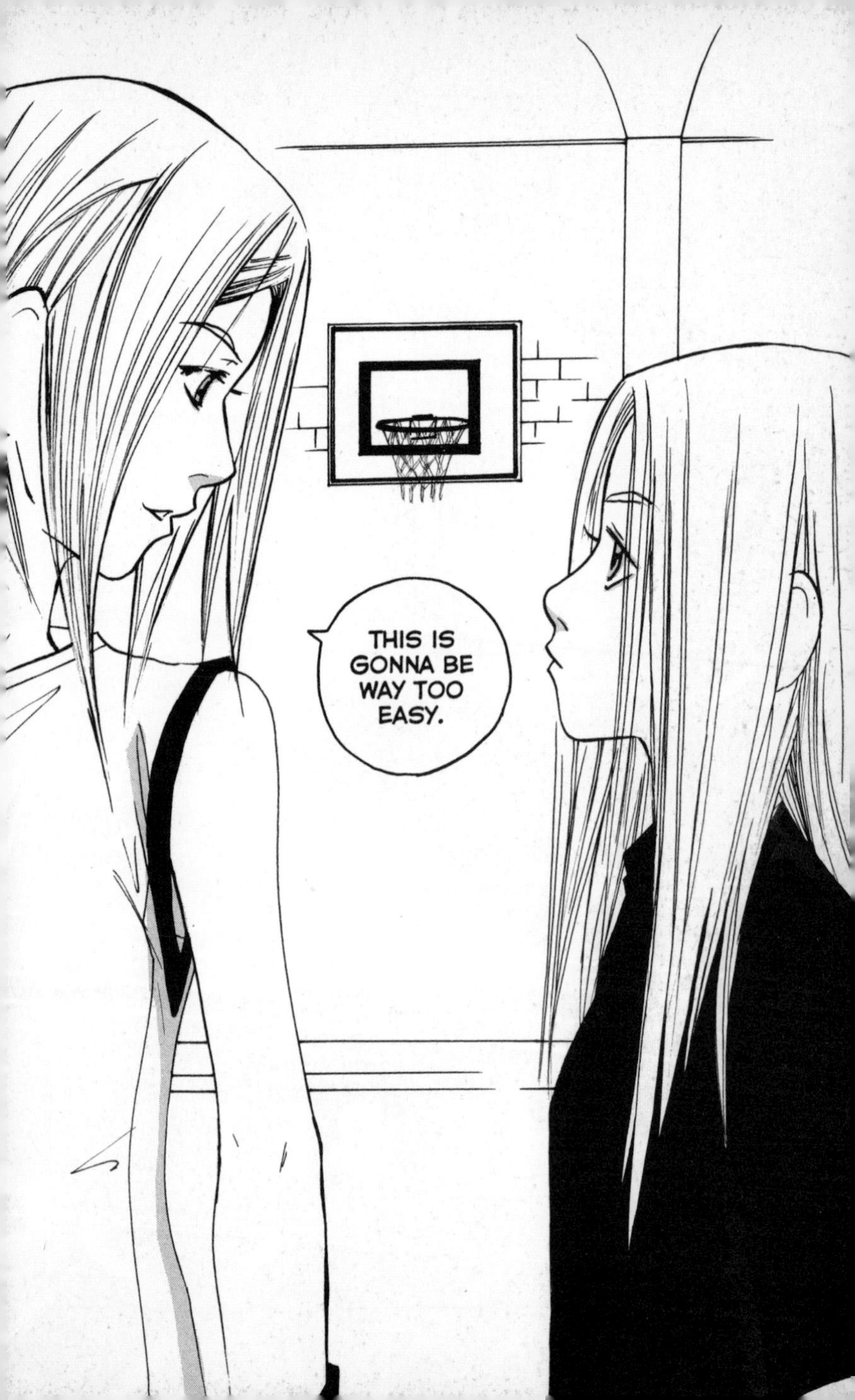
THIS IS GONNA BE WAY TOO EASY.

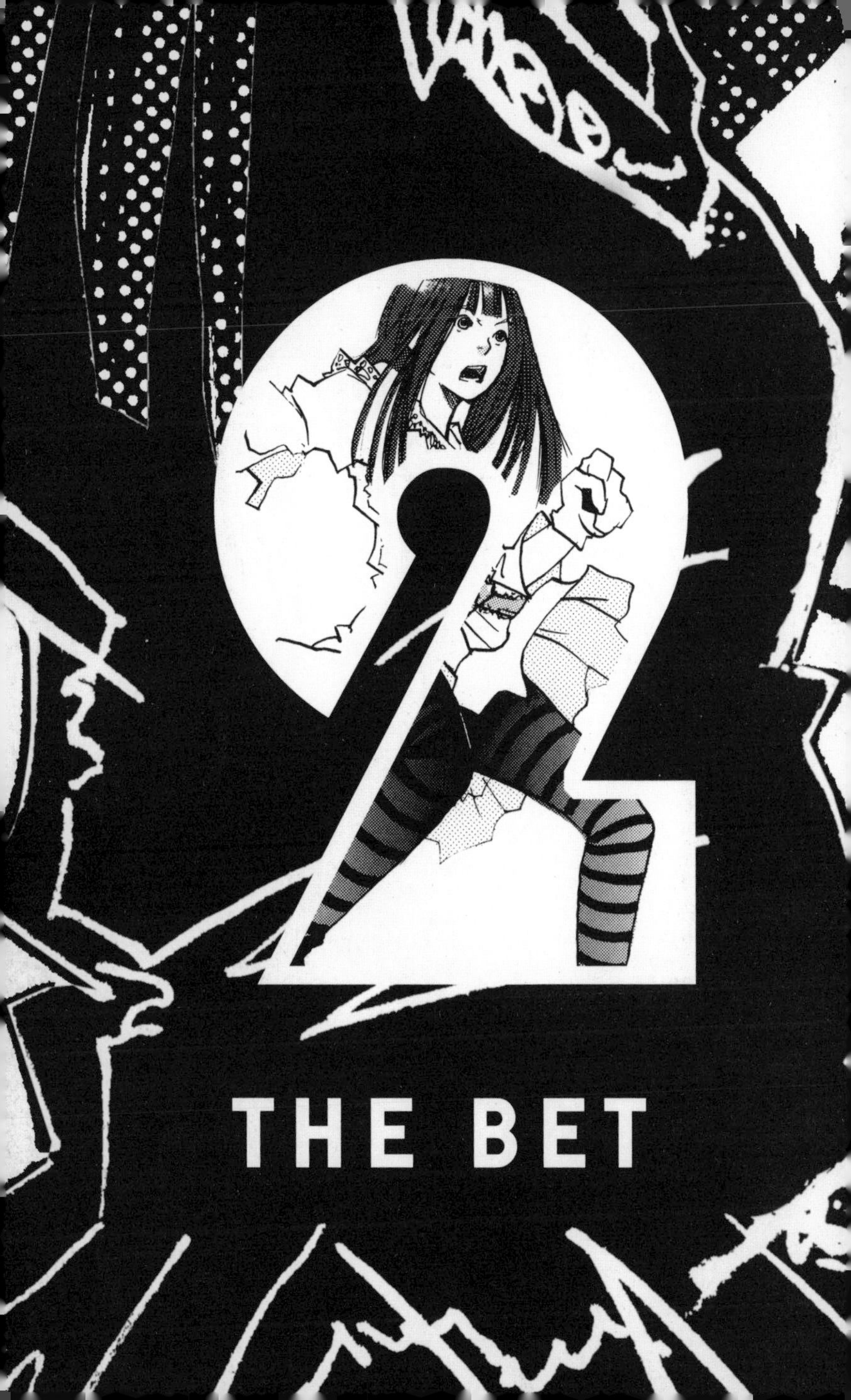

2 THE BET

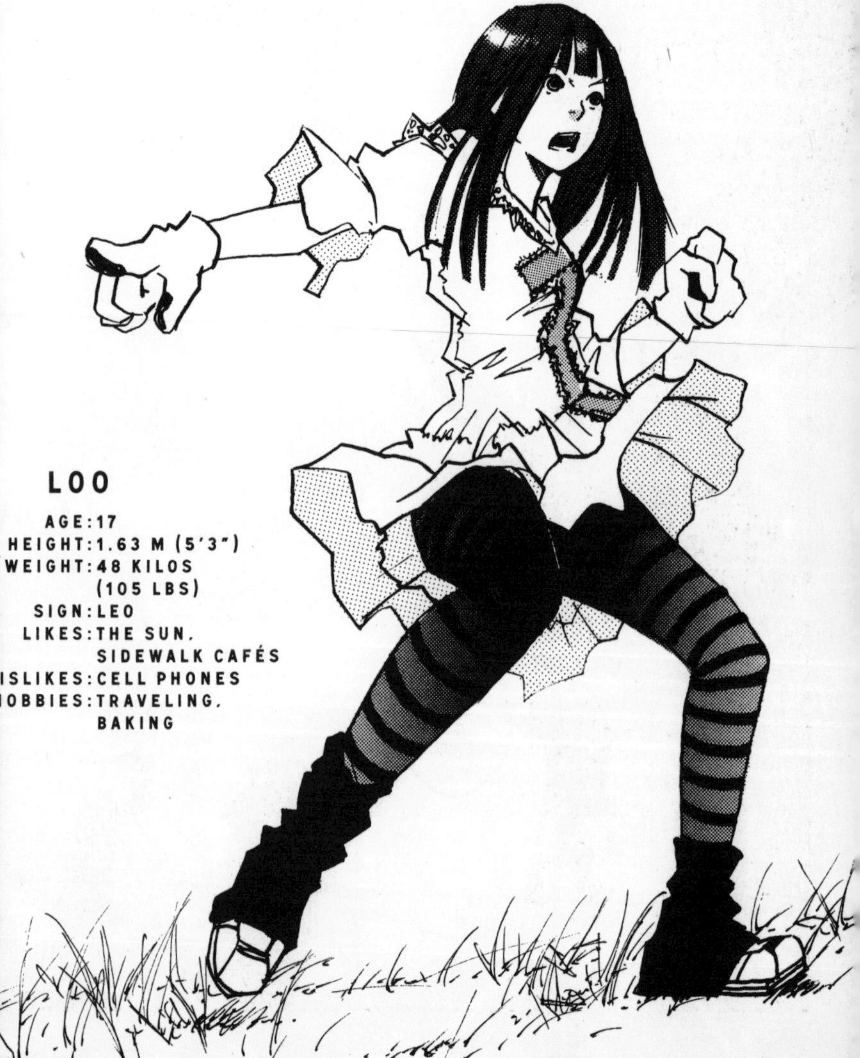

LOO

AGE:17
HEIGHT:1.63 M (5'3")
WEIGHT:48 KILOS
(105 LBS)
SIGN:LEO
LIKES:THE SUN,
SIDEWALK CAFÉS
ISLIKES:CELL PHONES
HOBBIES:TRAVELING,
BAKING

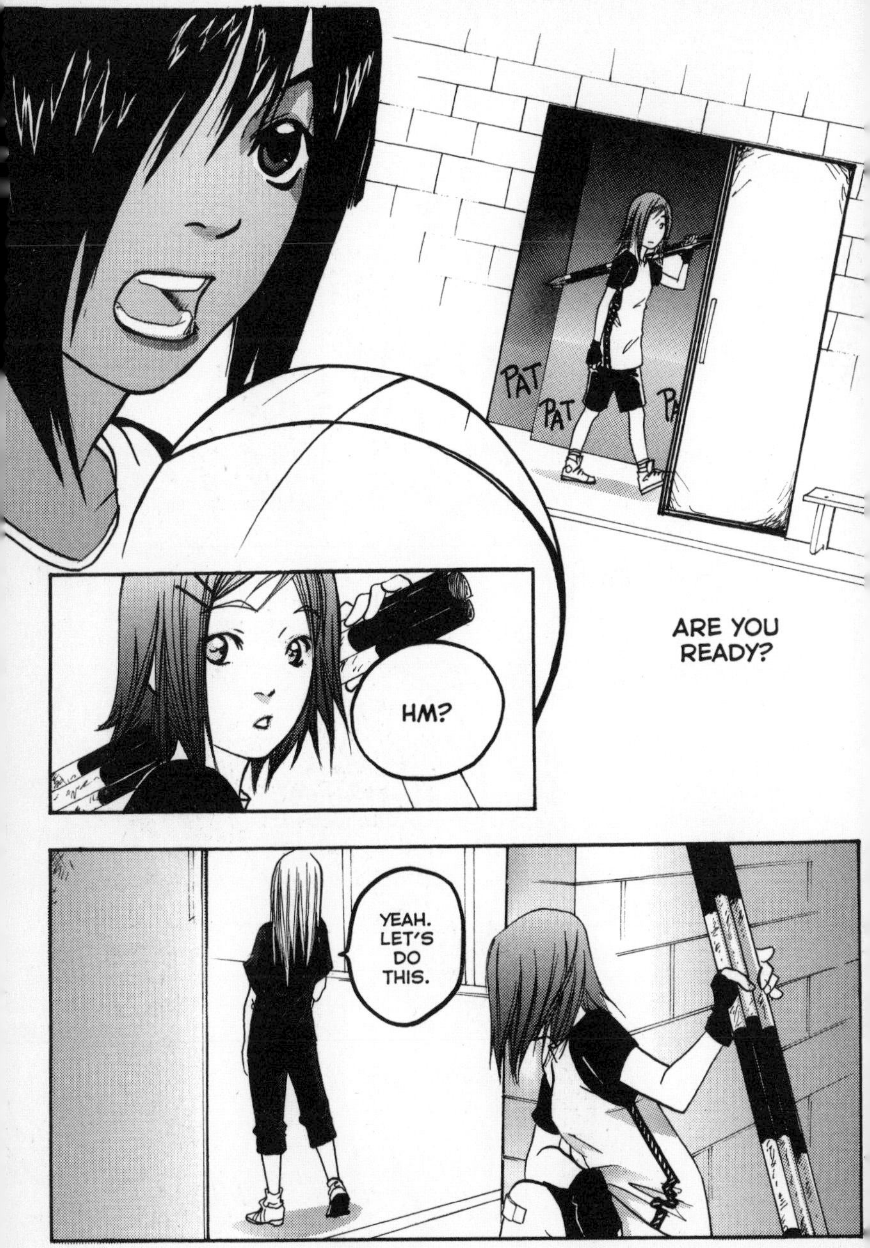
PAT PAT PA
ARE YOU READY?
HM?
YEAH. LET'S DO THIS.

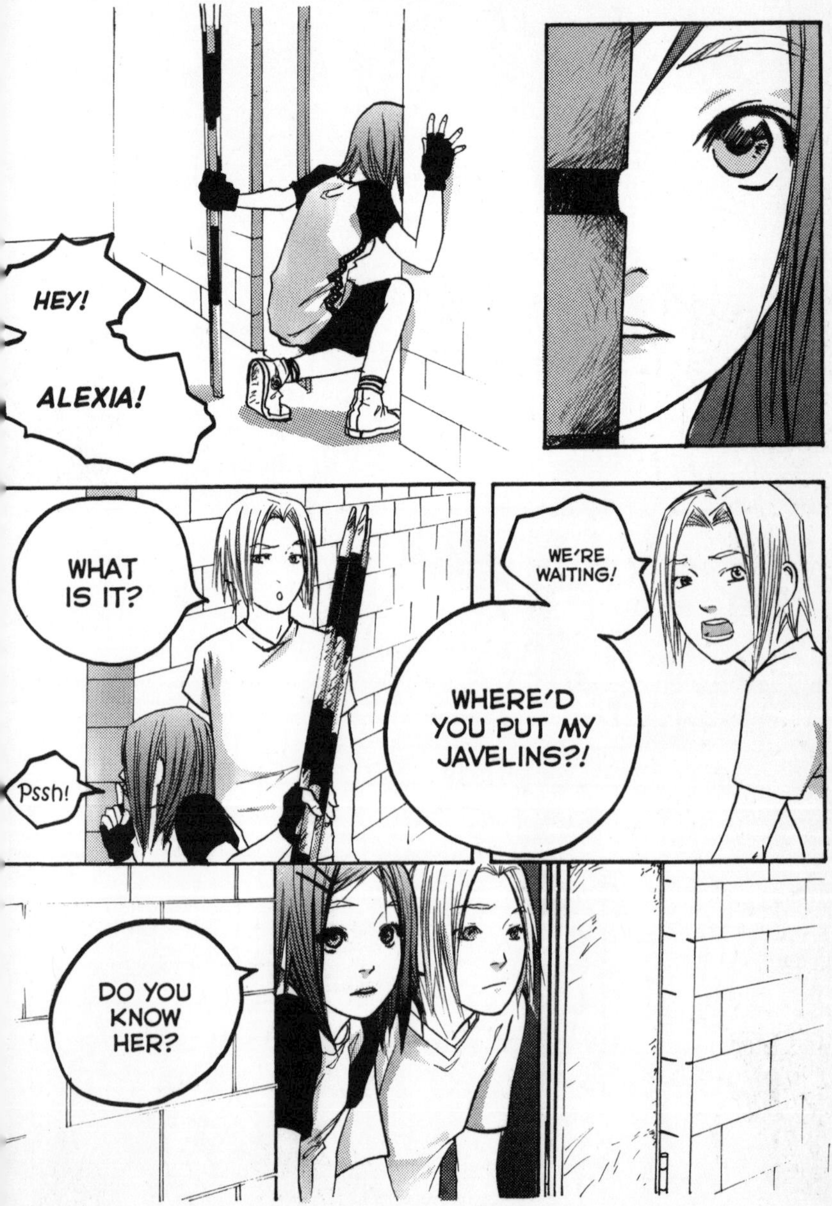
HEY!
ALEXIA!
WE'RE WAITING!
WHERE'D YOU PUT MY JAVELINS?!
WHAT IS IT?
Pssh!
DO YOU KNOW HER?

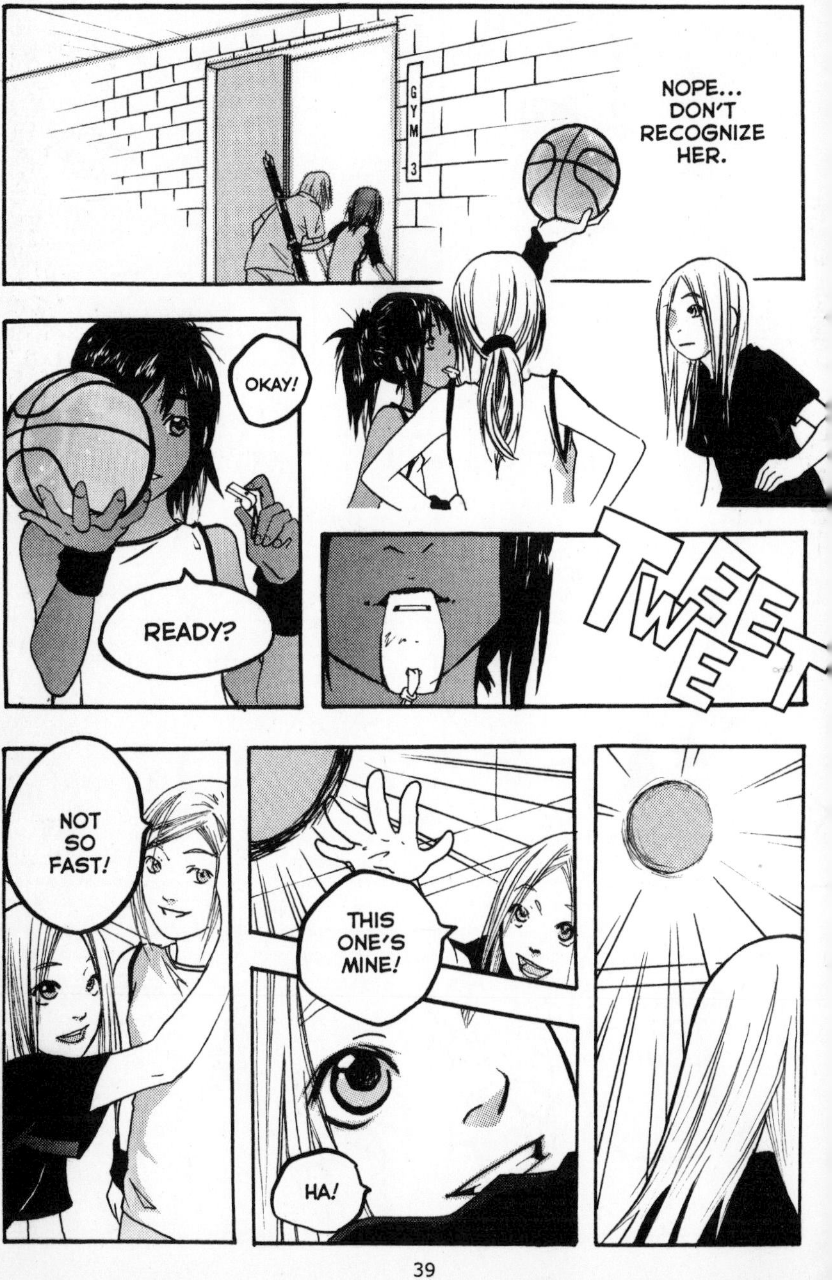
NOPE... DON'T RECOGNIZE HER.
GYM 3
OKAY!
READY?
TWEET
NOT SO FAST!
THIS ONE'S MINE!
HA!

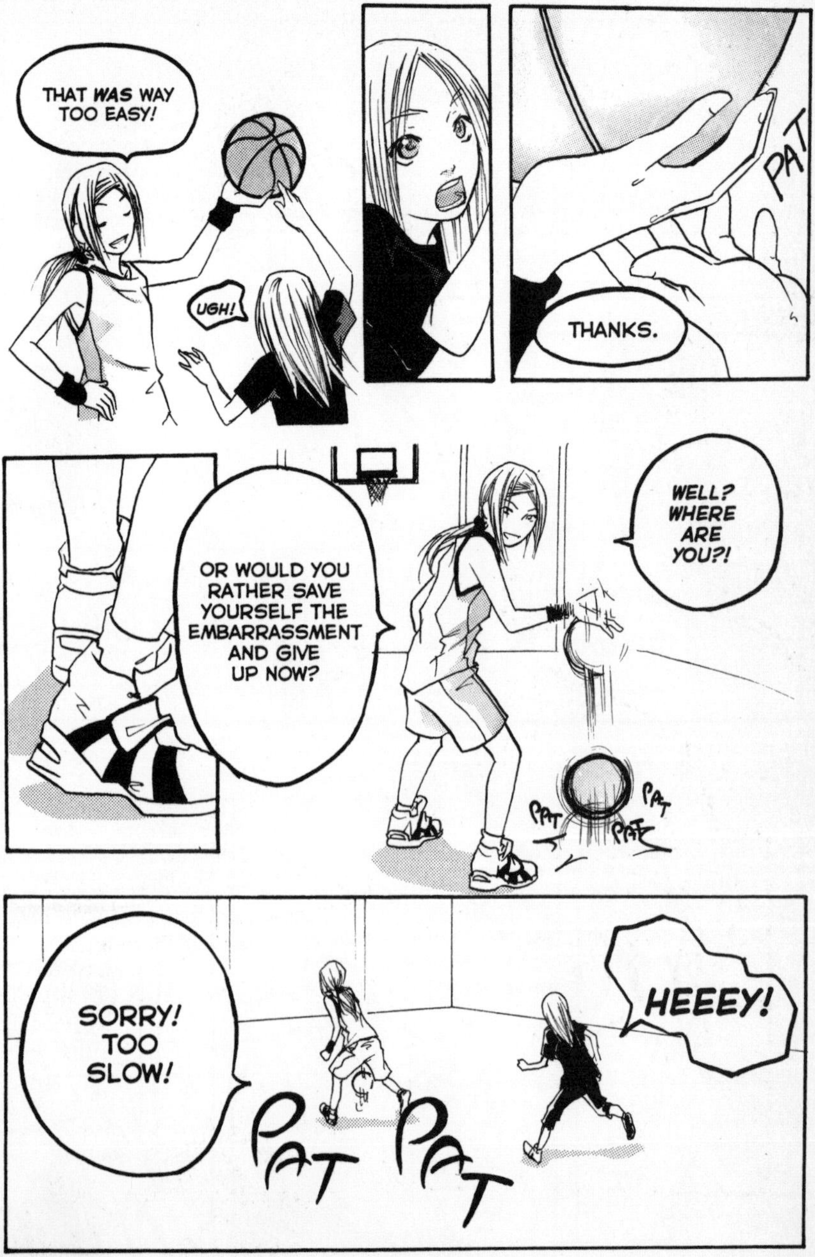
PAT
THANKS.
THAT WAS WAY TOO EASY!
UGH!
WELL? WHERE ARE YOU?!
PAT PAT PAT
OR WOULD YOU RATHER SAVE YOURSELF THE EMBARRASSMENT AND GIVE UP NOW?
HEEEY!
SORRY! TOO SLOW!
PAT PAT

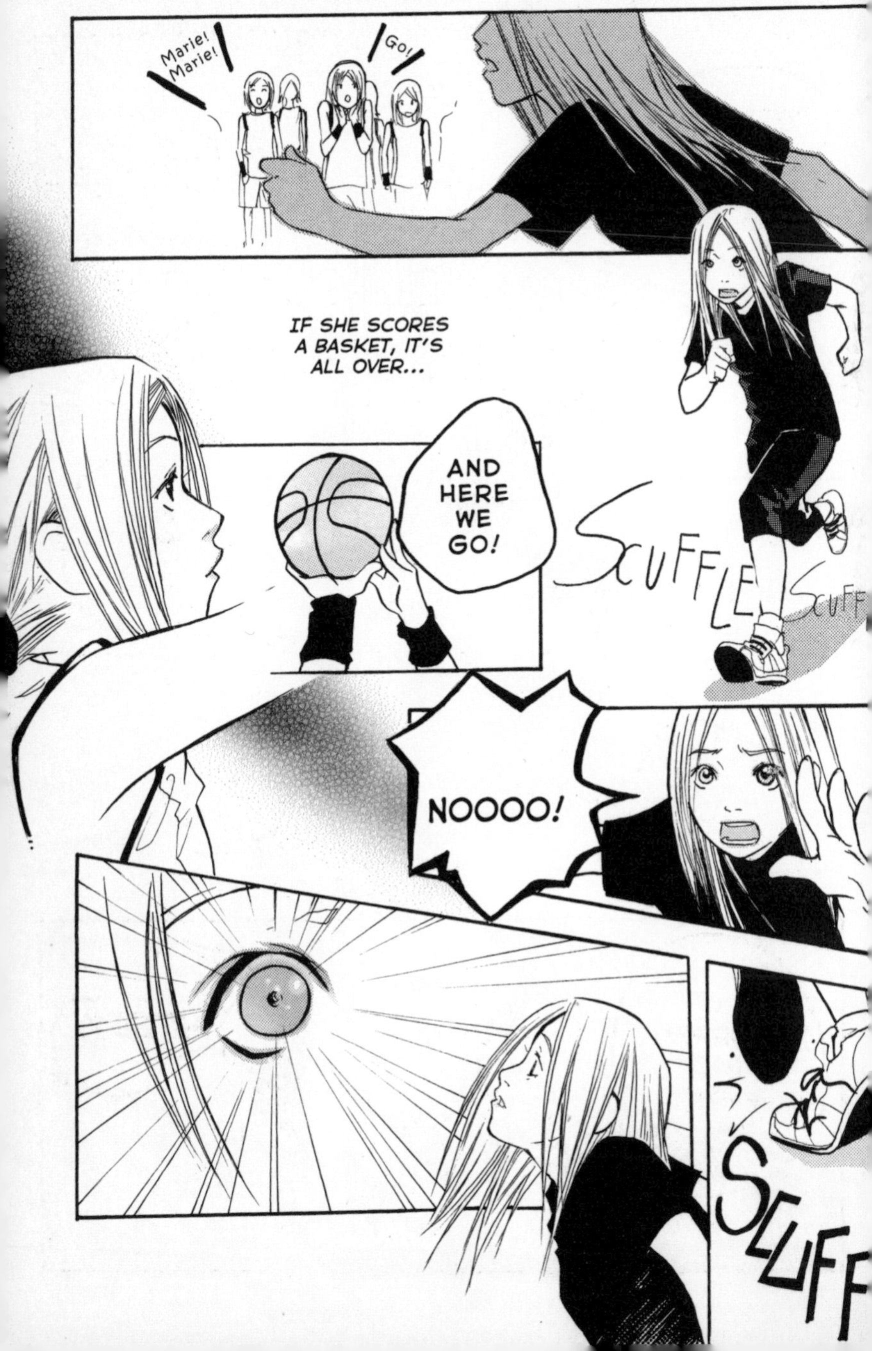
Go!
Marie! Marie!
IF SHE SCORES A BASKET, IT'S ALL OVER...
SCUFFLE SCUFF
AND HERE WE GO!
NOOOO!
SCUFF

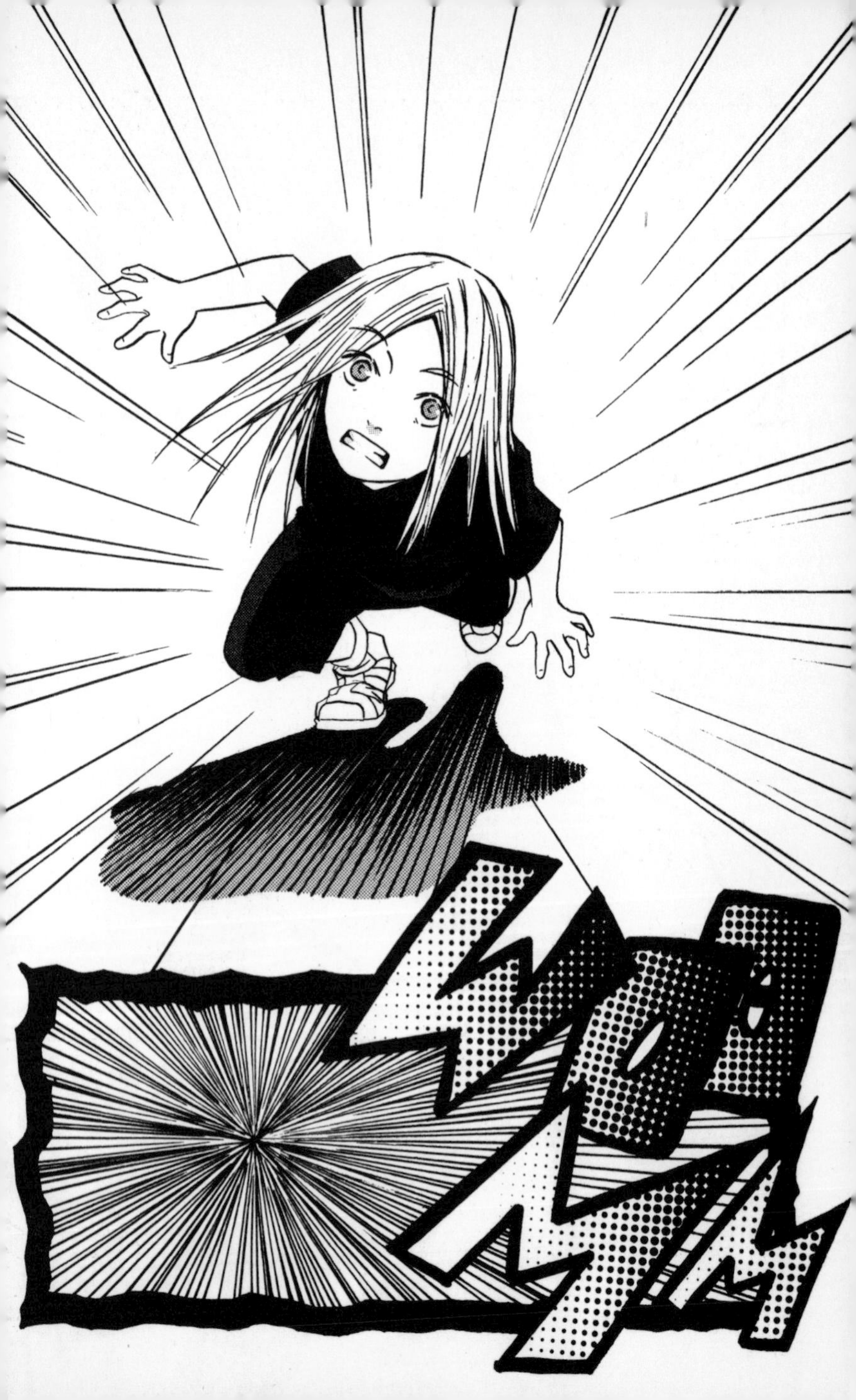

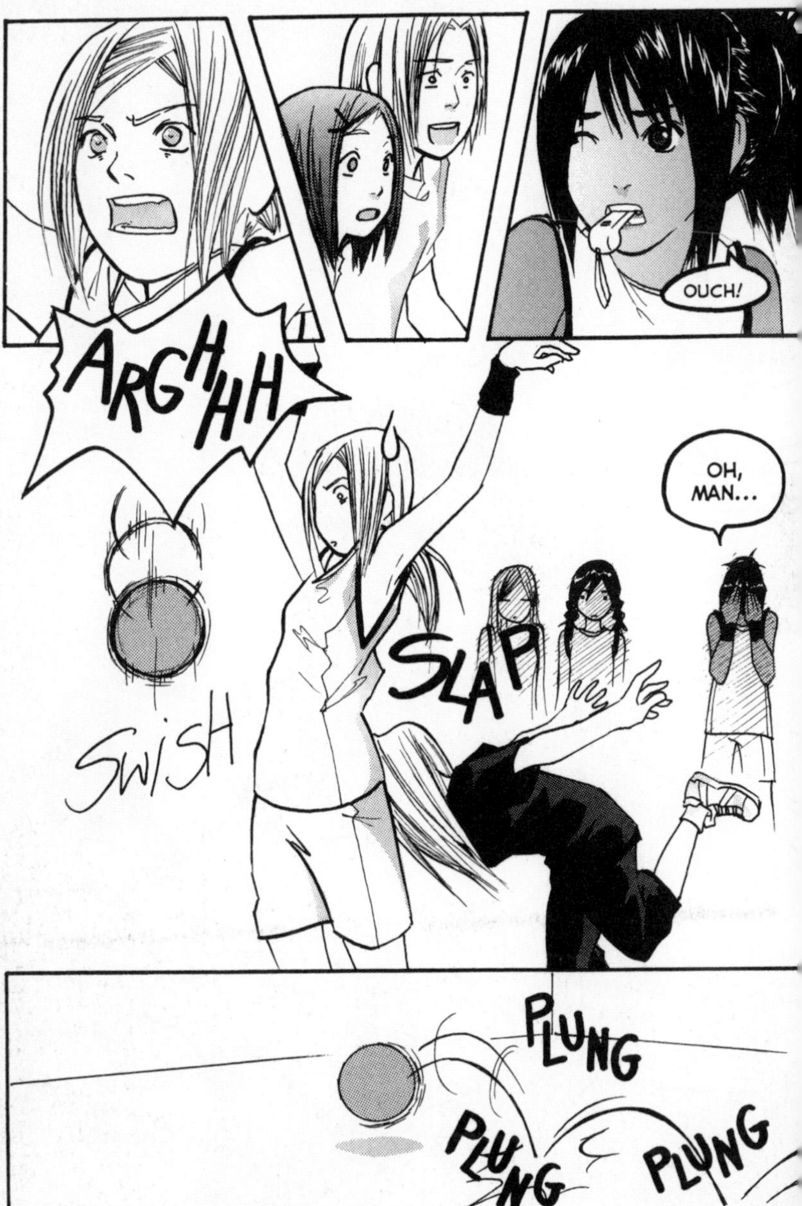
OUCH!
ARGHHHH
OH, MAN...
SLAP
SWISH
PLUNG
PLUNG
PLUNG

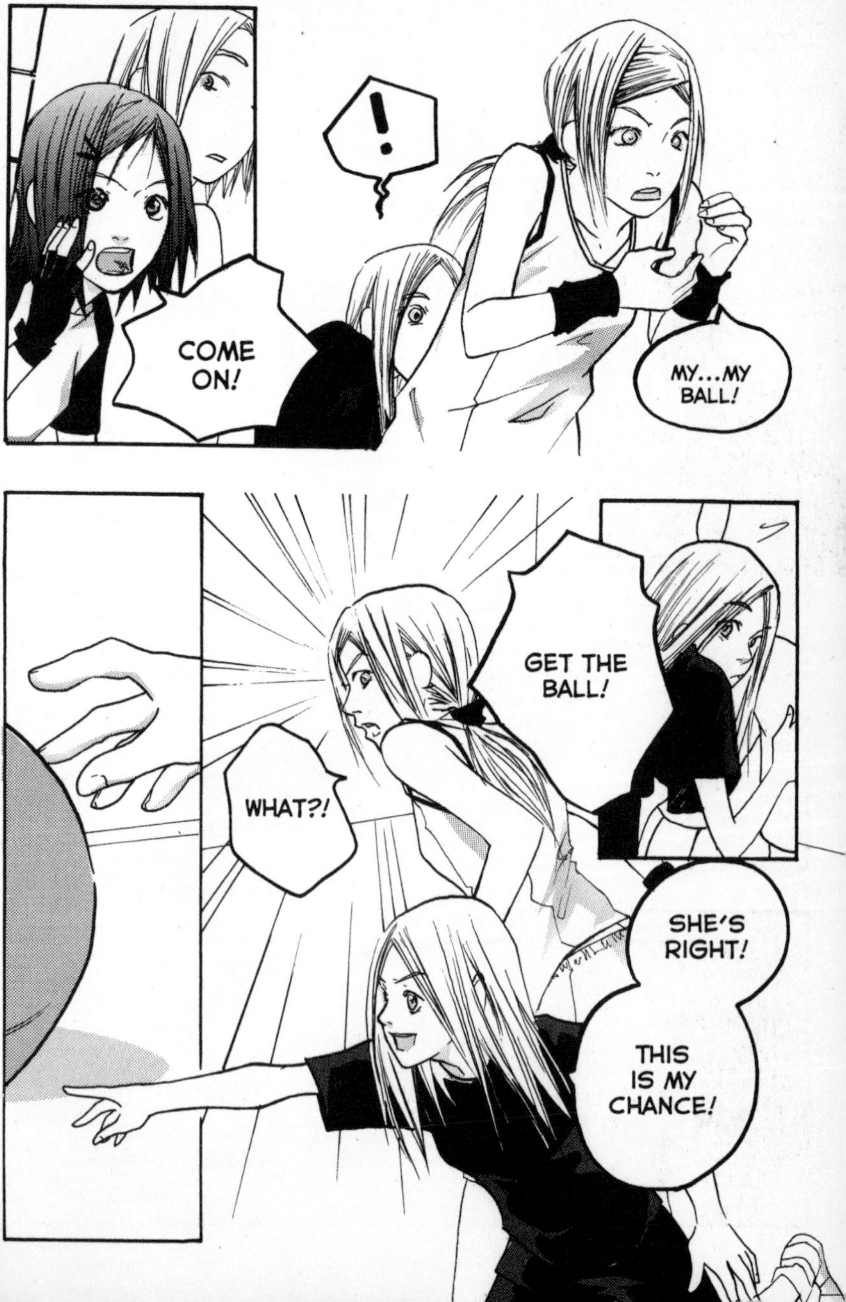
!
MY...MY BALL!
COME ON!
GET THE BALL!
WHAT?!
SHE'S RIGHT!
THIS IS MY CHANCE!

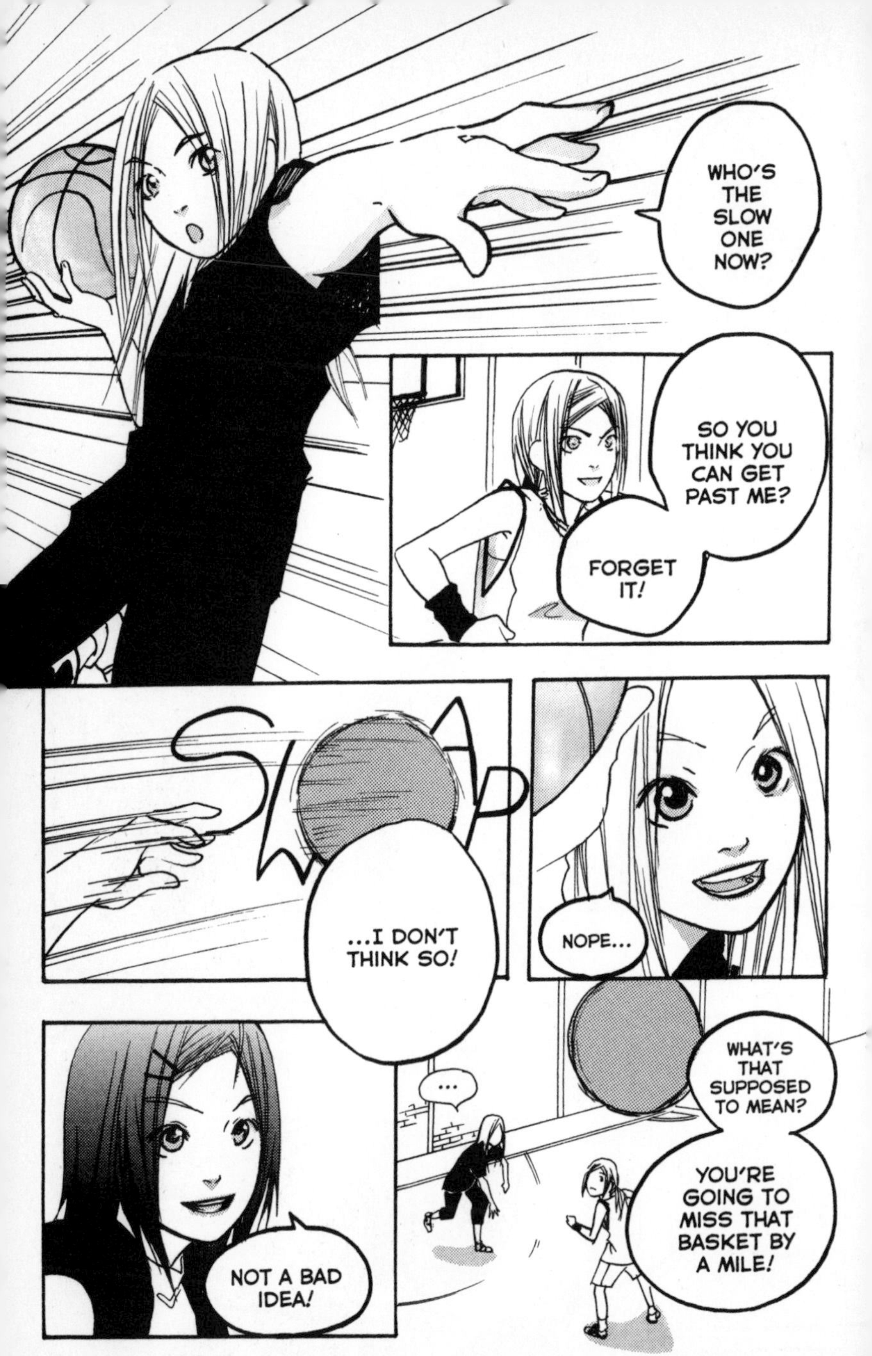
SO YOU THINK YOU CAN GET PAST ME?
FORGET IT!
WHO'S THE SLOW ONE NOW?
NOPE...
SLAP
...I DON'T THINK SO!
WHAT'S THAT SUPPOSED TO MEAN?
YOU'RE GOING TO MISS THAT BASKET BY A MILE!
...
NOT A BAD IDEA!

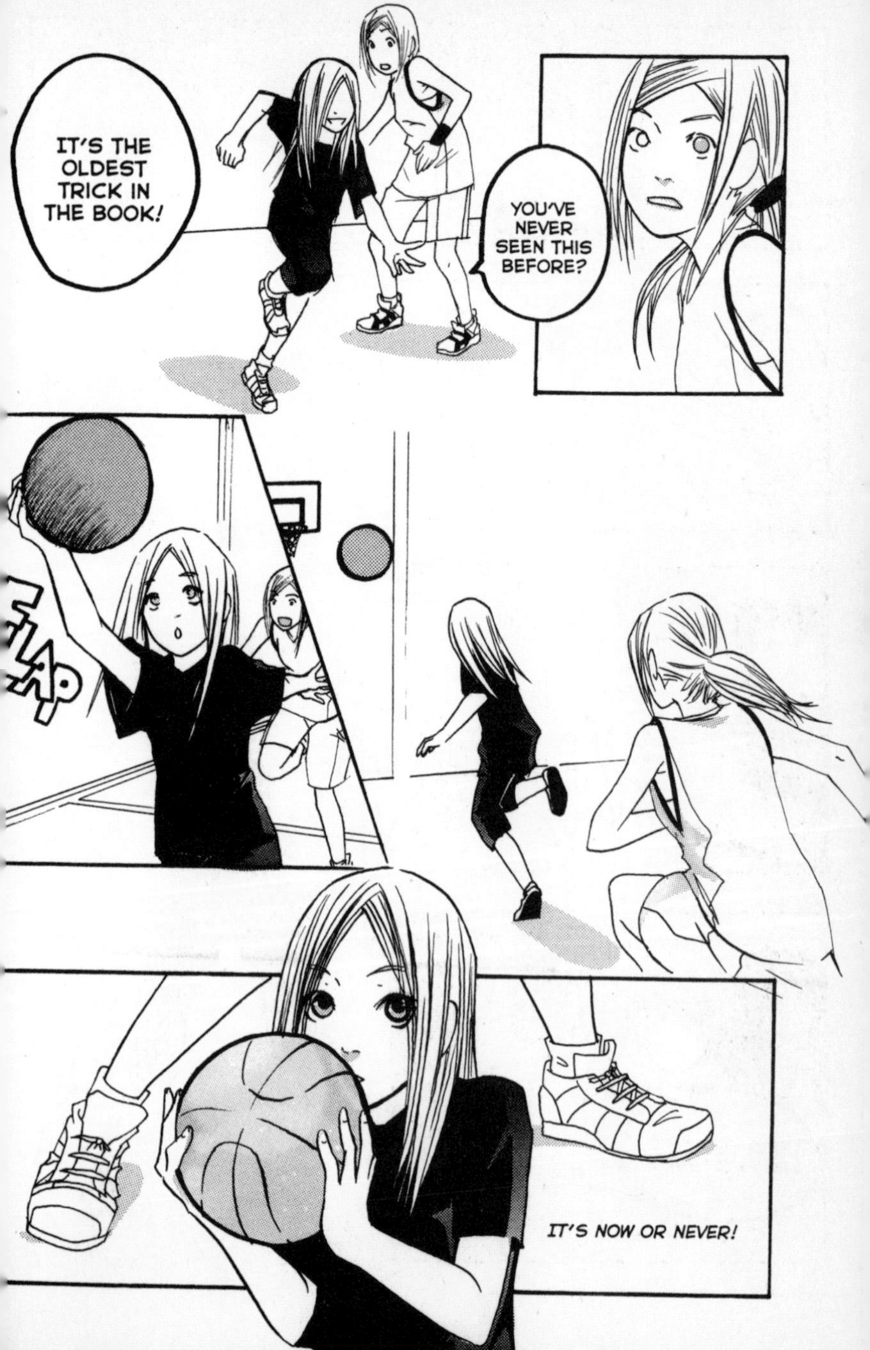
YOU'VE NEVER SEEN THIS BEFORE?
IT'S THE OLDEST TRICK IN THE BOOK!
FLAP
IT'S NOW OR NEVER!

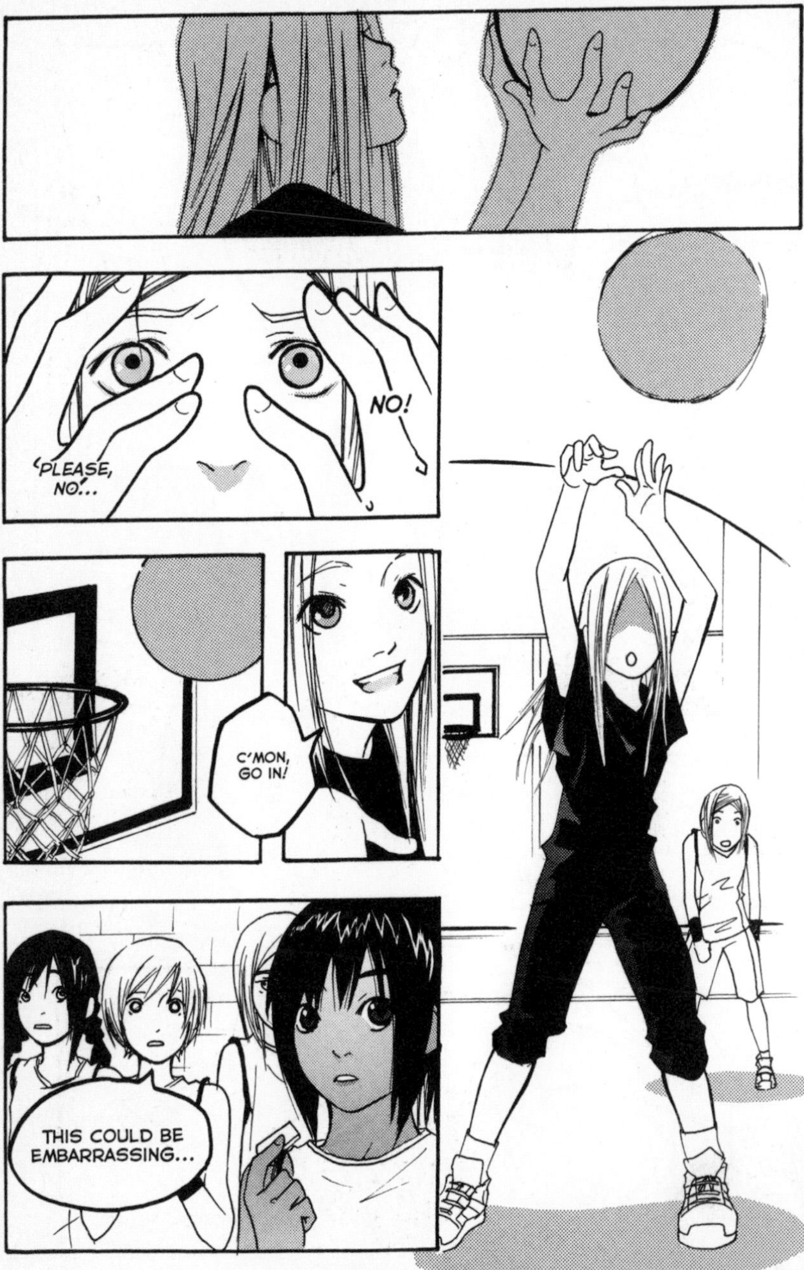
NO!
'PLEASE, NO!...
C'MON, GO IN!
THIS COULD BE EMBARRASSING...

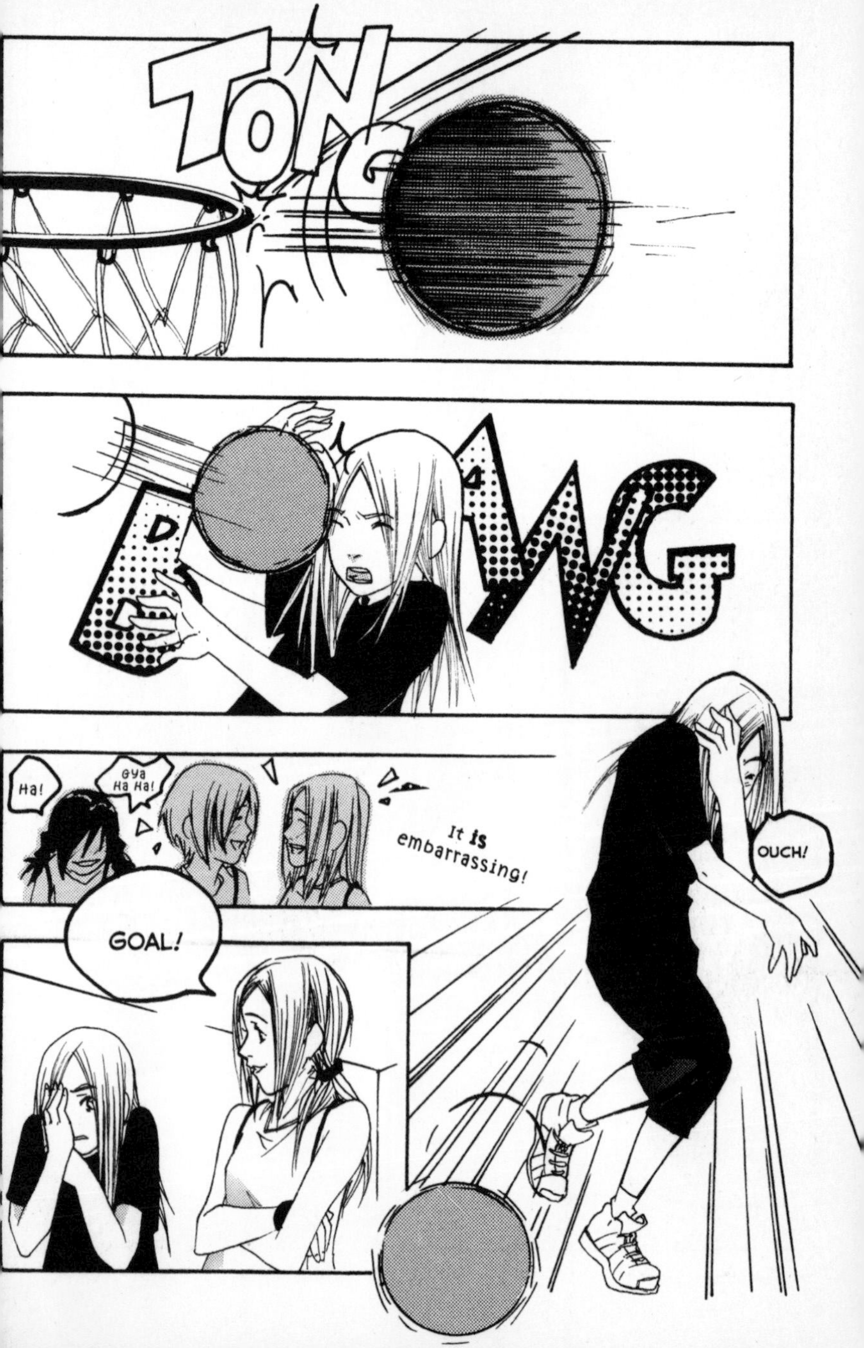
TONG
OUCH!
It is embarrassing!
GYA HA HA!
HA!
GOAL!

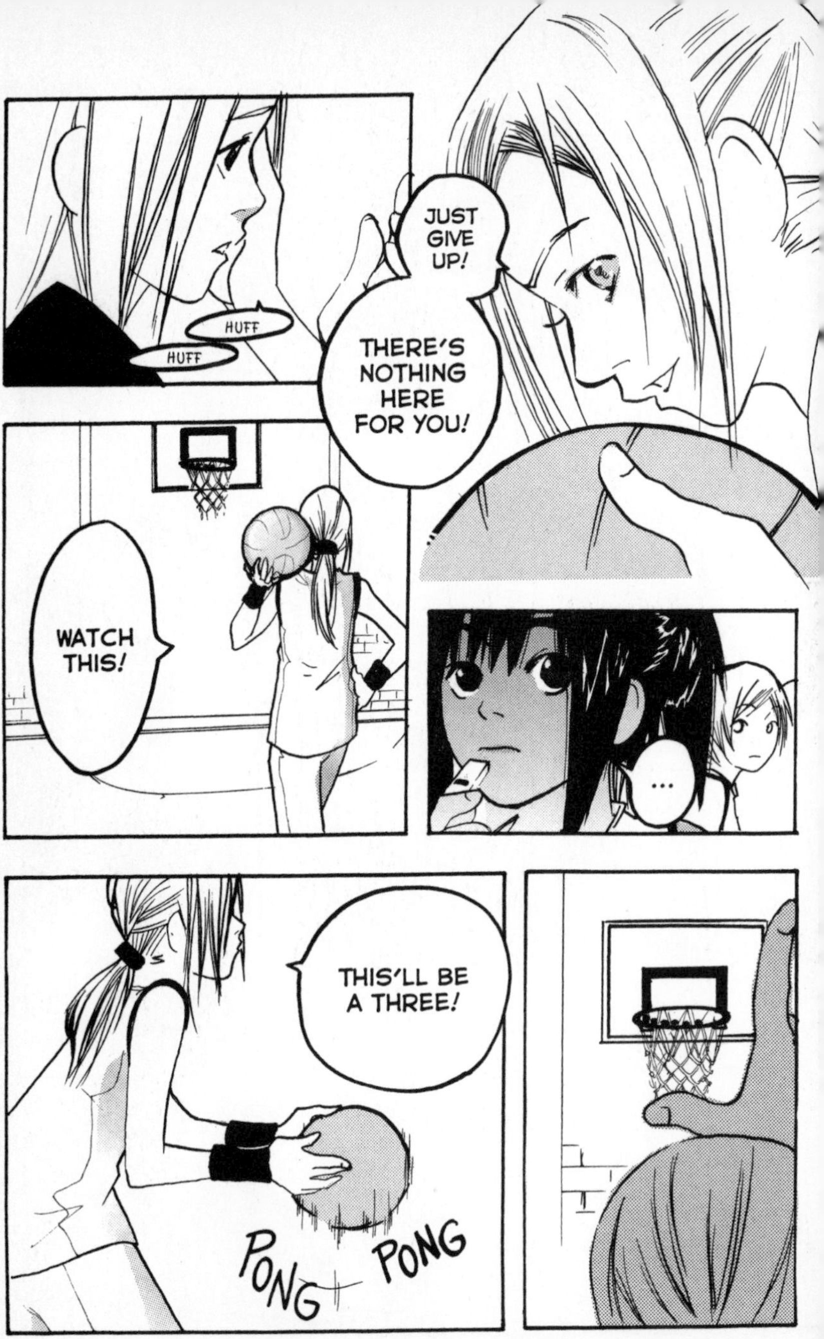
JUST GIVE UP!
THERE'S NOTHING HERE FOR YOU!
HUFF
HUFF
...
WATCH THIS!
THIS'LL BE A THREE!
PONG
PONG

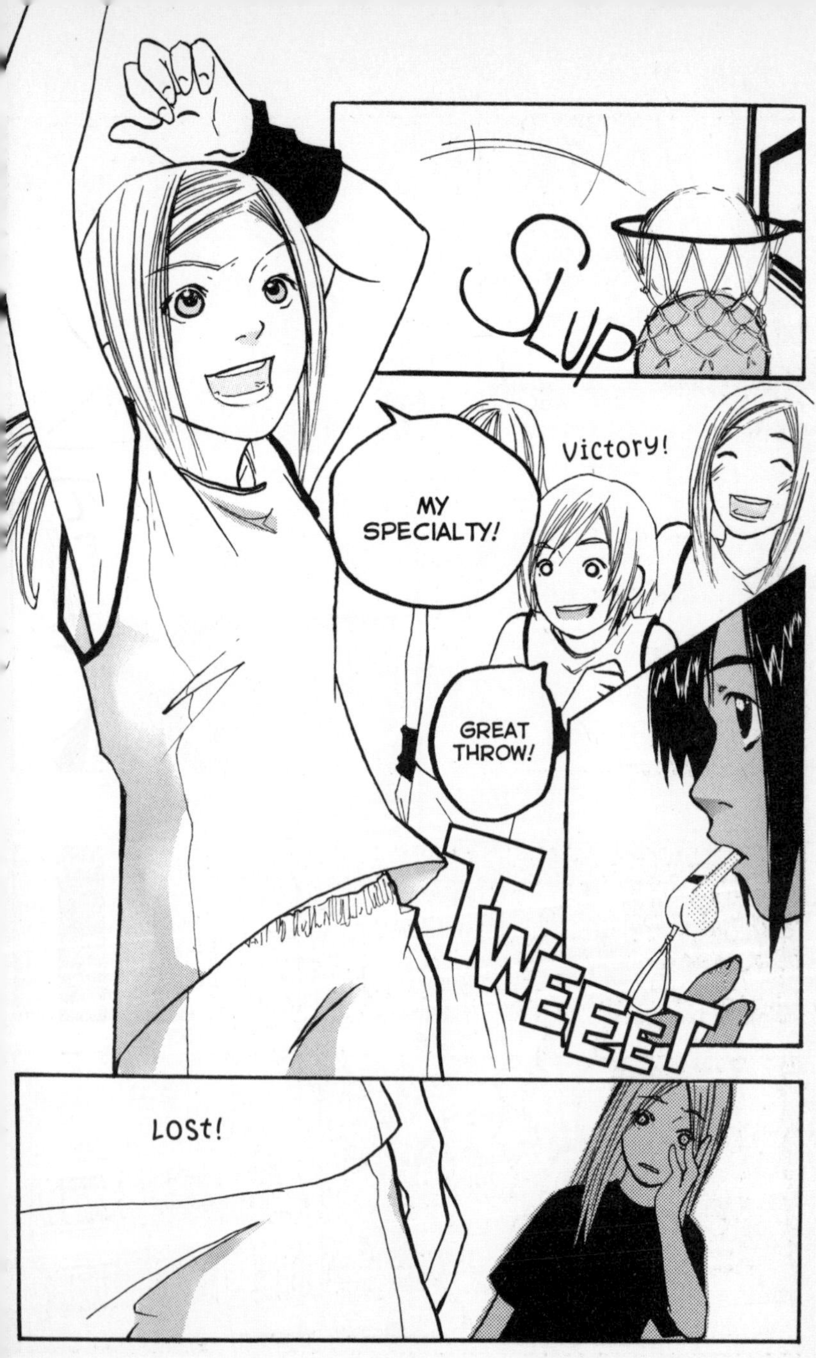
SLUP
Victory!
MY SPECIALTY!
GREAT THROW!
TWEEET
LOSt!

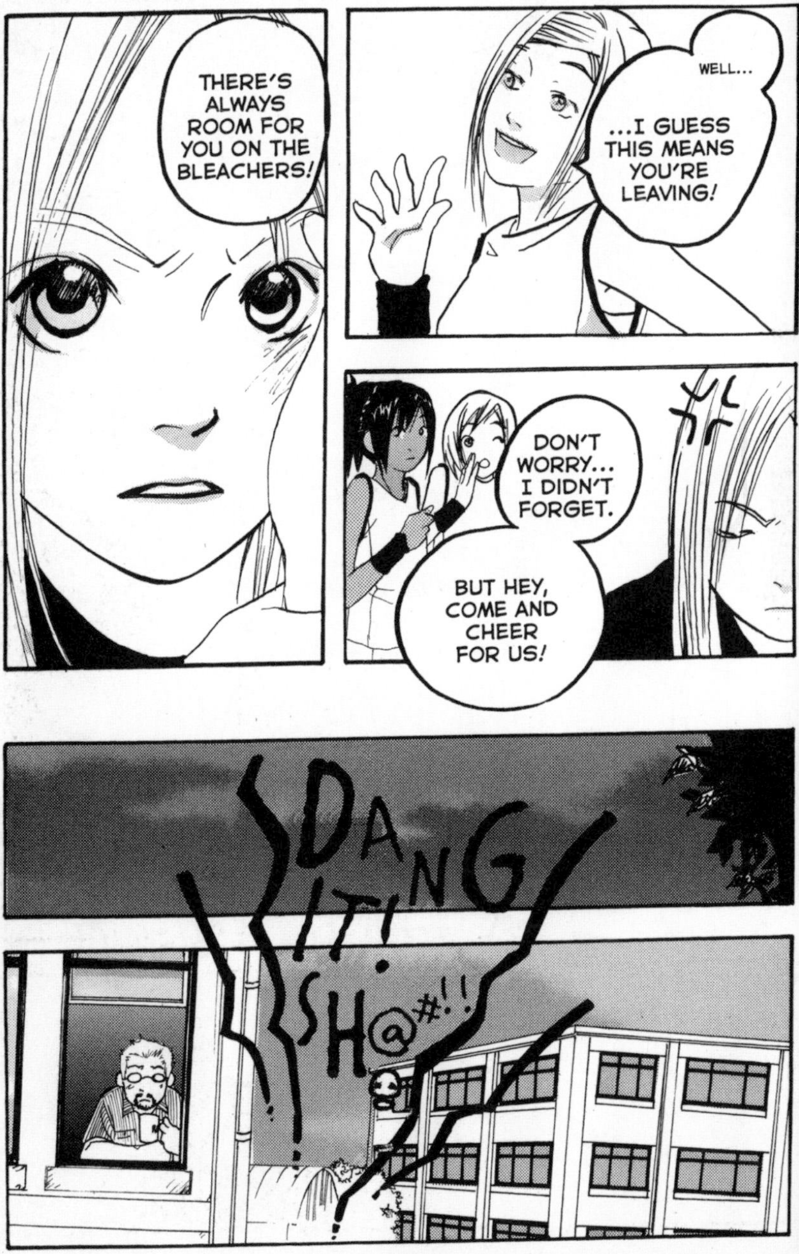
WELL...
...I GUESS THIS MEANS YOU'RE LEAVING!
DON'T WORRY... I DIDN'T FORGET.
BUT HEY, COME AND CHEER FOR US!
THERE'S ALWAYS ROOM FOR YOU ON THE BLEACHERS!
DANG IT! SH@#!!

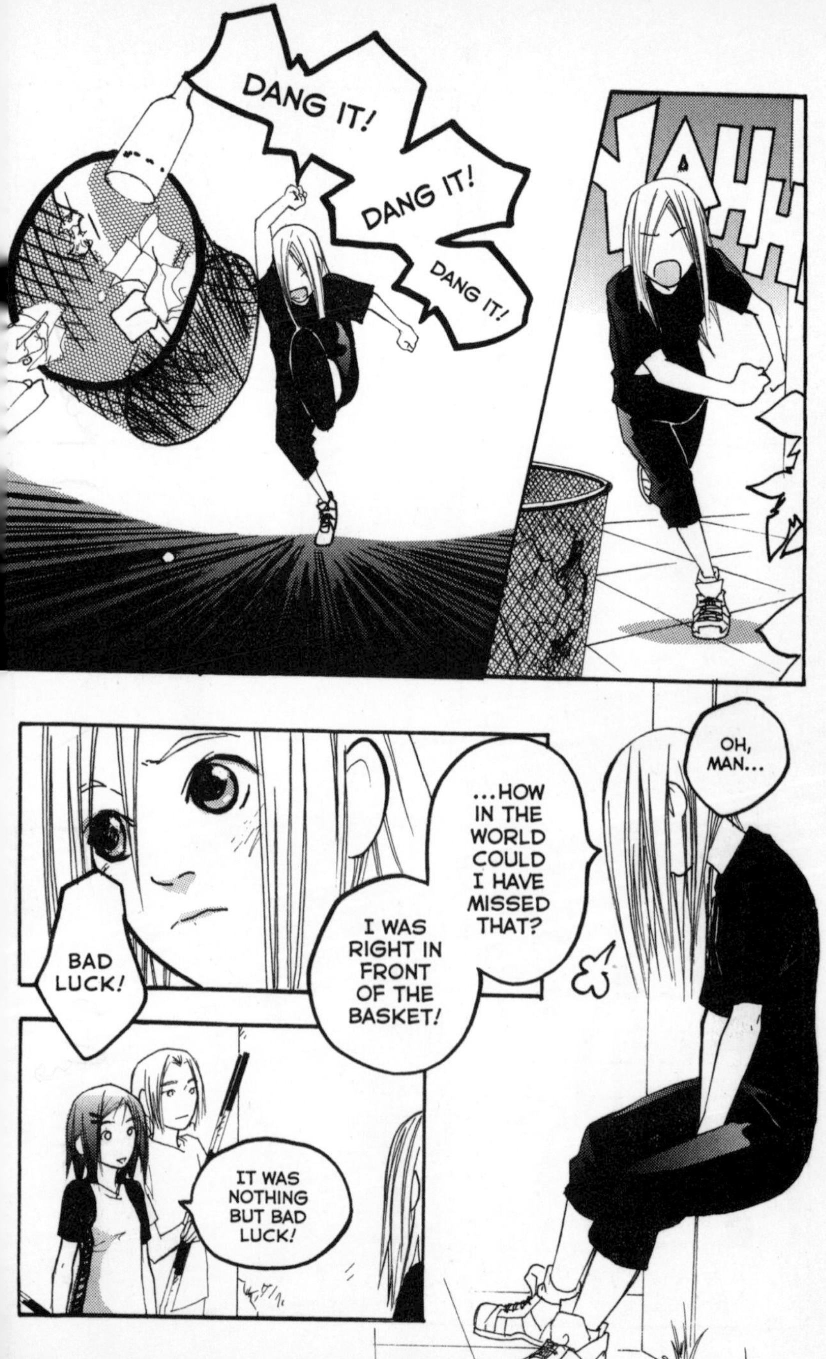
DANG IT!
DANG IT!
DANG IT!
OH, MAN...
...HOW IN THE WORLD COULD I HAVE MISSED THAT?
I WAS RIGHT IN FRONT OF THE BASKET!
BAD LUCK!
IT WAS NOTHING BUT BAD LUCK!

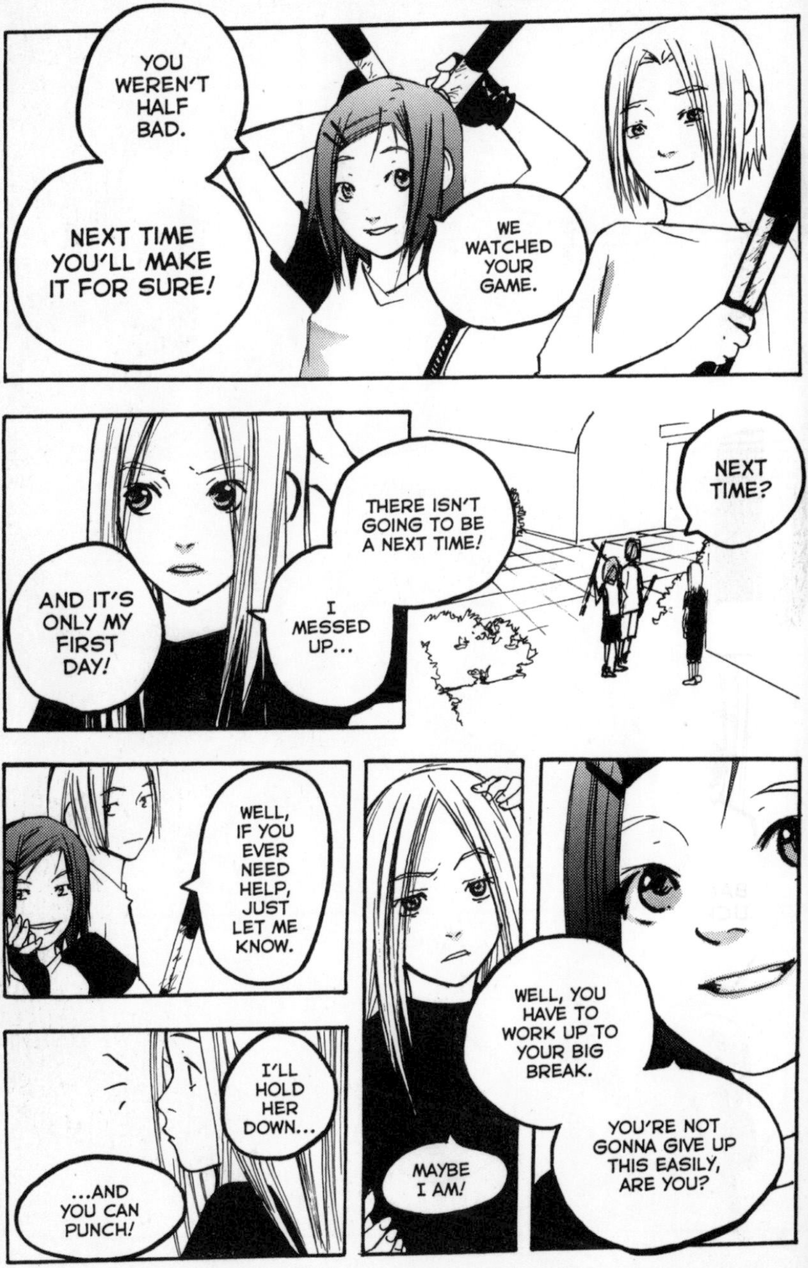
WE WATCHED YOUR GAME.
YOU WEREN'T HALF BAD.
NEXT TIME YOU'LL MAKE IT FOR SURE!
NEXT TIME?
THERE ISN'T GOING TO BE A NEXT TIME!
I MESSED UP...
AND IT'S ONLY MY FIRST DAY!
WELL, YOU HAVE TO WORK UP TO YOUR BIG BREAK.
YOU'RE NOT GONNA GIVE UP THIS EASILY, ARE YOU?
MAYBE I AM!
WELL, IF YOU EVER NEED HELP, JUST LET ME KNOW.
I'LL HOLD HER DOWN...
...AND YOU CAN PUNCH!

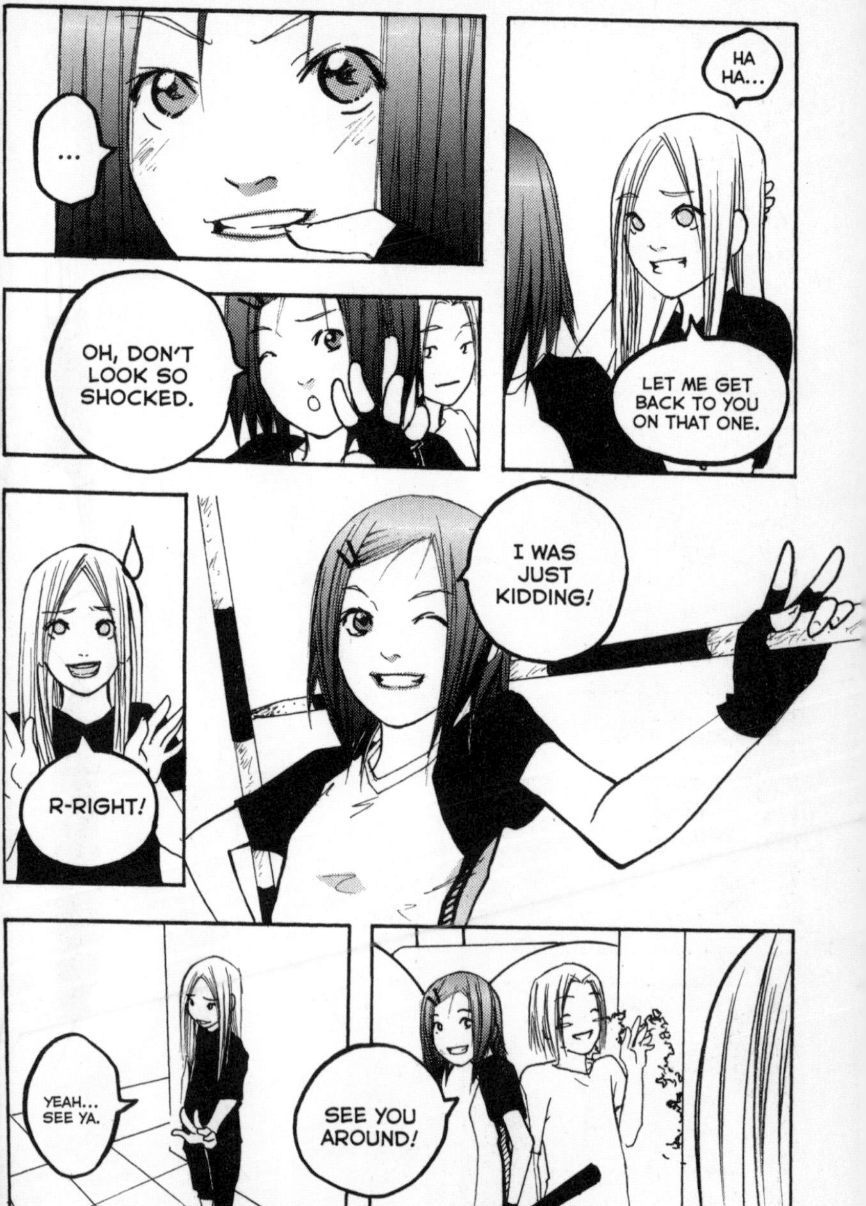
HA HA...
LET ME GET BACK TO YOU ON THAT ONE.
...
OH, DON'T LOOK SO SHOCKED.
I WAS JUST KIDDING!
R-RIGHT!
SEE YOU AROUND!
YEAH... SEE YA.

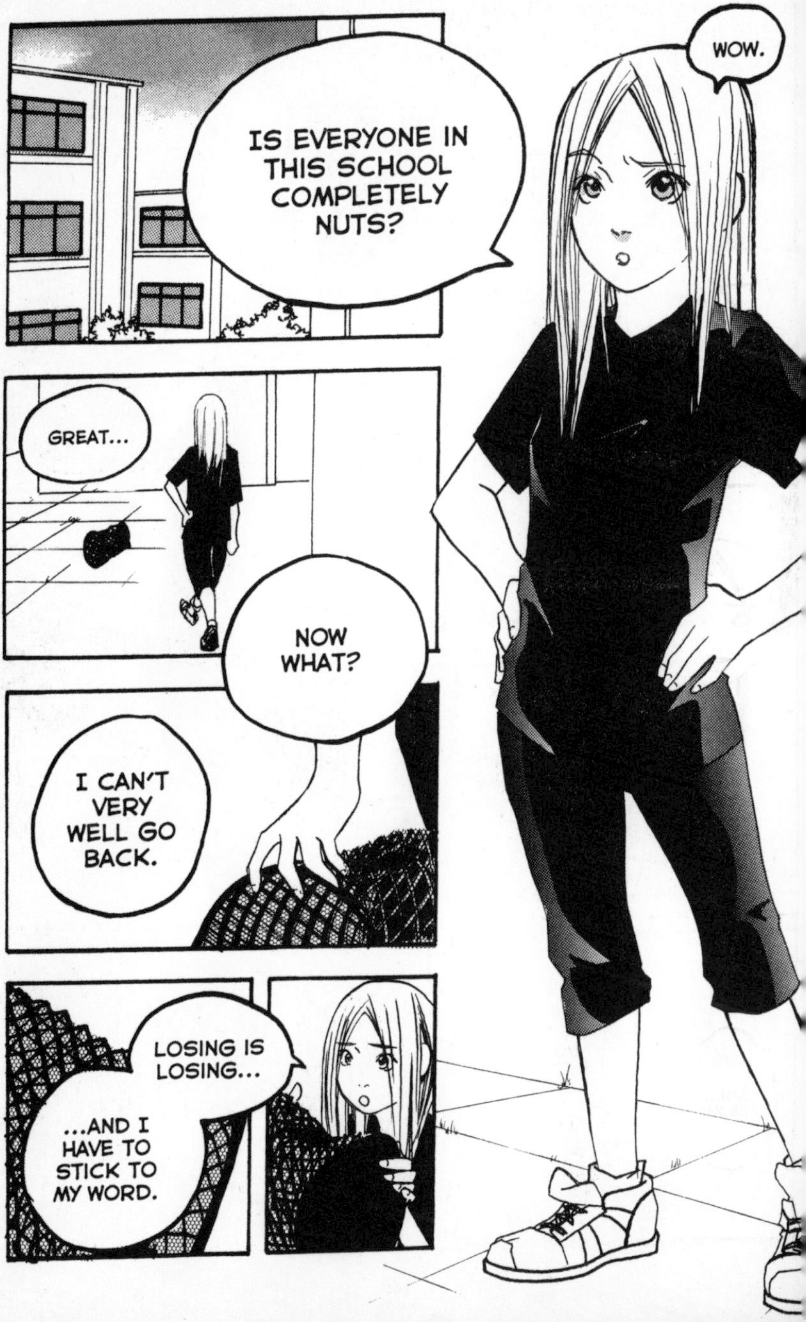
WOW.
IS EVERYONE IN THIS SCHOOL COMPLETELY NUTS?
GREAT...
NOW WHAT?
I CAN'T VERY WELL GO BACK.
LOSING IS LOSING...
...AND I HAVE TO STICK TO MY WORD.

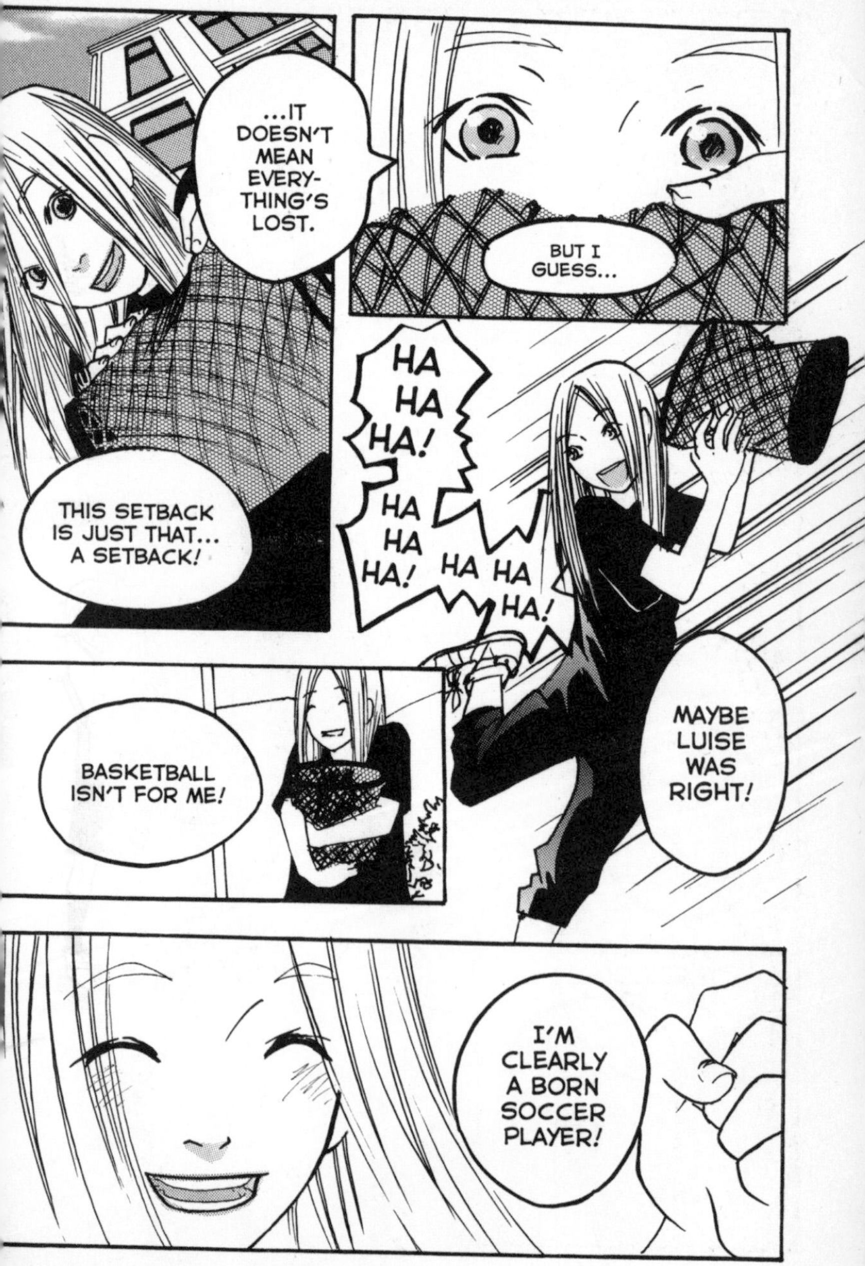
BUT I GUESS...
...IT DOESN'T MEAN EVERY-THING'S LOST.
THIS SETBACK IS JUST THAT... A SETBACK!
HA HA HA! HA HA HA! HA HA HA!
MAYBE LUISE WAS RIGHT!
BASKETBALL ISN'T FOR ME!
I'M CLEARLY A BORN SOCCER PLAYER!

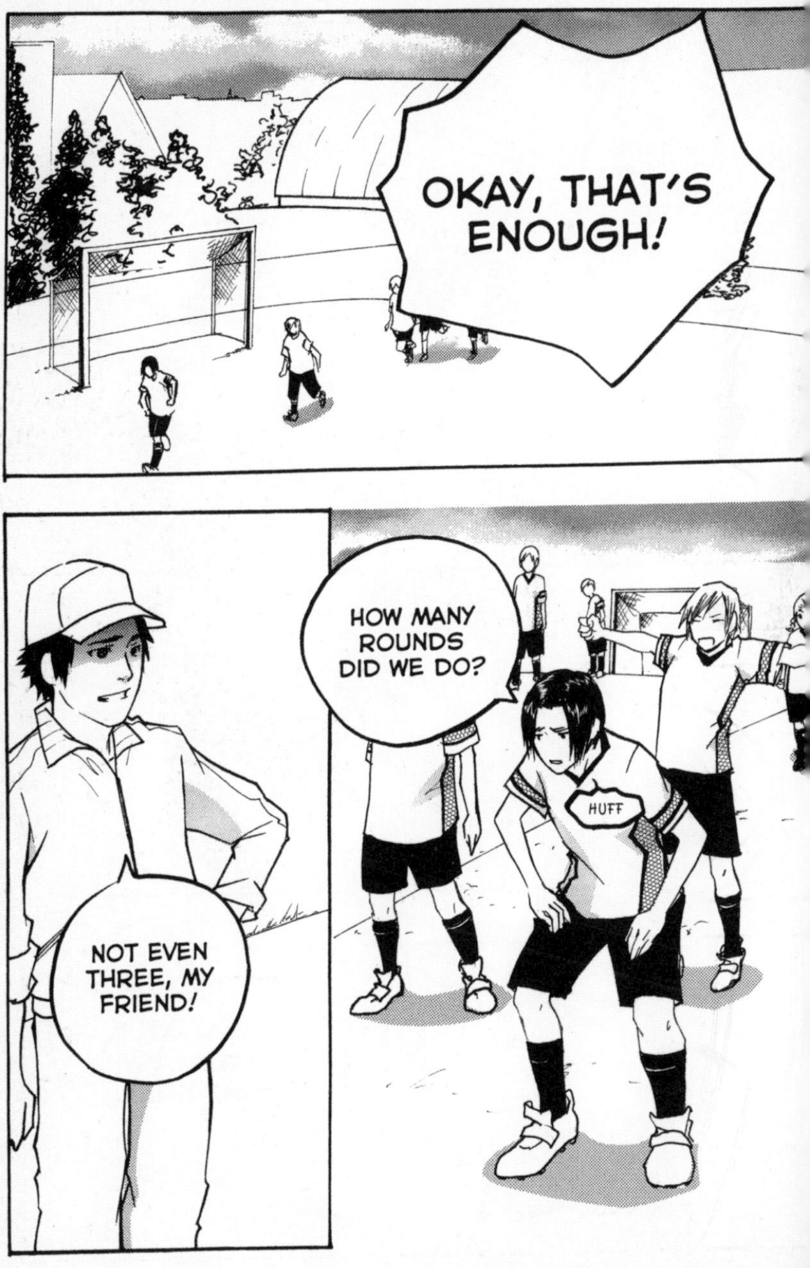
OKAY, THAT'S ENOUGH!
HOW MANY ROUNDS DID WE DO?
HUFF
NOT EVEN THREE, MY FRIEND!

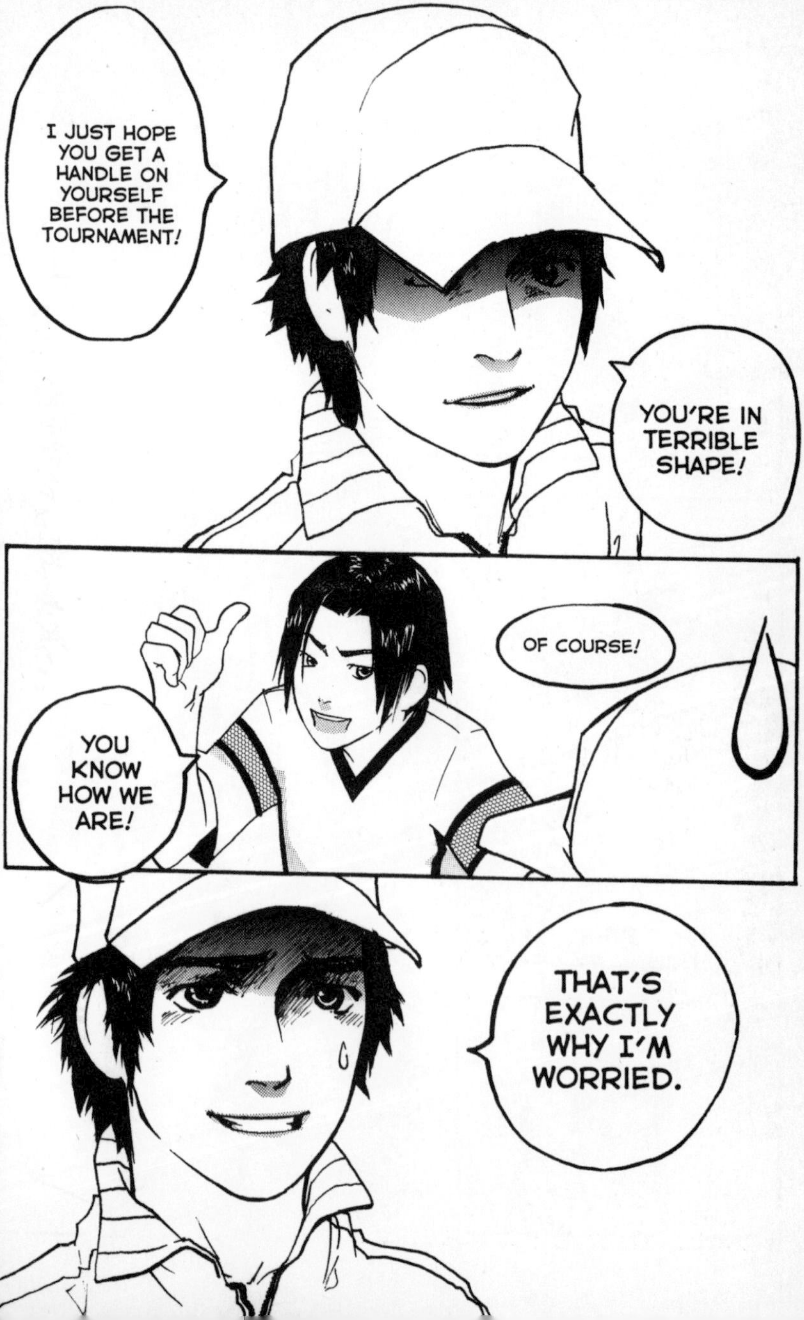
YOU'RE IN TERRIBLE SHAPE!
I JUST HOPE YOU GET A HANDLE ON YOURSELF BEFORE THE TOURNAMENT!
OF COURSE!
YOU KNOW HOW WE ARE!
THAT'S EXACTLY WHY I'M WORRIED.

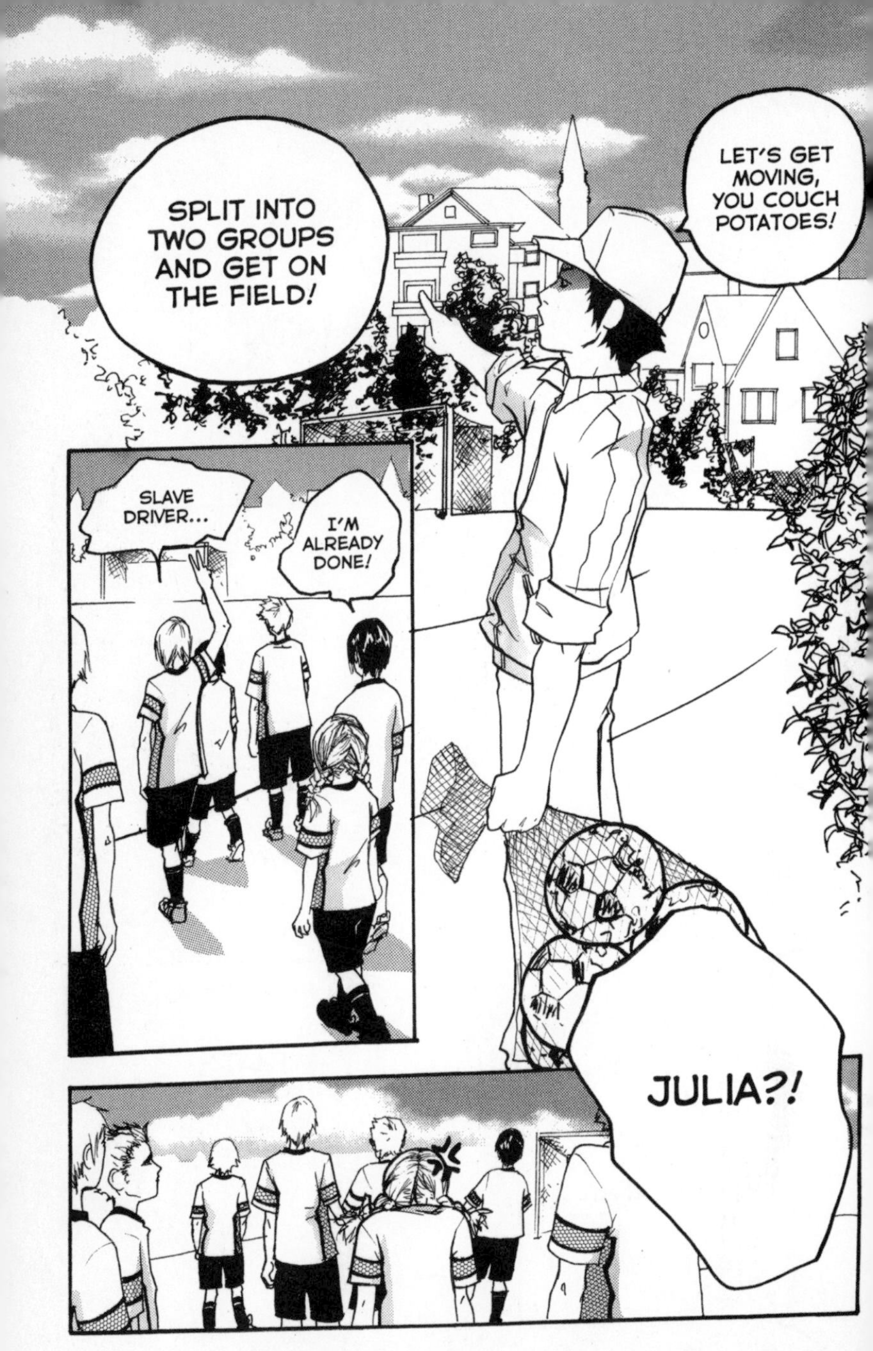
LET'S GET MOVING, YOU COUCH POTATOES!
SPLIT INTO TWO GROUPS AND GET ON THE FIELD!
I'M ALREADY DONE!
SLAVE DRIVER...
JULIA?!

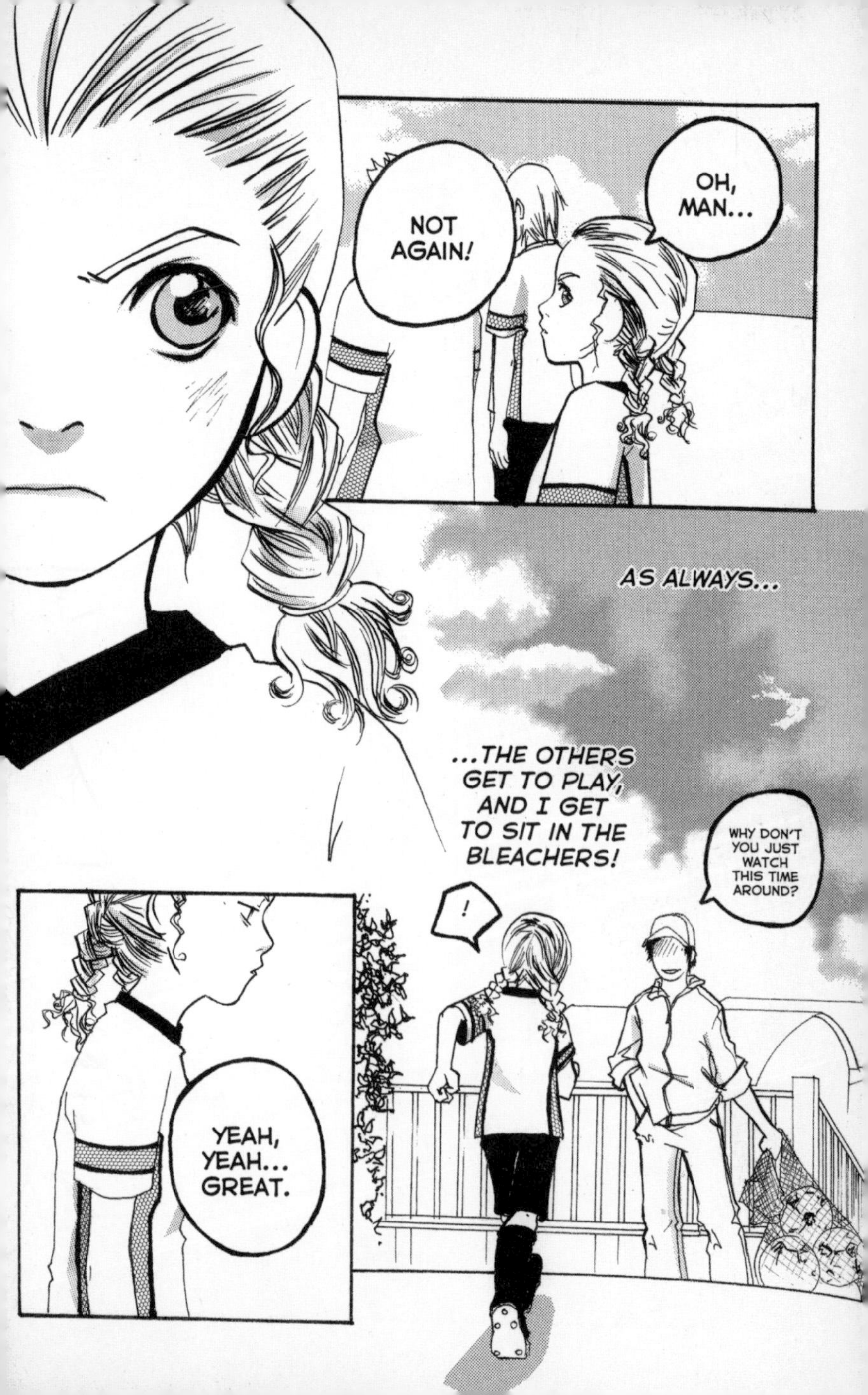
OH, MAN...
NOT AGAIN!
AS ALWAYS...
...THE OTHERS GET TO PLAY, AND I GET TO SIT IN THE BLEACHERS!
WHY DON'T YOU JUST WATCH THIS TIME AROUND?
!
YEAH, YEAH... GREAT.

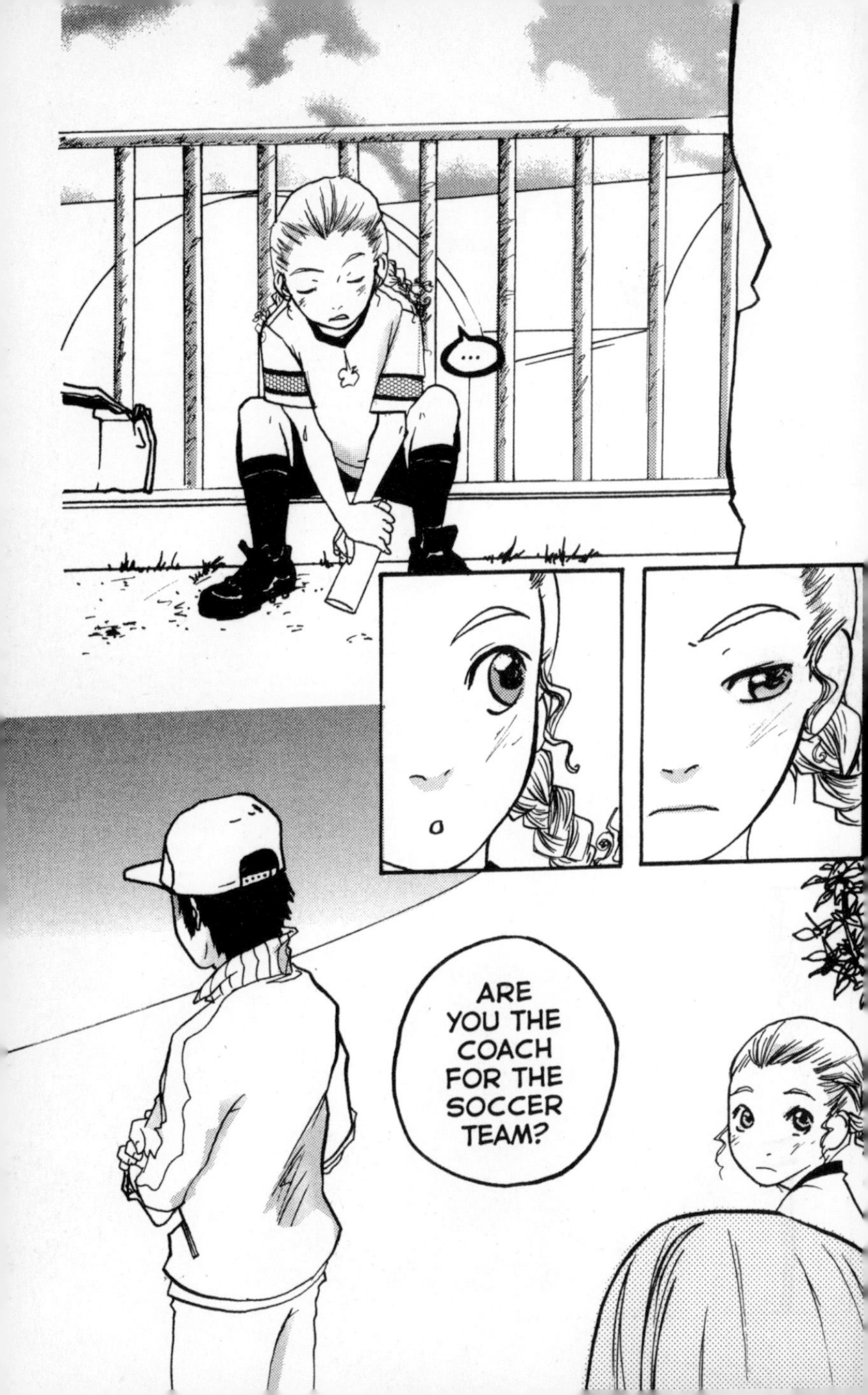
...
ARE YOU THE COACH FOR THE SOCCER TEAM?

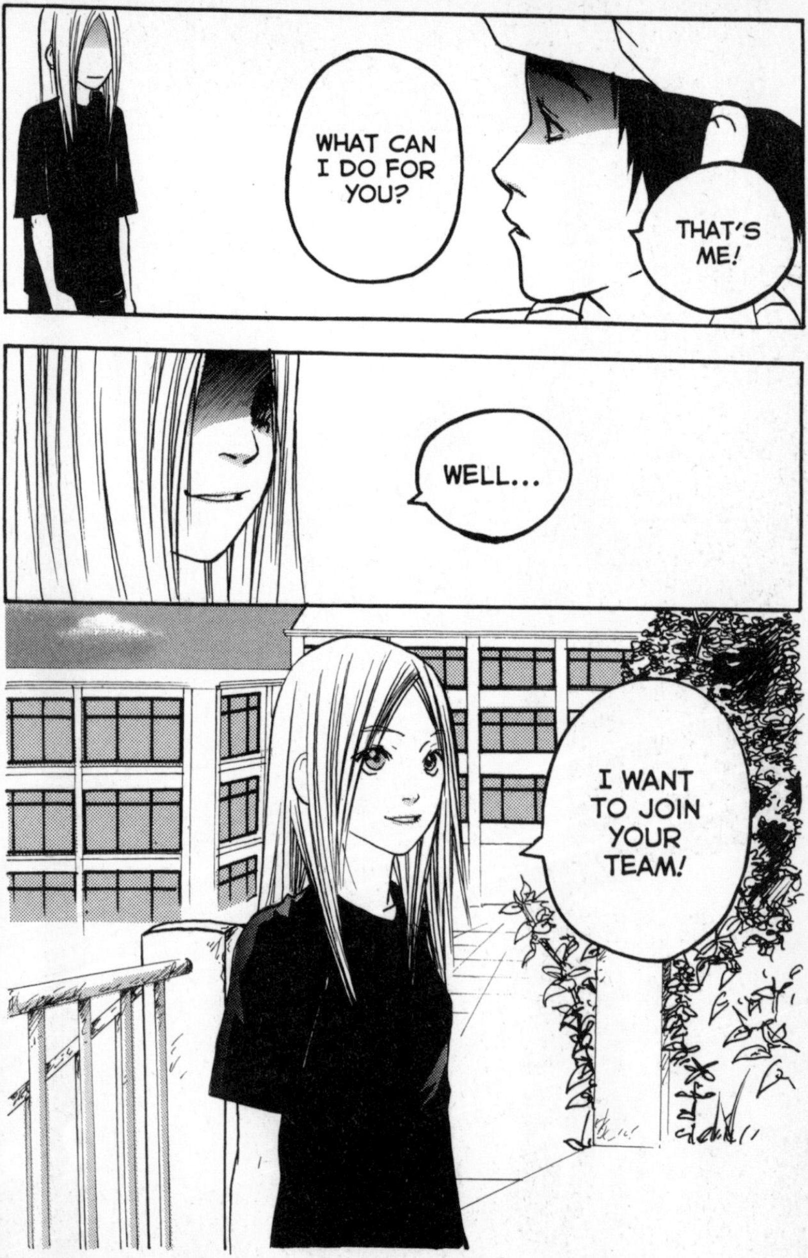
THAT'S ME!
WHAT CAN I DO FOR YOU?
WELL...
I WANT TO JOIN YOUR TEAM!

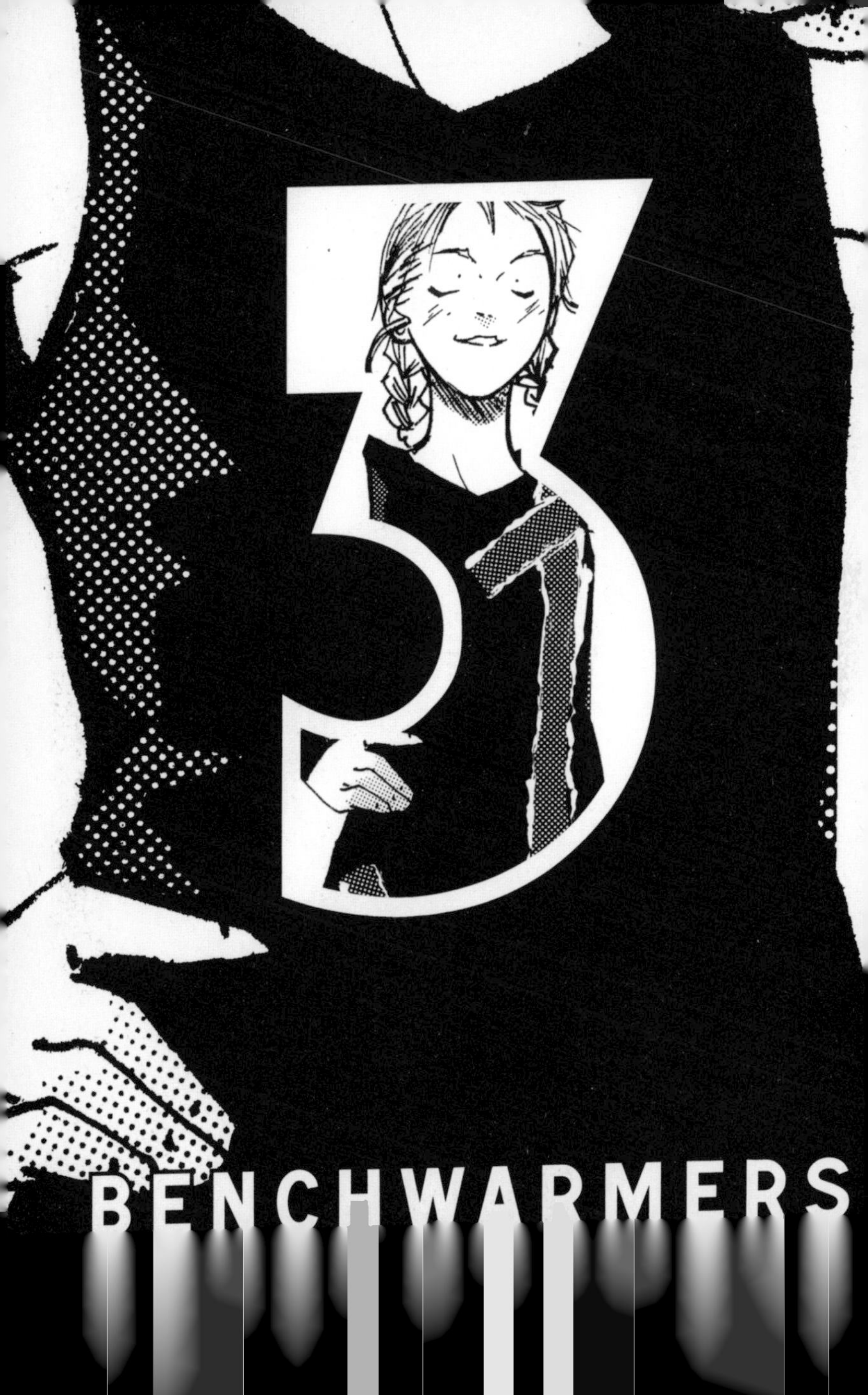
BENCHWARMERS

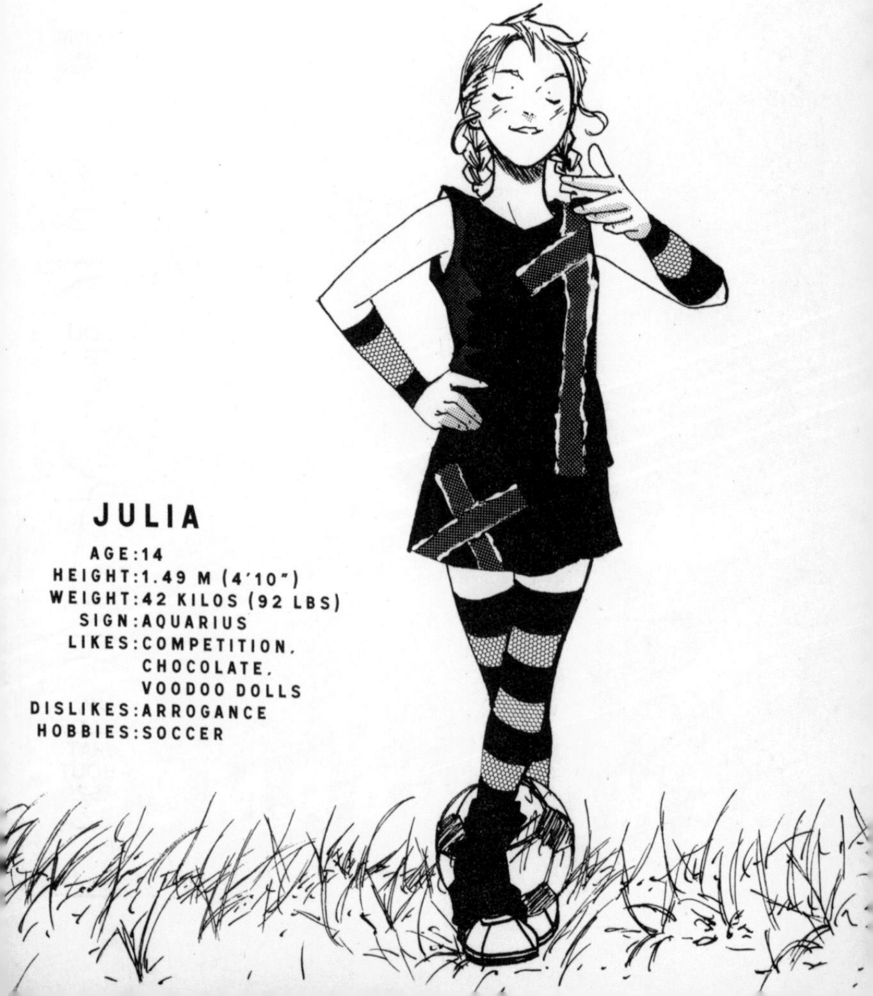

JULIA

AGE: 14
HEIGHT: 1.49 M (4'10")
WEIGHT: 42 KILOS (92 LBS)
SIGN: AQUARIUS
LIKES: COMPETITION, CHOCOLATE, VOODOO DOLLS
DISLIKES: ARROGANCE
HOBBIES: SOCCER

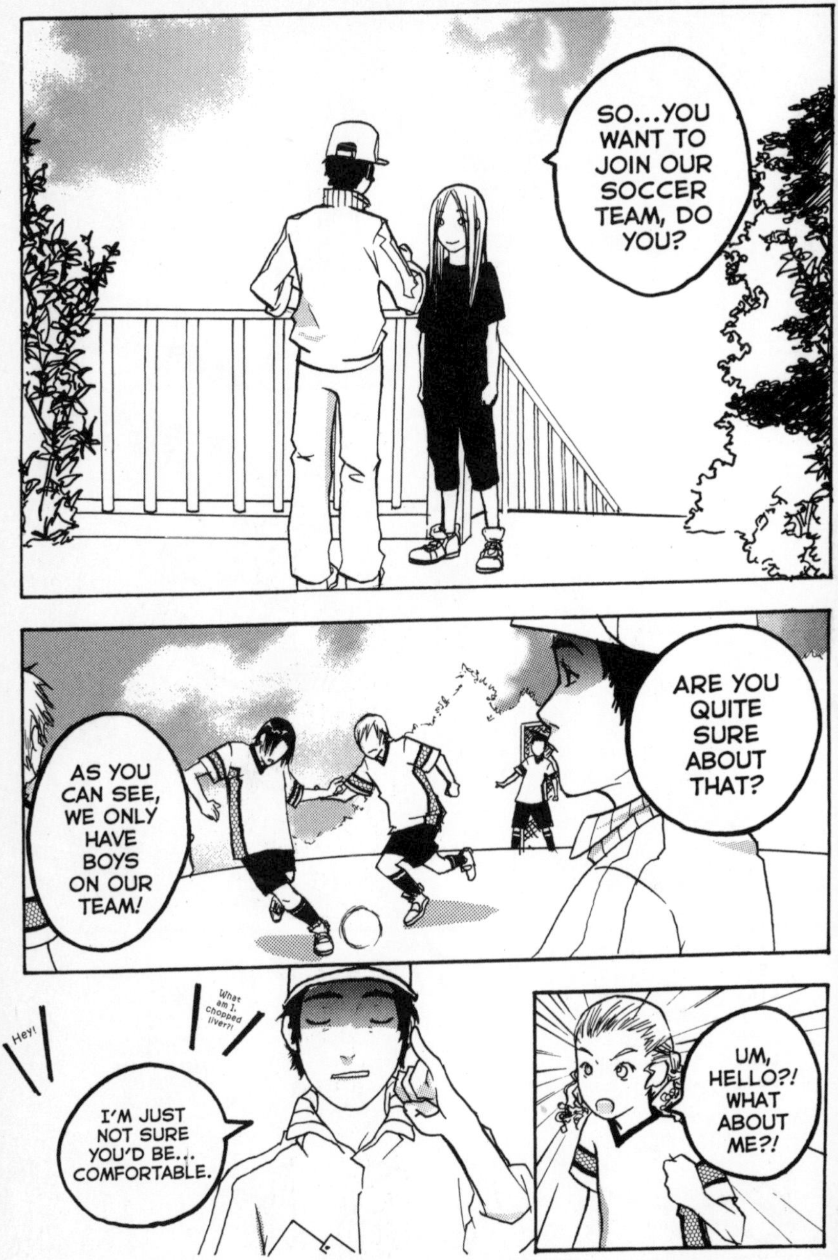
SO...YOU WANT TO JOIN OUR SOCCER TEAM, DO YOU?
ARE YOU QUITE SURE ABOUT THAT?
AS YOU CAN SEE, WE ONLY HAVE BOYS ON OUR TEAM!
UM, HELLO?! WHAT ABOUT ME?!
What am I. Chopped liver?!
Hey!
I'M JUST NOT SURE YOU'D BE... COMFORTABLE.

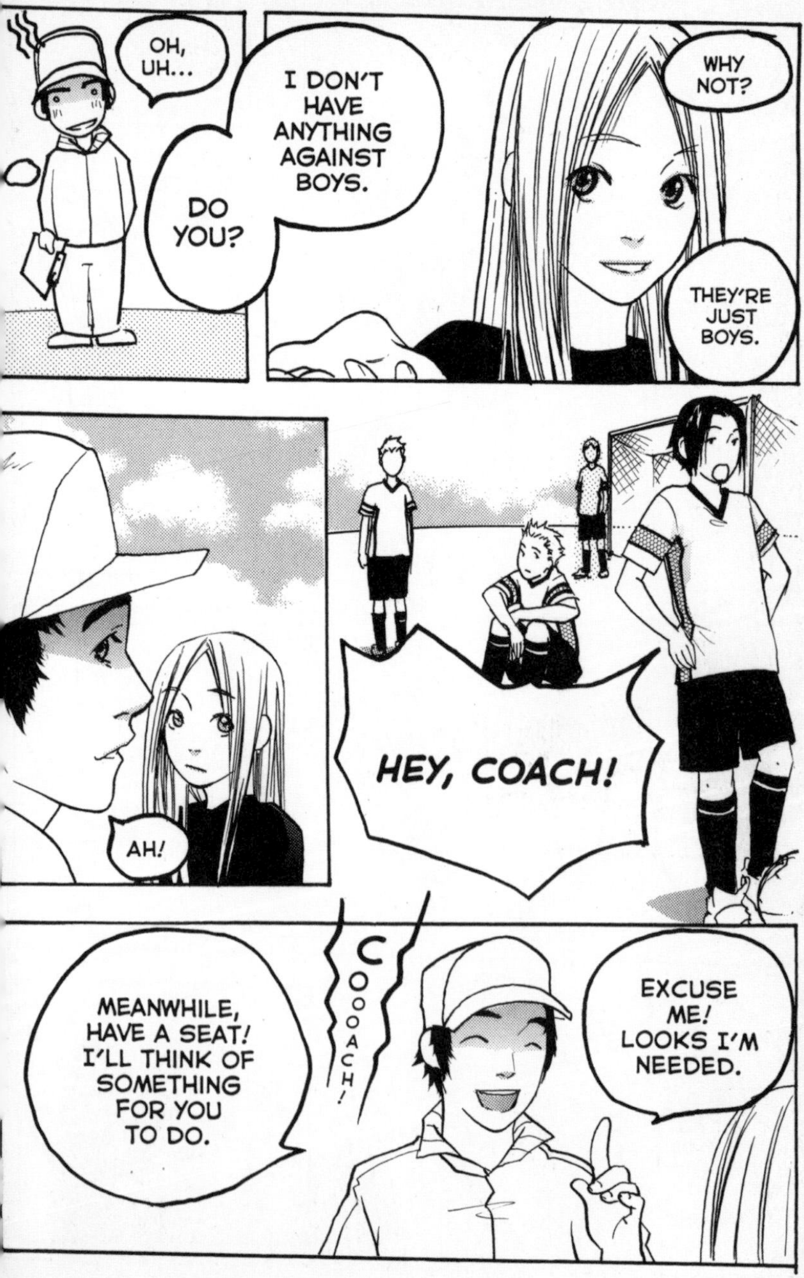
WHY NOT?
THEY'RE JUST BOYS.
I DON'T HAVE ANYTHING AGAINST BOYS.
DO YOU?
OH, UH...
HEY, COACH!
AH!
COOOOACH!
EXCUSE ME! LOOKS I'M NEEDED.
MEANWHILE, HAVE A SEAT! I'LL THINK OF SOMETHING FOR YOU TO DO.

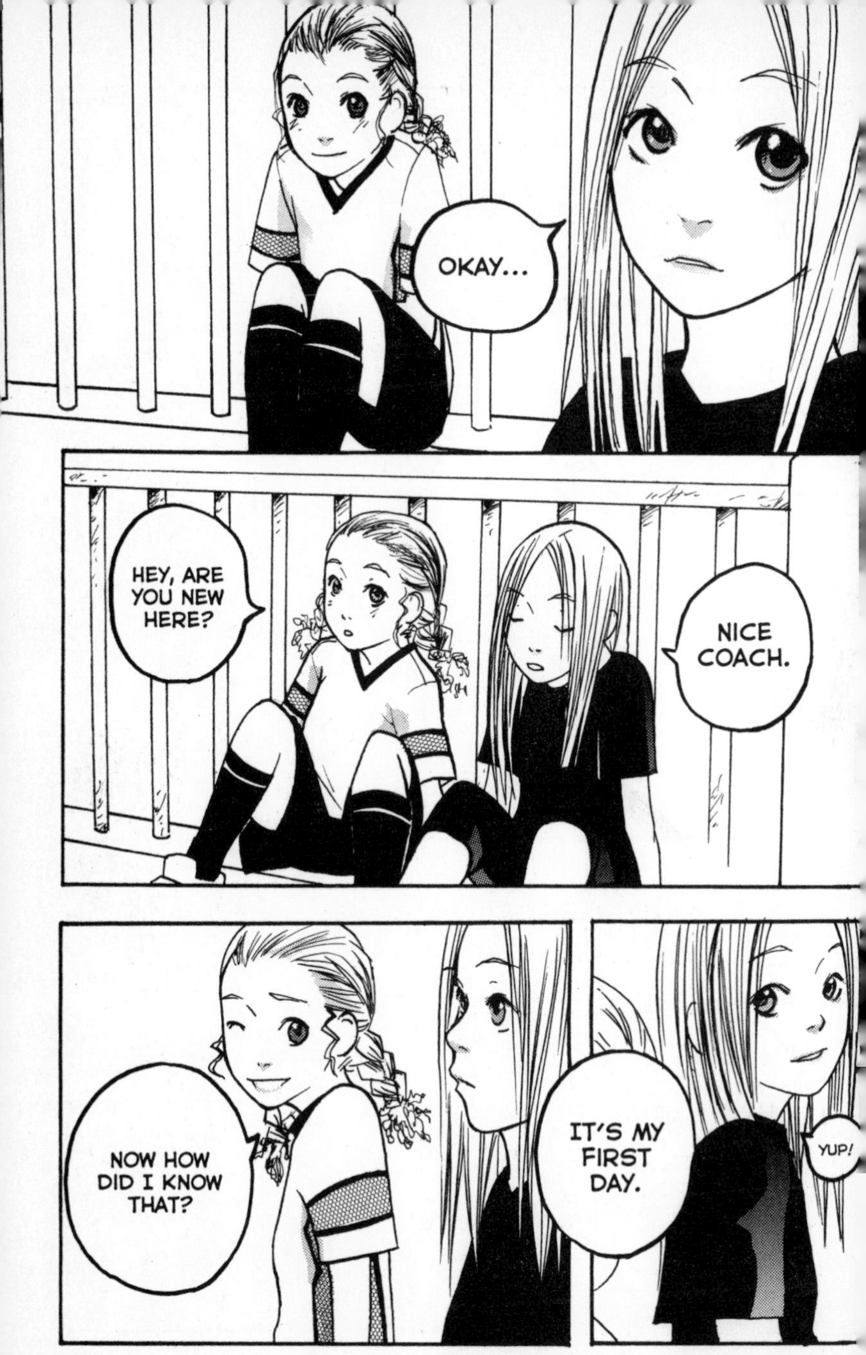
OKAY...
NICE COACH.
HEY, ARE YOU NEW HERE?
YUP!
IT'S MY FIRST DAY.
NOW HOW DID I KNOW THAT?

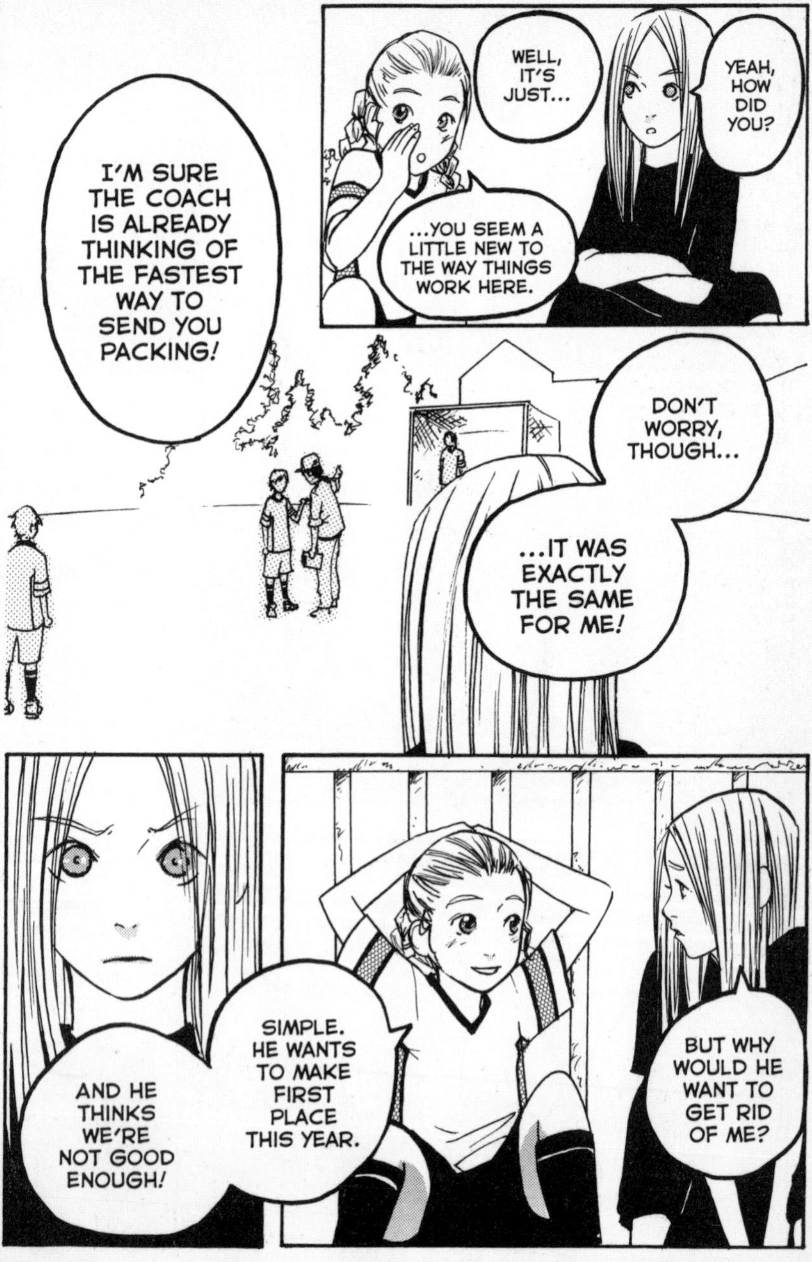
YEAH, HOW DID YOU?
WELL, IT'S JUST...
...YOU SEEM A LITTLE NEW TO THE WAY THINGS WORK HERE.
I'M SURE THE COACH IS ALREADY THINKING OF THE FASTEST WAY TO SEND YOU PACKING!
DON'T WORRY, THOUGH...
...IT WAS EXACTLY THE SAME FOR ME!
BUT WHY WOULD HE WANT TO GET RID OF ME?
SIMPLE. HE WANTS TO MAKE FIRST PLACE THIS YEAR.
AND HE THINKS WE'RE NOT GOOD ENOUGH!

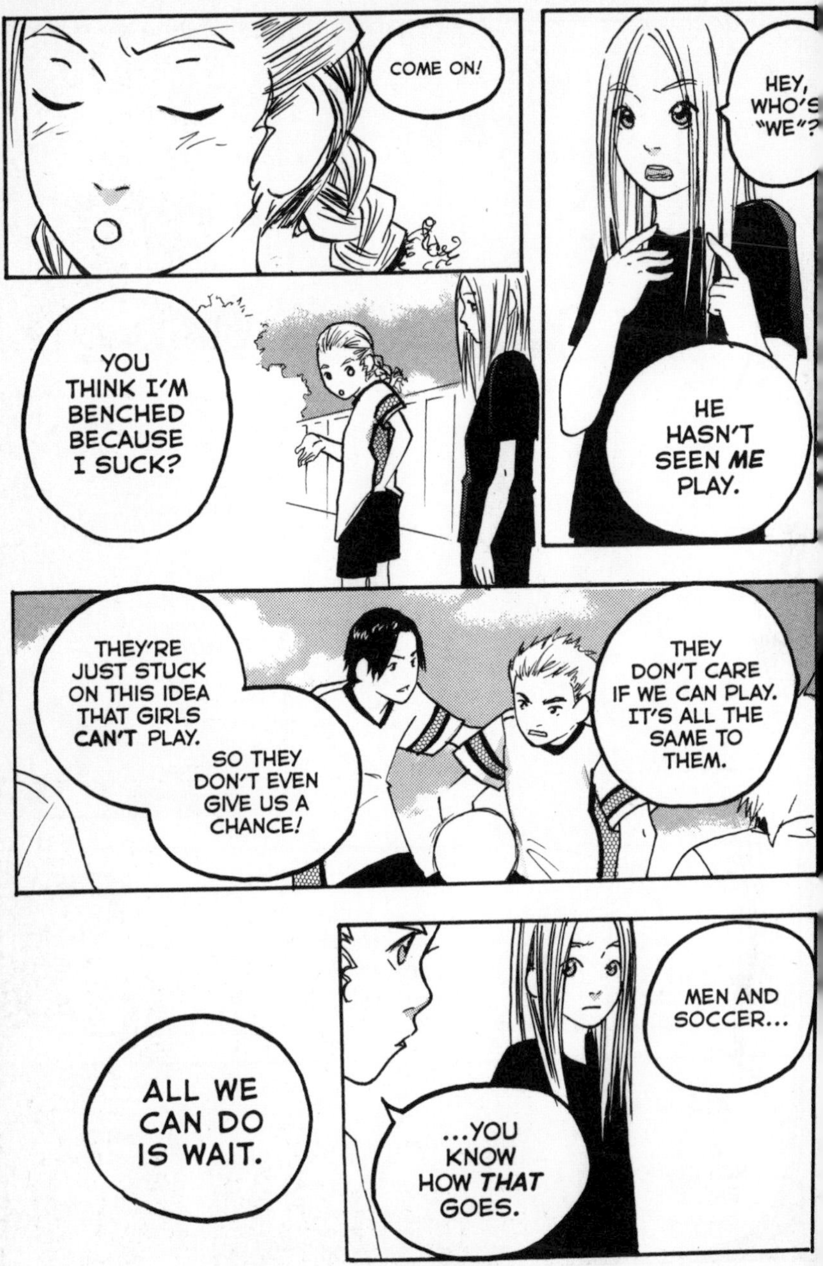
HEY, WHO'S "WE"?
HE HASN'T SEEN *ME* PLAY.
COME ON!
YOU THINK I'M BENCHED BECAUSE I SUCK?
THEY DON'T CARE IF WE CAN PLAY. IT'S ALL THE SAME TO THEM.
THEY'RE JUST STUCK ON THIS IDEA THAT GIRLS **CAN'T** PLAY.
SO THEY DON'T EVEN GIVE US A CHANCE!
MEN AND SOCCER...
...YOU KNOW HOW *THAT* GOES.
ALL WE CAN DO IS WAIT.

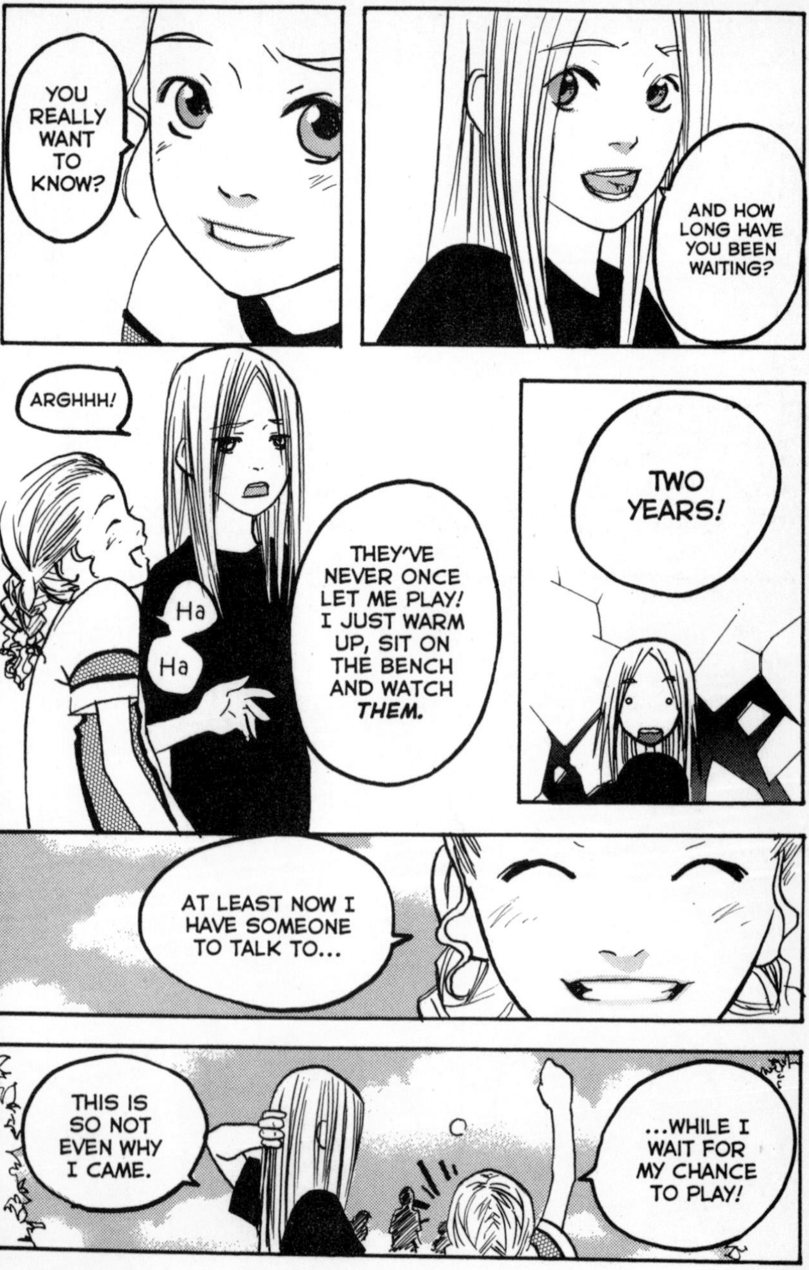
AND HOW LONG HAVE YOU BEEN WAITING?
YOU REALLY WANT TO KNOW?
TWO YEARS!
ARGHHH!
THEY'VE NEVER ONCE LET ME PLAY! I JUST WARM UP, SIT ON THE BENCH AND WATCH *THEM.*
Ha
Ha
AT LEAST NOW I HAVE SOMEONE TO TALK TO...
...WHILE I WAIT FOR MY CHANCE TO PLAY!
THIS IS SO NOT EVEN WHY I CAME.

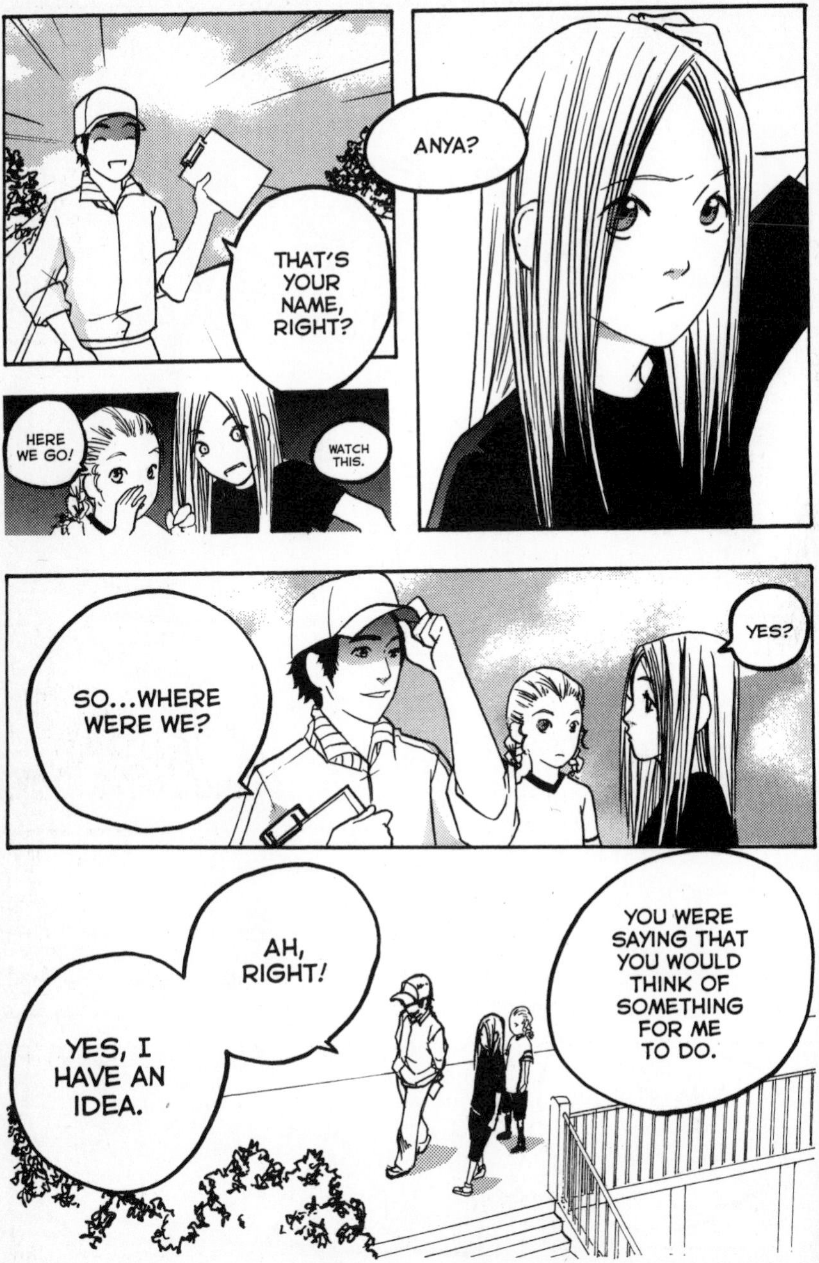
ANYA?
THAT'S YOUR NAME, RIGHT?
WATCH THIS.
HERE WE GO!
YES?
SO...WHERE WERE WE?
YOU WERE SAYING THAT YOU WOULD THINK OF SOMETHING FOR ME TO DO.
AH, RIGHT!
YES, I HAVE AN IDEA.

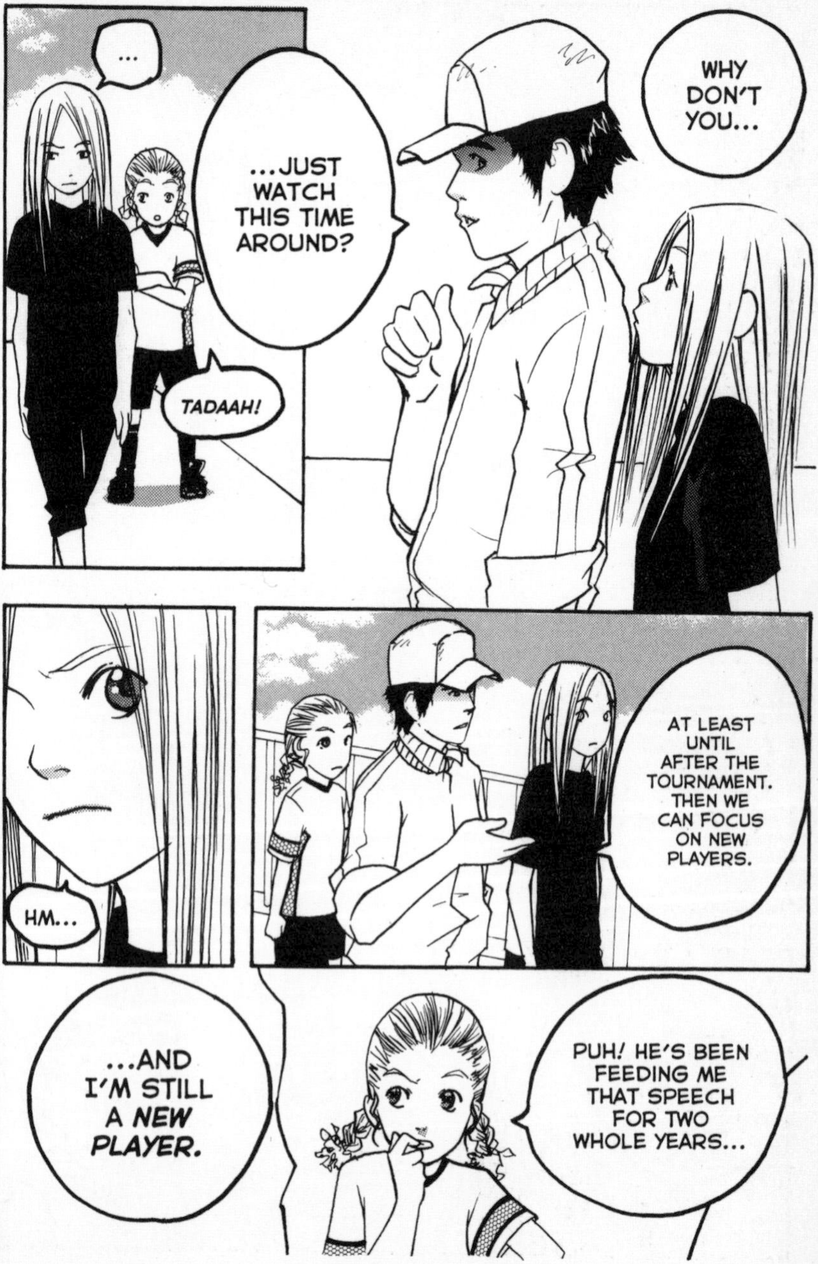
WHY DON'T YOU...
...JUST WATCH THIS TIME AROUND?
...
TADAAH!
AT LEAST UNTIL AFTER THE TOURNAMENT. THEN WE CAN FOCUS ON NEW PLAYERS.
HM...
PUH! HE'S BEEN FEEDING ME THAT SPEECH FOR TWO WHOLE YEARS...
...AND I'M STILL A ***NEW PLAYER.***

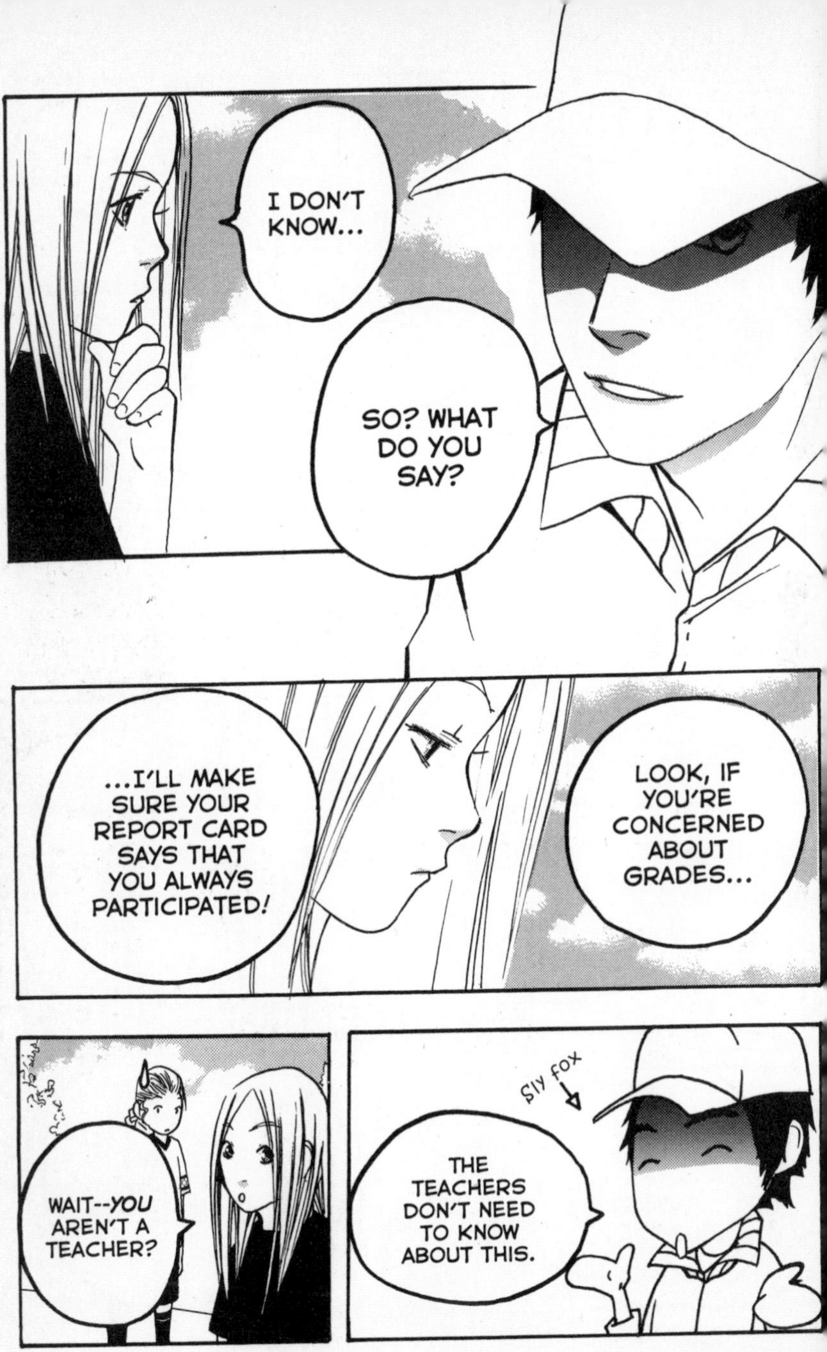
SO? WHAT DO YOU SAY?
I DON'T KNOW...
LOOK, IF YOU'RE CONCERNED ABOUT GRADES...
...I'LL MAKE SURE YOUR REPORT CARD SAYS THAT YOU ALWAYS PARTICIPATED!
Sly fox
THE TEACHERS DON'T NEED TO KNOW ABOUT THIS.
WAIT--*YOU* AREN'T A TEACHER?

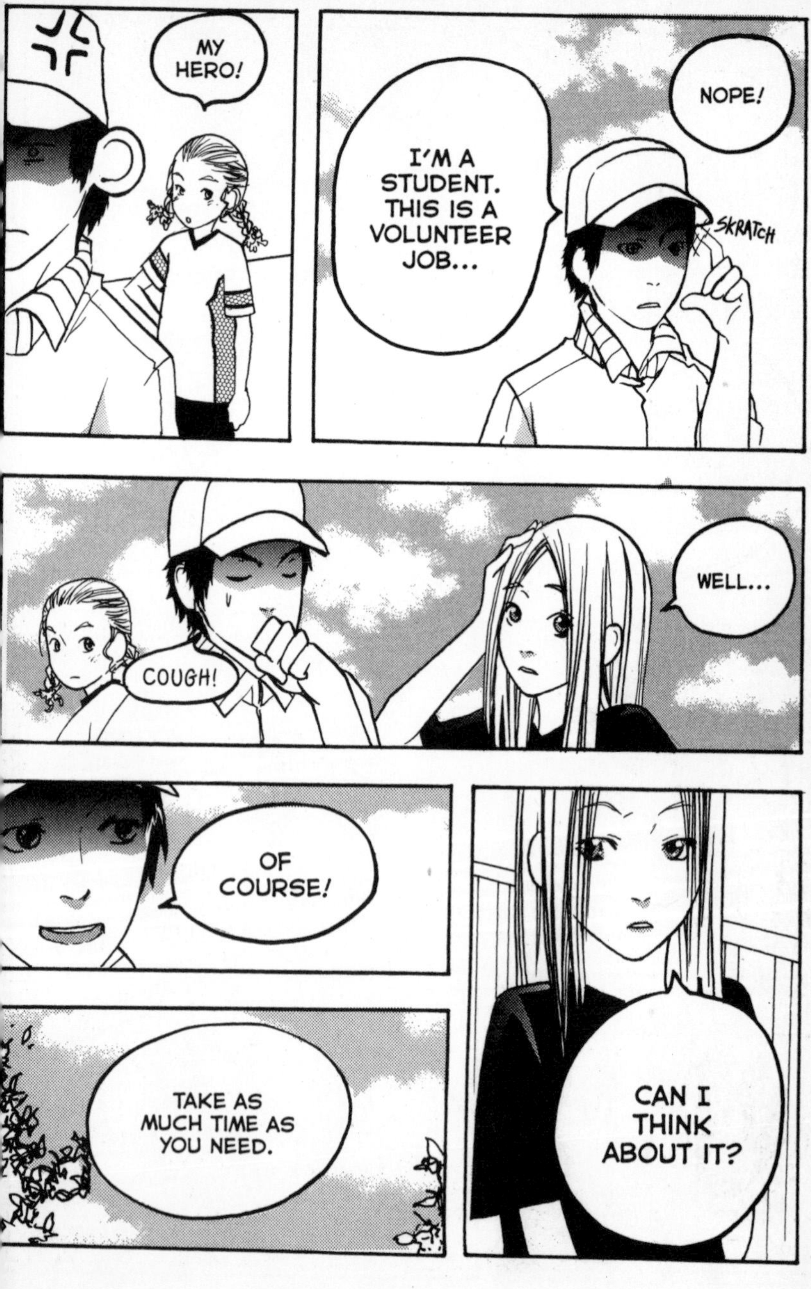
NOPE!
I'M A STUDENT. THIS IS A VOLUNTEER JOB...
SKRATCH
MY HERO!
WELL...
COUGH!
CAN I THINK ABOUT IT?
OF COURSE!
TAKE AS MUCH TIME AS YOU NEED.

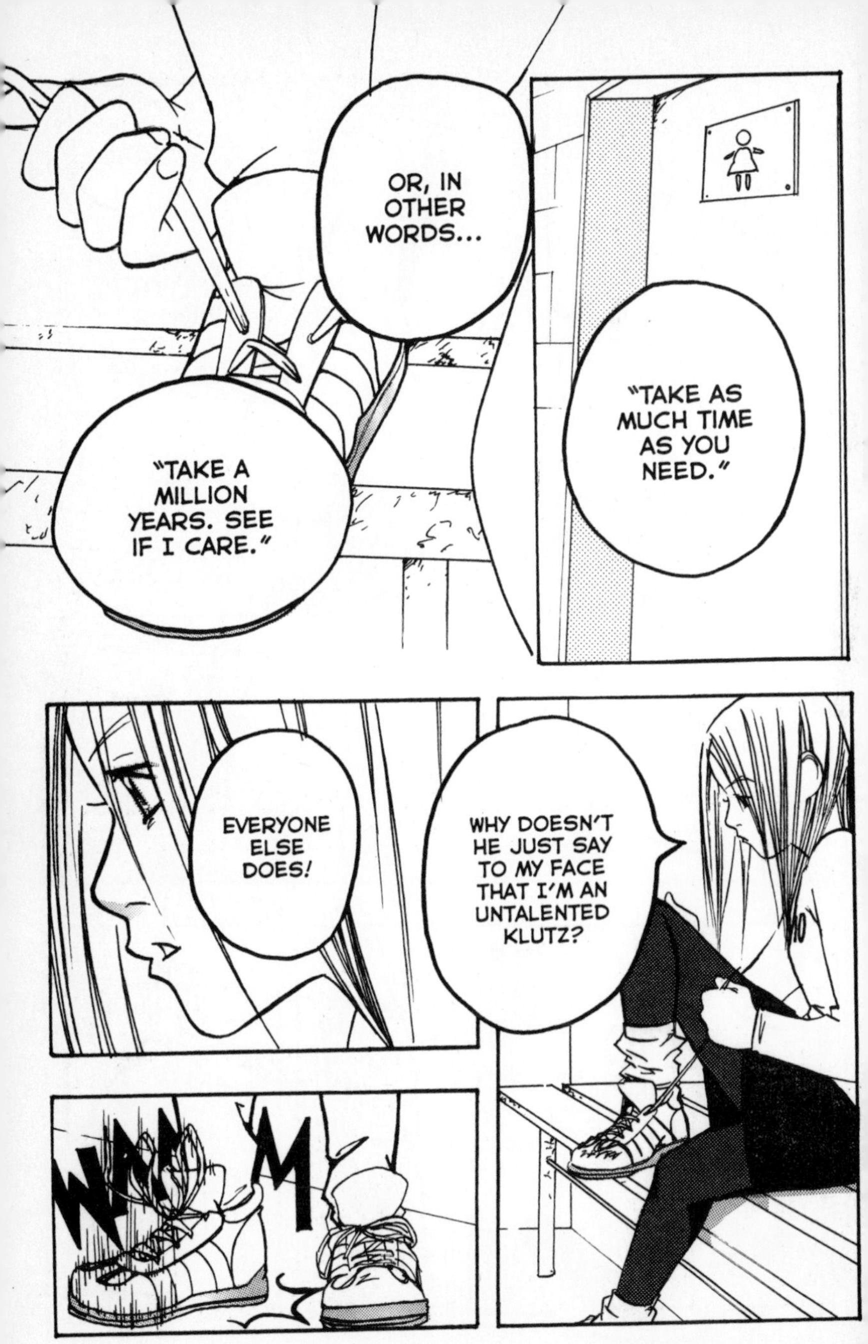
"TAKE AS MUCH TIME AS YOU NEED."
OR, IN OTHER WORDS...
"TAKE A MILLION YEARS. SEE IF I CARE."
WHY DOESN'T HE JUST SAY TO MY FACE THAT I'M AN UNTALENTED KLUTZ?
EVERYONE ELSE DOES!
WHAM

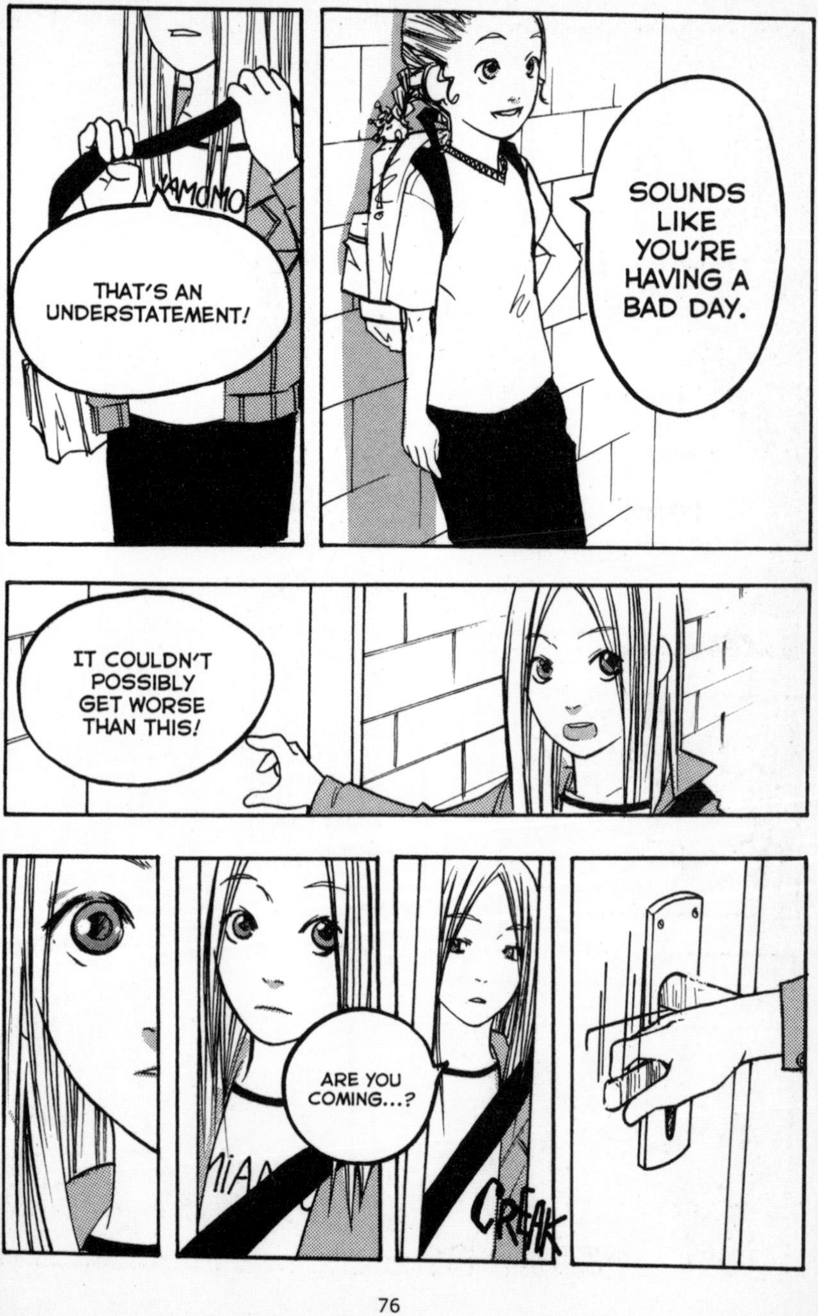
SOUNDS LIKE YOU'RE HAVING A BAD DAY.
THAT'S AN UNDERSTATEMENT!
IT COULDN'T POSSIBLY GET WORSE THAN THIS!
CREAK
ARE YOU COMING...?

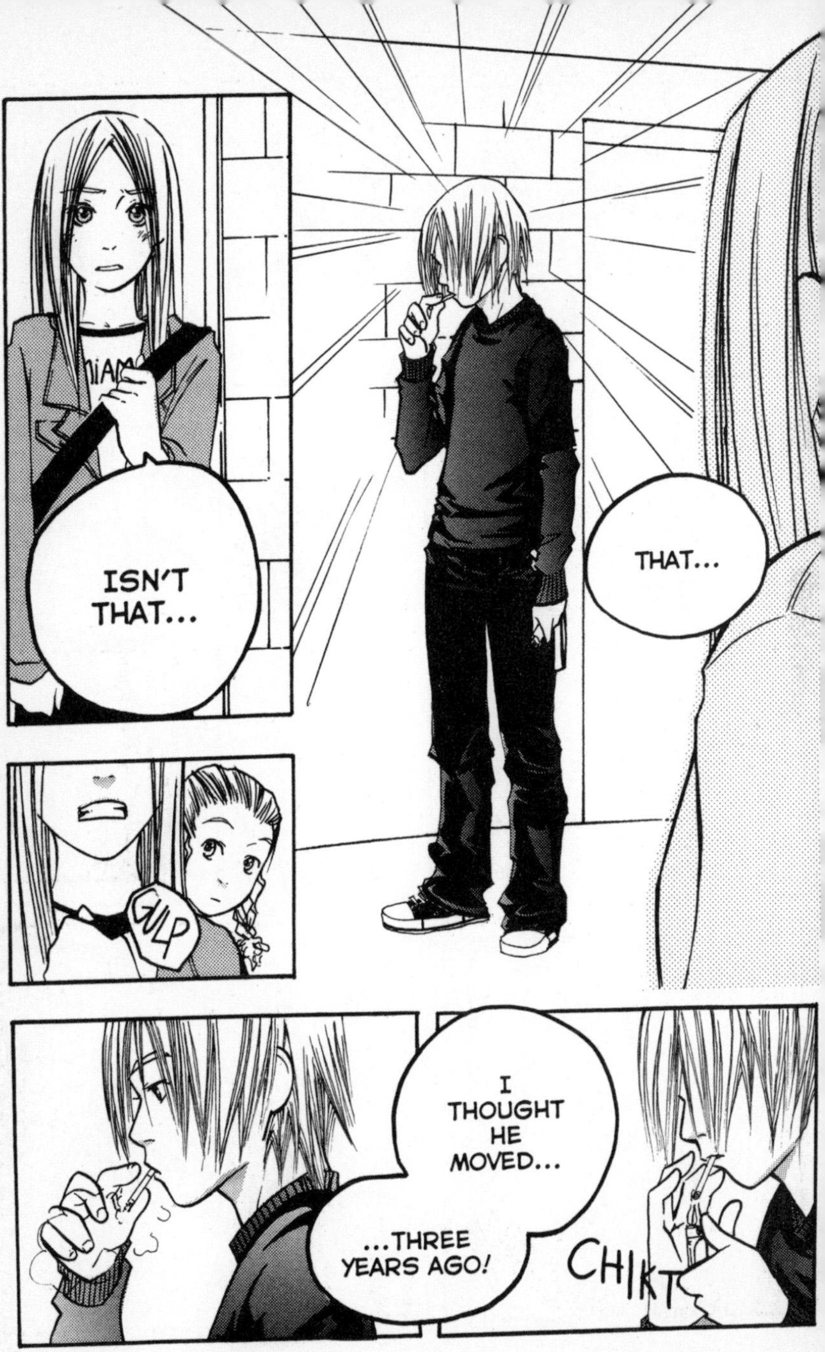
THAT...
ISN'T THAT...
GULP
CHIKT
I THOUGHT HE MOVED...
...THREE YEARS AGO!

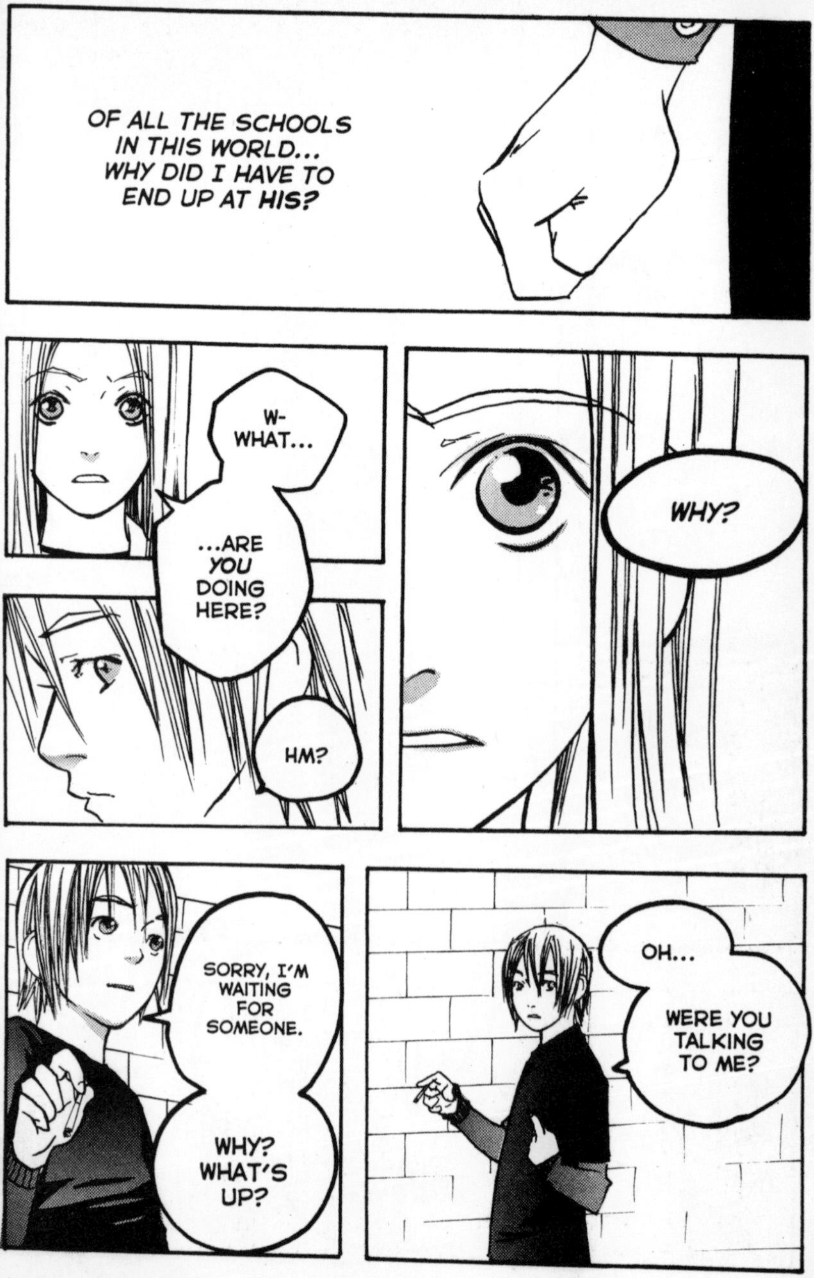
OF ALL THE SCHOOLS IN THIS WORLD... WHY DID I HAVE TO END UP AT *HIS*?
WHY?
W- WHAT...
...ARE *YOU* DOING HERE?
HM?
OH...
WERE YOU TALKING TO ME?
SORRY, I'M WAITING FOR SOMEONE.
WHY? WHAT'S UP?

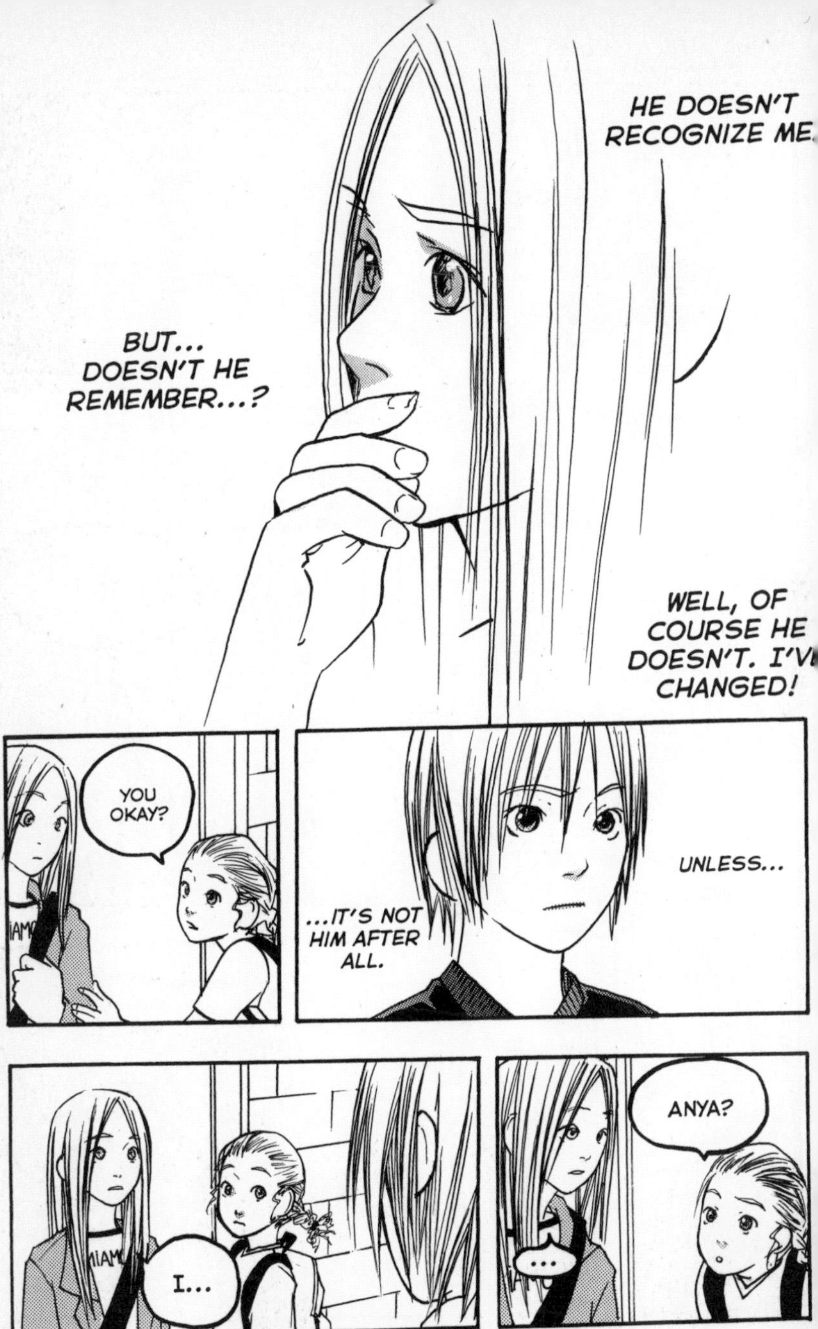
HE DOESN'T RECOGNIZE ME.
BUT... DOESN'T HE REMEMBER...?
WELL, OF COURSE HE DOESN'T. I'V
CHANGED!
UNLESS...
...IT'S NOT HIM AFTER ALL.
YOU OKAY?
ANYA?
...
I...

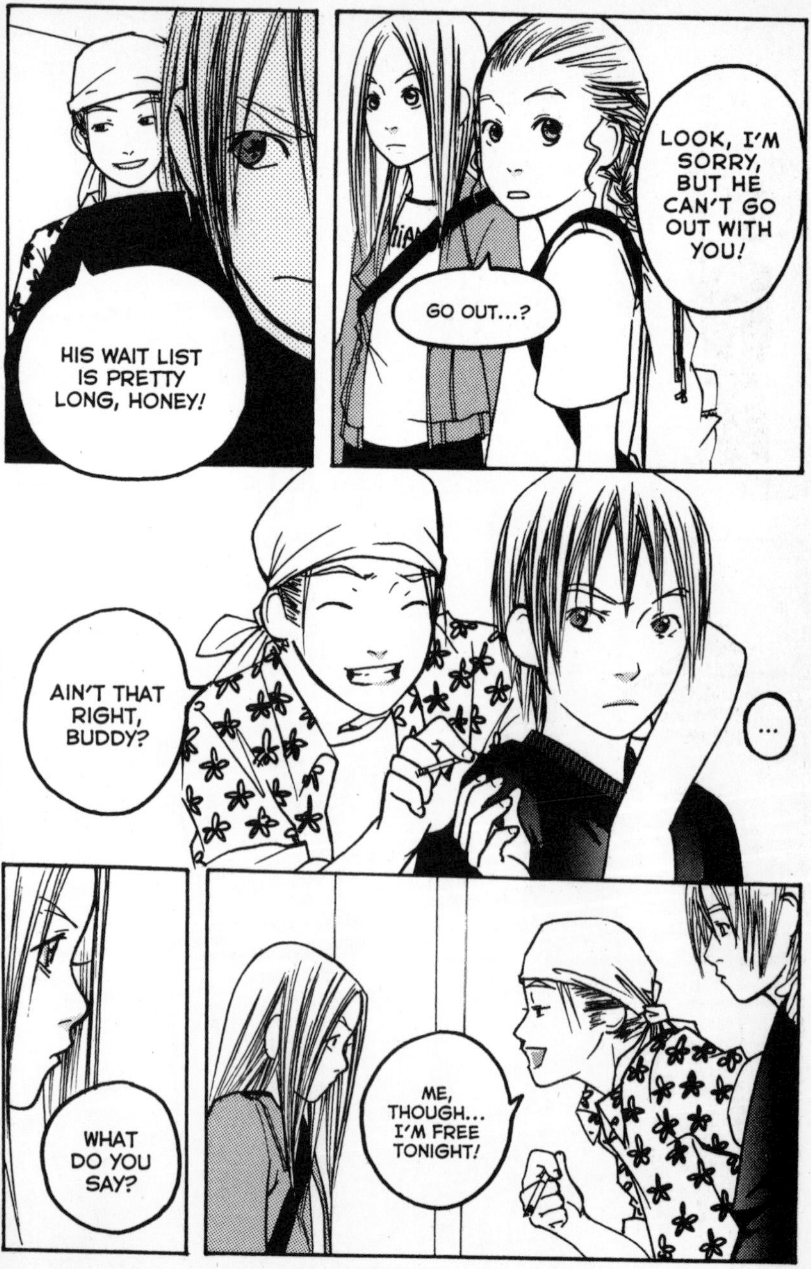
LOOK, I'M SORRY, BUT HE CAN'T GO OUT WITH YOU!
GO OUT...?
HIS WAIT LIST IS PRETTY LONG, HONEY!
AIN'T THAT RIGHT, BUDDY?
...
ME, THOUGH... I'M FREE TONIGHT!
WHAT DO YOU SAY?

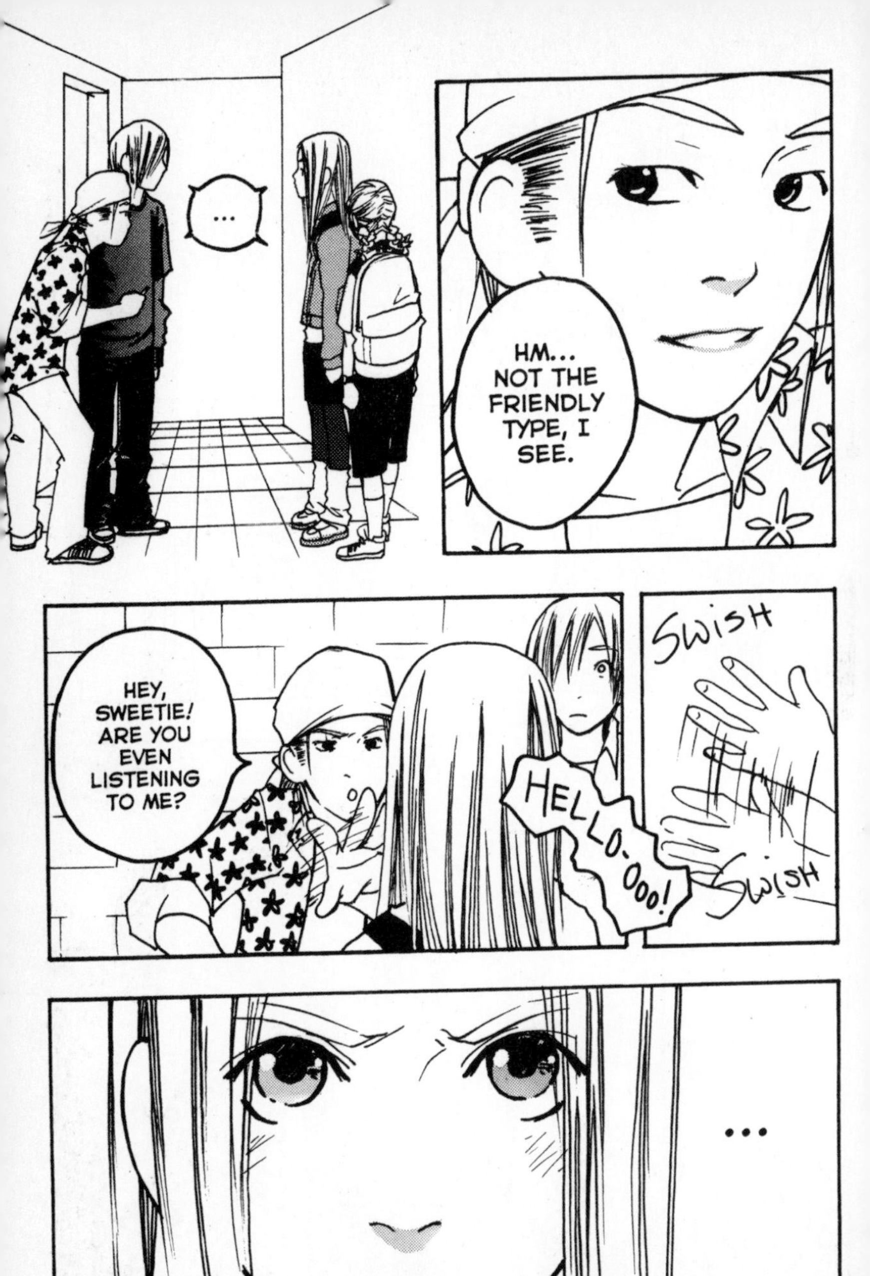
...
HM... NOT THE FRIENDLY TYPE, I SEE.
HEY, SWEETIE! ARE YOU EVEN LISTENING TO ME?
HELLO-OOO!
SWISH
SWISH
...

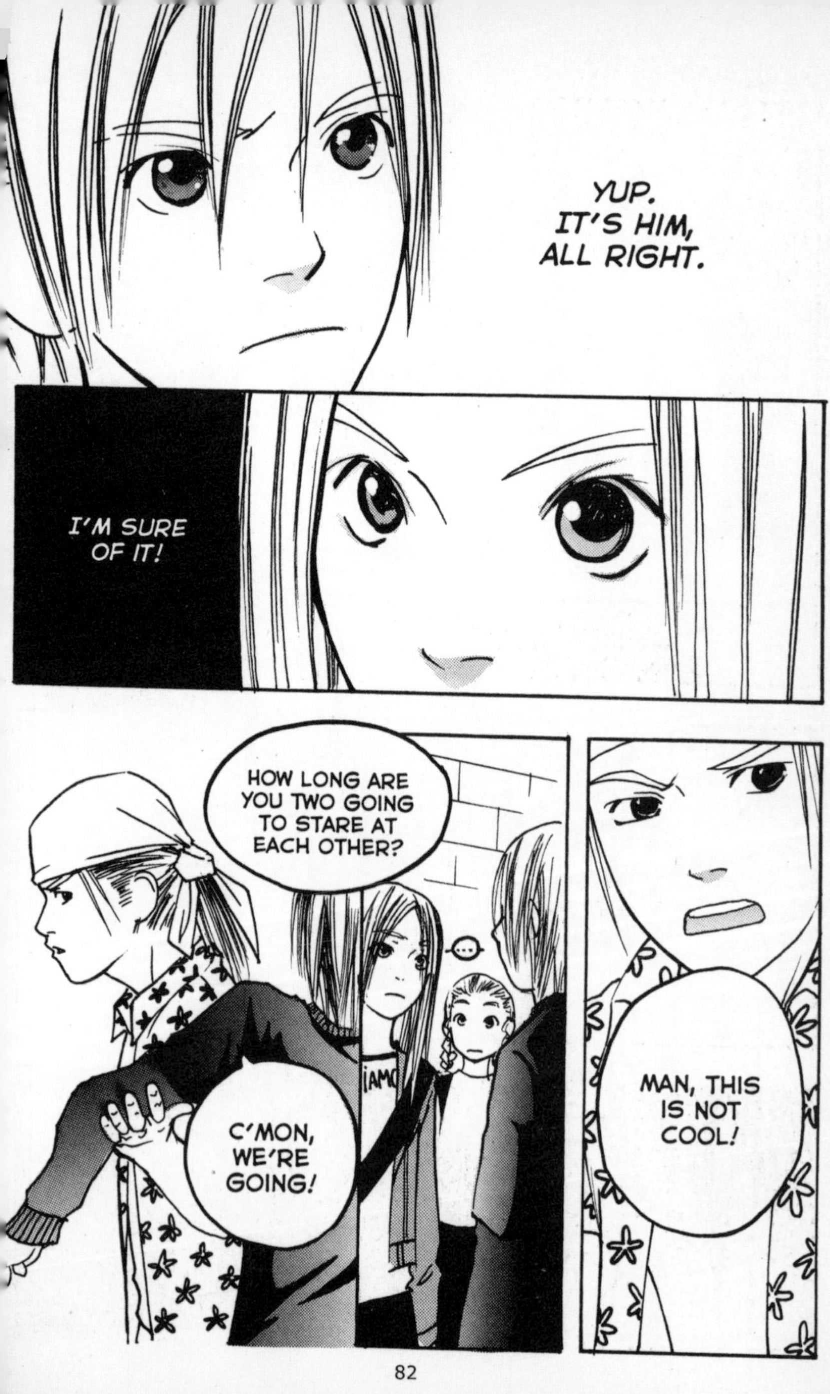
YUP. IT'S HIM, ALL RIGHT.
I'M SURE OF IT!
MAN, THIS IS NOT COOL!
HOW LONG ARE YOU TWO GOING TO STARE AT EACH OTHER?
...
C'MON, WE'RE GOING!

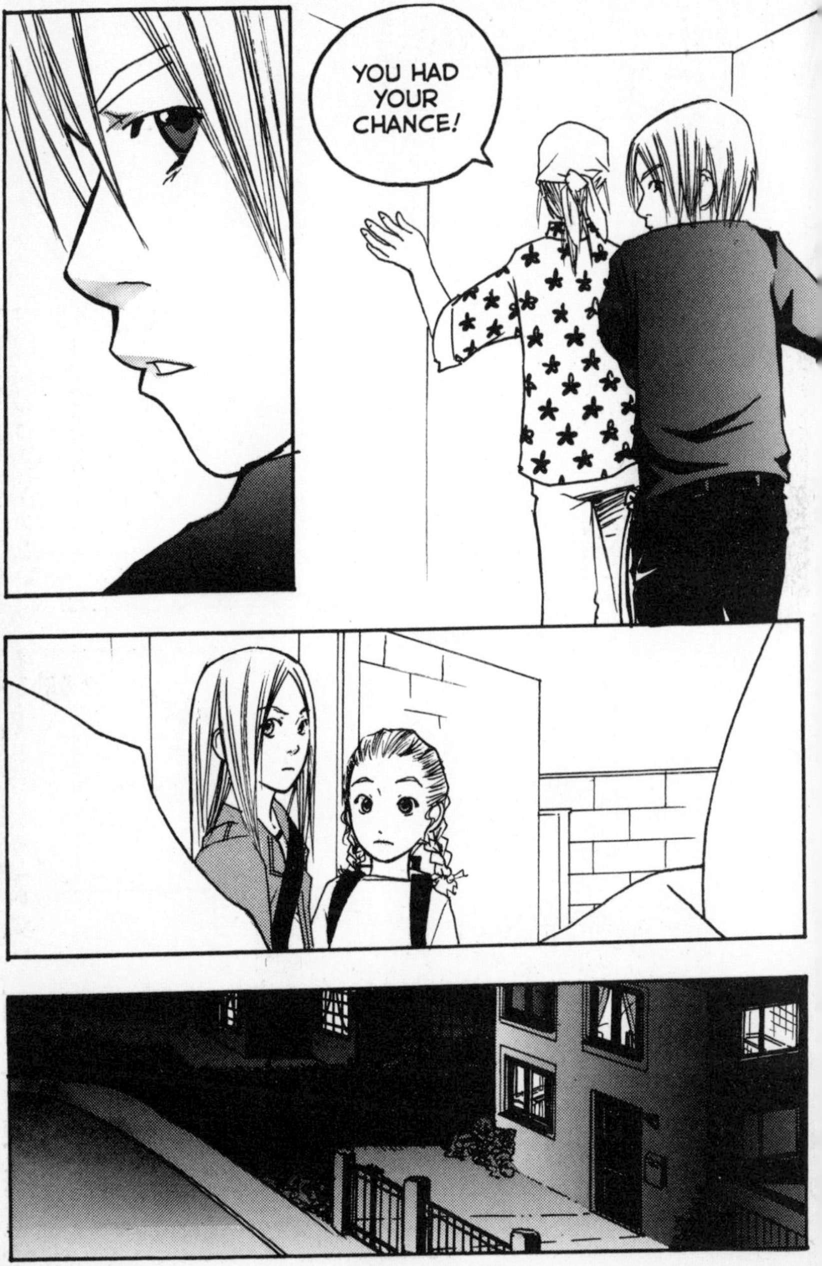
YOU HAD YOUR CHANCE!

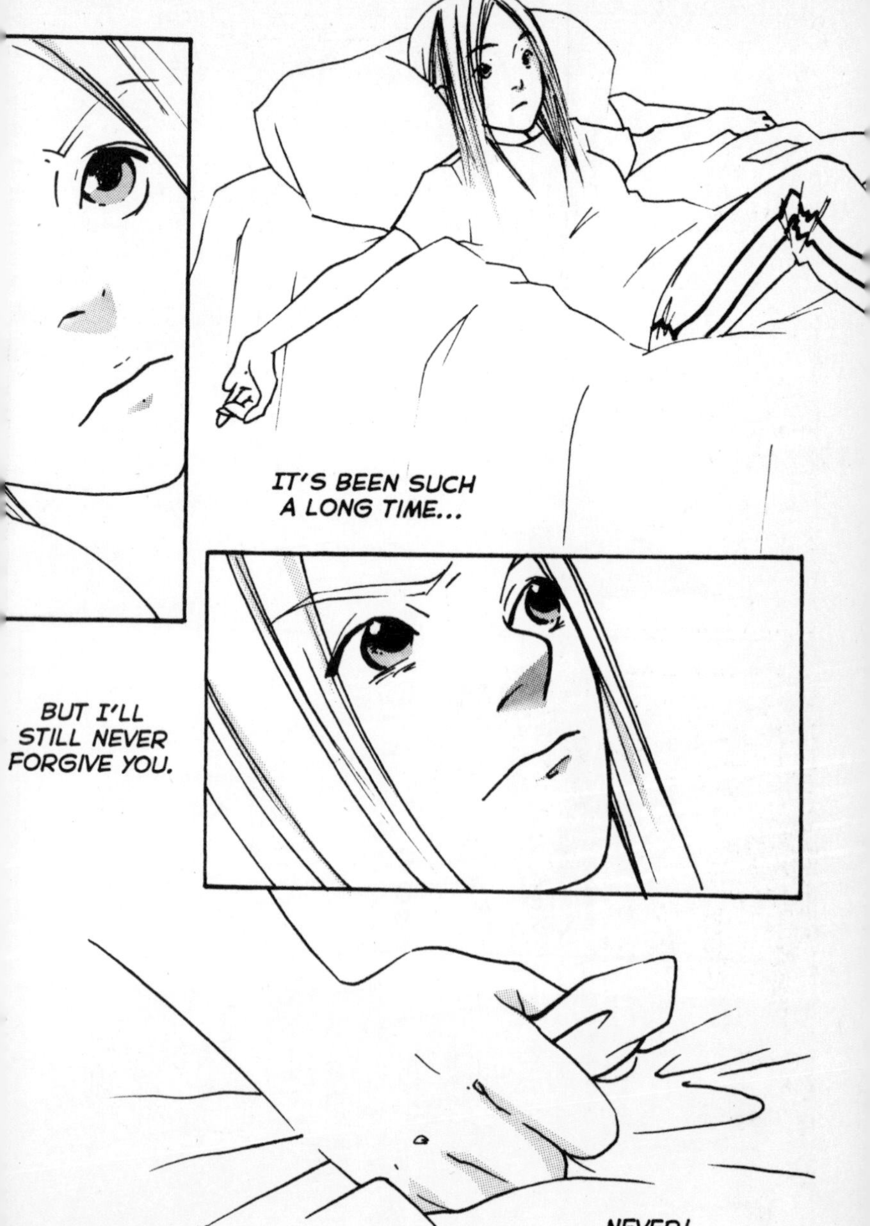
IT'S BEEN SUCH A LONG TIME...
BUT I'LL STILL NEVER FORGIVE YOU.
NEVER!

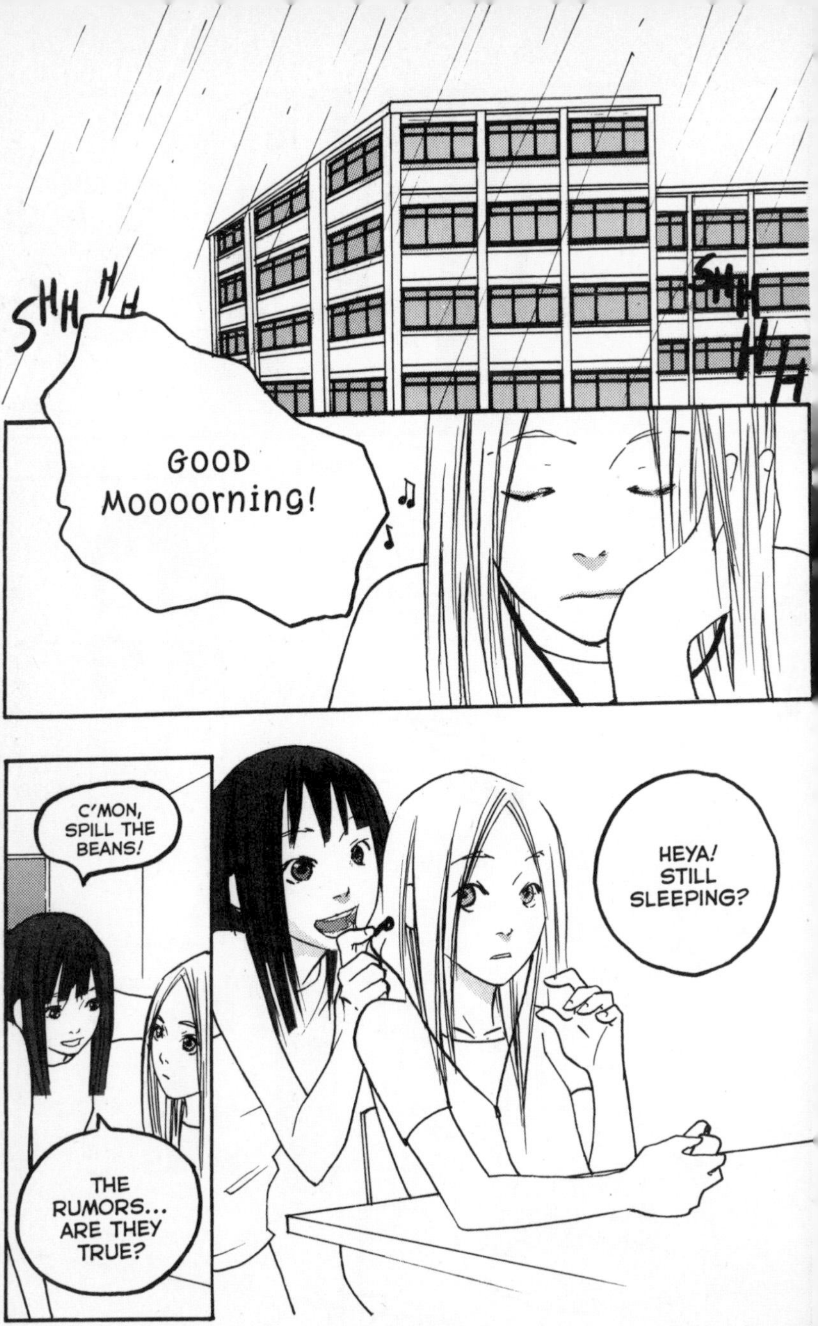
SHHHH
SHHHH
GOOD Moooorning!
HEYA! STILL SLEEPING?
C'MON, SPILL THE BEANS!
THE RUMORS... ARE THEY TRUE?

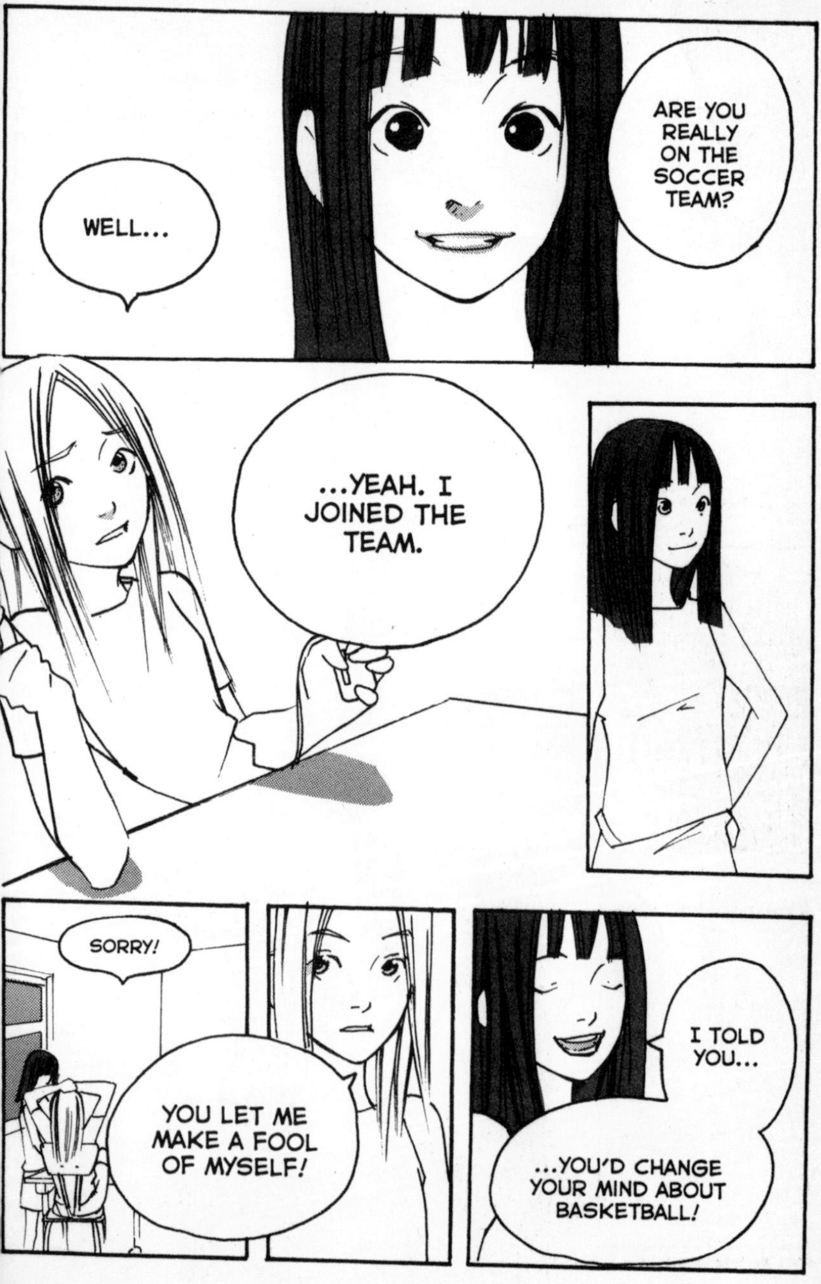
ARE YOU REALLY ON THE SOCCER TEAM?
WELL...
...YEAH. I JOINED THE TEAM.
I TOLD YOU...
...YOU'D CHANGE YOUR MIND ABOUT BASKETBALL!
YOU LET ME MAKE A FOOL OF MYSELF!
SORRY!

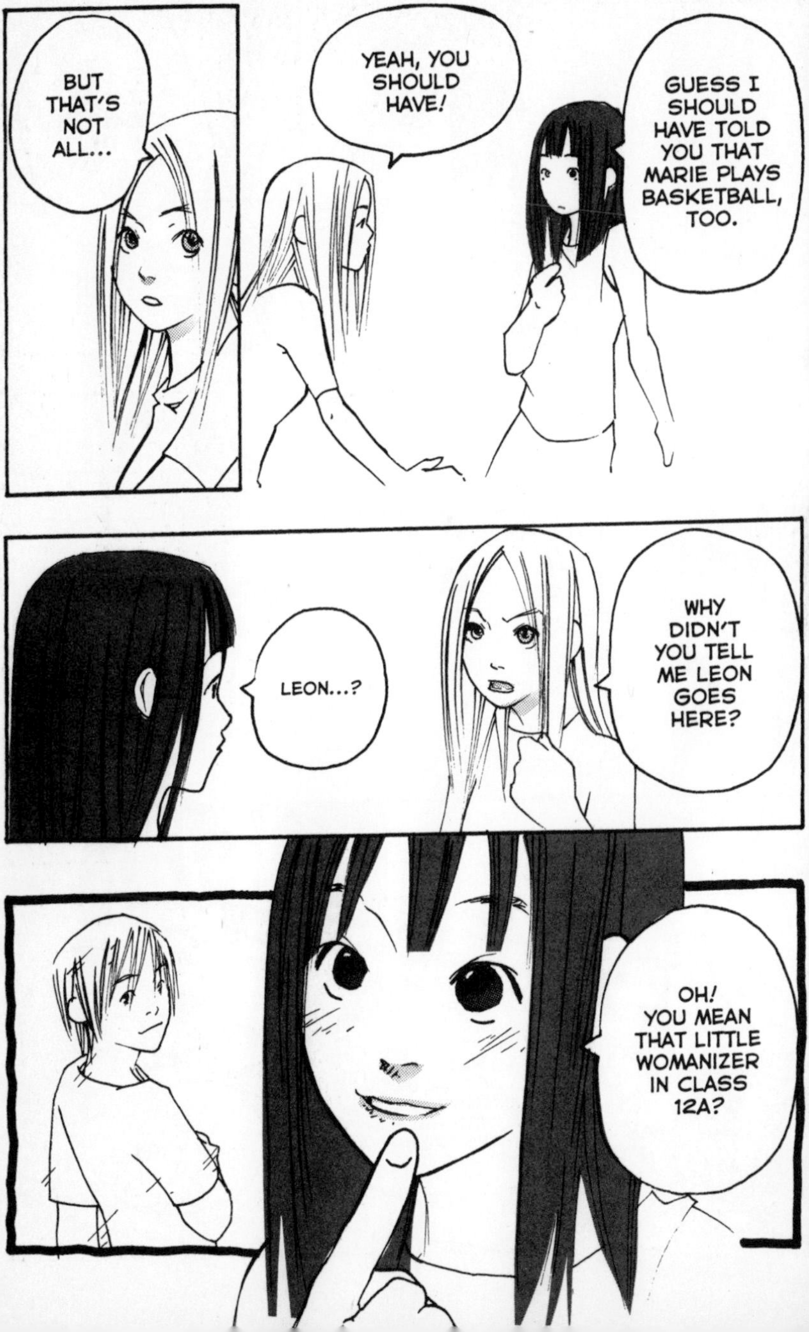
GUESS I SHOULD HAVE TOLD YOU THAT MARIE PLAYS BASKETBALL, TOO.
YEAH, YOU SHOULD HAVE!
BUT THAT'S NOT ALL...
WHY DIDN'T YOU TELL ME LEON GOES HERE?
LEON...?
OH! YOU MEAN THAT LITTLE WOMANIZER IN CLASS 12A?

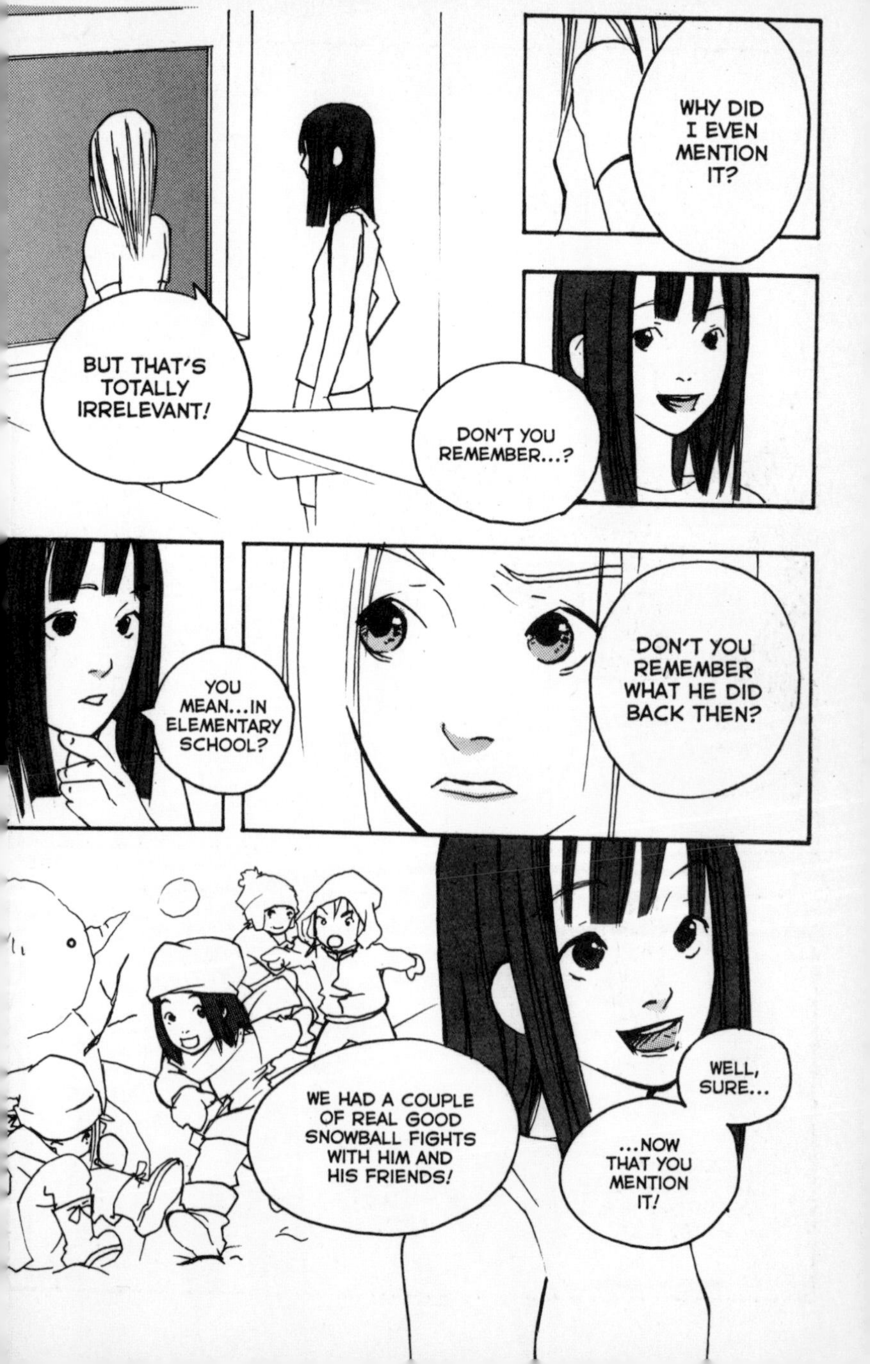
WHY DID I EVEN MENTION IT?
DON'T YOU REMEMBER...?
BUT THAT'S TOTALLY IRRELEVANT!
DON'T YOU REMEMBER WHAT HE DID BACK THEN?
YOU MEAN...IN ELEMENTARY SCHOOL?
WELL, SURE...
...NOW THAT YOU MENTION IT!
WE HAD A COUPLE OF REAL GOOD SNOWBALL FIGHTS WITH HIM AND HIS FRIENDS!

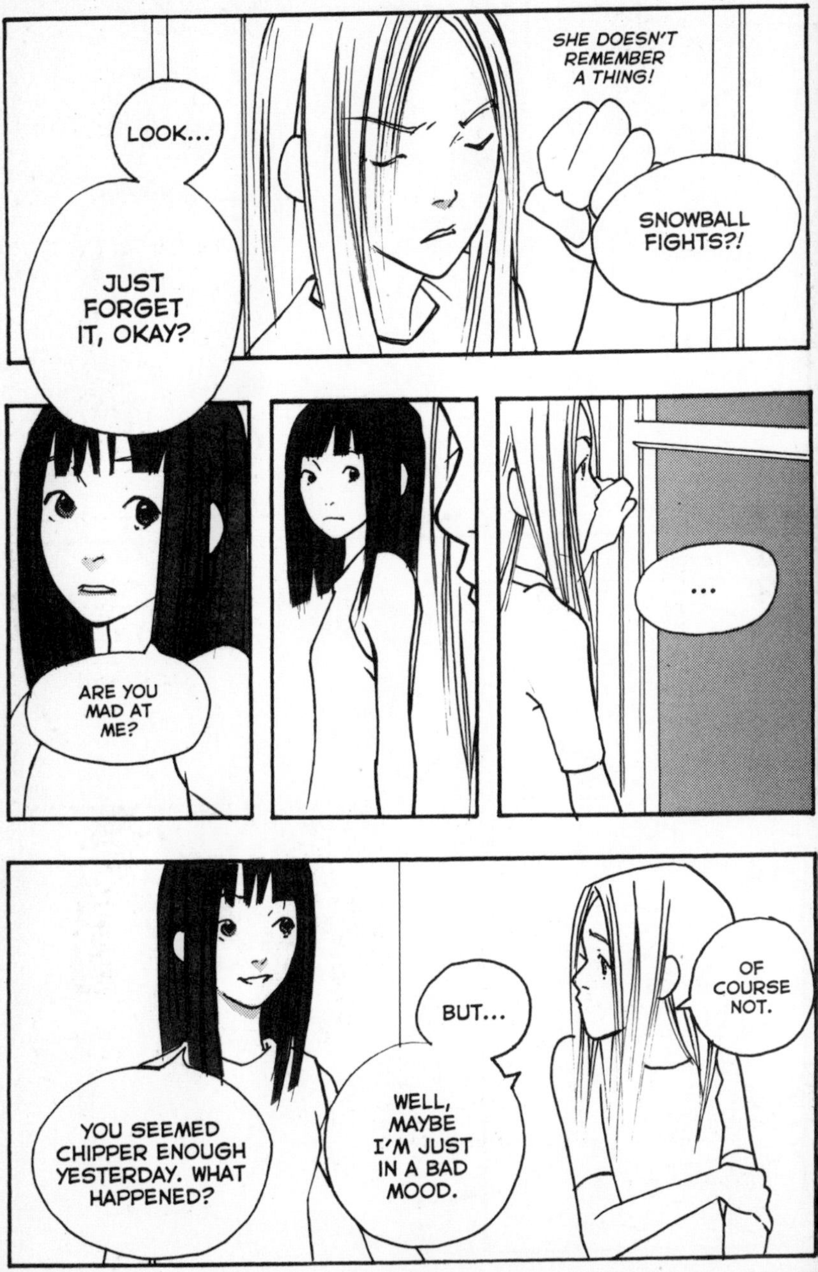
SHE DOESN'T REMEMBER A THING!
SNOWBALL FIGHTS?!
LOOK...
JUST FORGET IT, OKAY?
...
ARE YOU MAD AT ME?
OF COURSE NOT.
BUT...
YOU SEEMED CHIPPER ENOUGH YESTERDAY. WHAT HAPPENED?
WELL, MAYBE I'M JUST IN A BAD MOOD.

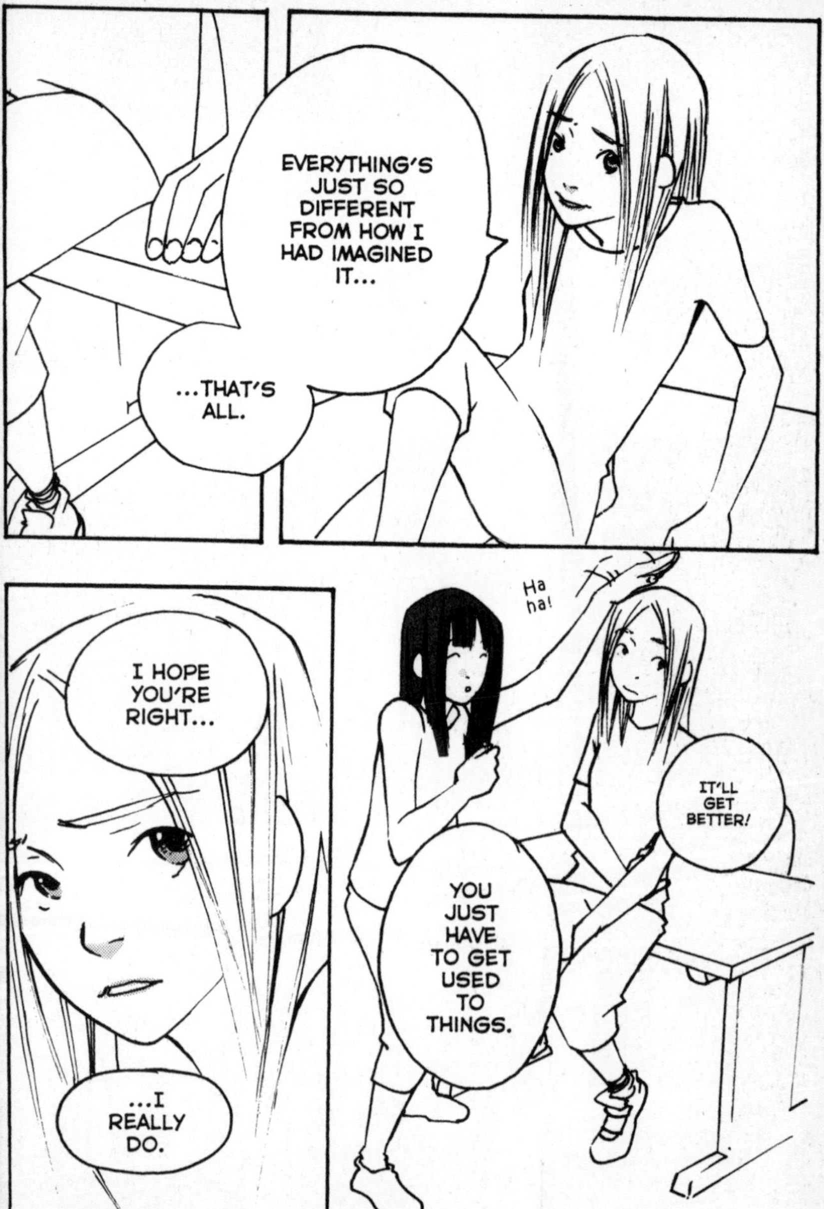
EVERYTHING'S JUST SO DIFFERENT FROM HOW I HAD IMAGINED IT...
...THAT'S ALL.
Ha ha!
IT'LL GET BETTER!
YOU JUST HAVE TO GET USED TO THINGS.
I HOPE YOU'RE RIGHT...
...I REALLY DO.

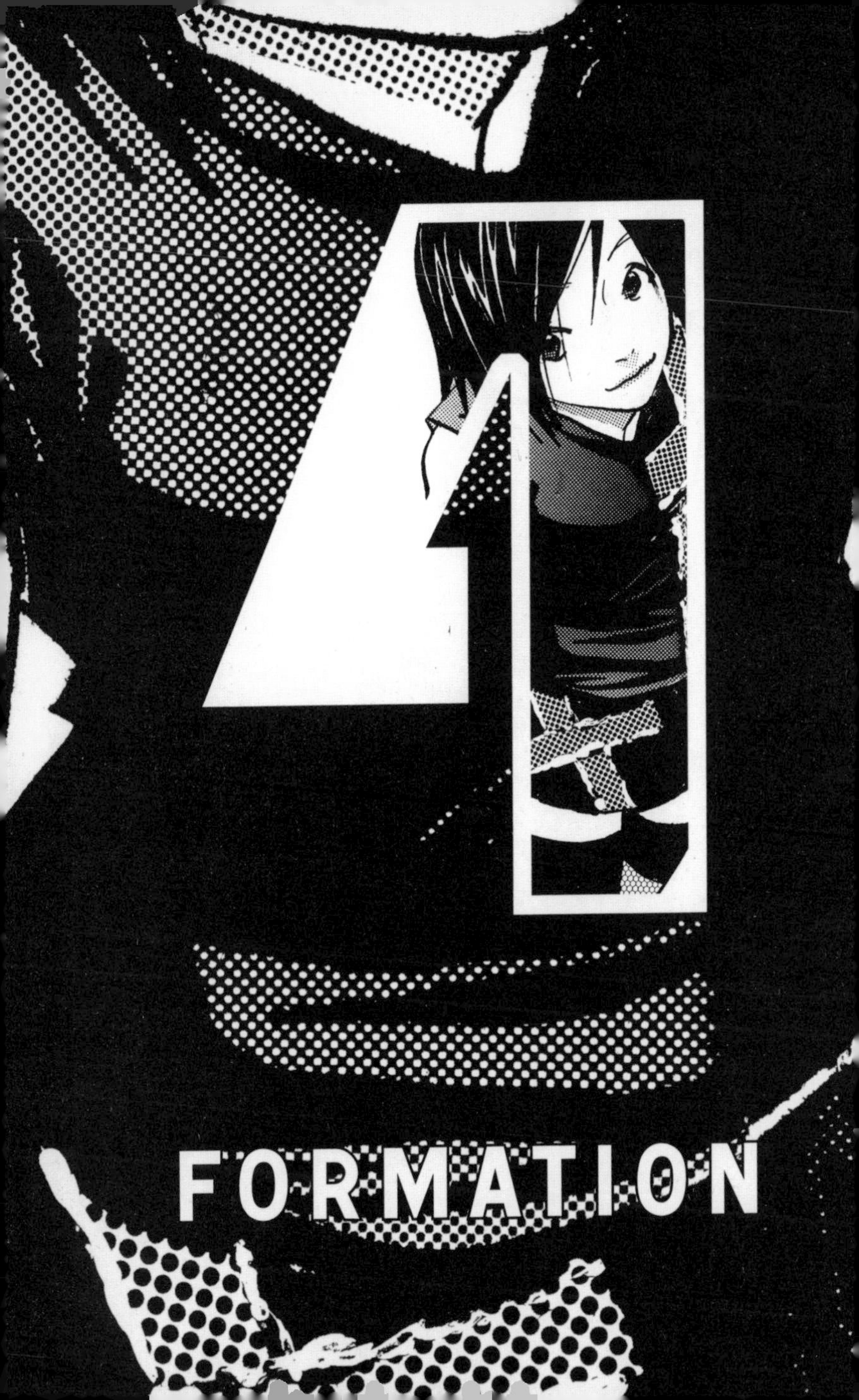
4
FORMATION

FILIZ

AGE:16
HEIGHT:1.60 M (5'2")
WEIGHT:46 KILOS (101 LBS)
SIGN:VIRGO
LIKES:COSPLAY, MANGA,
FASHION MAGAZINES
DISLIKES:MOTHS, TOMATO
SAUCE, BIGOTRY
HOBBIES:SEWING, DESIGNING,
STANDING OUT

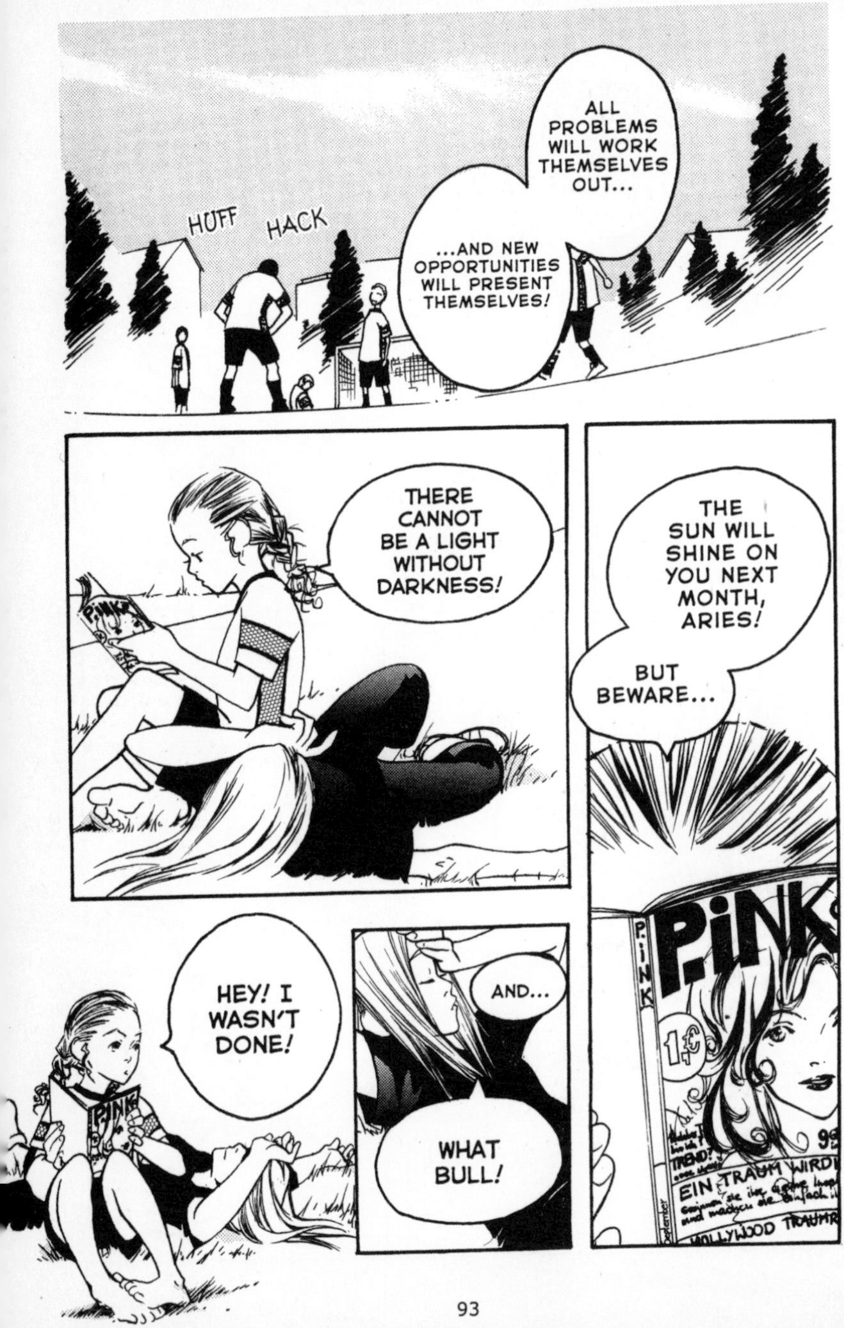
HUFF
HACK
ALL PROBLEMS WILL WORK THEMSELVES OUT...
...AND NEW OPPORTUNITIES WILL PRESENT THEMSELVES!
THERE CANNOT BE A LIGHT WITHOUT DARKNESS!
THE SUN WILL SHINE ON YOU NEXT MONTH, ARIES!
BUT BEWARE...
AND...
WHAT BULL!
HEY! I WASN'T DONE!

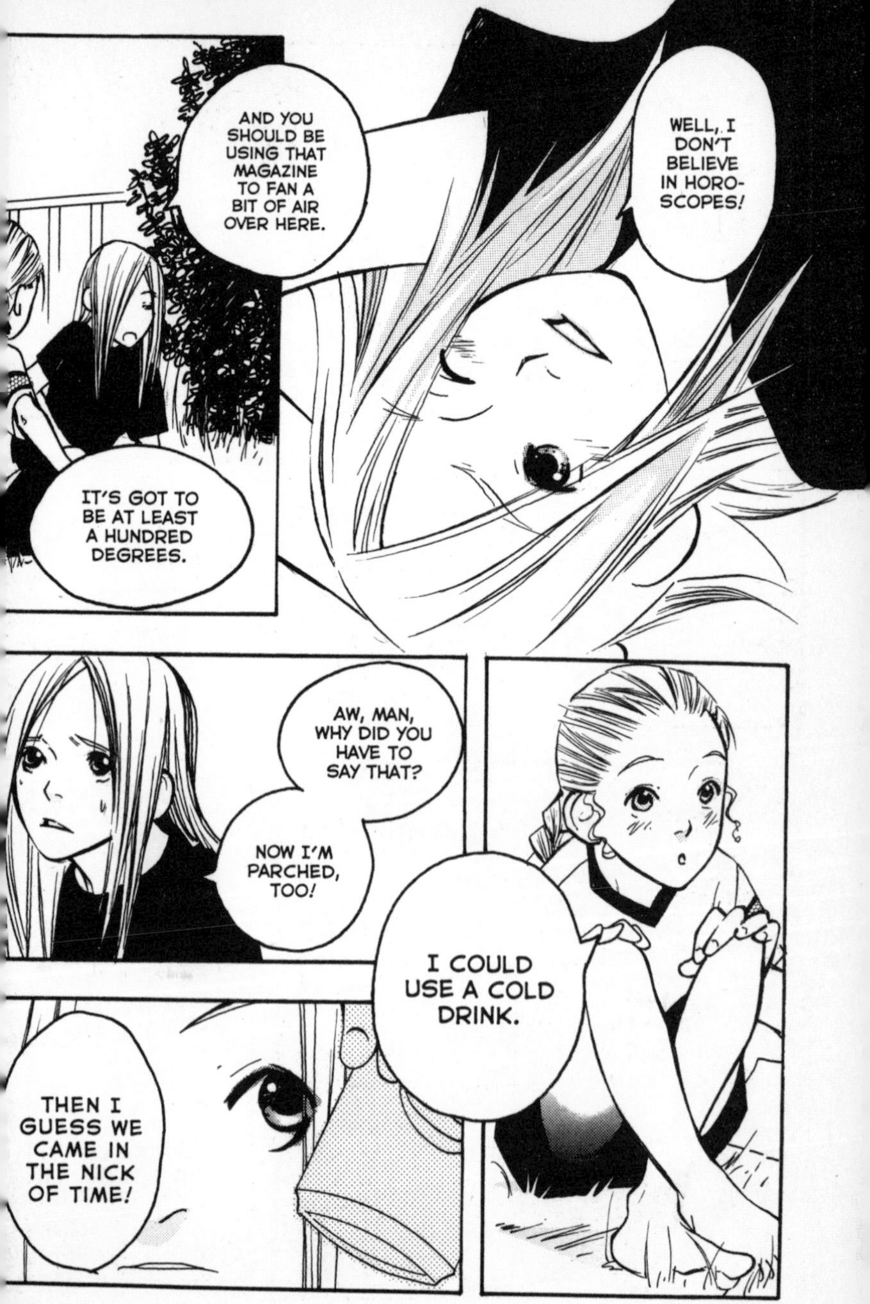
WELL, I DON'T BELIEVE IN HORO-SCOPES!
AND YOU SHOULD BE USING THAT MAGAZINE TO FAN A BIT OF AIR OVER HERE.
IT'S GOT TO BE AT LEAST A HUNDRED DEGREES.
AW, MAN, WHY DID YOU HAVE TO SAY THAT?
NOW I'M PARCHED, TOO!
I COULD USE A COLD DRINK.
THEN I GUESS WE CAME IN THE NICK OF TIME!

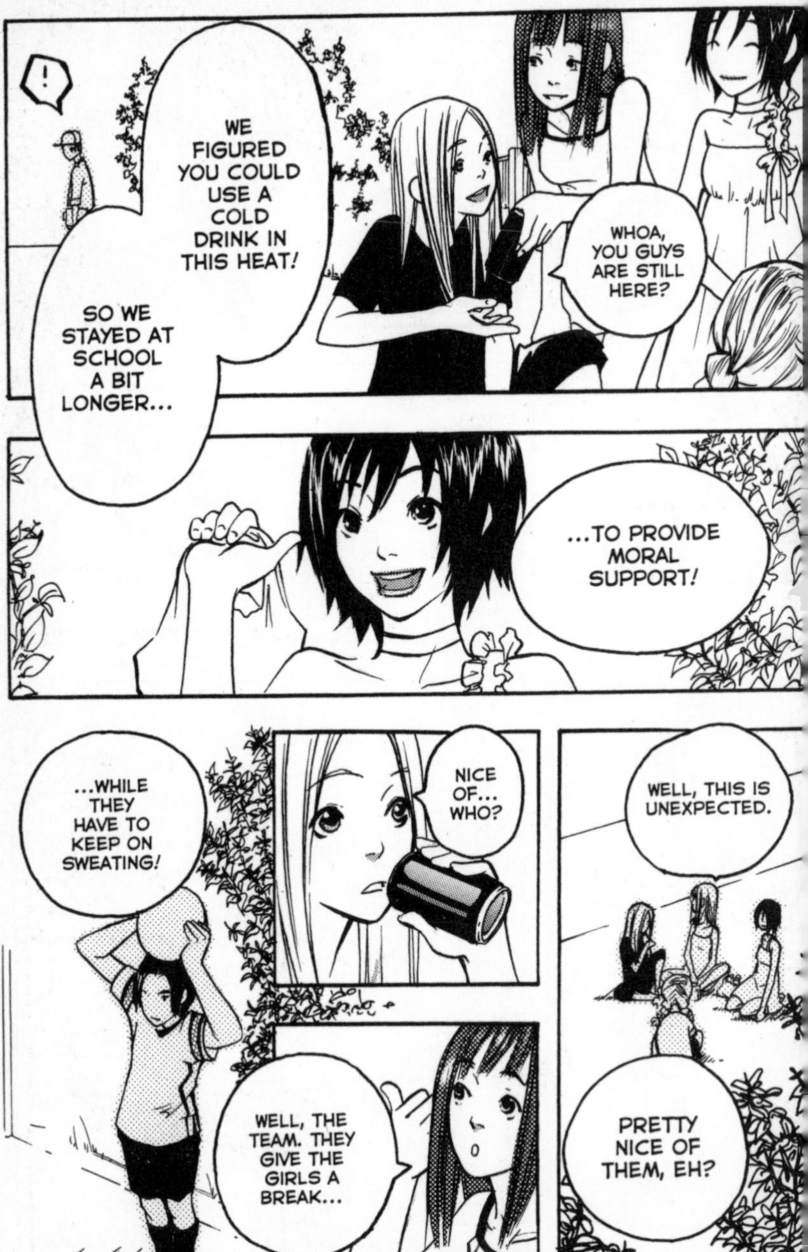
WHOA, YOU GUYS ARE STILL HERE?
!
WE FIGURED YOU COULD USE A COLD DRINK IN THIS HEAT!
SO WE STAYED AT SCHOOL A BIT LONGER...
...TO PROVIDE MORAL SUPPORT!
WELL, THIS IS UNEXPECTED.
PRETTY NICE OF THEM, EH?
NICE OF... WHO?
WELL, THE TEAM. THEY GIVE THE GIRLS A BREAK...
...WHILE THEY HAVE TO KEEP ON SWEATING!

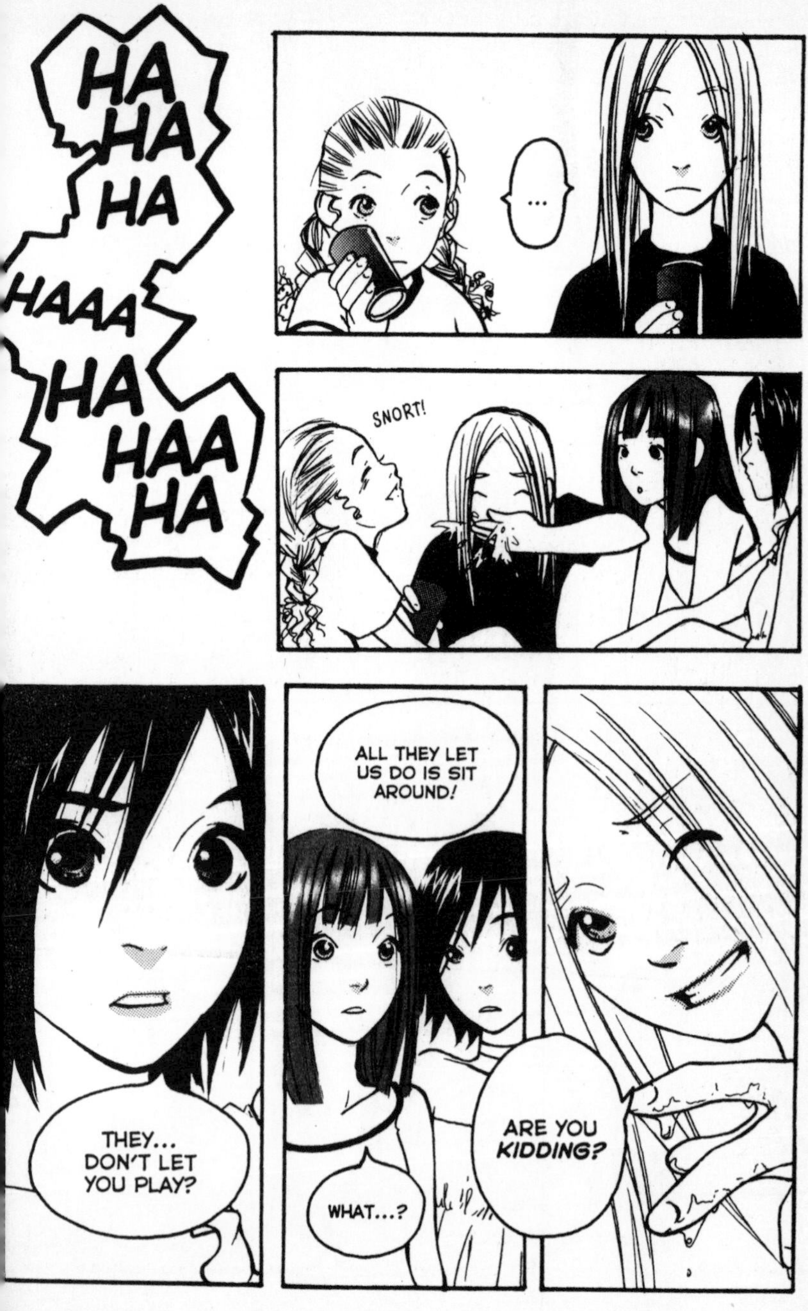
...
SNORT!
HA HA HA HAAA HA HAA HA
ARE YOU KIDDING?
ALL THEY LET US DO IS SIT AROUND!
WHAT...?
THEY... DON'T LET YOU PLAY?

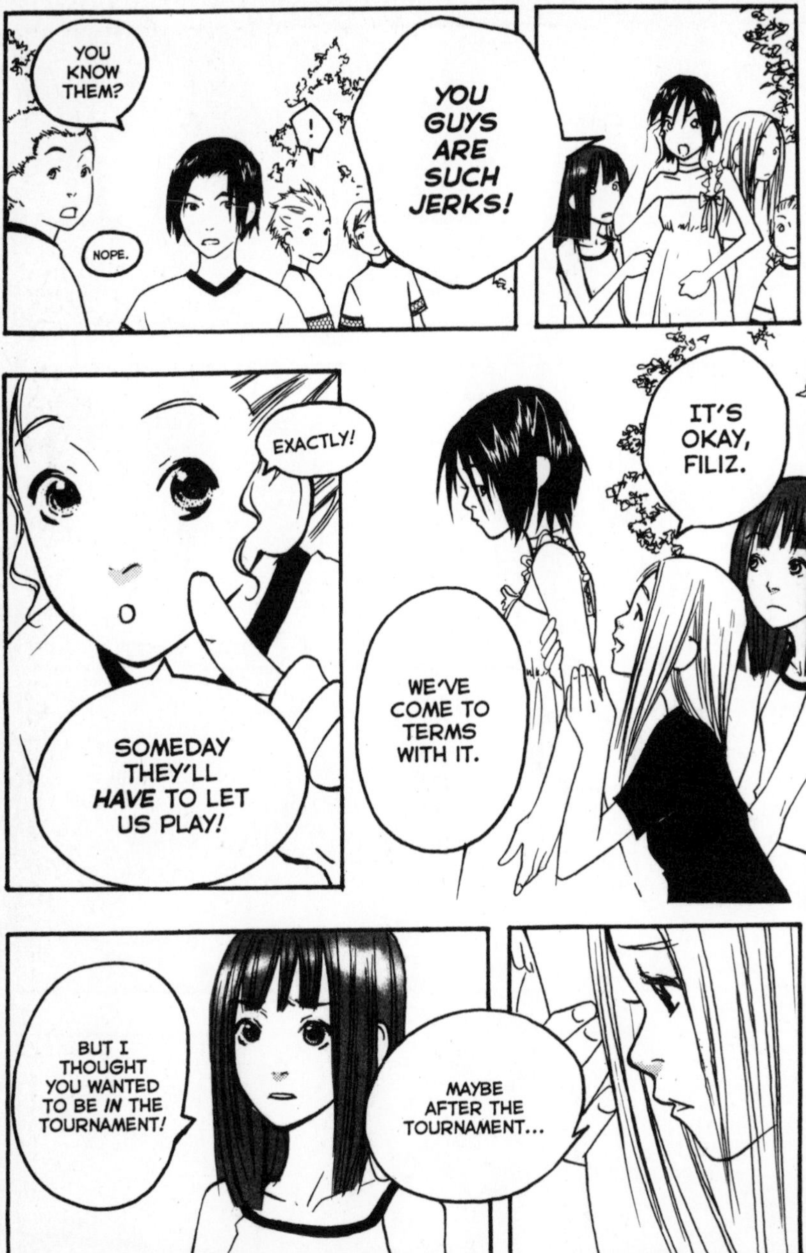
YOU KNOW THEM?
NOPE.
!
YOU GUYS ARE SUCH JERKS!
EXACTLY!
SOMEDAY THEY'LL *HAVE* TO LET US PLAY!
IT'S OKAY, FILIZ.
WE'VE COME TO TERMS WITH IT.
BUT I THOUGHT YOU WANTED TO BE *IN* THE TOURNAMENT!
MAYBE AFTER THE TOURNAMENT...

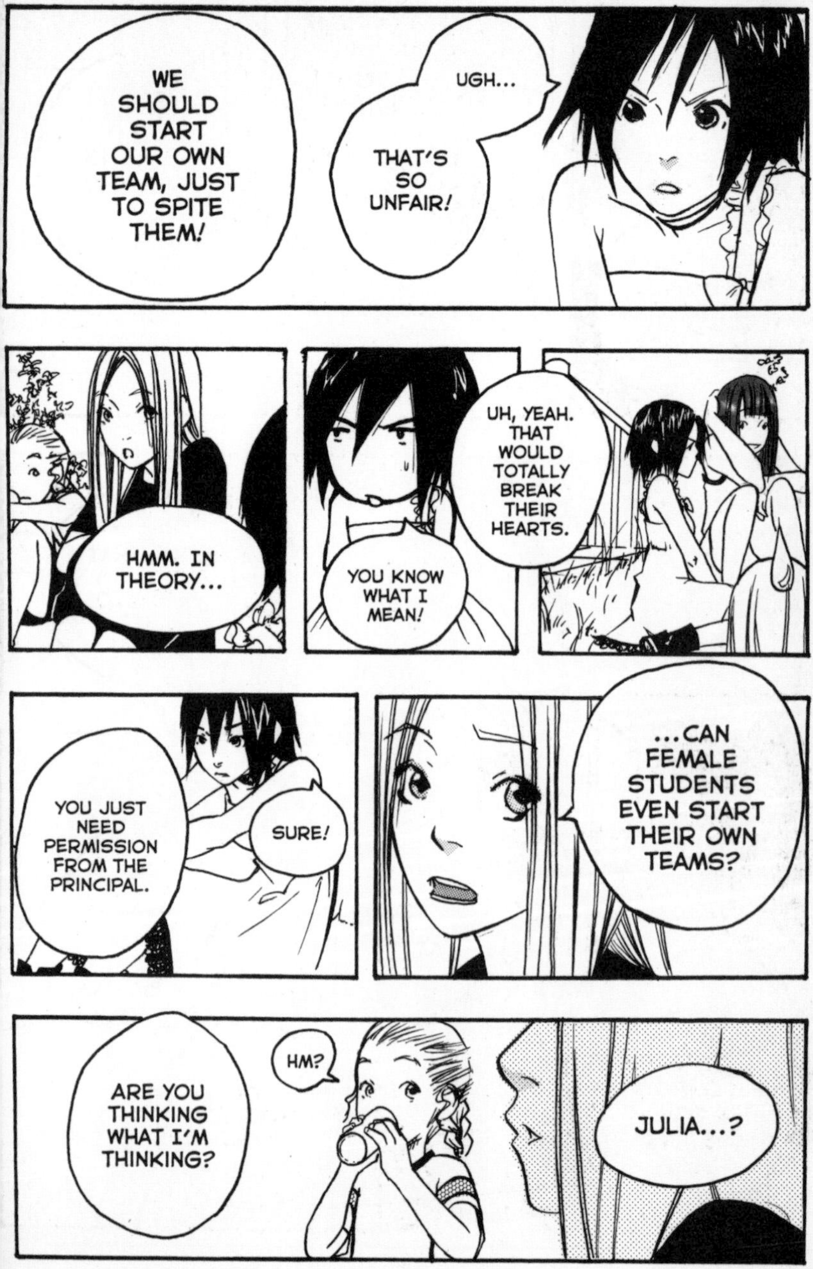
UGH...
THAT'S SO UNFAIR!
WE SHOULD START OUR OWN TEAM, JUST TO SPITE THEM!
UH, YEAH. THAT WOULD TOTALLY BREAK THEIR HEARTS.
YOU KNOW WHAT I MEAN!
HMM. IN THEORY...
...CAN FEMALE STUDENTS EVEN START THEIR OWN TEAMS?
SURE!
YOU JUST NEED PERMISSION FROM THE PRINCIPAL.
JULIA...?
HM?
ARE YOU THINKING WHAT I'M THINKING?

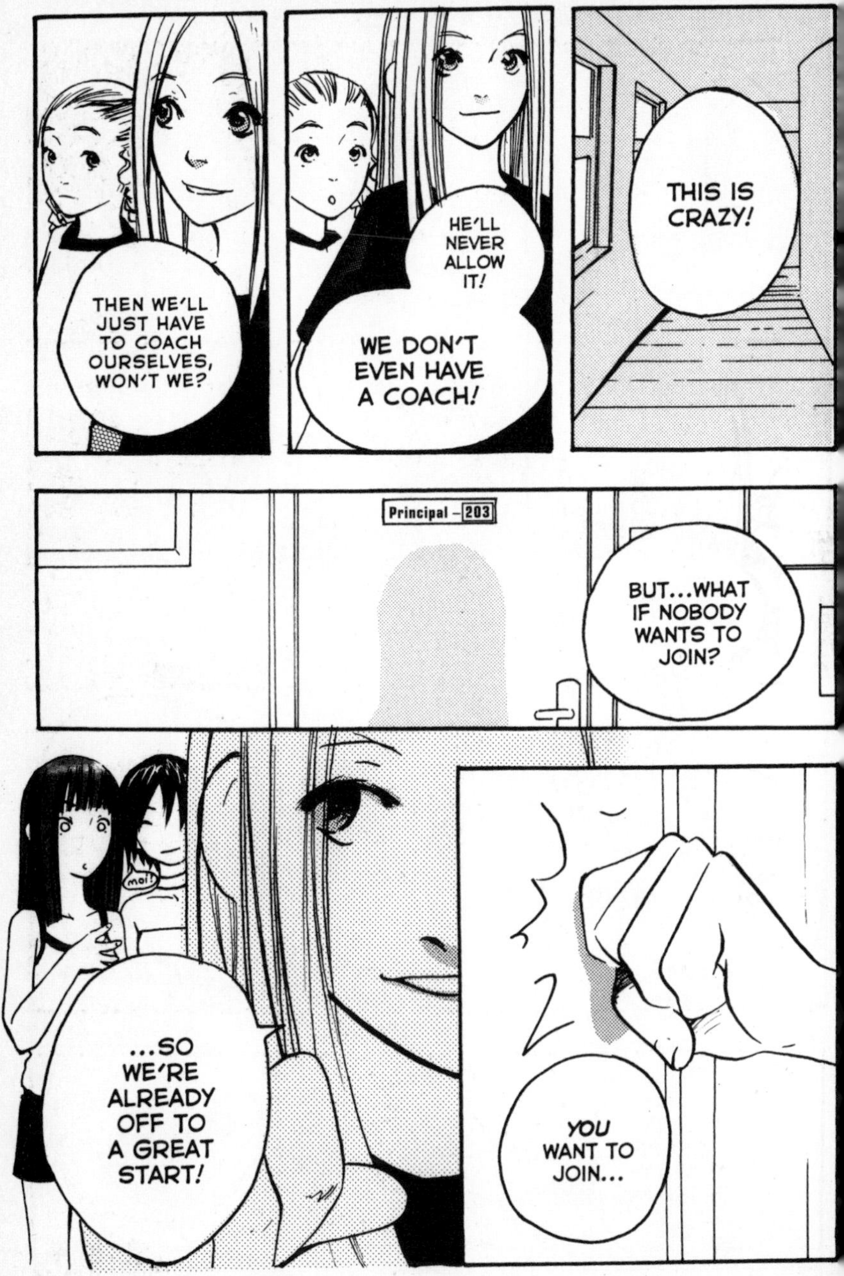
THIS IS CRAZY!
HE'LL NEVER ALLOW IT!
WE DON'T EVEN HAVE A COACH!
THEN WE'LL JUST HAVE TO COACH OURSELVES, WON'T WE?
Principal – 203
BUT...WHAT IF NOBODY WANTS TO JOIN?
YOU WANT TO JOIN...
...SO WE'RE ALREADY OFF TO A GREAT START!
moi!

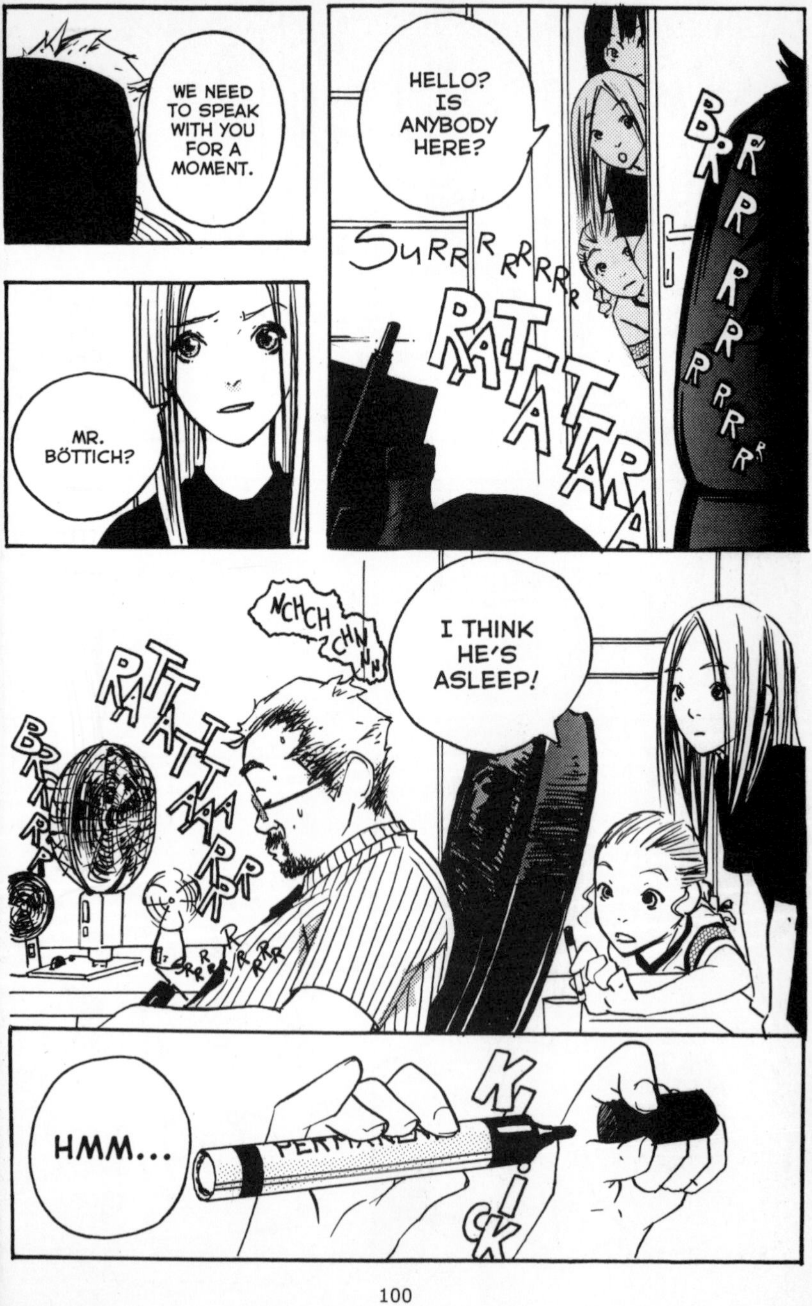
HELLO? IS ANYBODY HERE?
BRRRRRRRRRR
SURRRRRRRRR
RATTATTARA
WE NEED TO SPEAK WITH YOU FOR A MOMENT.
MR. BÖTTICH?
I THINK HE'S ASLEEP!
NCHCH CHNN
RATTATTAAARRR
BRRRRP
SRRRRRRRR
KICK
HMM...

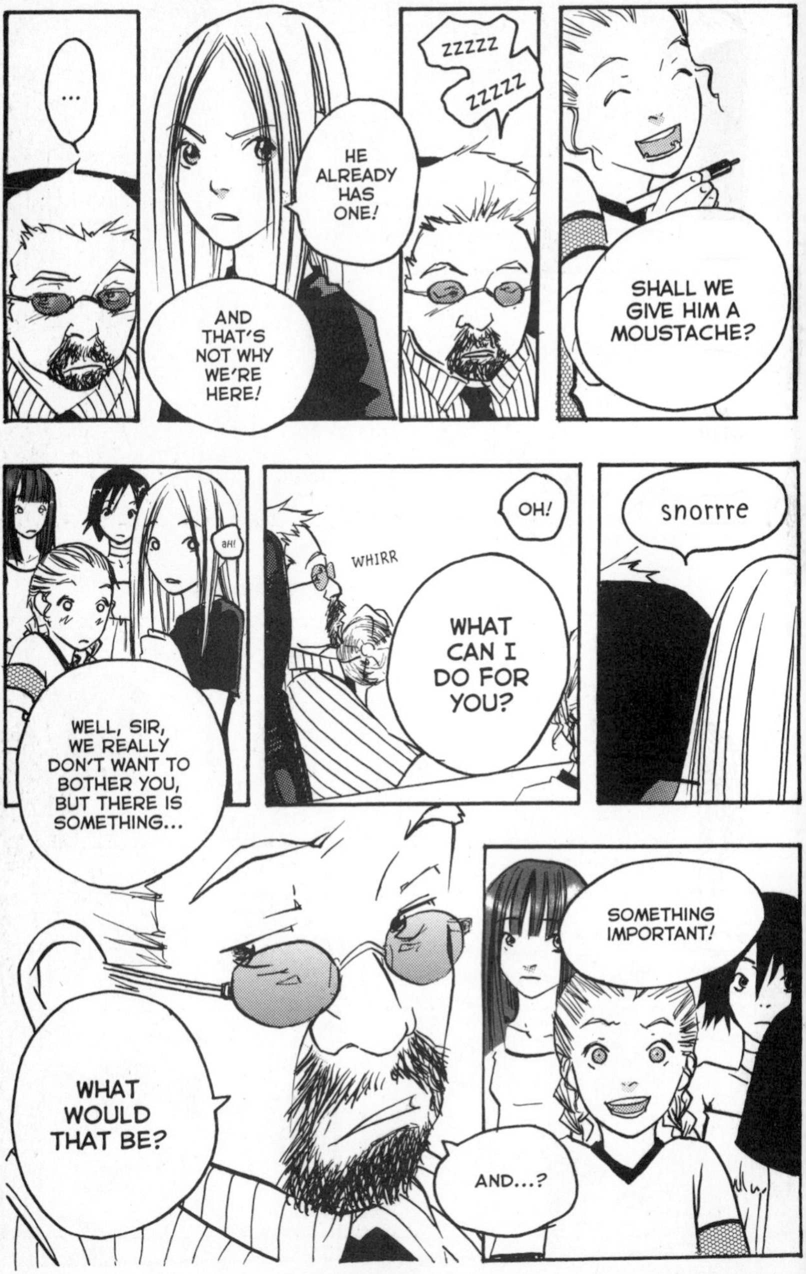
SHALL WE GIVE HIM A MOUSTACHE?
ZZZZZ
ZZZZZ
HE ALREADY HAS ONE!
AND THAT'S NOT WHY WE'RE HERE!
...
snorrre
OH!
WHIRR
WHAT CAN I DO FOR YOU?
ah!
WELL, SIR, WE REALLY DON'T WANT TO BOTHER YOU, BUT THERE IS SOMETHING...
SOMETHING IMPORTANT!
AND...?
WHAT WOULD THAT BE?

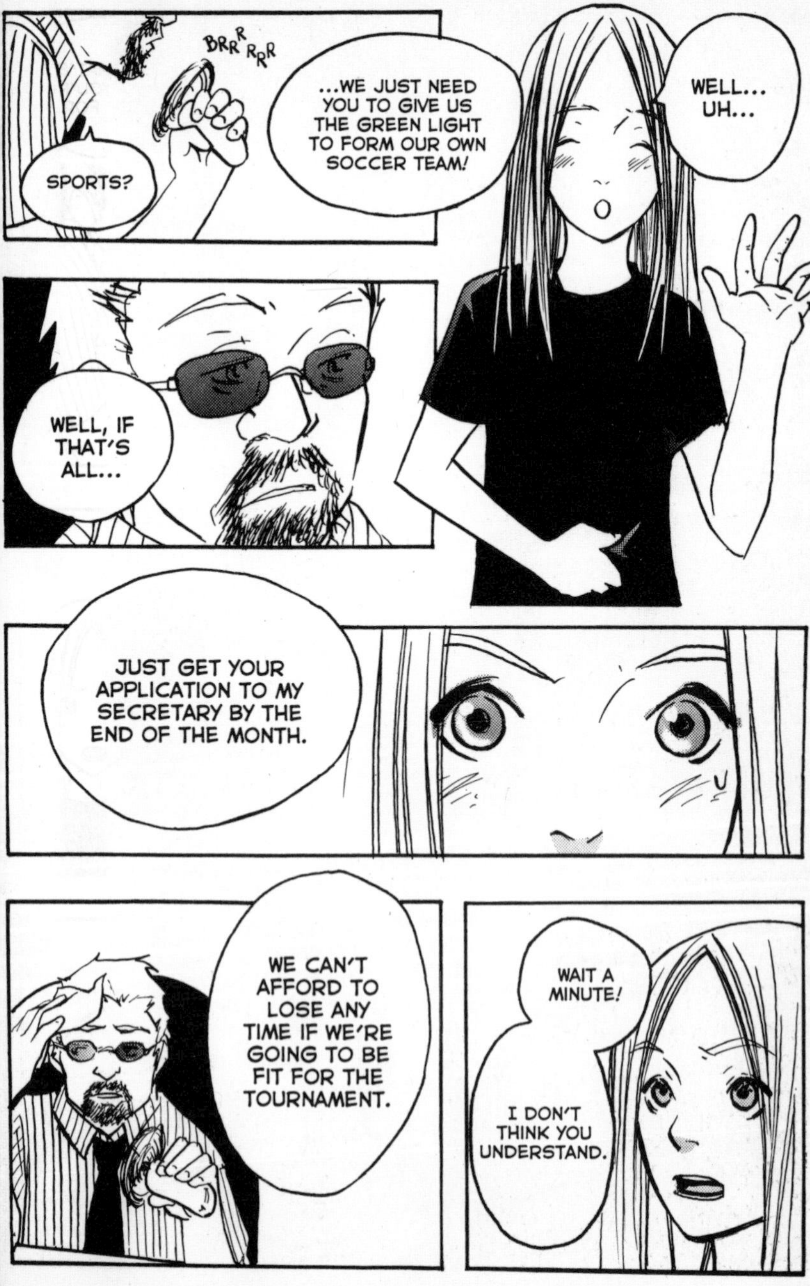
BRRRRRR
SPORTS?
...WE JUST NEED YOU TO GIVE US THE GREEN LIGHT TO FORM OUR OWN SOCCER TEAM!
WELL... UH...
WELL, IF THAT'S ALL...
JUST GET YOUR APPLICATION TO MY SECRETARY BY THE END OF THE MONTH.
WE CAN'T AFFORD TO LOSE ANY TIME IF WE'RE GOING TO BE FIT FOR THE TOURNAMENT.
WAIT A MINUTE!
I DON'T THINK YOU UNDERSTAND.

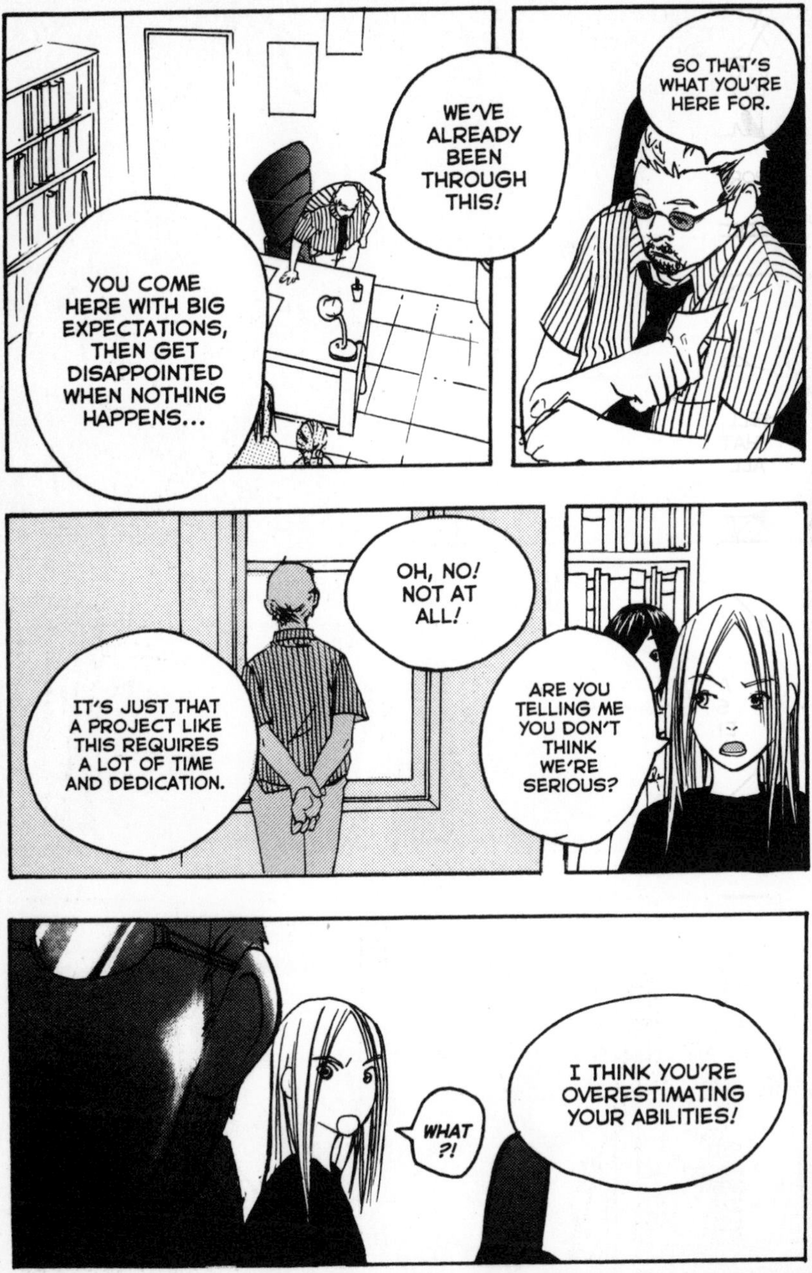
SO THAT'S WHAT YOU'RE HERE FOR.
WE'VE ALREADY BEEN THROUGH THIS!
YOU COME HERE WITH BIG EXPECTATIONS, THEN GET DISAPPOINTED WHEN NOTHING HAPPENS...
ARE YOU TELLING ME YOU DON'T THINK WE'RE SERIOUS?
OH, NO! NOT AT ALL!
IT'S JUST THAT A PROJECT LIKE THIS REQUIRES A LOT OF TIME AND DEDICATION.
I THINK YOU'RE OVERESTIMATING YOUR ABILITIES!
WHAT ?!

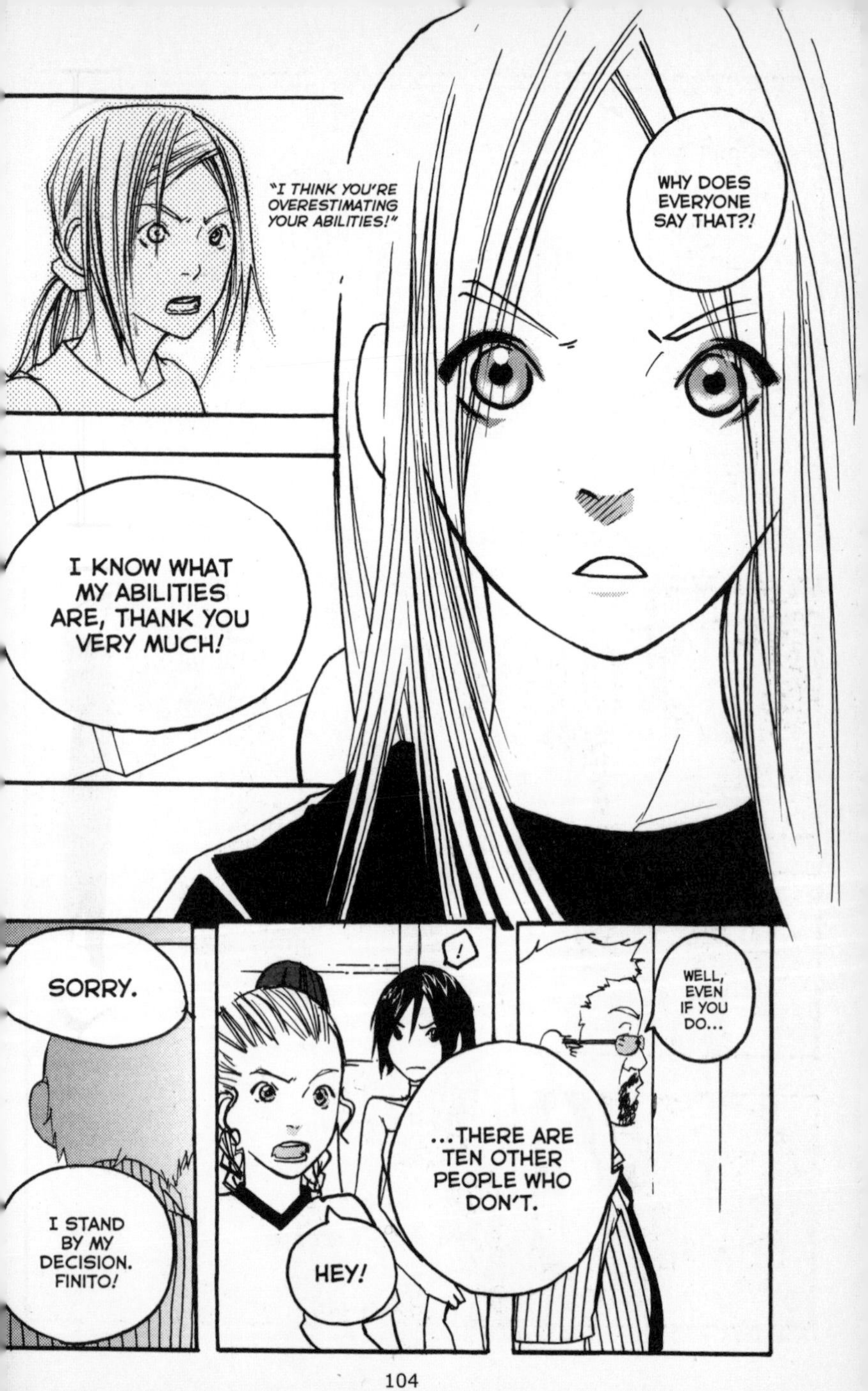
WHY DOES EVERYONE SAY THAT?!
"I THINK YOU'RE OVERESTIMATING YOUR ABILITIES!"
I KNOW WHAT MY ABILITIES ARE, THANK YOU VERY MUCH!
WELL, EVEN IF YOU DO...
...THERE ARE TEN OTHER PEOPLE WHO DON'T.
!
HEY!
SORRY.
I STAND BY MY DECISION. FINITO!

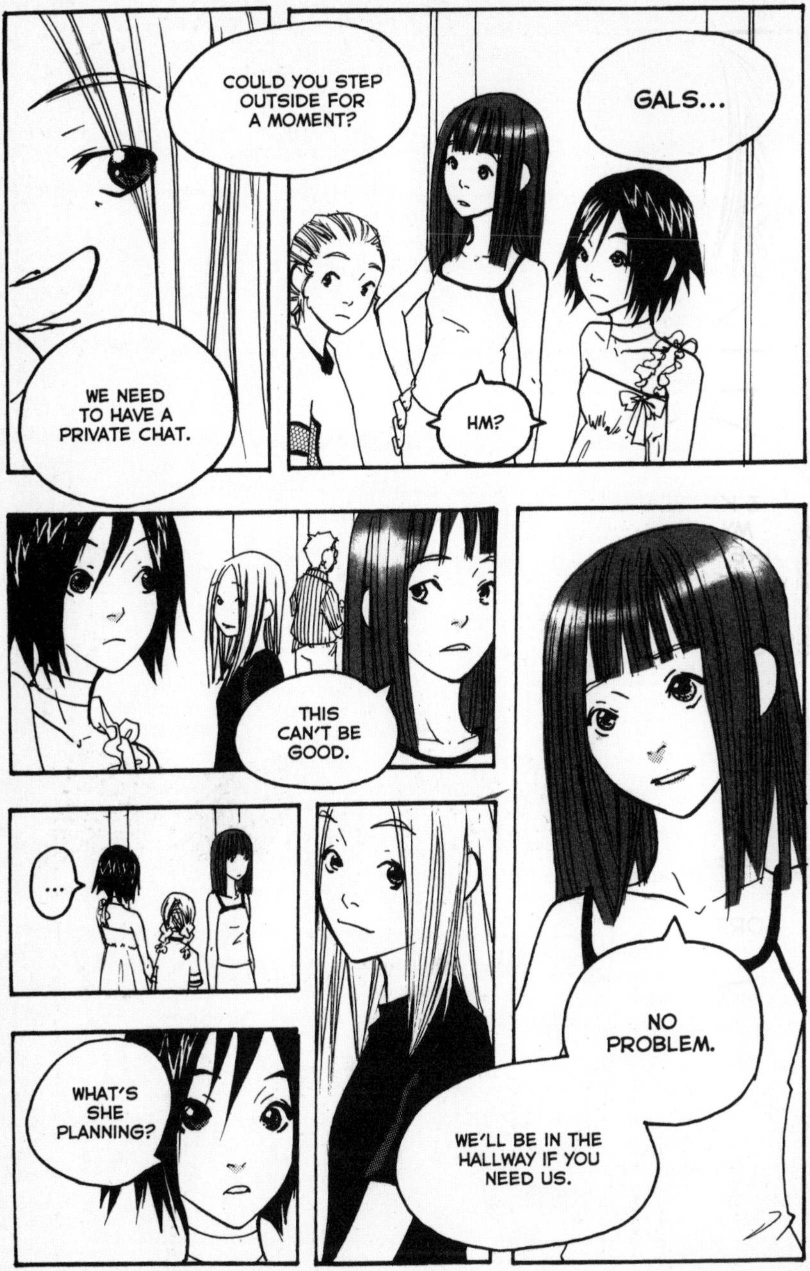
GALS...
HM?
COULD YOU STEP OUTSIDE FOR A MOMENT?
WE NEED TO HAVE A PRIVATE CHAT.
NO PROBLEM.
WE'LL BE IN THE HALLWAY IF YOU NEED US.
THIS CAN'T BE GOOD.
...
WHAT'S SHE PLANNING?

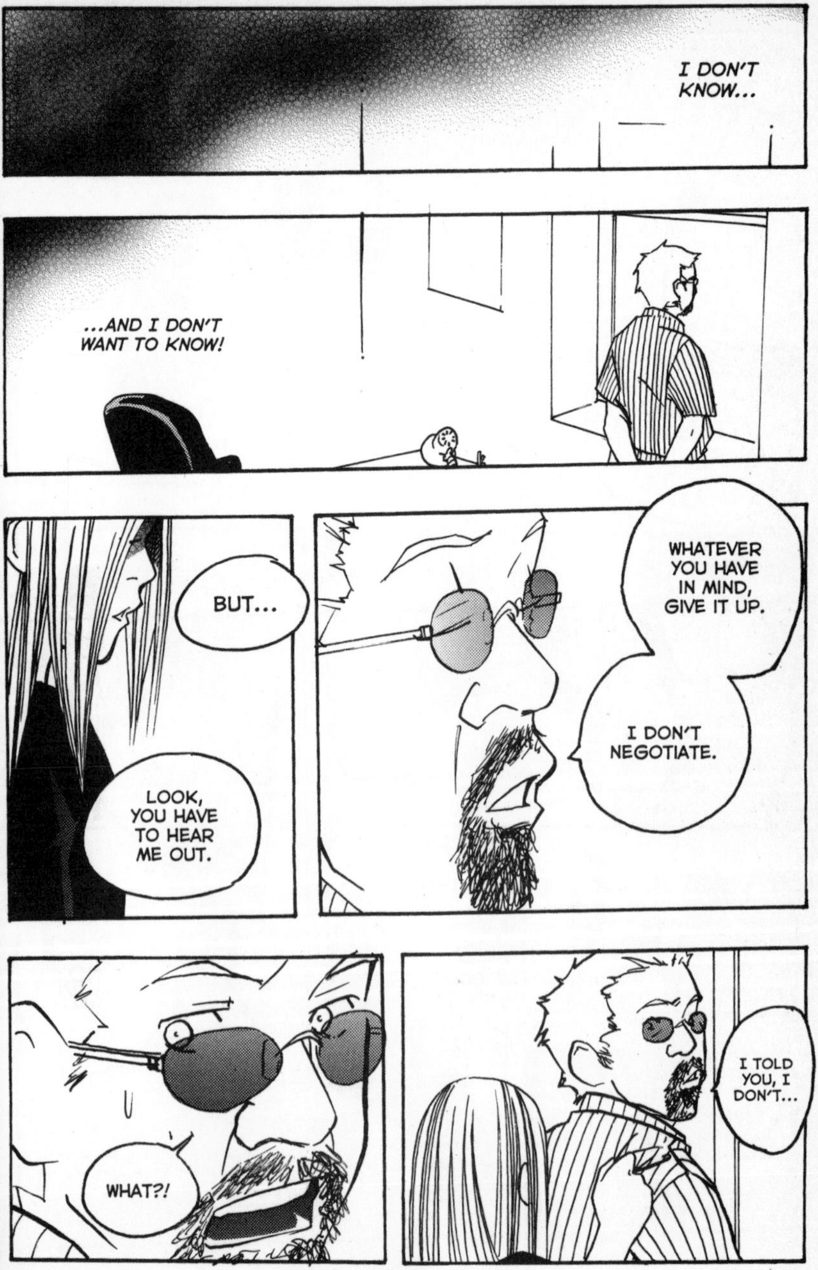
I DON'T KNOW...
...AND I DON'T WANT TO KNOW!
WHATEVER YOU HAVE IN MIND, GIVE IT UP.
I DON'T NEGOTIATE.
BUT...
LOOK, YOU HAVE TO HEAR ME OUT.
I TOLD YOU, I DON'T...
WHAT?!

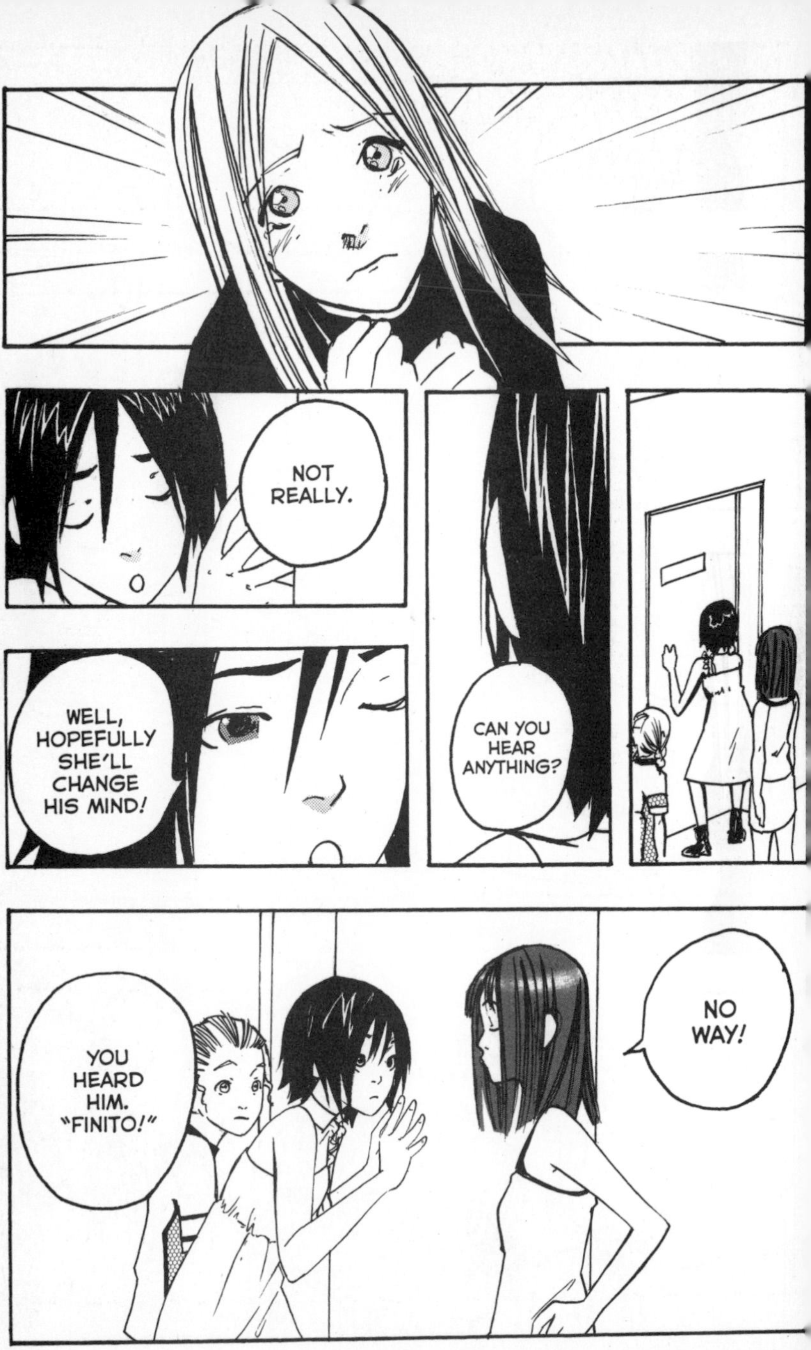
CAN YOU HEAR ANYTHING?
NOT REALLY.
WELL, HOPEFULLY SHE'LL CHANGE HIS MIND!
NO WAY!
YOU HEARD HIM. "FINITO!"

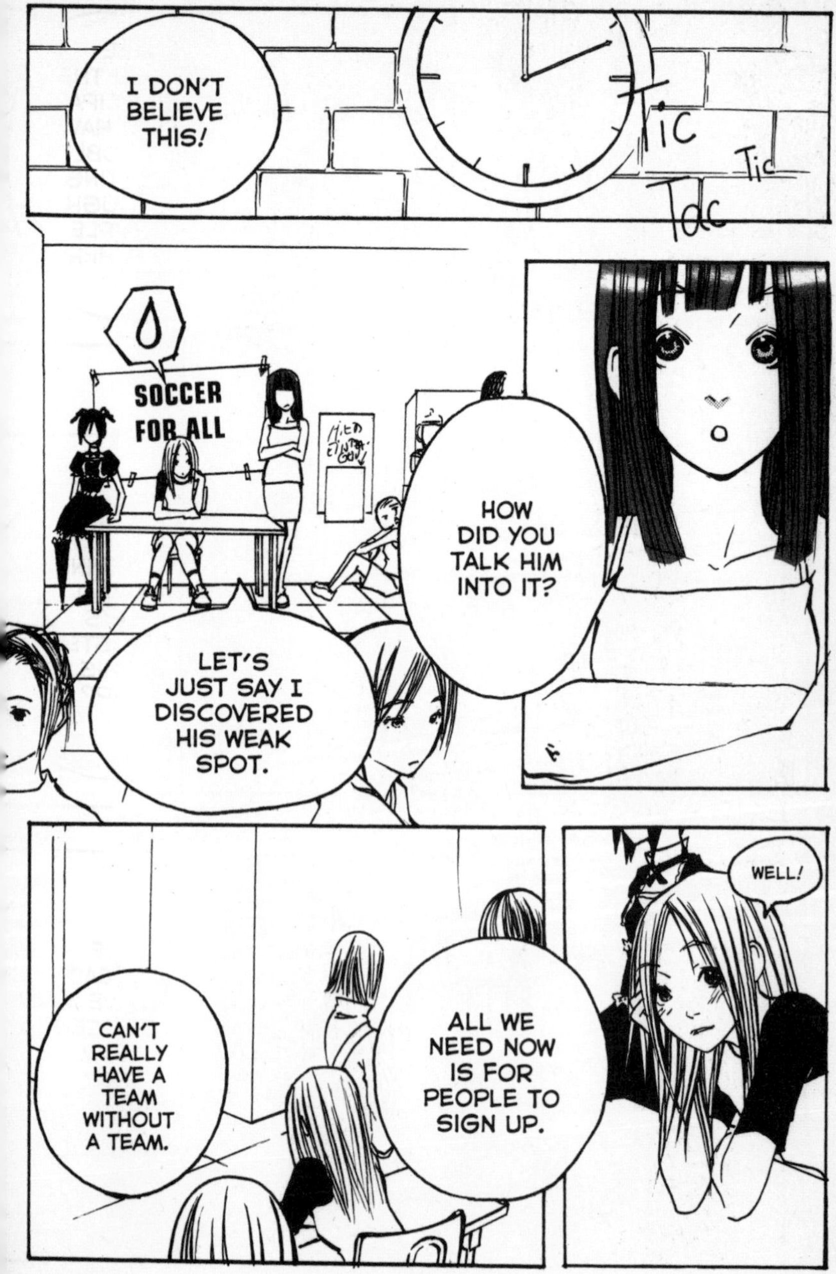
Tic
Tac
Tic
I DON'T BELIEVE THIS!
HOW DID YOU TALK HIM INTO IT?
SOCCER FOR ALL
LET'S JUST SAY I DISCOVERED HIS WEAK SPOT.
WELL!
ALL WE NEED NOW IS FOR PEOPLE TO SIGN UP.
CAN'T REALLY HAVE A TEAM WITHOUT A TEAM.

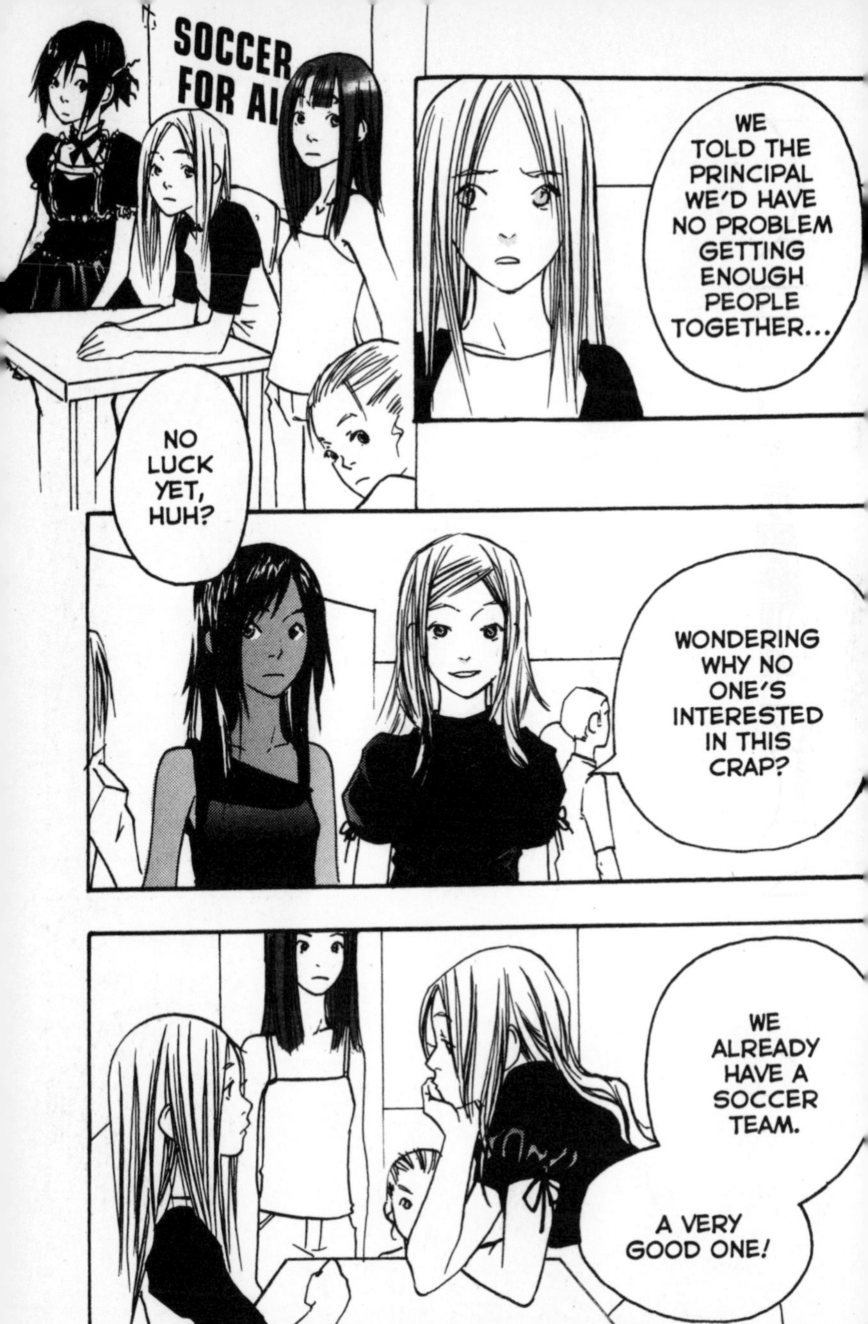
WE TOLD THE PRINCIPAL WE'D HAVE NO PROBLEM GETTING ENOUGH PEOPLE TOGETHER...
SOCCER
FOR AL
NO LUCK YET, HUH?
WONDERING WHY NO ONE'S INTERESTED IN THIS CRAP?
WE ALREADY HAVE A SOCCER TEAM.
A VERY GOOD ONE!

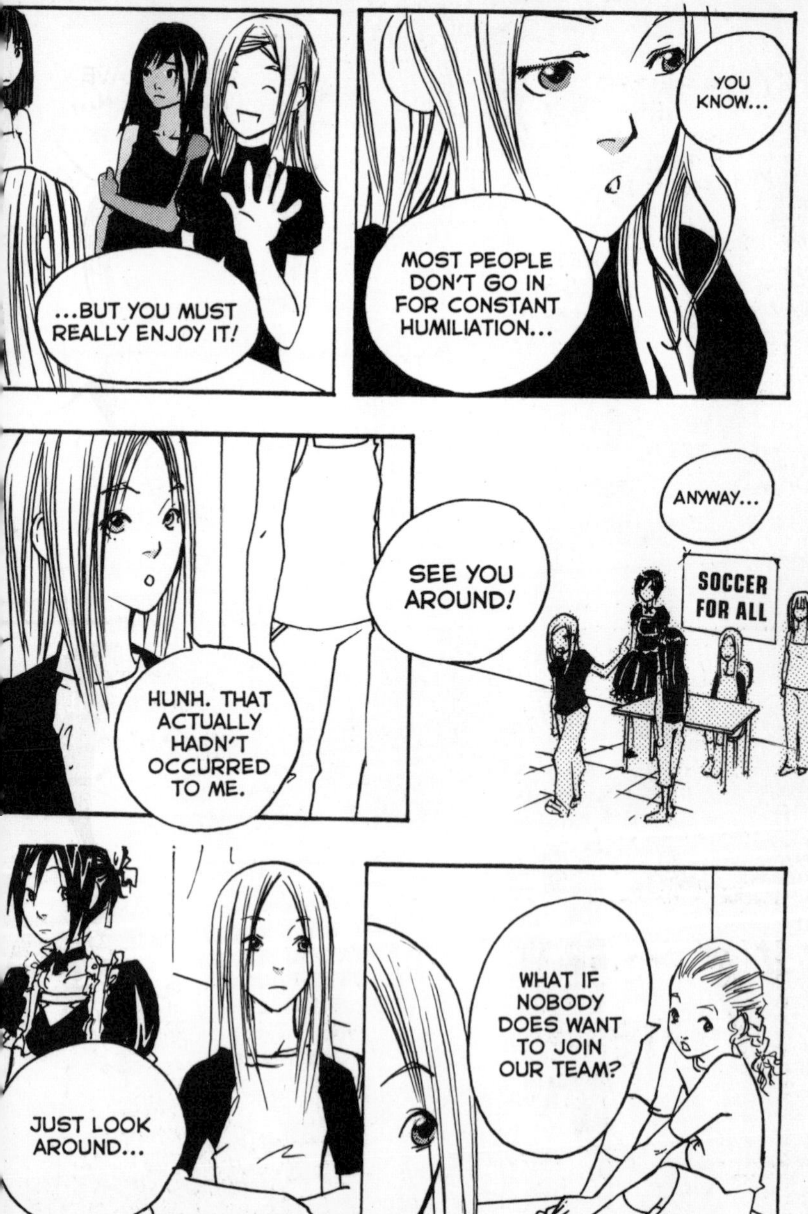
YOU KNOW...
MOST PEOPLE DON'T GO IN FOR CONSTANT HUMILIATION...
...BUT YOU MUST REALLY ENJOY IT!
ANYWAY...
SOCCER FOR ALL
SEE YOU AROUND!
HUNH. THAT ACTUALLY HADN'T OCCURRED TO ME.
WHAT IF NOBODY DOES WANT TO JOIN OUR TEAM?
JUST LOOK AROUND...

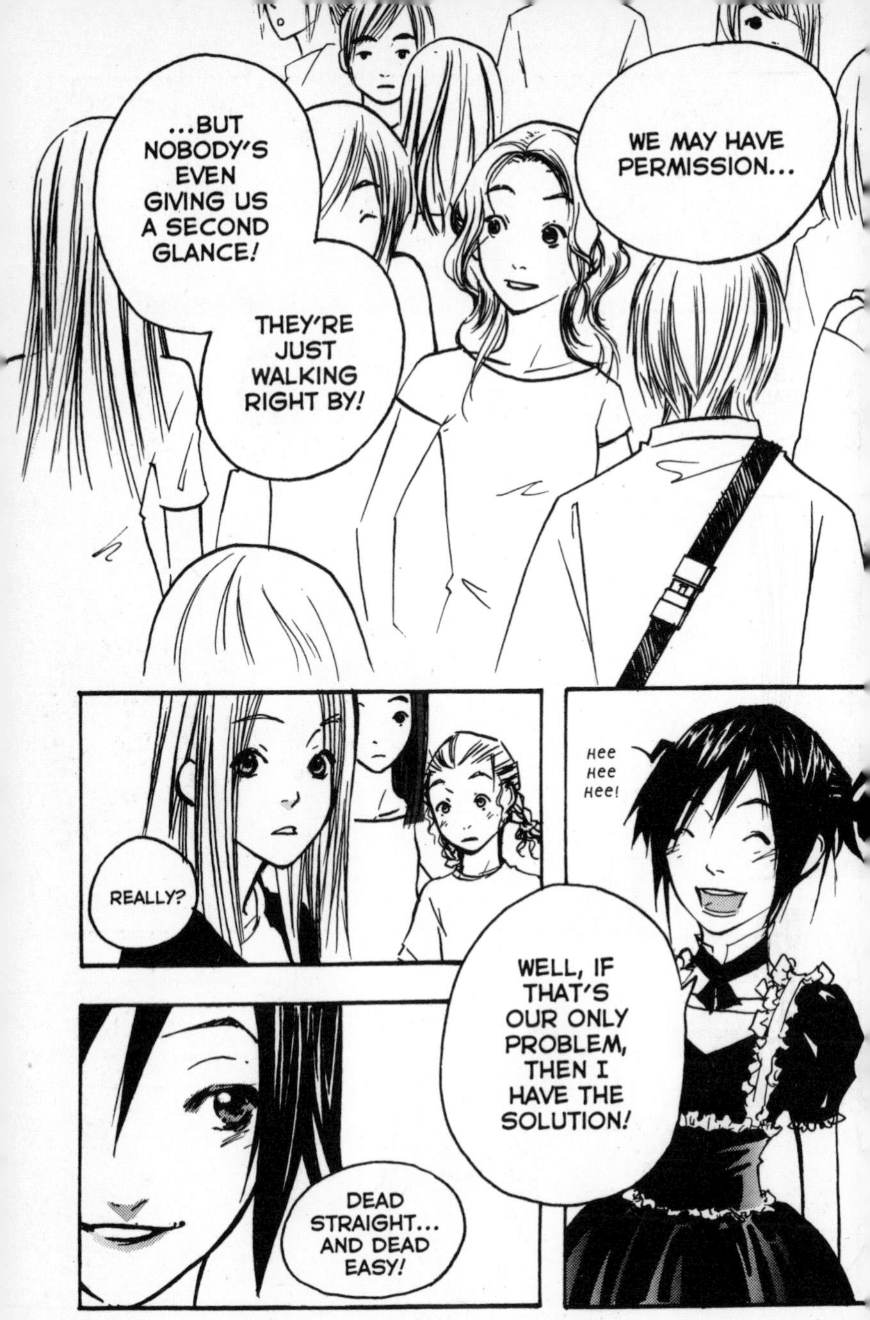
WE MAY HAVE PERMISSION...
...BUT NOBODY'S EVEN GIVING US A SECOND GLANCE!
THEY'RE JUST WALKING RIGHT BY!
Hee Hee Hee!
WELL, IF THAT'S OUR ONLY PROBLEM, THEN I HAVE THE SOLUTION!
REALLY?
DEAD STRAIGHT... AND DEAD EASY!

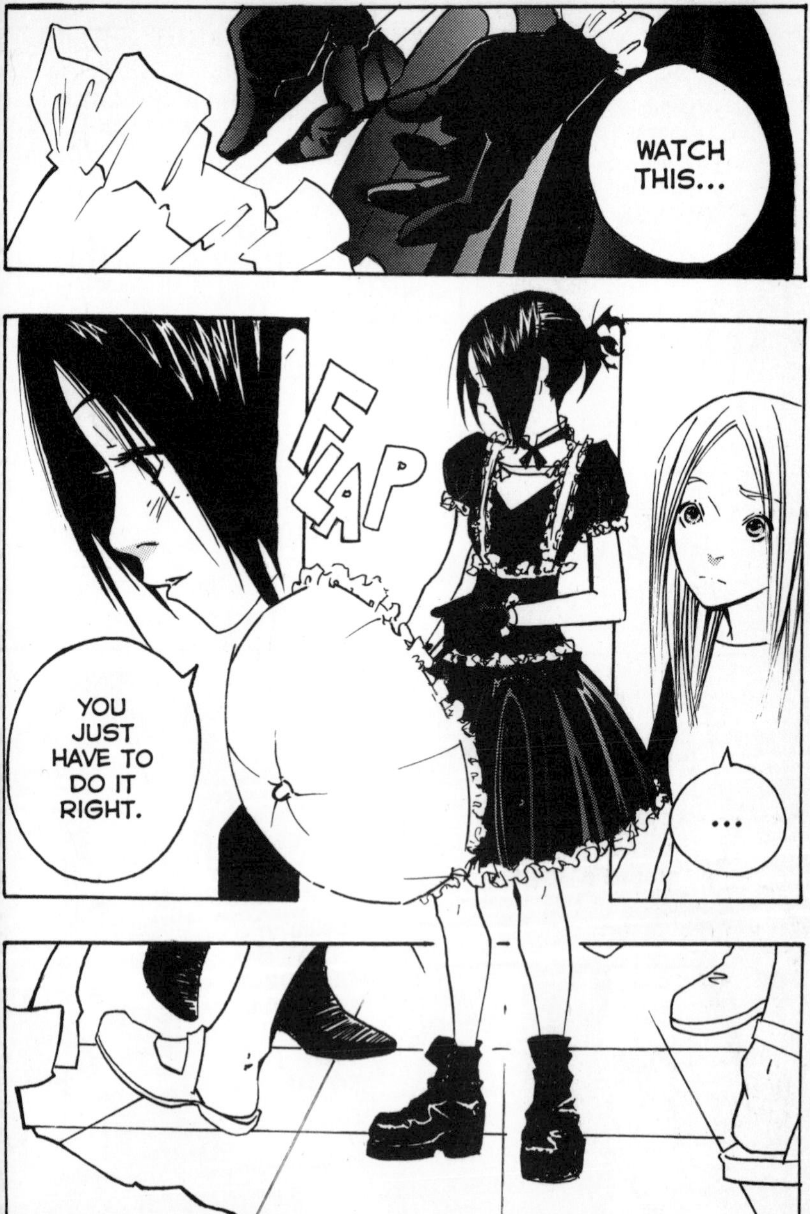
WATCH THIS...
FLAP
YOU JUST HAVE TO DO IT RIGHT.
...

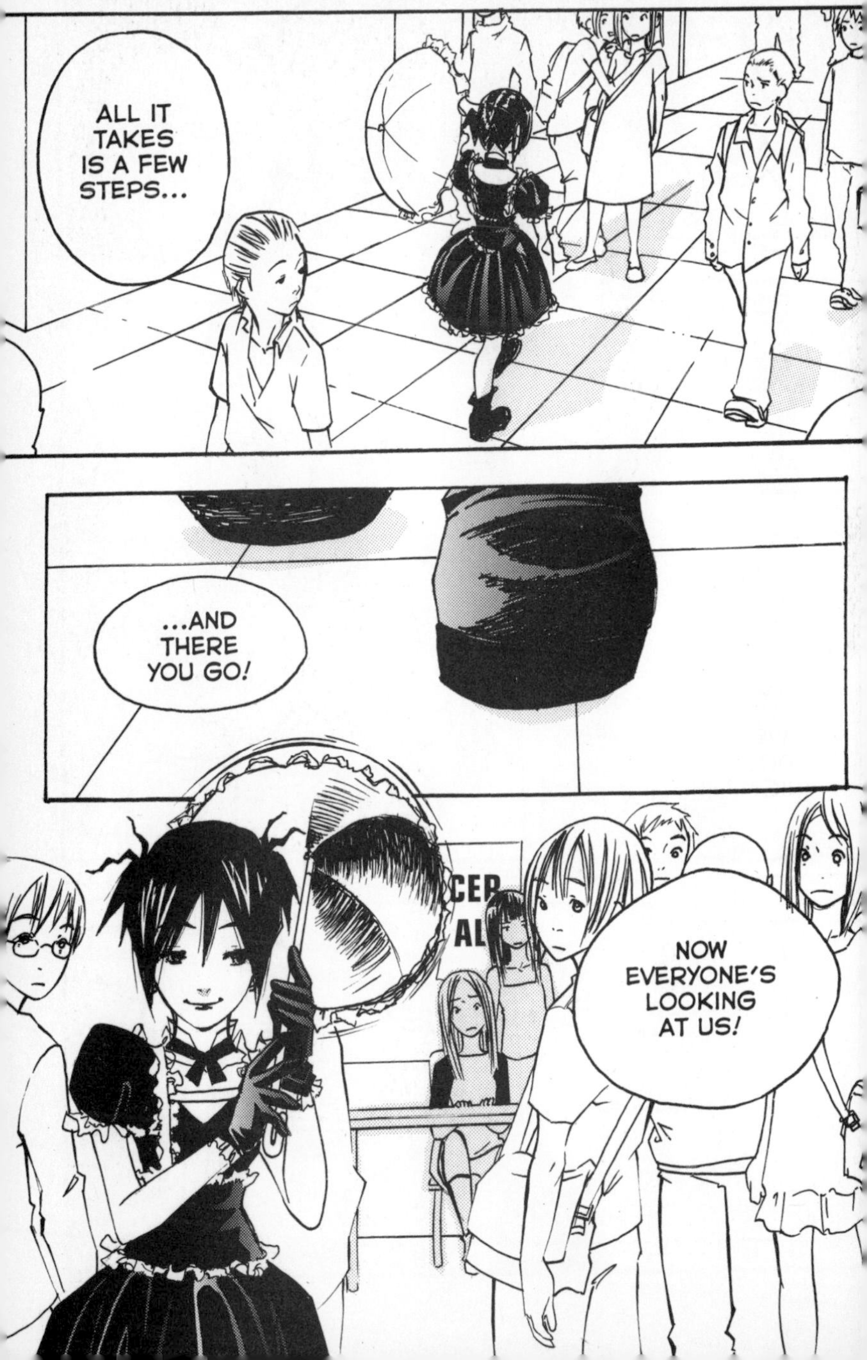
ALL IT TAKES IS A FEW STEPS...
...AND THERE YOU GO!
NOW EVERYONE'S LOOKING AT US!

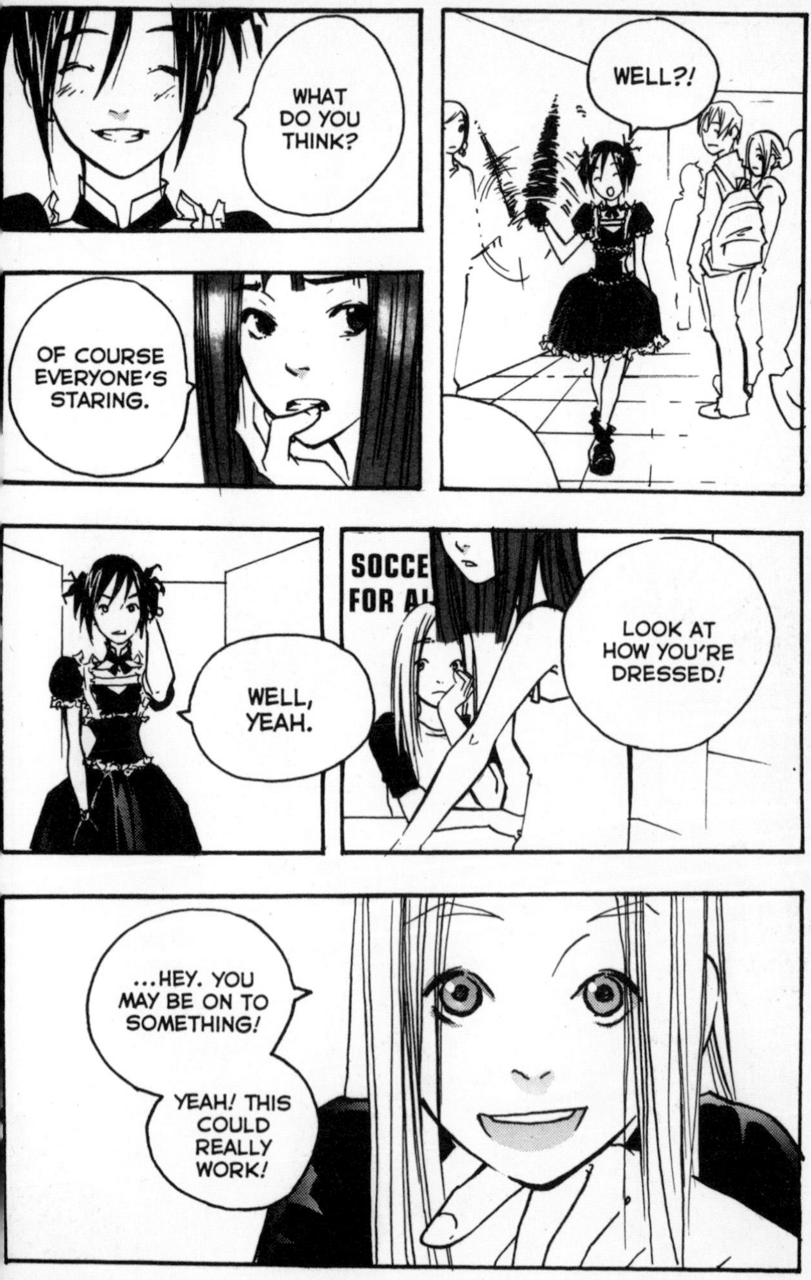
WELL?!
WHAT DO YOU THINK?
OF COURSE EVERYONE'S STARING.
LOOK AT HOW YOU'RE DRESSED!
WELL, YEAH.
...HEY. YOU MAY BE ON TO SOMETHING!
YEAH! THIS COULD REALLY WORK!

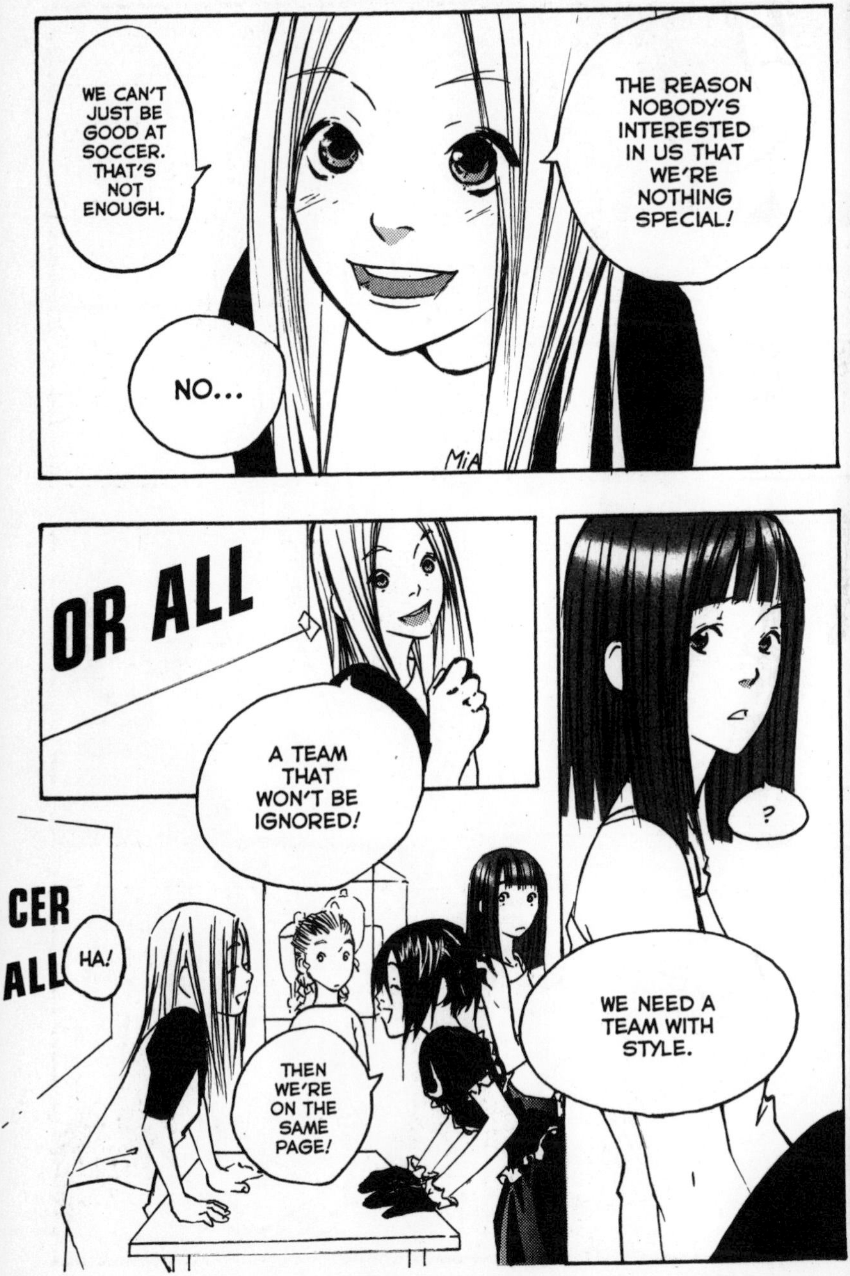
THE REASON NOBODY'S INTERESTED IN US THAT WE'RE NOTHING SPECIAL!
WE CAN'T JUST BE GOOD AT SOCCER. THAT'S NOT ENOUGH.
NO...
MiA
?
WE NEED A TEAM WITH STYLE.
OR ALL
A TEAM THAT WON'T BE IGNORED!
CER
ALL
HA!
THEN WE'RE ON THE SAME PAGE!

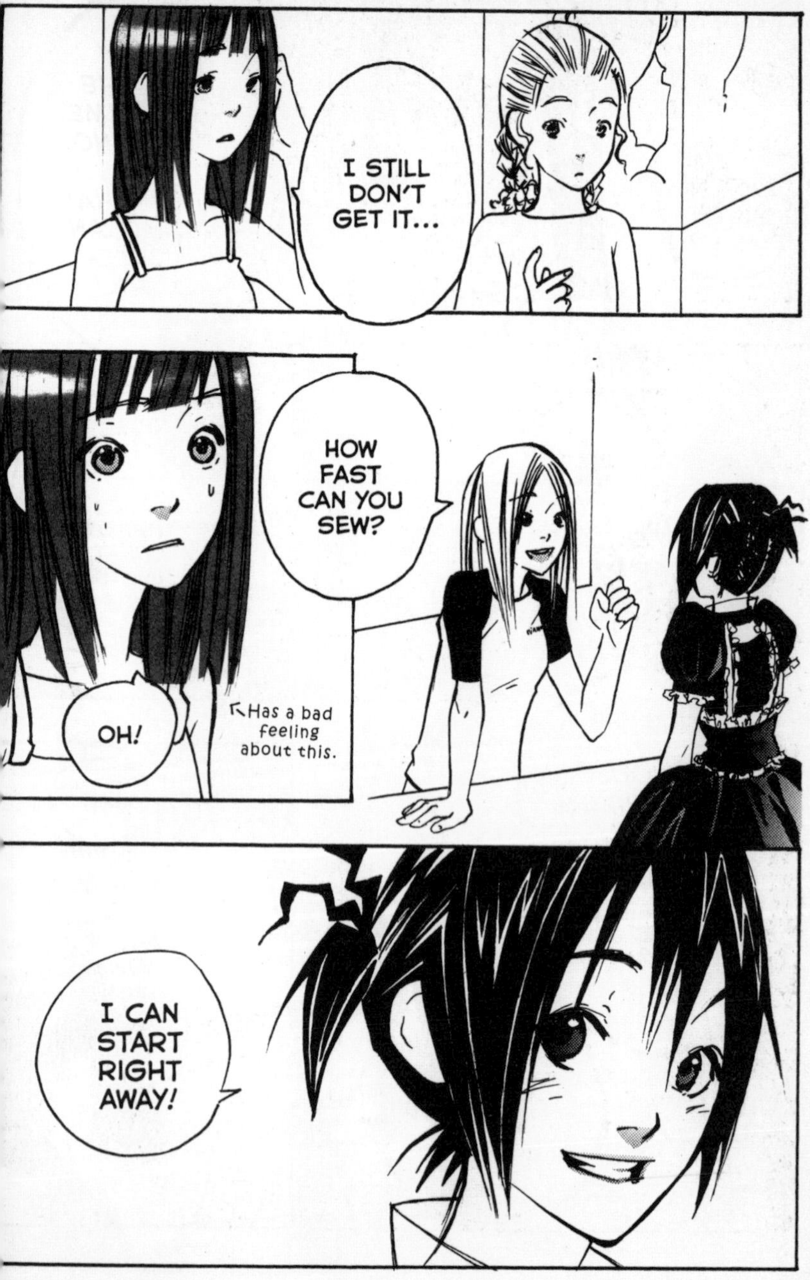
I STILL DON'T GET IT...
HOW FAST CAN YOU SEW?
OH!
↖Has a bad feeling about this.
I CAN START RIGHT AWAY!

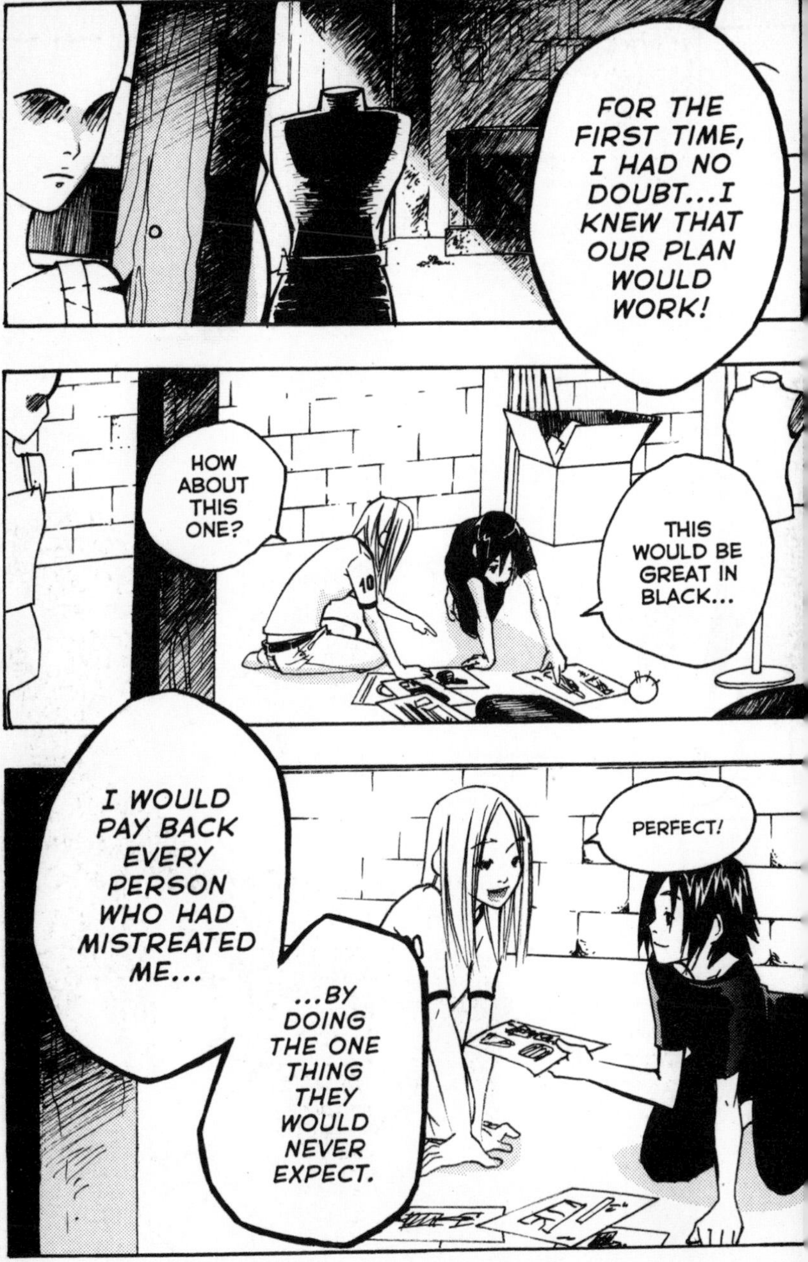
FOR THE FIRST TIME, I HAD NO DOUBT...I KNEW THAT OUR PLAN WOULD WORK!
THIS WOULD BE GREAT IN BLACK...
HOW ABOUT THIS ONE?
PERFECT!
I WOULD PAY BACK EVERY PERSON WHO HAD MISTREATED ME...
...BY DOING THE ONE THING THEY WOULD NEVER EXPECT.

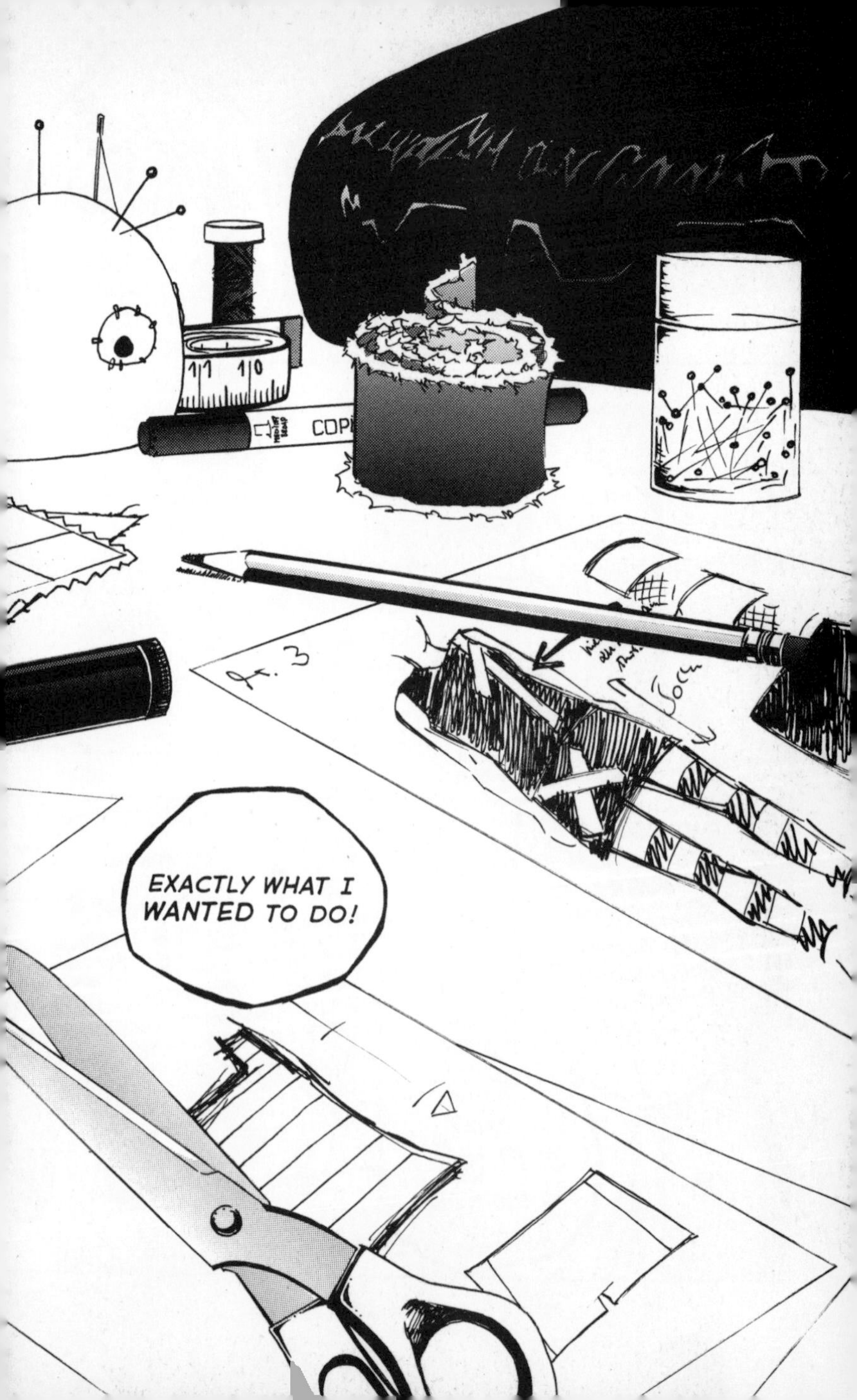
EXACTLY WHAT I WANTED TO DO!

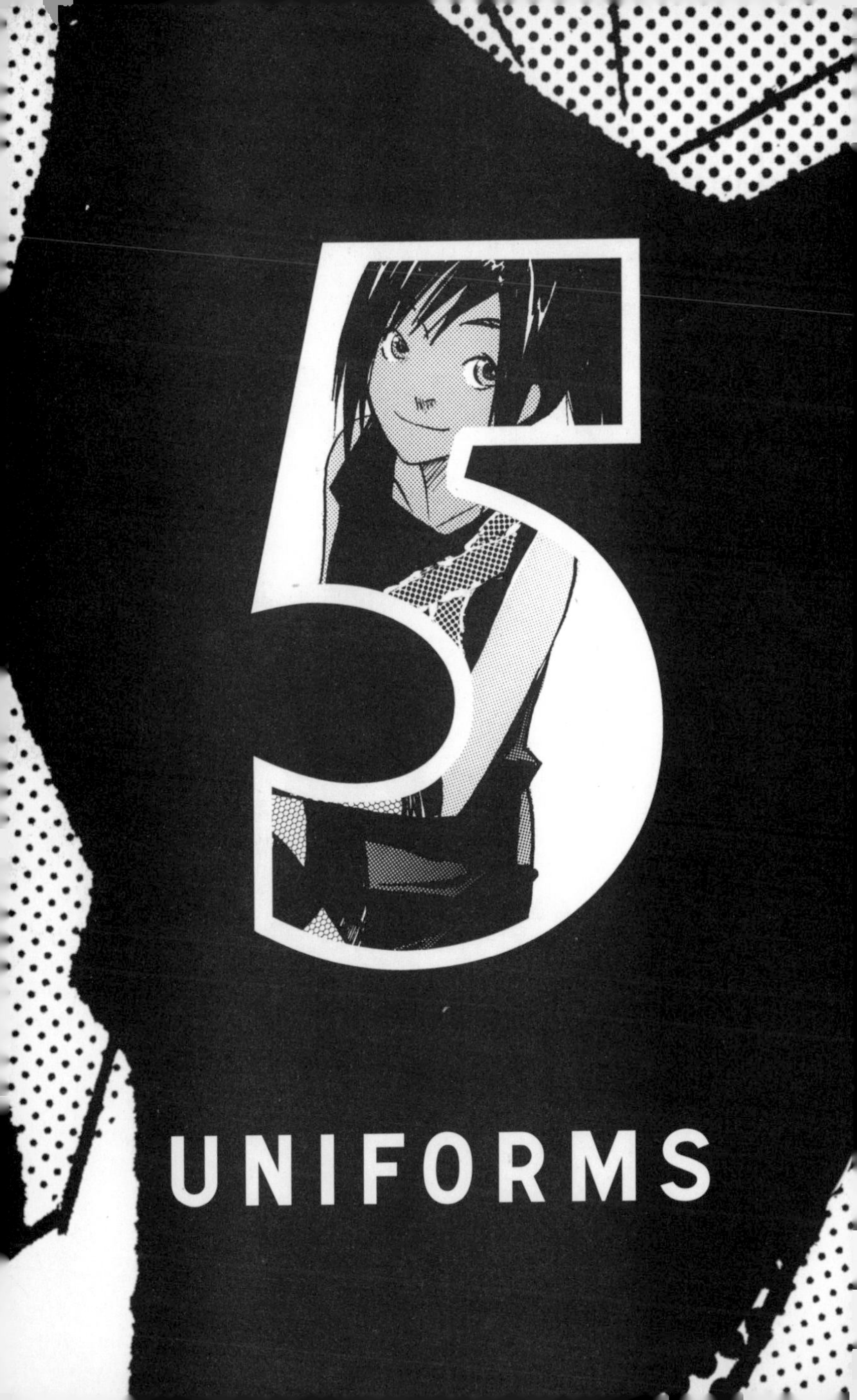
5
UNIFORMS

DELIA

AGE: 20
HEIGHT: 1.73 M (5′8″)
WEIGHT: 58 KILOS (128 LBS)
SIGN: TAURUS
LIKES: SPORTS, PEOPLE, FAST FOOD
DISLIKES: NEEDLES, ARGUMENTS, CIGARETTES
HOBBIES: BASKETBALL, KARAOKE, DANCING

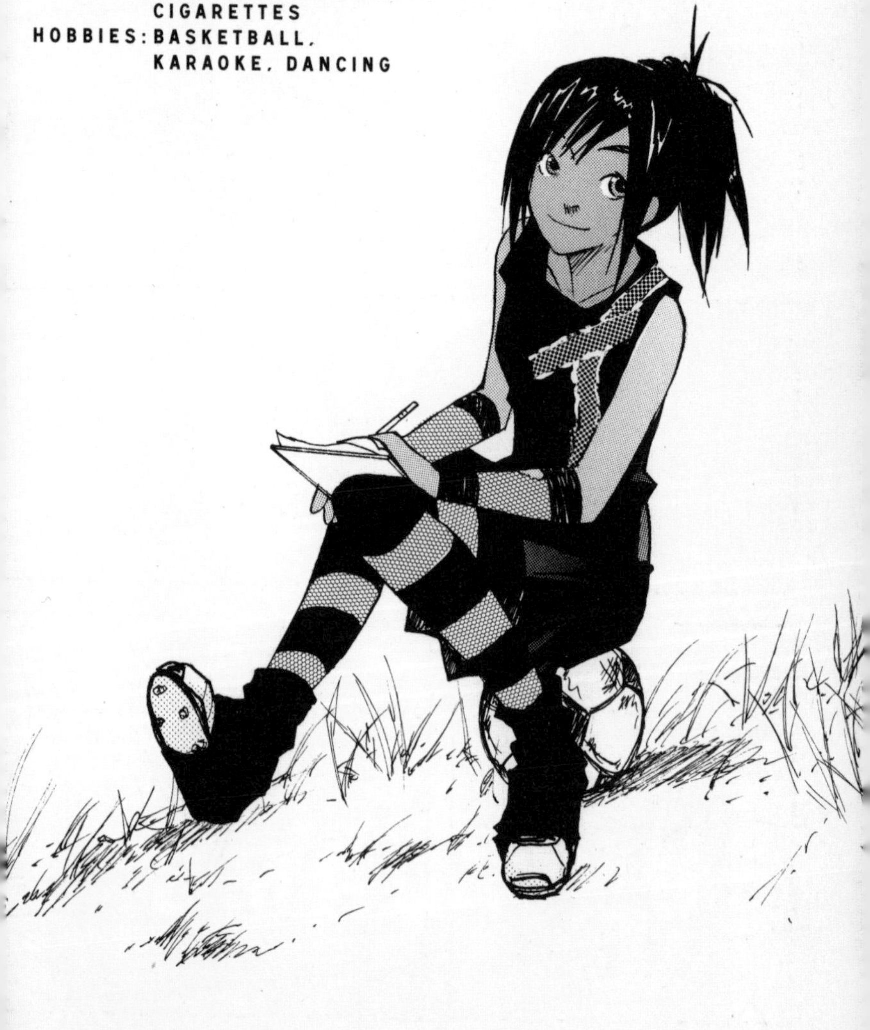

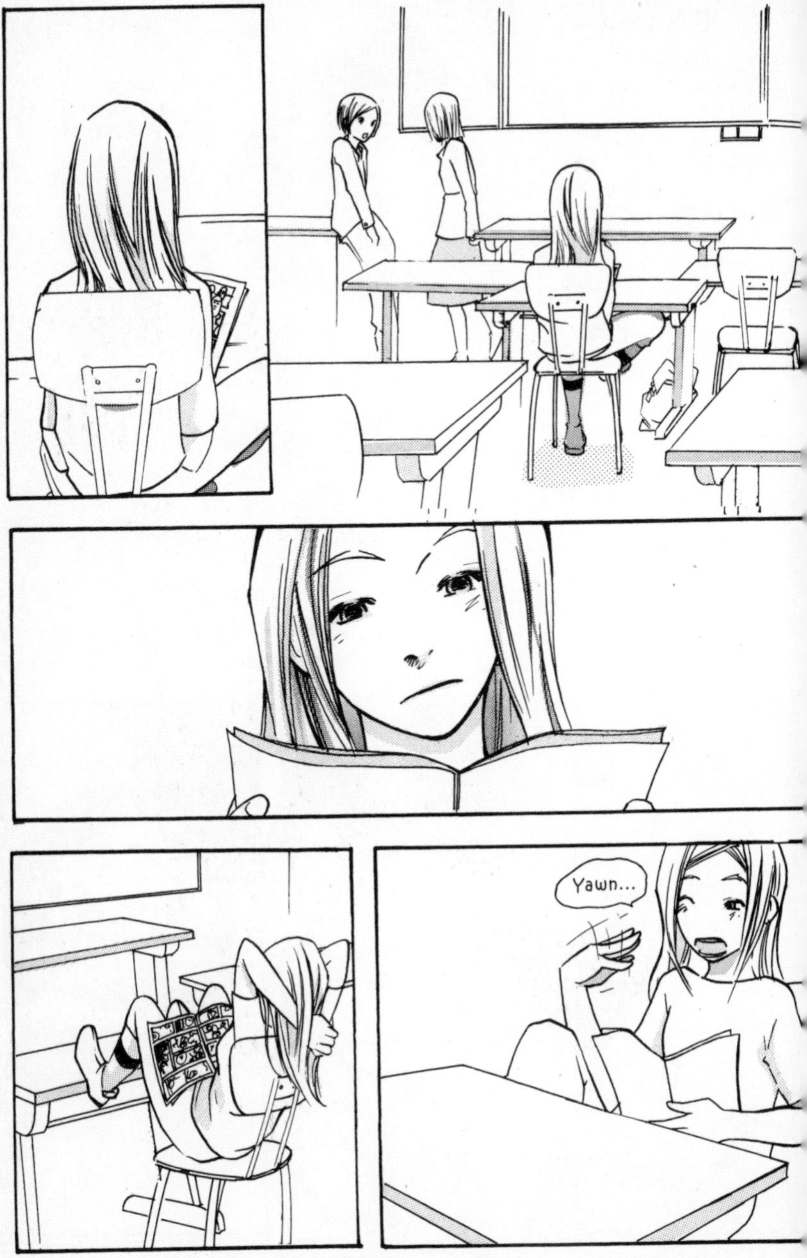
Yawn...

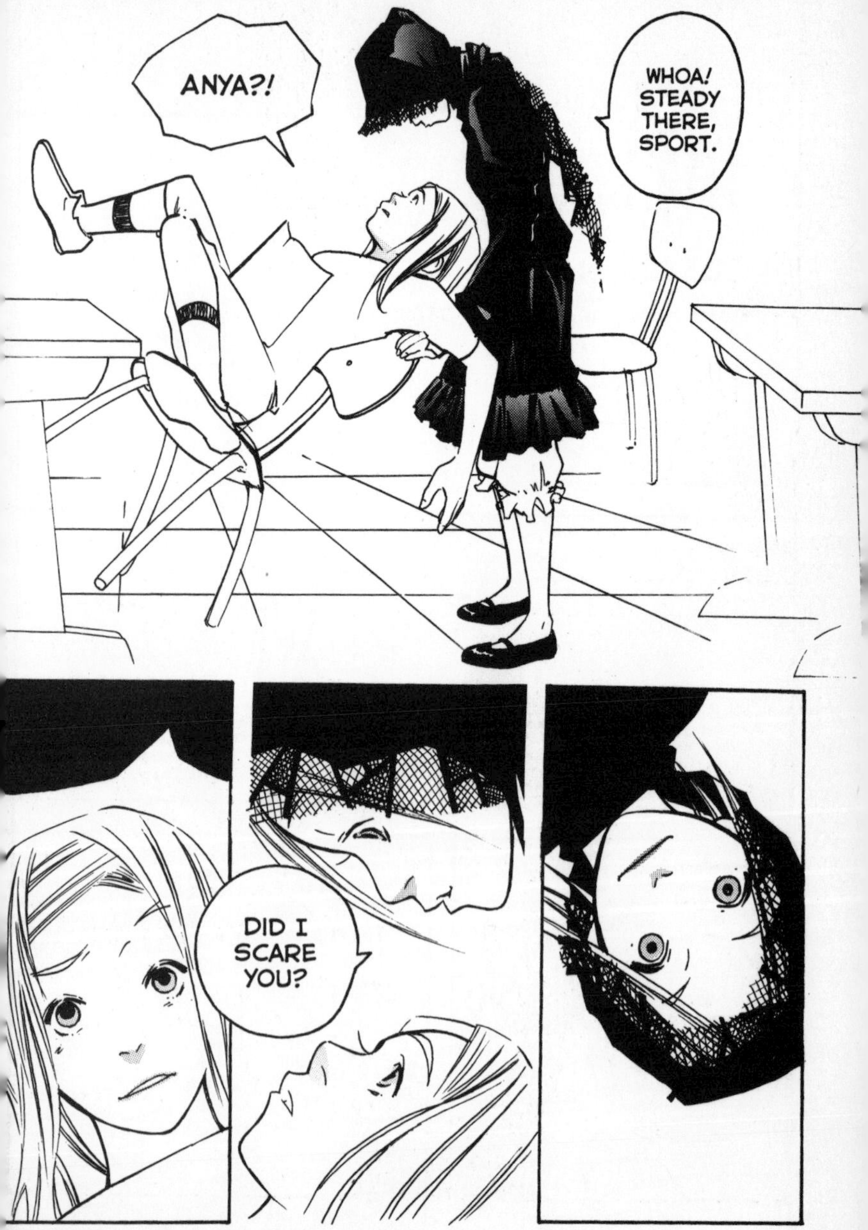
WHOA! STEADY THERE, SPORT.
ANYA?!
DID I SCARE YOU?

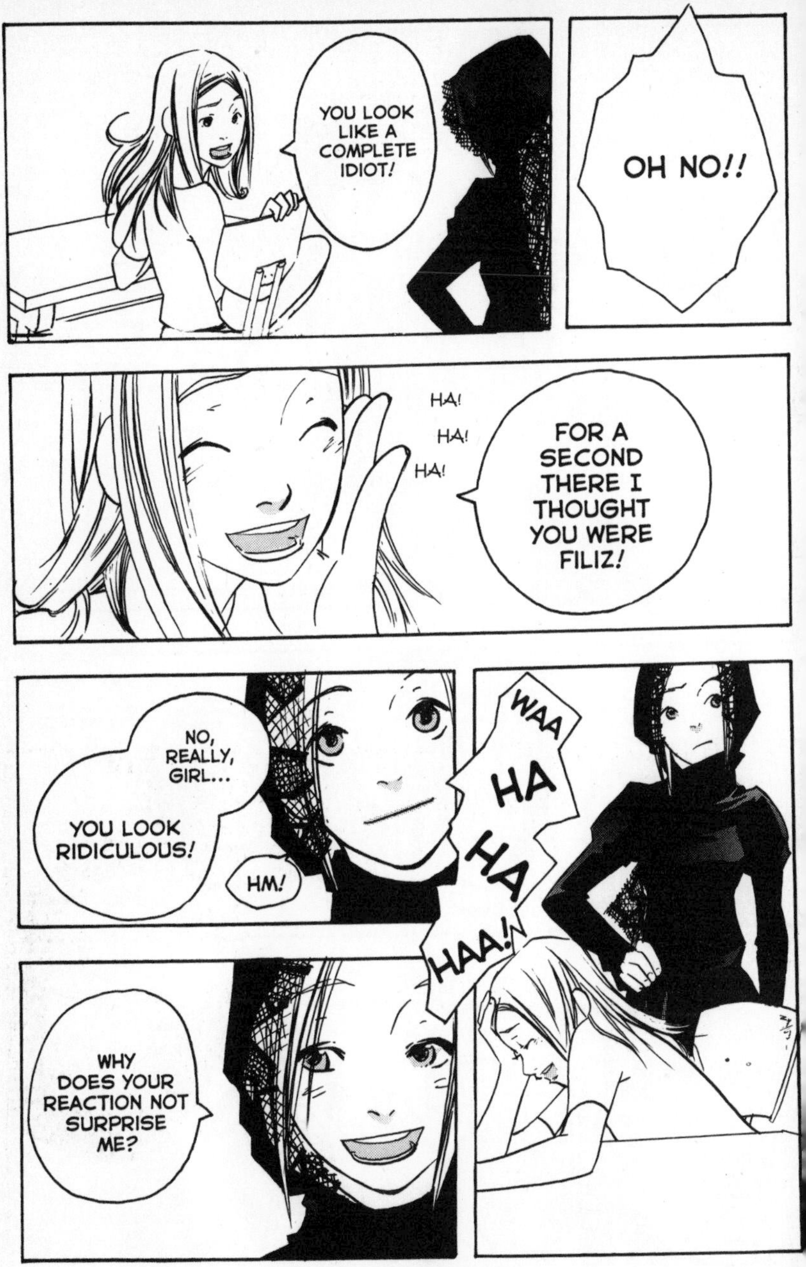
OH NO!!
YOU LOOK LIKE A COMPLETE IDIOT!
HA! HA! HA!
FOR A SECOND THERE I THOUGHT YOU WERE FILIZ!
WAA HA HA HAA!
NO, REALLY, GIRL... YOU LOOK RIDICULOUS!
HM!
WHY DOES YOUR REACTION NOT SURPRISE ME?

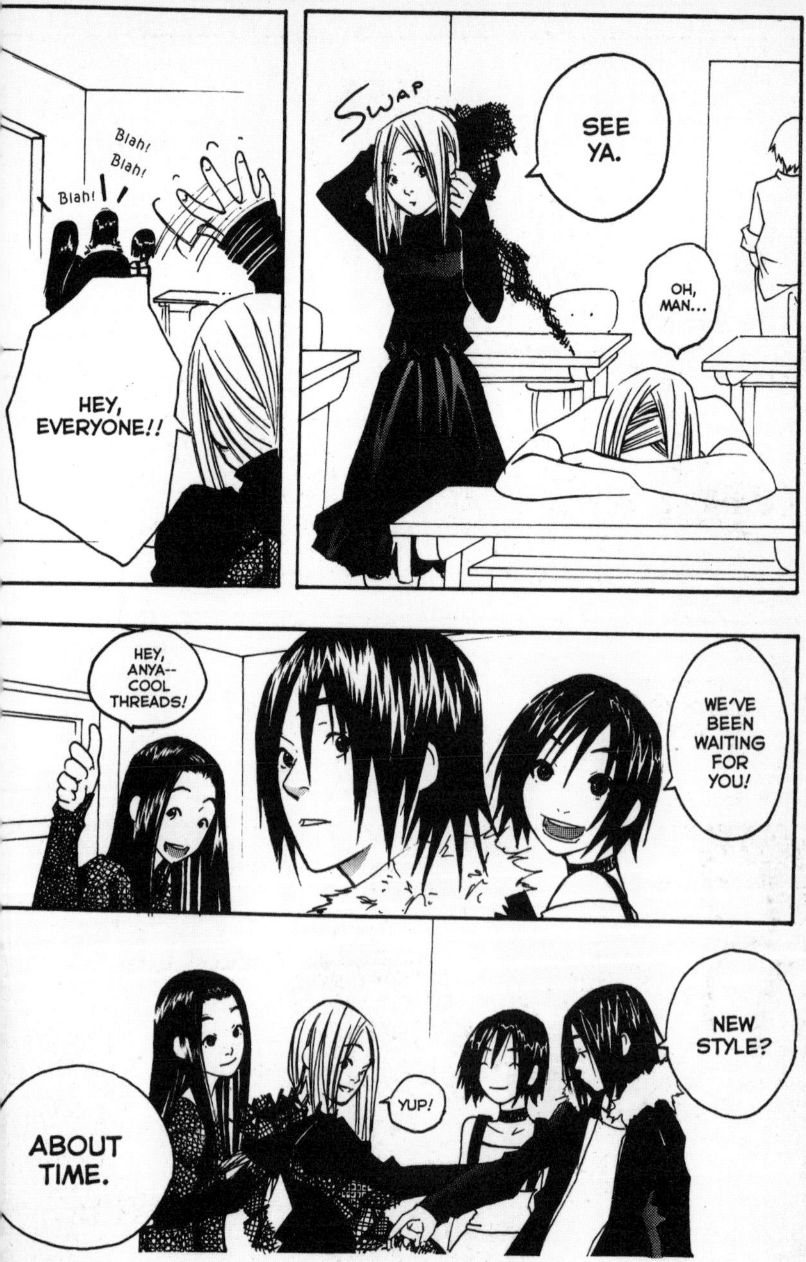
SWAP
SEE YA.
...
OH, MAN...
Blah!
Blah!
Blah!
HEY, EVERYONE!!
WE'VE BEEN WAITING FOR YOU!
HEY, ANYA-- COOL THREADS!
NEW STYLE?
YUP!
ABOUT TIME.

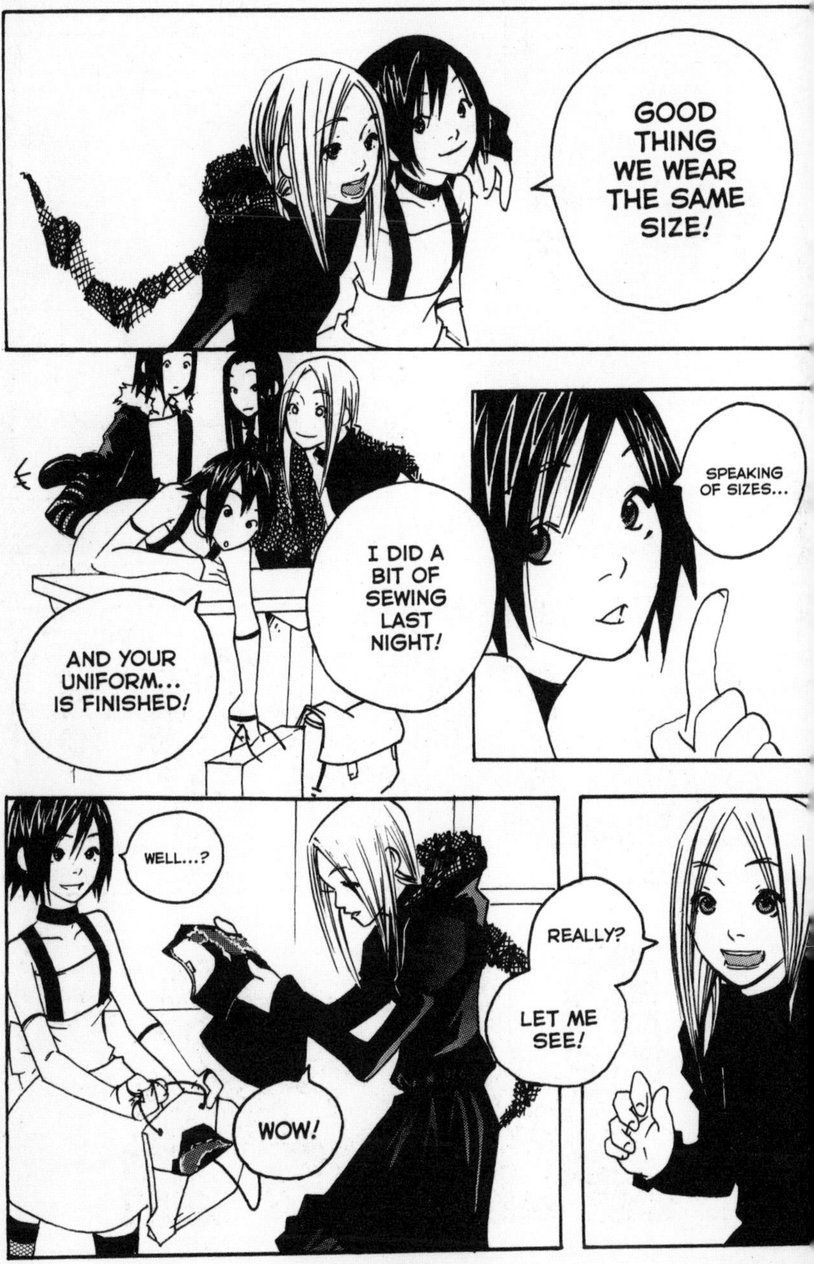
GOOD THING WE WEAR THE SAME SIZE!
SPEAKING OF SIZES...
I DID A BIT OF SEWING LAST NIGHT!
AND YOUR UNIFORM... IS FINISHED!
REALLY?
LET ME SEE!
WELL...?
WOW!

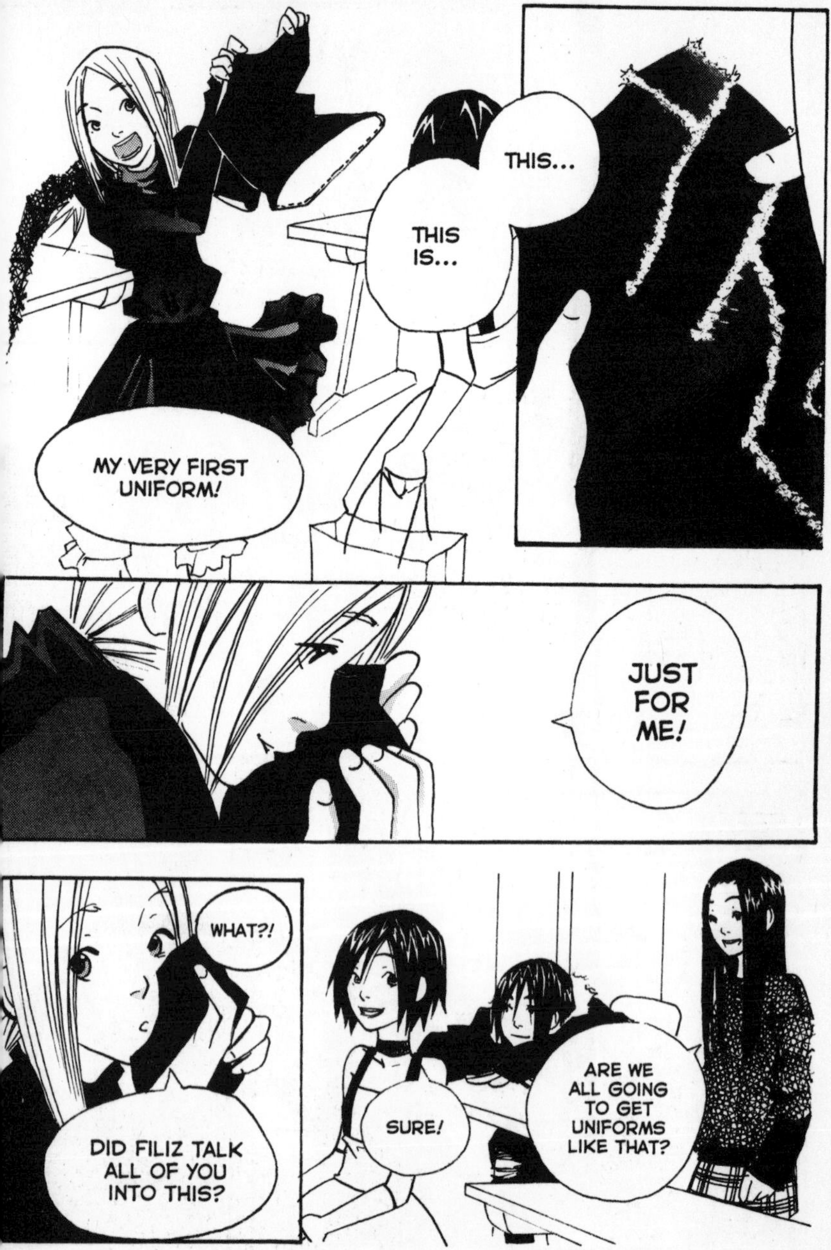
THIS...
THIS IS...
MY VERY FIRST UNIFORM!
JUST FOR ME!
ARE WE ALL GOING TO GET UNIFORMS LIKE THAT?
SURE!
WHAT?!
DID FILIZ TALK ALL OF YOU INTO THIS?

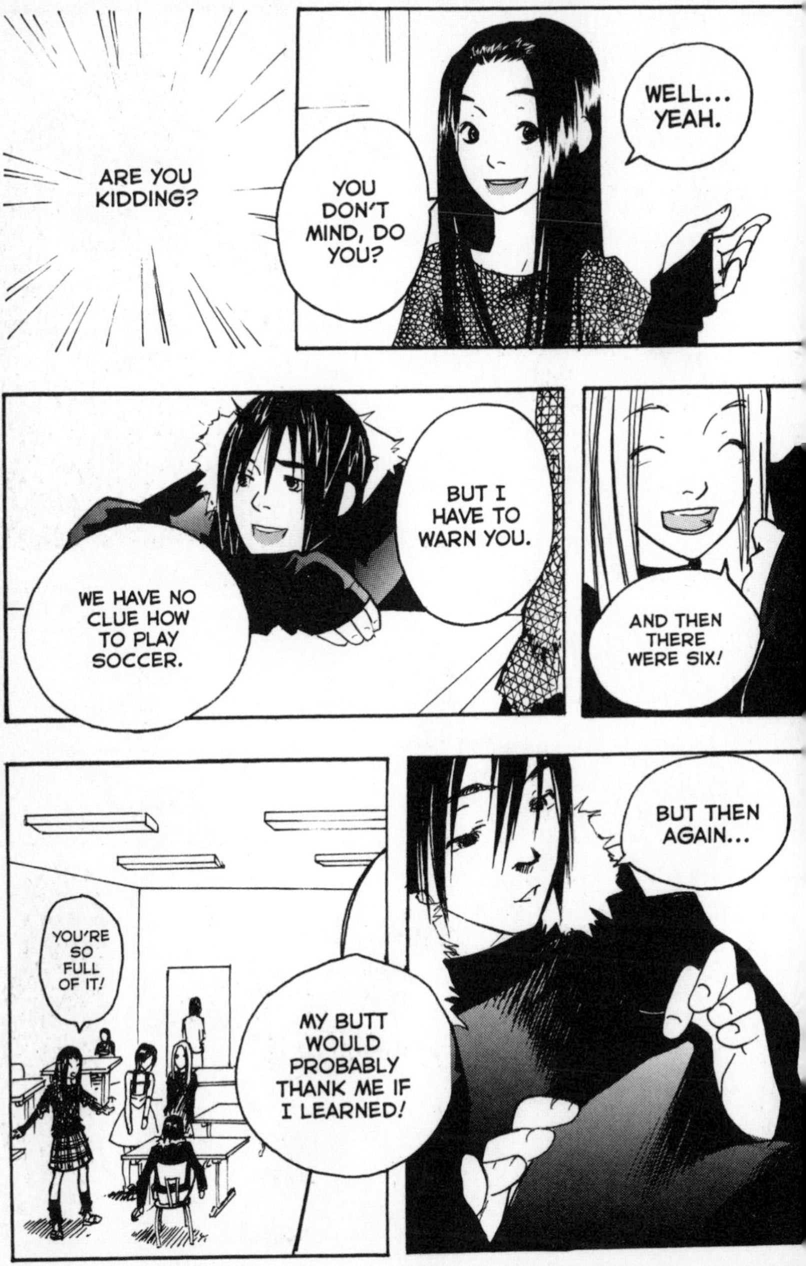
WELL... YEAH.
YOU DON'T MIND, DO YOU?
ARE YOU KIDDING?
AND THEN THERE WERE SIX!
BUT I HAVE TO WARN YOU.
WE HAVE NO CLUE HOW TO PLAY SOCCER.
BUT THEN AGAIN...
MY BUTT WOULD PROBABLY THANK ME IF I LEARNED!
YOU'RE SO FULL OF IT!

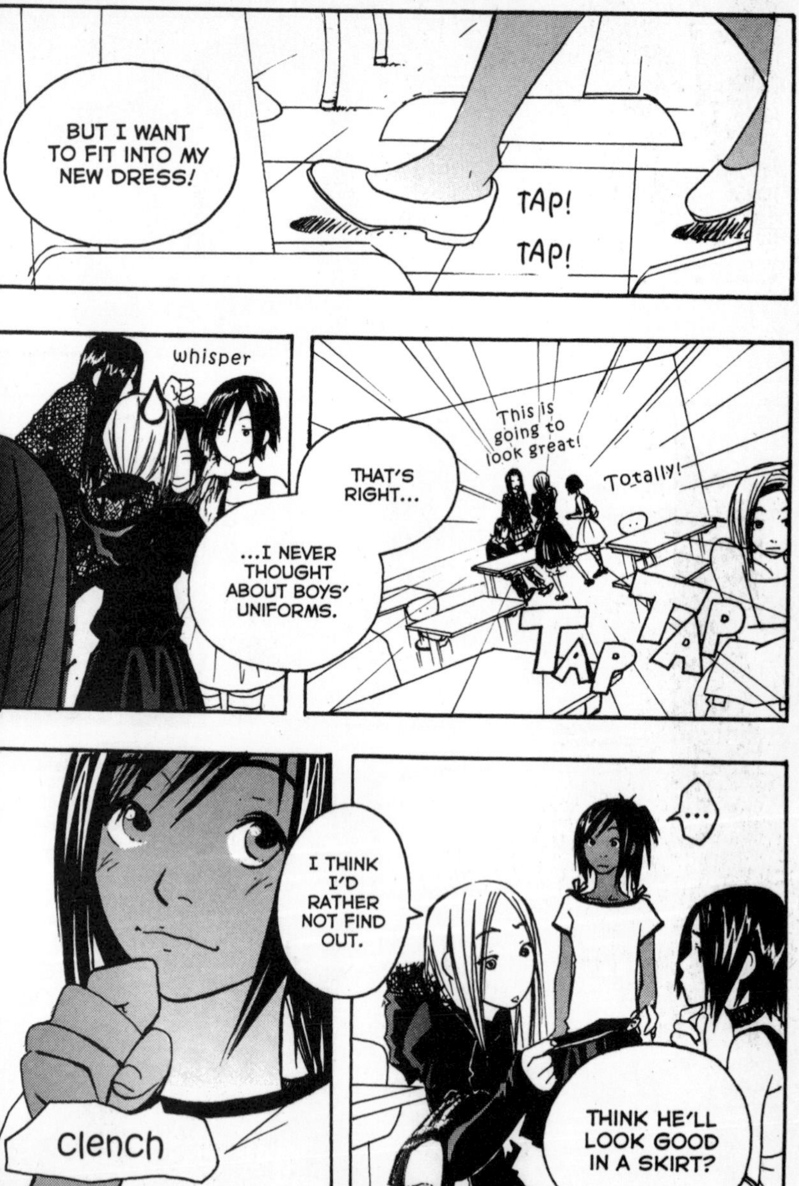
BUT I WANT TO FIT INTO MY NEW DRESS!
TAP!
TAP!
Totally!
This is going to look great!
...
...
THAT'S RIGHT...
...I NEVER THOUGHT ABOUT BOYS' UNIFORMS.
TAP TAP
whisper
...
THINK HE'LL LOOK GOOD IN A SKIRT?
I THINK I'D RATHER NOT FIND OUT.
clench

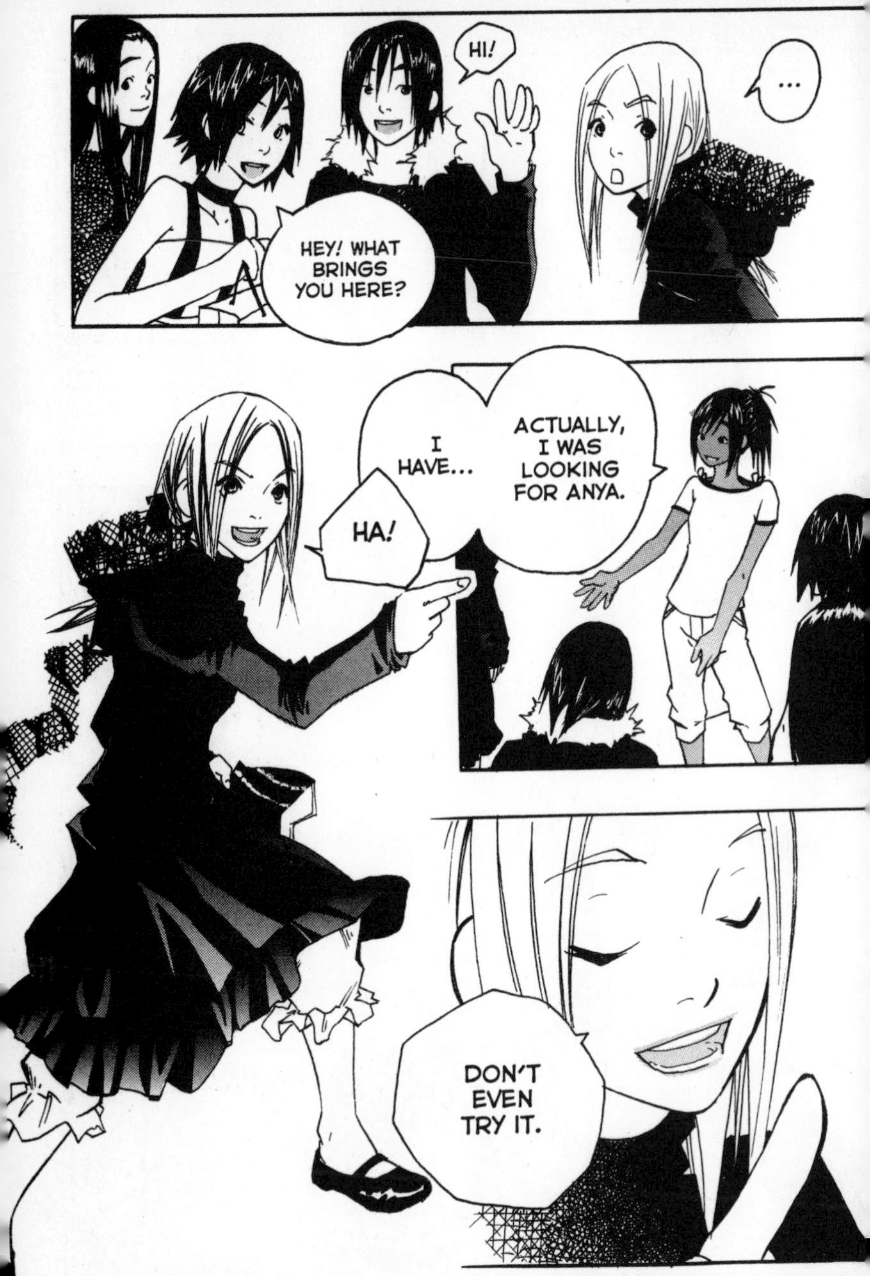
...
HI!
HEY! WHAT BRINGS YOU HERE?
ACTUALLY, I WAS LOOKING FOR ANYA.
I HAVE...
HA!
DON'T EVEN TRY IT.

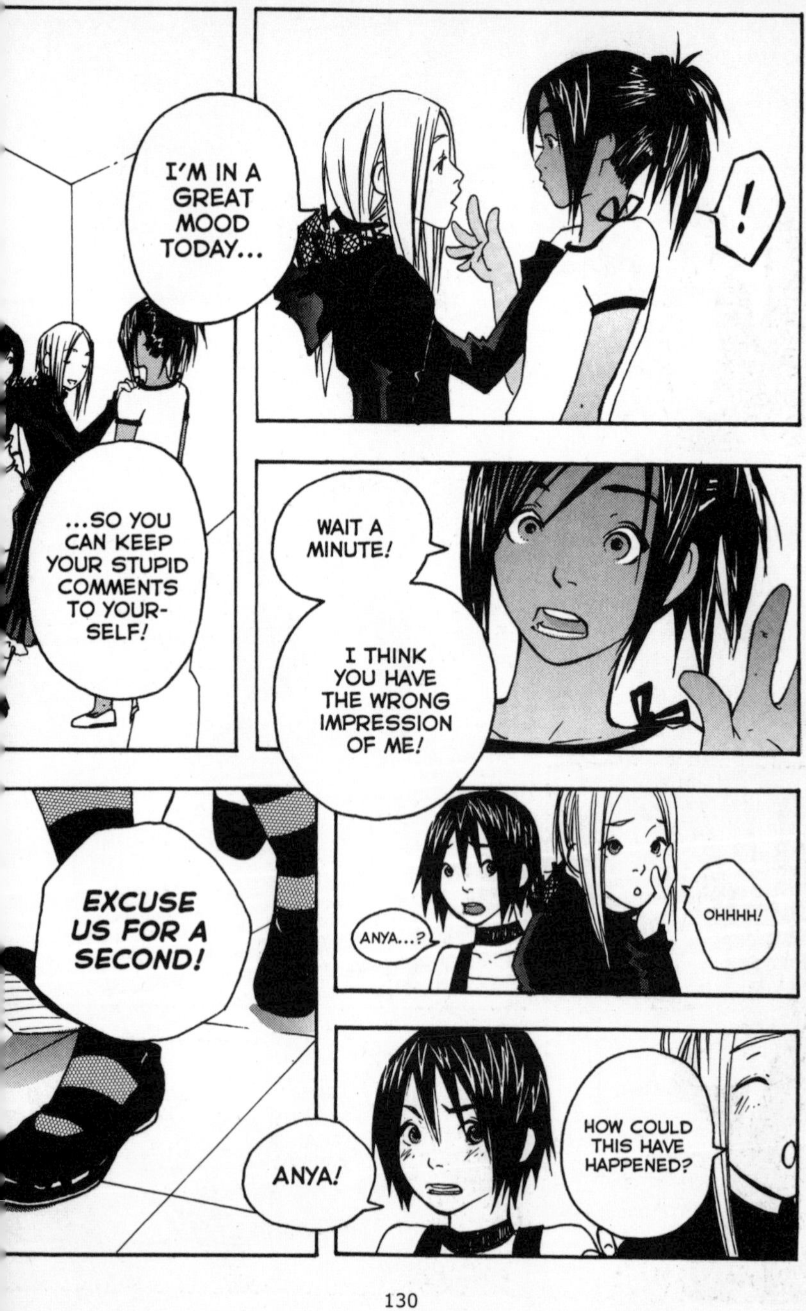
I'M IN A GREAT MOOD TODAY...
...SO YOU CAN KEEP YOUR STUPID COMMENTS TO YOURSELF!
!
WAIT A MINUTE!
I THINK YOU HAVE THE WRONG IMPRESSION OF ME!
OHHHH!
ANYA...?
HOW COULD THIS HAVE HAPPENED?
ANYA!
EXCUSE US FOR A SECOND!

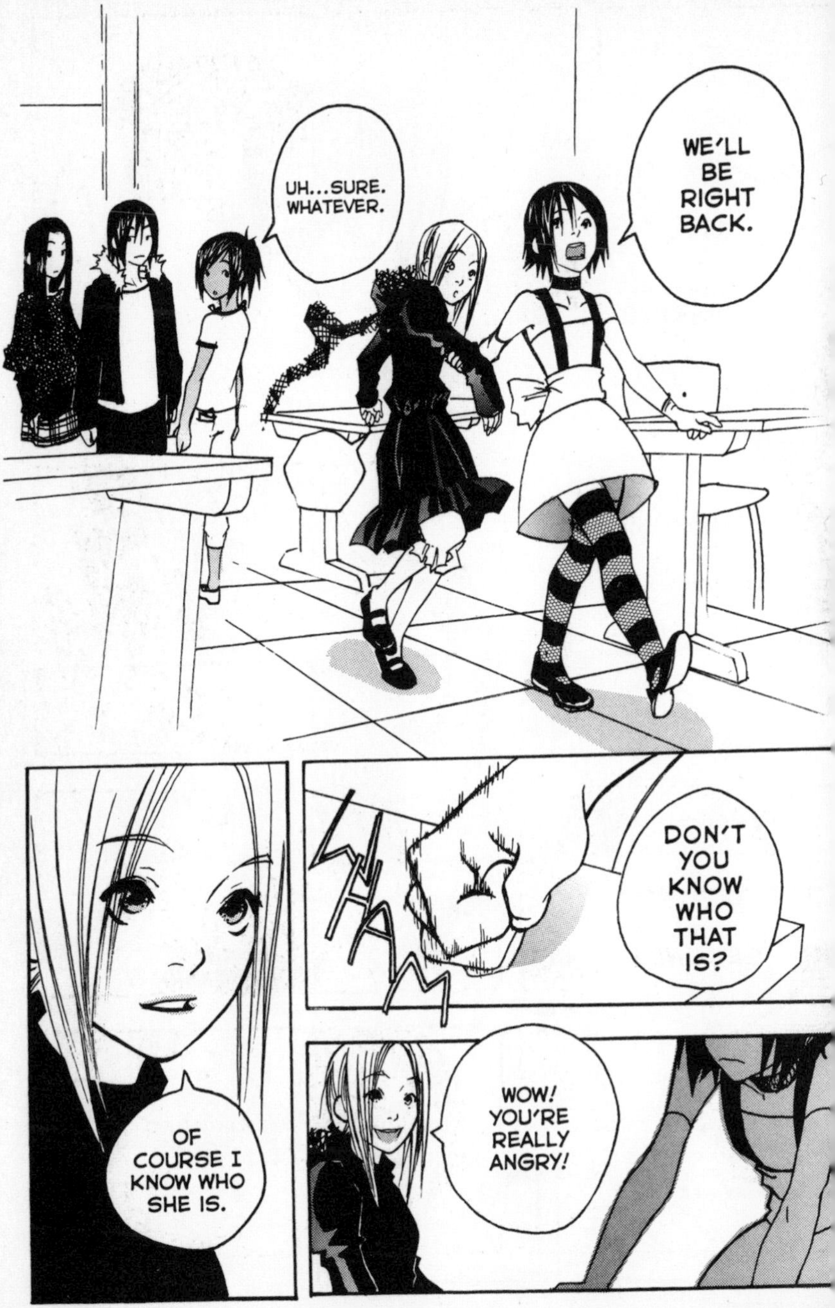

WE'LL BE RIGHT BACK.
UH...SURE. WHATEVER.
DON'T YOU KNOW WHO THAT IS?
WHAM
WOW! YOU'RE REALLY ANGRY!
OF COURSE I KNOW WHO SHE IS.

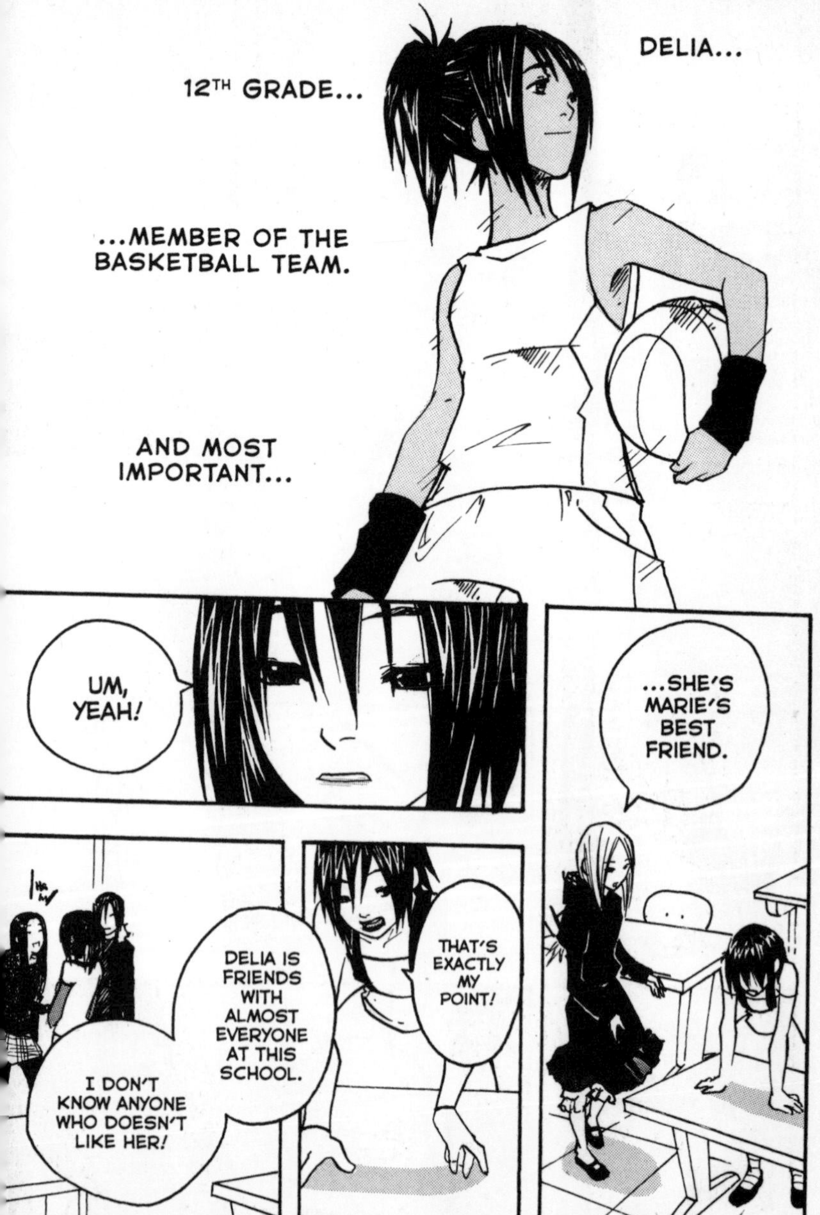
DELIA...
12TH GRADE...
...MEMBER OF THE BASKETBALL TEAM.
AND MOST IMPORTANT...
...SHE'S MARIE'S BEST FRIEND.
UM, YEAH!
THAT'S EXACTLY MY POINT!
DELIA IS FRIENDS WITH ALMOST EVERYONE AT THIS SCHOOL.
I DON'T KNOW ANYONE WHO DOESN'T LIKE HER!

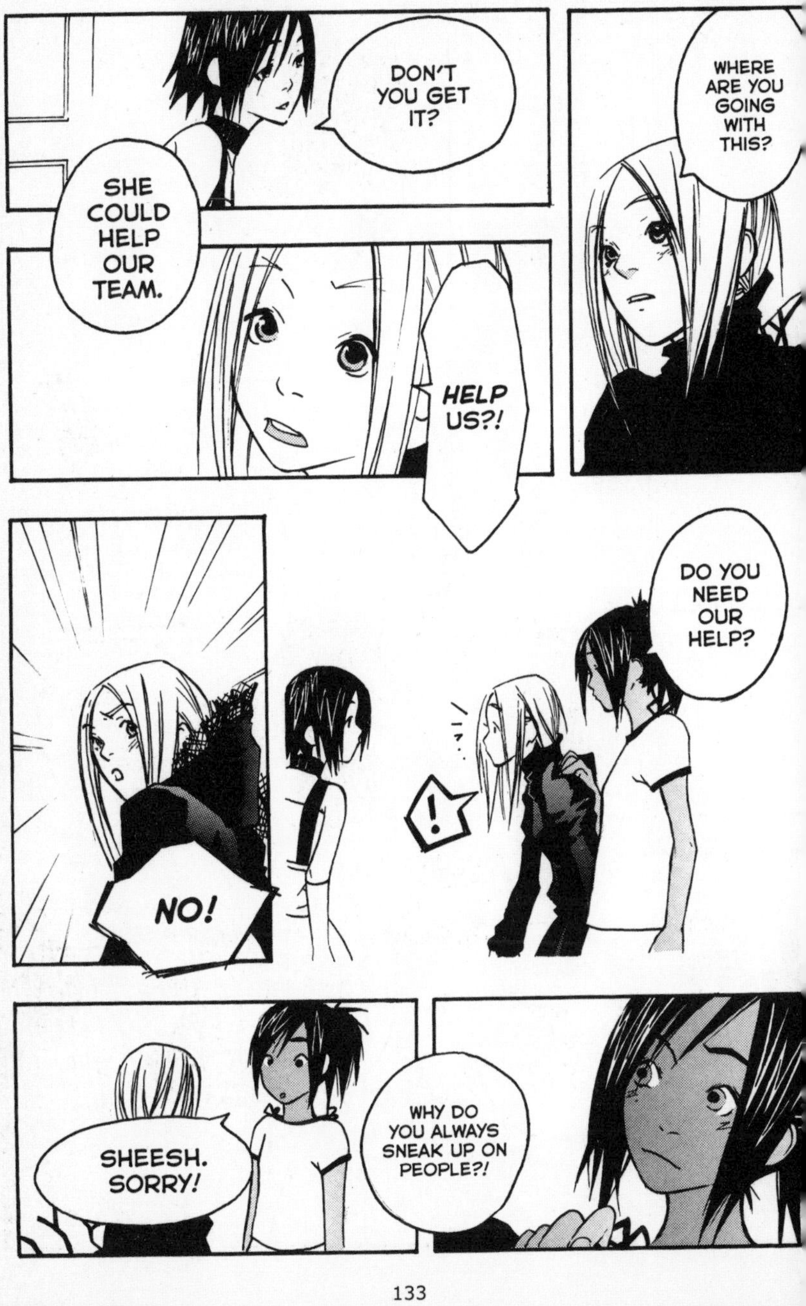
WHERE ARE YOU GOING WITH THIS?
DON'T YOU GET IT?
SHE COULD HELP OUR TEAM.
HELP US?!
DO YOU NEED OUR HELP?
!
NO!
WHY DO YOU ALWAYS SNEAK UP ON PEOPLE?!
SHEESH. SORRY!

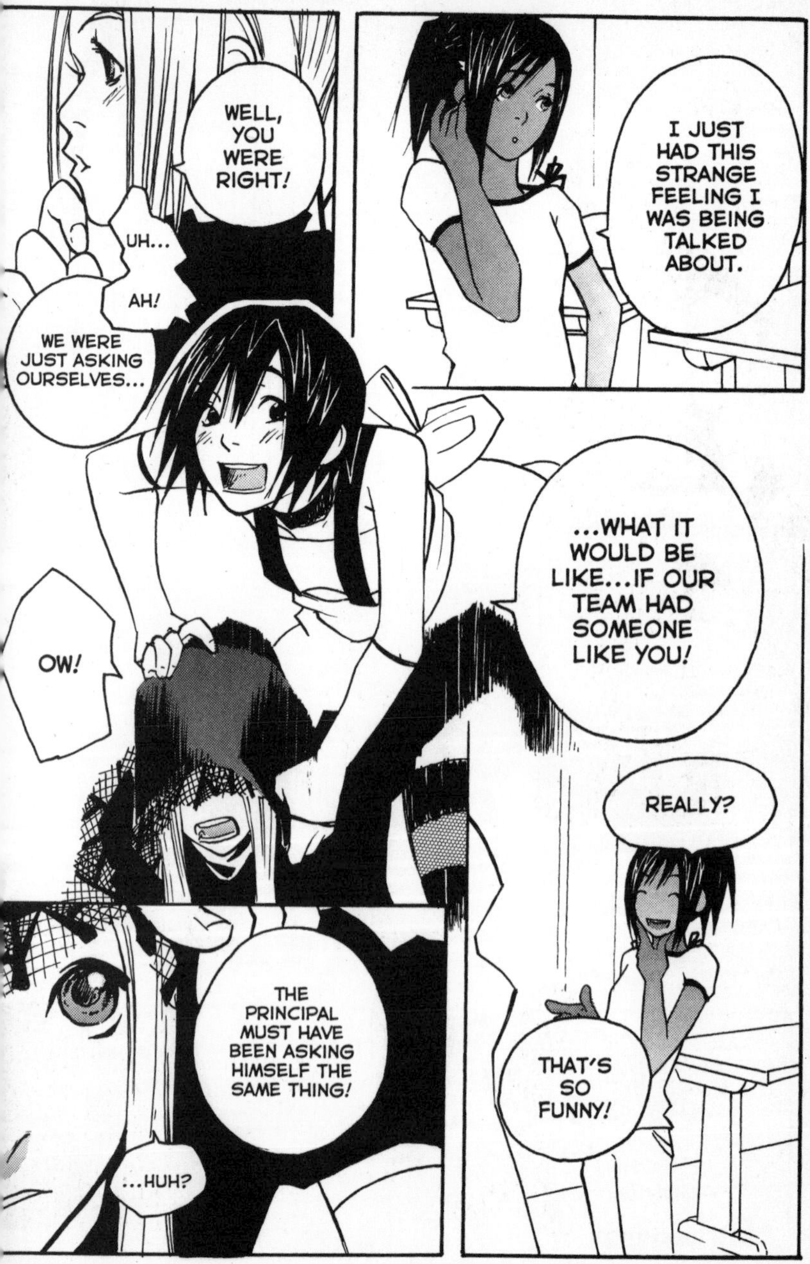
I JUST HAD THIS STRANGE FEELING I WAS BEING TALKED ABOUT.
WELL, YOU WERE RIGHT!
UH...
AH!
WE WERE JUST ASKING OURSELVES...
...WHAT IT WOULD BE LIKE...IF OUR TEAM HAD SOMEONE LIKE YOU!
OW!
REALLY?
THAT'S SO FUNNY!
THE PRINCIPAL MUST HAVE BEEN ASKING HIMSELF THE SAME THING!
...HUH?

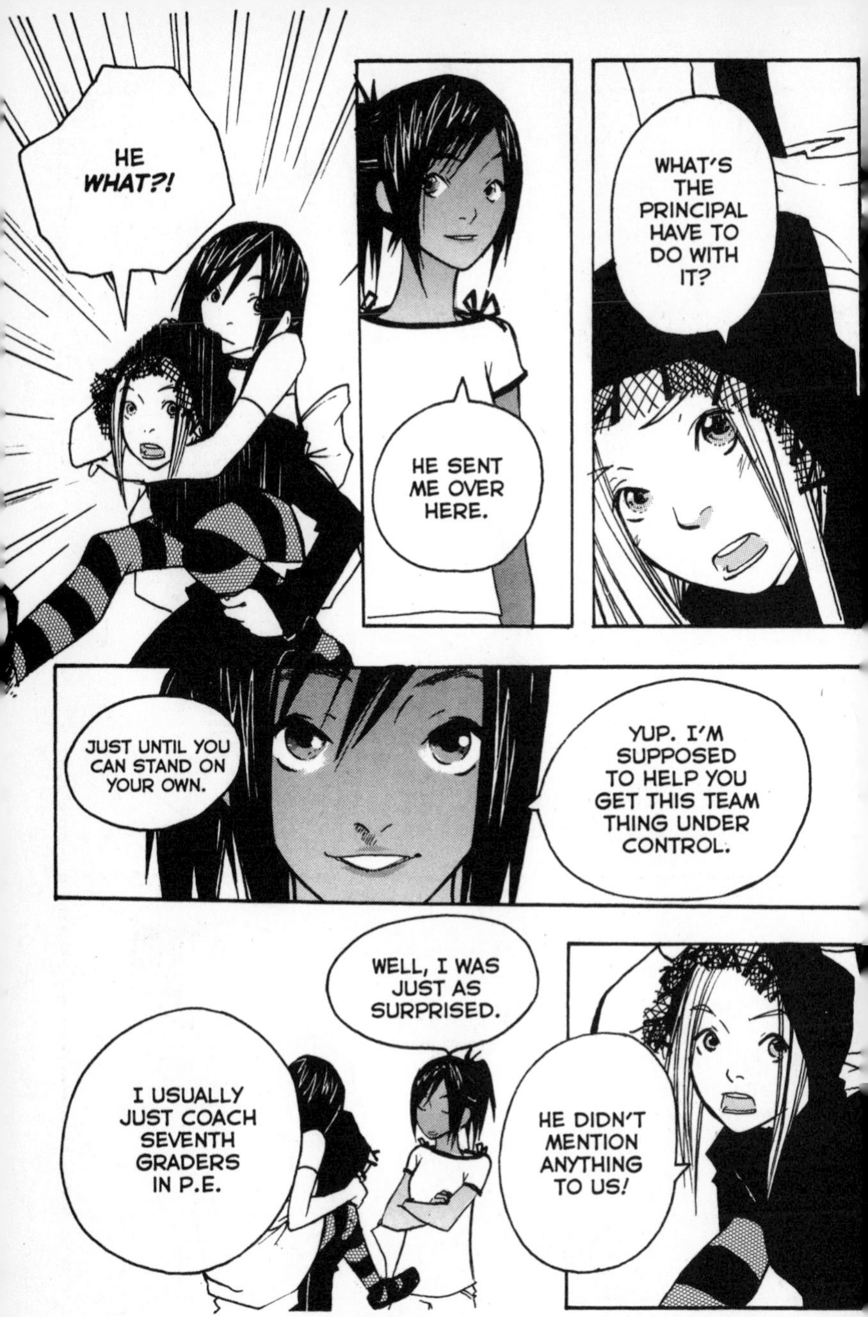
WHAT'S THE PRINCIPAL HAVE TO DO WITH IT?
HE SENT ME OVER HERE.
HE *WHAT?!*
YUP. I'M SUPPOSED TO HELP YOU GET THIS TEAM THING UNDER CONTROL.
JUST UNTIL YOU CAN STAND ON YOUR OWN.
HE DIDN'T MENTION ANYTHING TO US!
WELL, I WAS JUST AS SURPRISED.
I USUALLY JUST COACH SEVENTH GRADERS IN P.E.

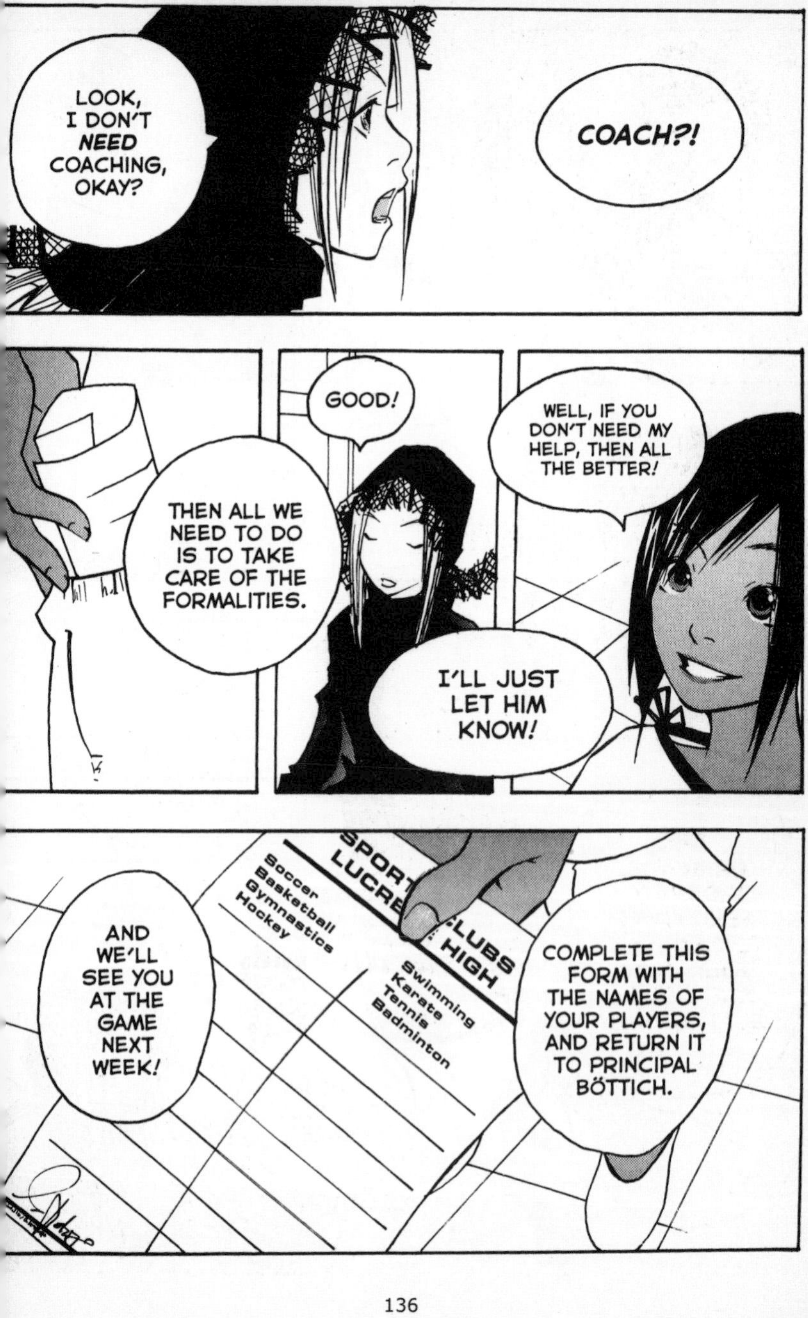
COACH?!
LOOK, I DON'T NEED COACHING, OKAY?
WELL, IF YOU DON'T NEED MY HELP, THEN ALL THE BETTER!
I'LL JUST LET HIM KNOW!
GOOD!
THEN ALL WE NEED TO DO IS TO TAKE CARE OF THE FORMALITIES.
COMPLETE THIS FORM WITH THE NAMES OF YOUR PLAYERS, AND RETURN IT TO PRINCIPAL BÖTTICH.
AND WE'LL SEE YOU AT THE GAME NEXT WEEK!

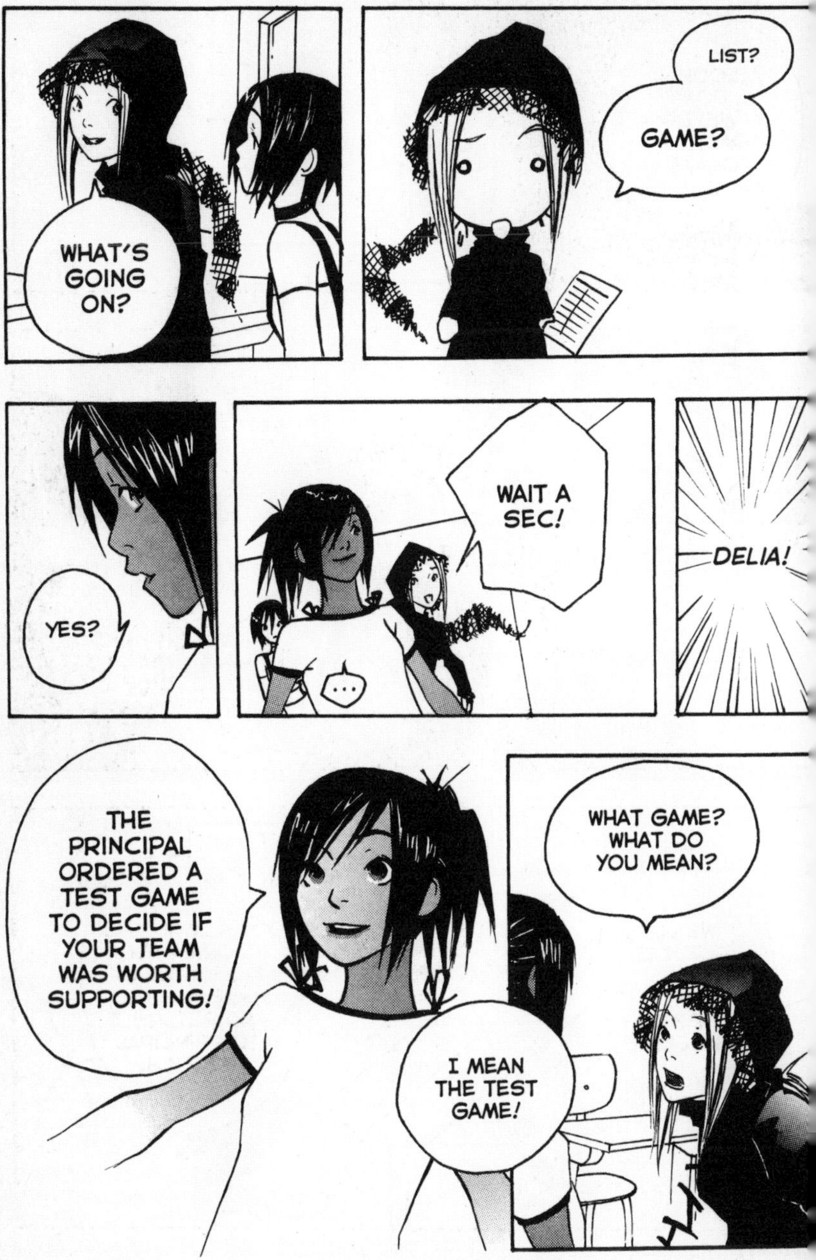
WHAT'S GOING ON?
GAME?
LIST?
YES?
WAIT A SEC!
DELIA!
THE PRINCIPAL ORDERED A TEST GAME TO DECIDE IF YOUR TEAM WAS WORTH SUPPORTING!
WHAT GAME? WHAT DO YOU MEAN?
I MEAN THE TEST GAME!

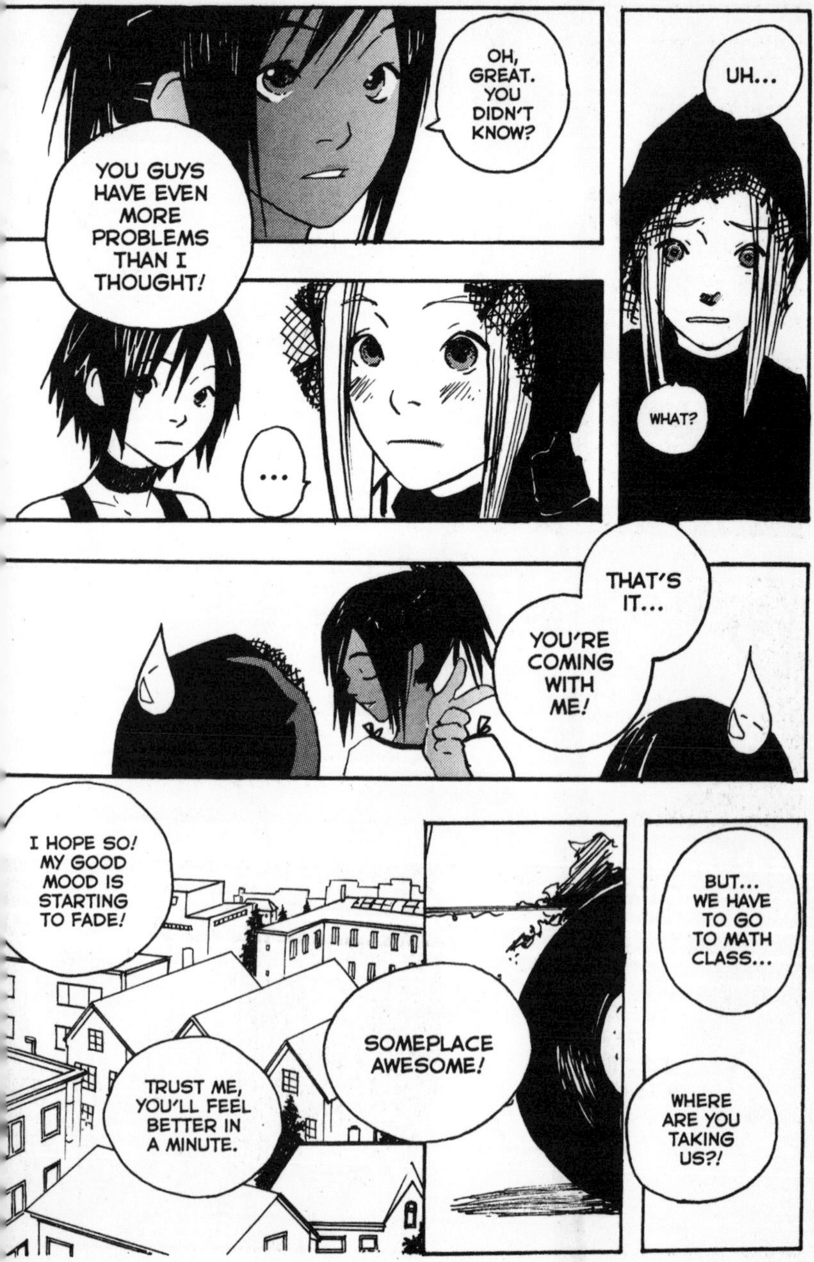
UH...
WHAT?
OH, GREAT. YOU DIDN'T KNOW?
YOU GUYS HAVE EVEN MORE PROBLEMS THAN I THOUGHT!
...
THAT'S IT...
YOU'RE COMING WITH ME!
BUT... WE HAVE TO GO TO MATH CLASS...
WHERE ARE YOU TAKING US?!
SOMEPLACE AWESOME!
TRUST ME, YOU'LL FEEL BETTER IN A MINUTE.
I HOPE SO! MY GOOD MOOD IS STARTING TO FADE!

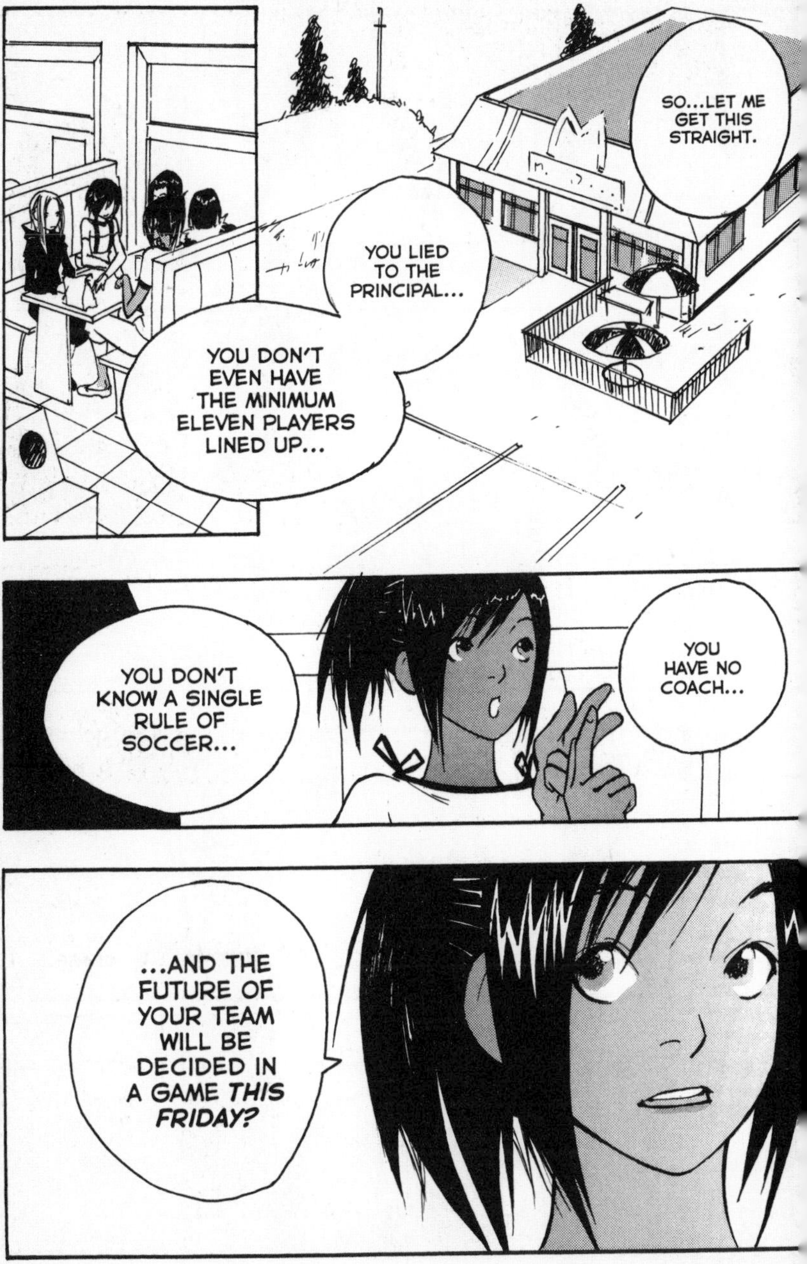
SO...LET ME GET THIS STRAIGHT.
YOU LIED TO THE PRINCIPAL...
YOU DON'T EVEN HAVE THE MINIMUM ELEVEN PLAYERS LINED UP...
YOU HAVE NO COACH...
YOU DON'T KNOW A SINGLE RULE OF SOCCER...
...AND THE FUTURE OF YOUR TEAM WILL BE DECIDED IN A GAME *THIS FRIDAY?*

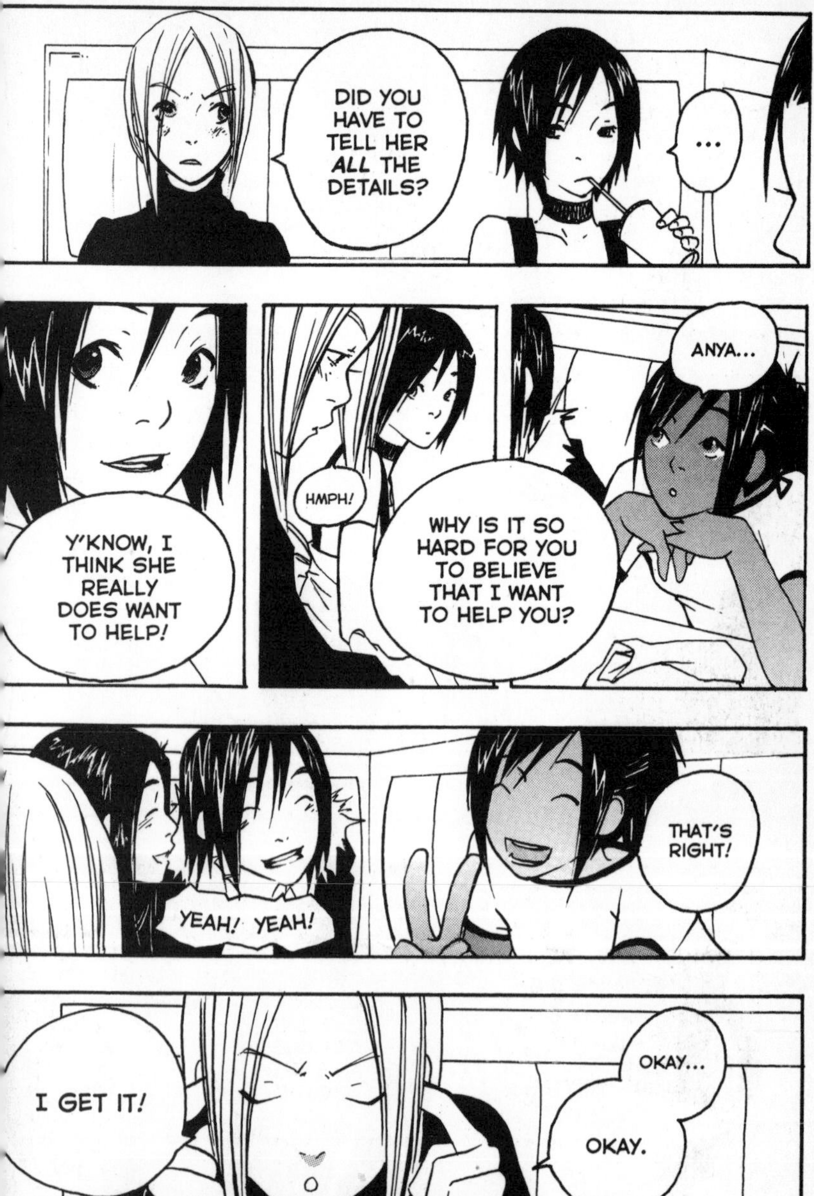
DID YOU HAVE TO TELL HER *ALL* THE DETAILS?
...
Y'KNOW, I THINK SHE REALLY DOES WANT TO HELP!
HMPH!
WHY IS IT SO HARD FOR YOU TO BELIEVE THAT I WANT TO HELP YOU?
ANYA...
YEAH! YEAH!
THAT'S RIGHT!
I GET IT!
OKAY...
OKAY.

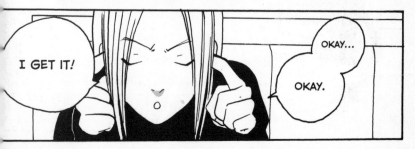

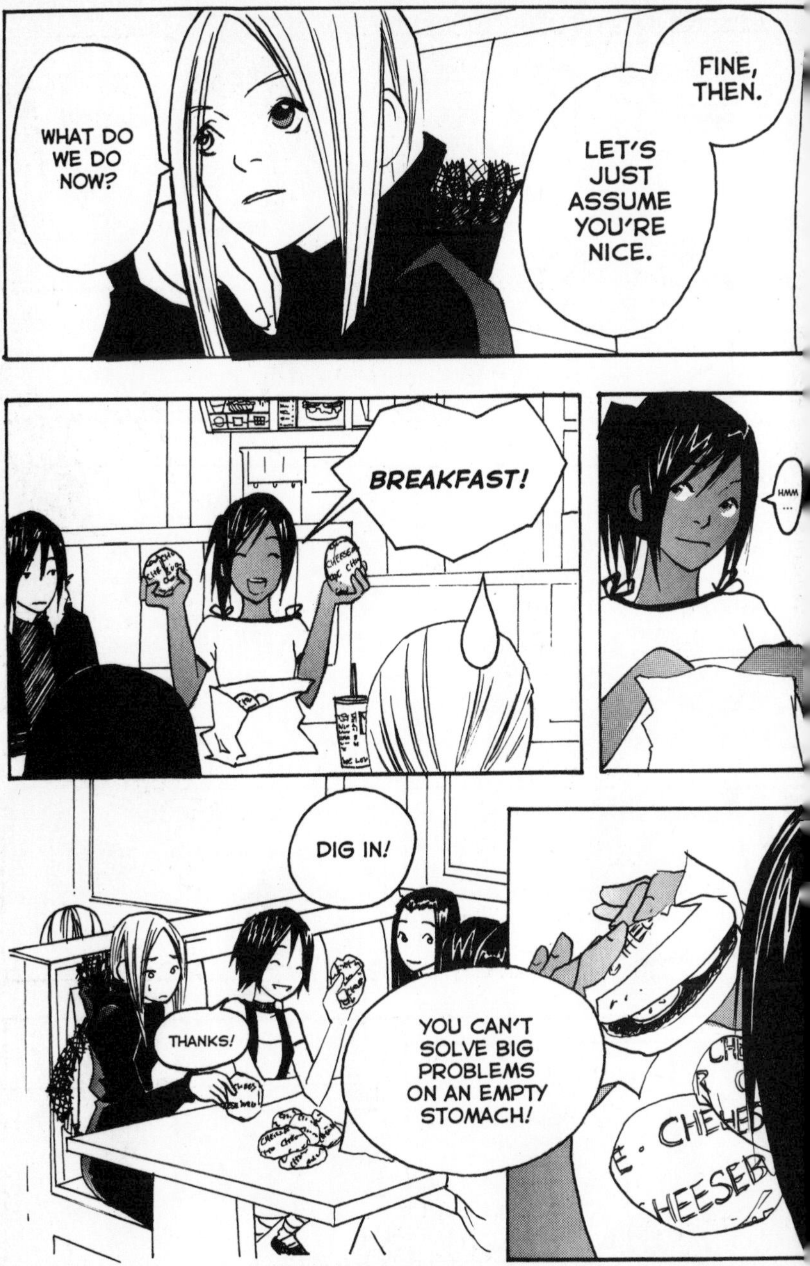
FINE, THEN.
LET'S JUST ASSUME YOU'RE NICE.
WHAT DO WE DO NOW?
HMM ...
BREAKFAST!
DIG IN!
YOU CAN'T SOLVE BIG PROBLEMS ON AN EMPTY STOMACH!
THANKS!

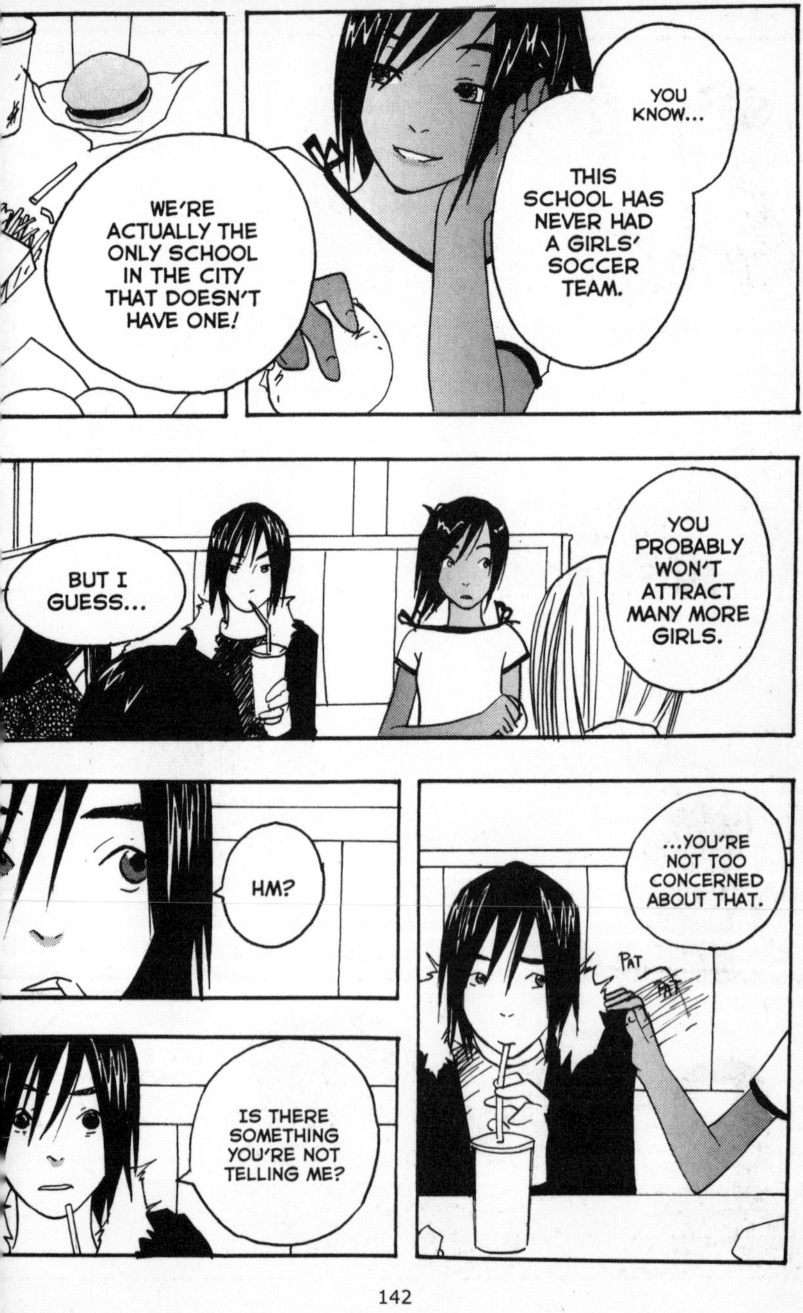
YOU KNOW...
THIS SCHOOL HAS NEVER HAD A GIRLS' SOCCER TEAM.
WE'RE ACTUALLY THE ONLY SCHOOL IN THE CITY THAT DOESN'T HAVE ONE!
YOU PROBABLY WON'T ATTRACT MANY MORE GIRLS.
BUT I GUESS...
...YOU'RE NOT TOO CONCERNED ABOUT THAT.
PAT
PAT
HM?
IS THERE SOMETHING YOU'RE NOT TELLING ME?

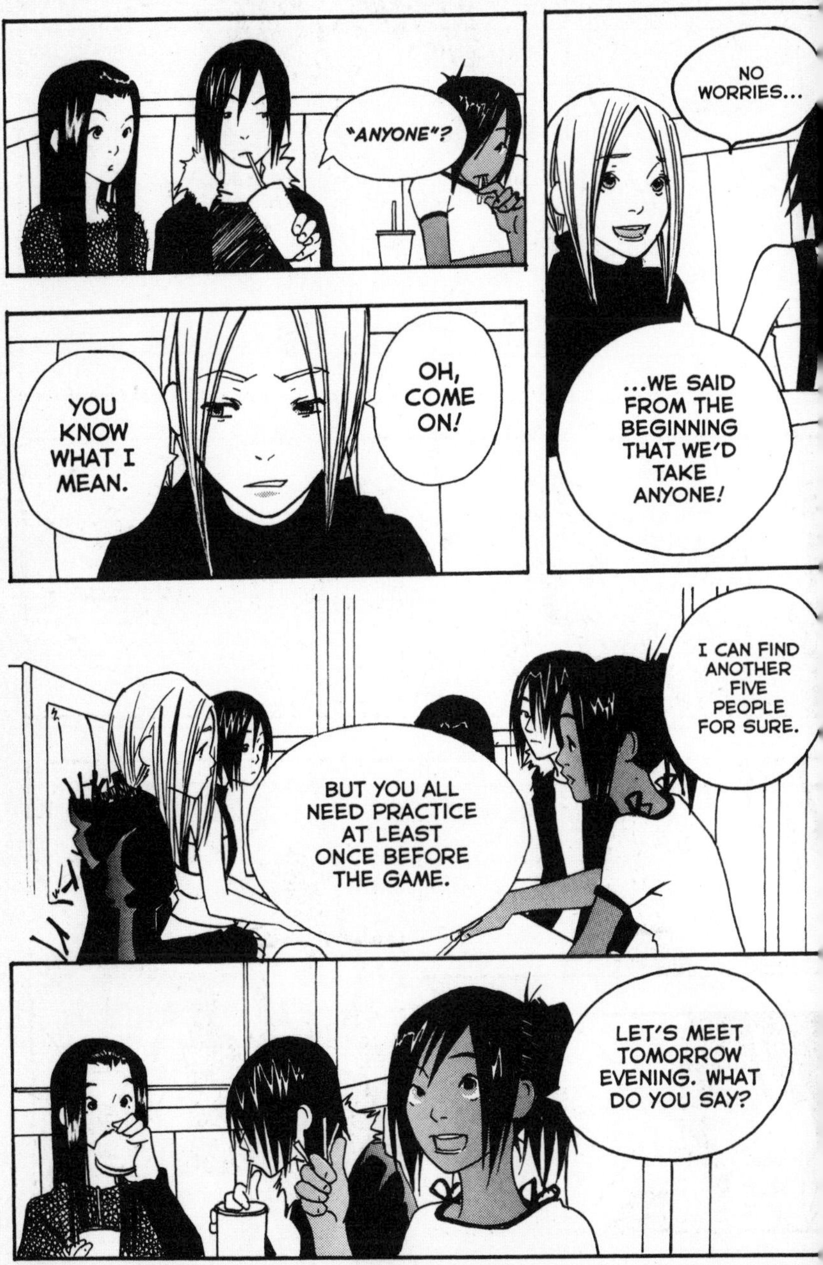
NO WORRIES...
...WE SAID FROM THE BEGINNING THAT WE'D TAKE ANYONE!
"ANYONE"?
OH, COME ON!
YOU KNOW WHAT I MEAN.
I CAN FIND ANOTHER FIVE PEOPLE FOR SURE.
BUT YOU ALL NEED PRACTICE AT LEAST ONCE BEFORE THE GAME.
LET'S MEET TOMORROW EVENING. WHAT DO YOU SAY?

ON THE FIELD BEHIND THE SCHOOL?

SIX P.M.?

DELIA!

YOU TRAITOR.

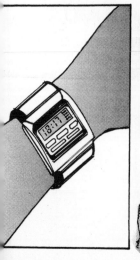

WHERE IS SHE?

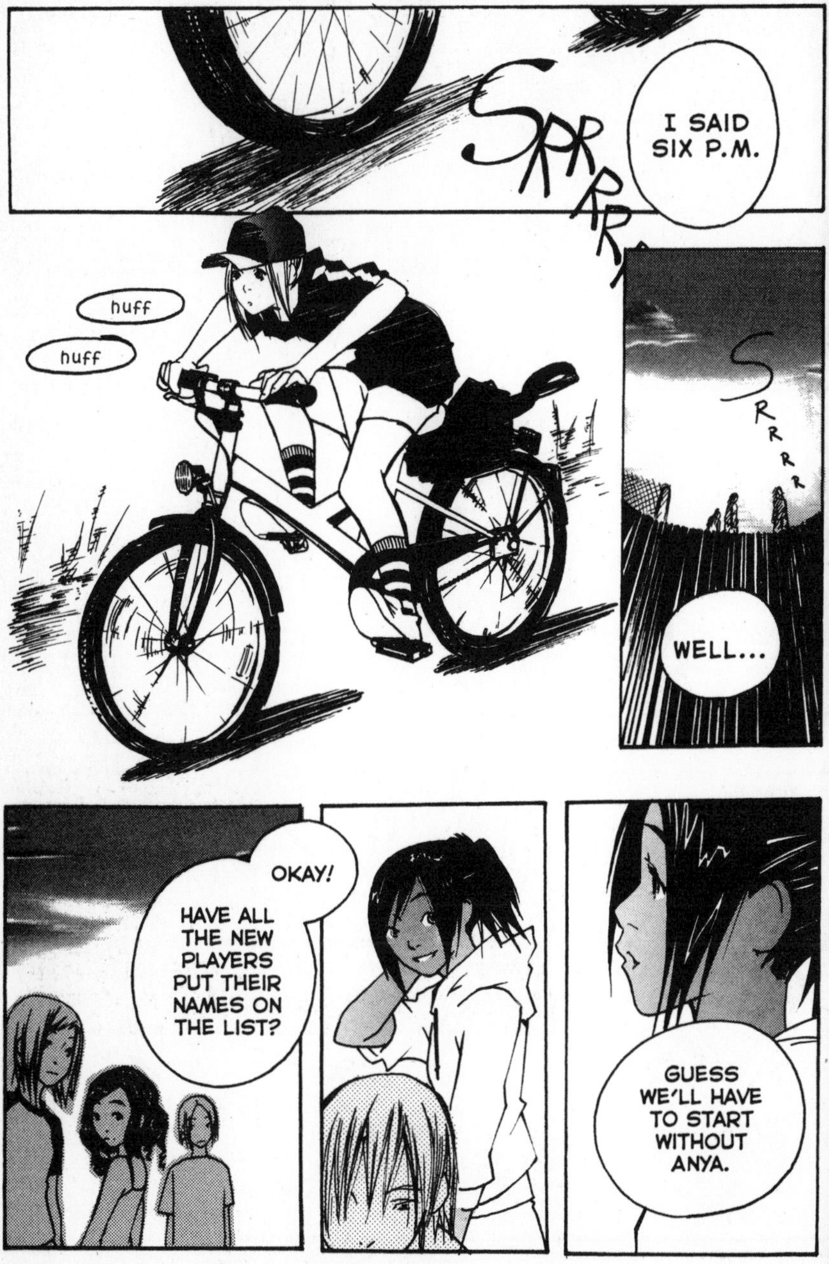
I SAID SIX P.M.
SRRRR
SRRRR
WELL...
huff
huff
GUESS WE'LL HAVE TO START WITHOUT ANYA.
OKAY!
HAVE ALL THE NEW PLAYERS PUT THEIR NAMES ON THE LIST?

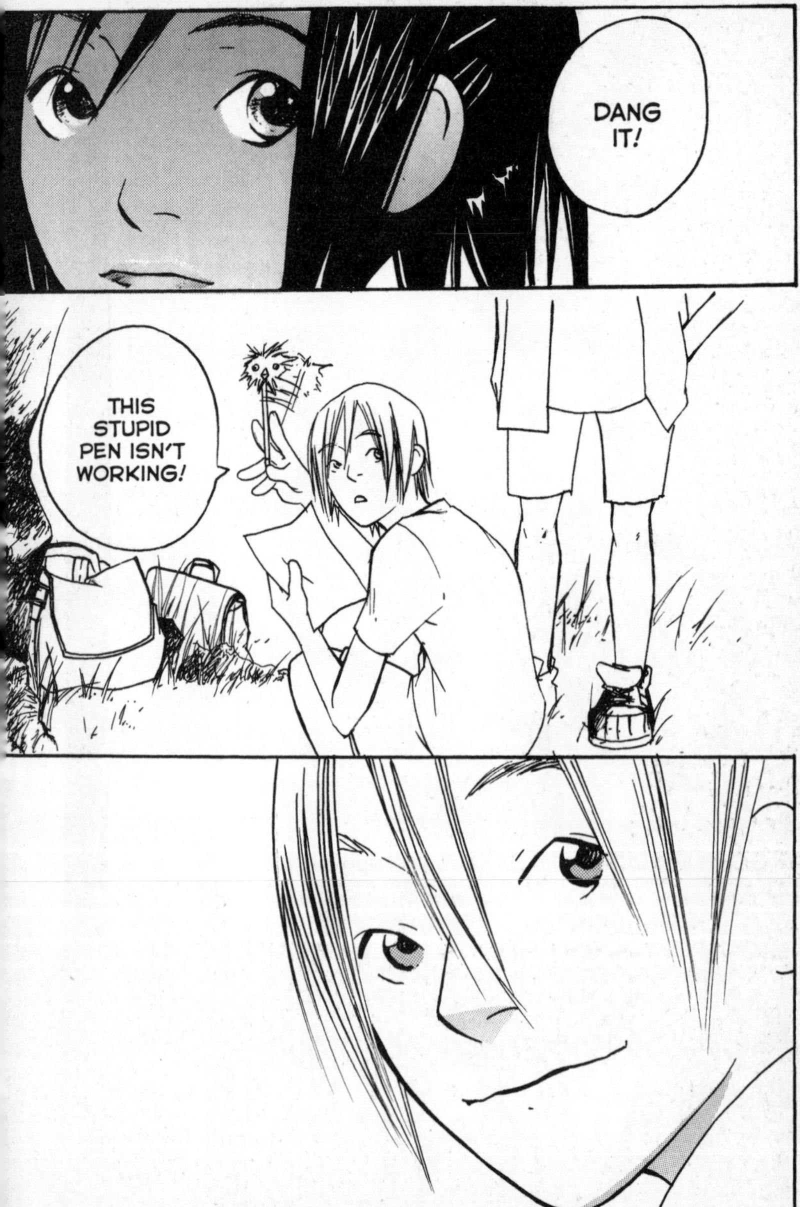
DANG IT!
THIS STUPID PEN ISN'T WORKING!

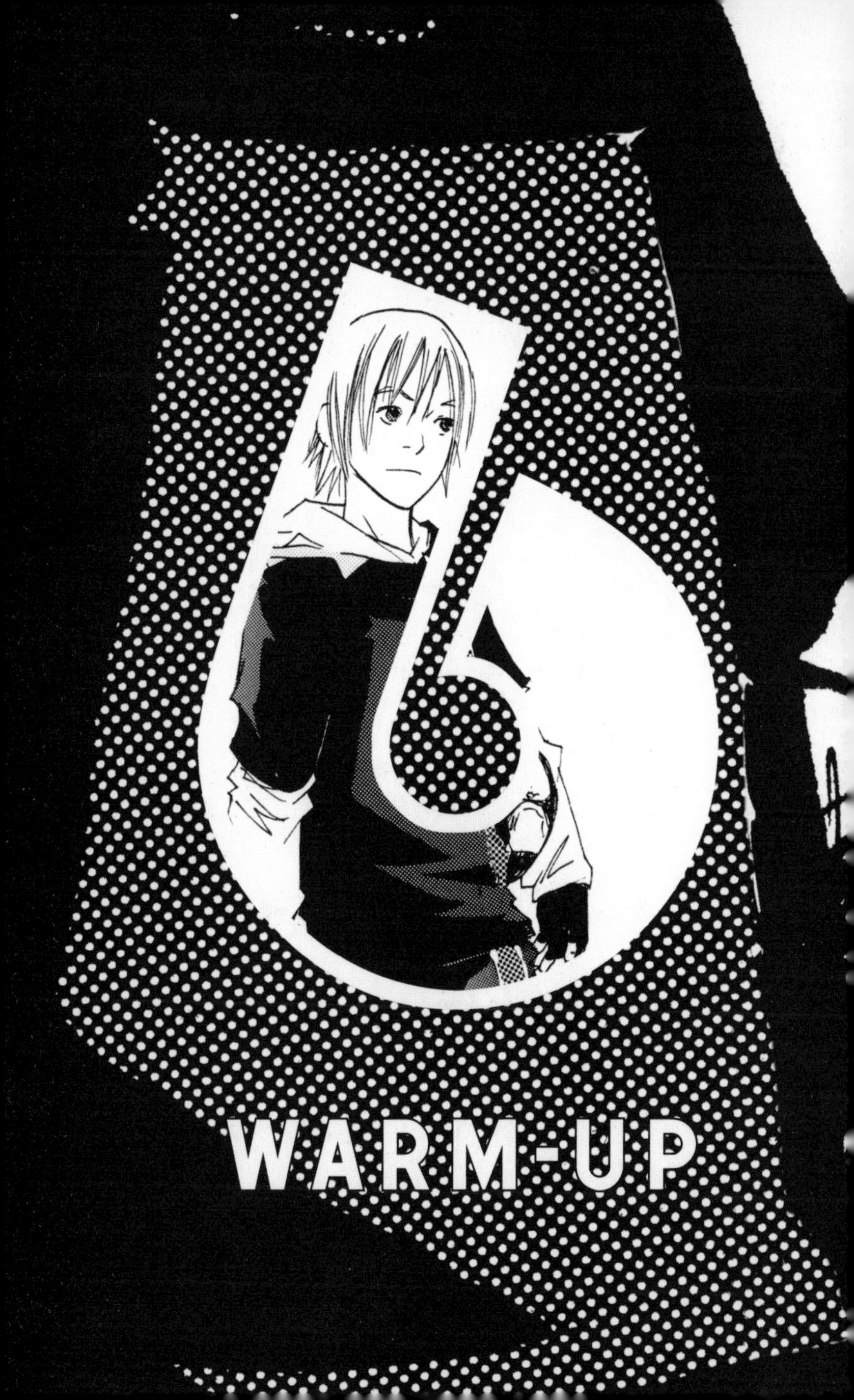
6
WARM-UP

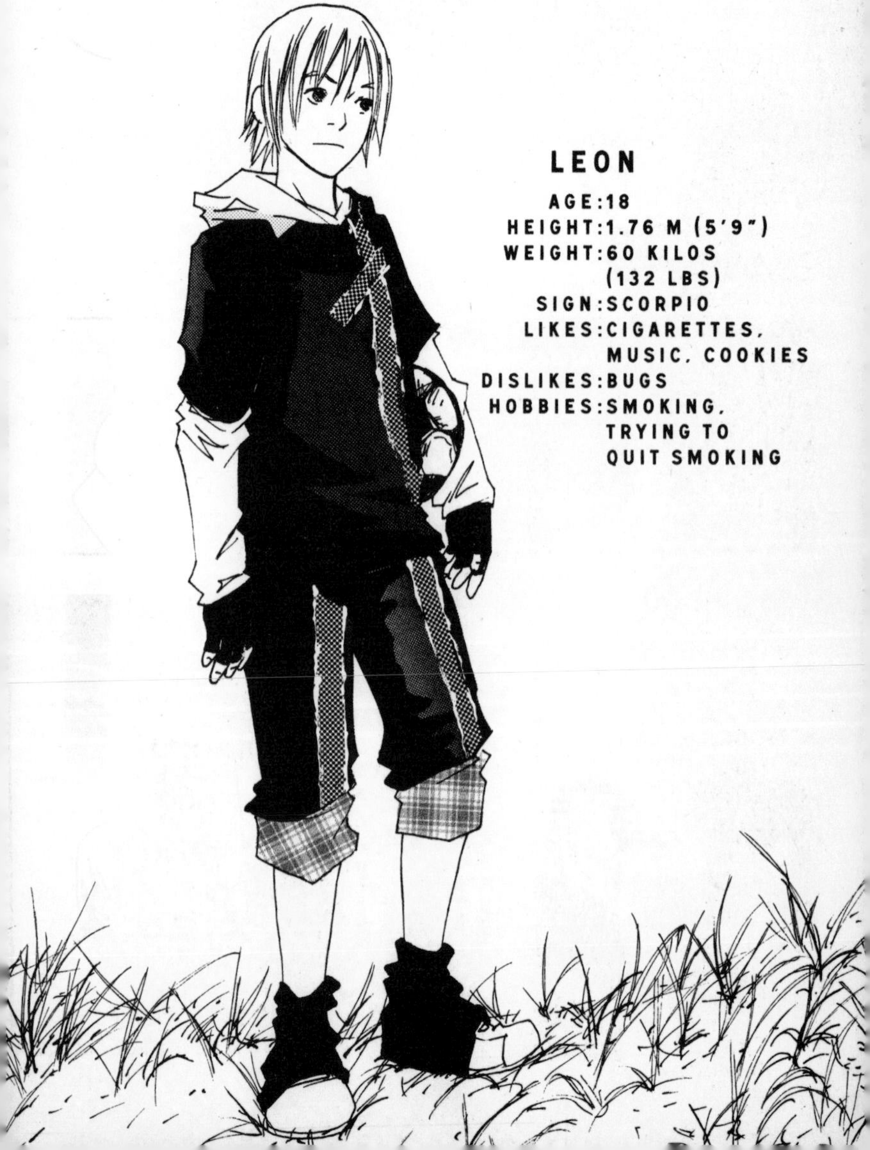

LEON

AGE:18
HEIGHT:1.76 M (5′9″)
WEIGHT:60 KILOS (132 LBS)
SIGN:SCORPIO
LIKES:CIGARETTES, MUSIC, COOKIES
DISLIKES:BUGS
HOBBIES:SMOKING, TRYING TO QUIT SMOKING

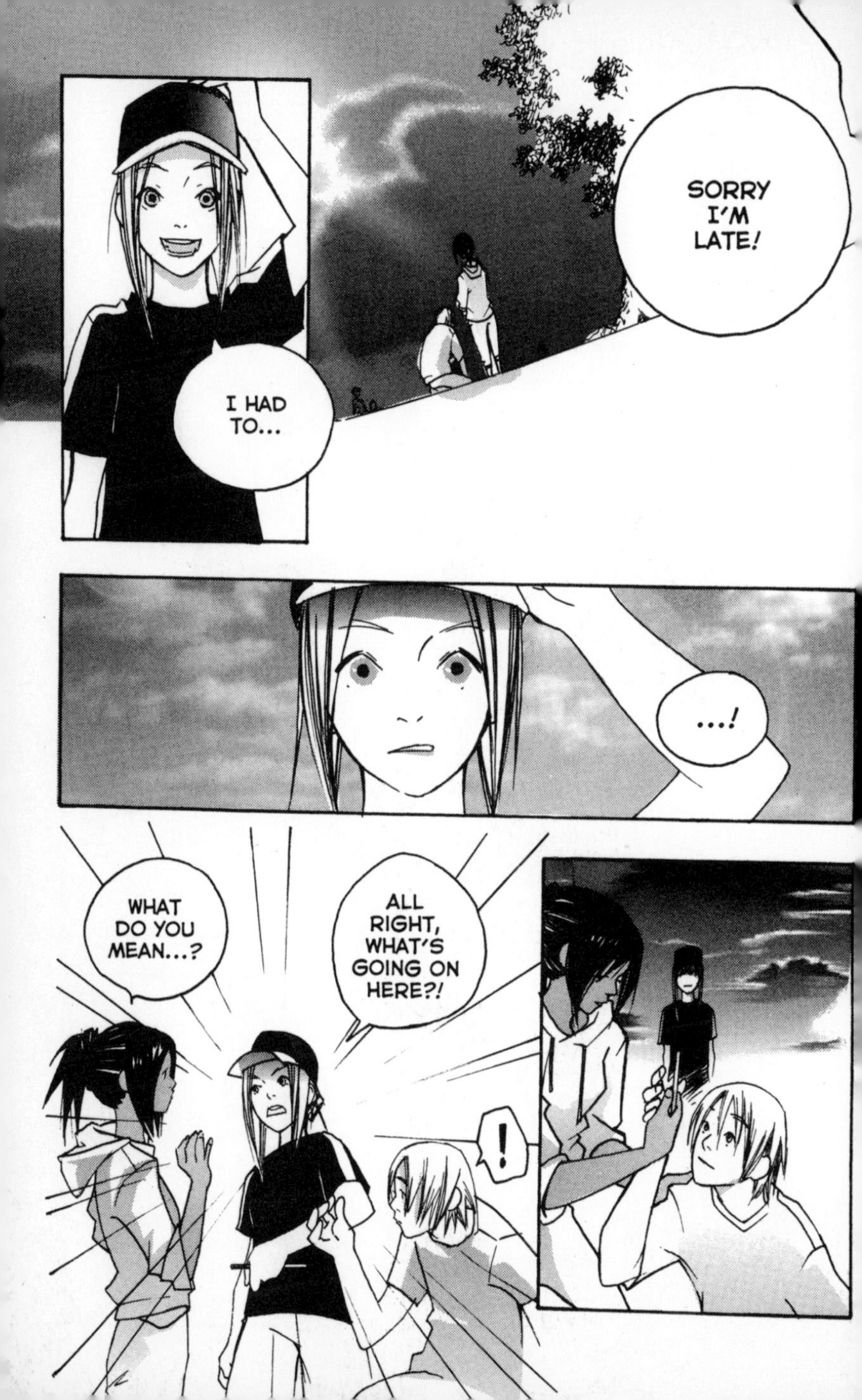
SORRY I'M LATE!
I HAD TO...
...!
!
ALL RIGHT, WHAT'S GOING ON HERE?!
WHAT DO YOU MEAN...?

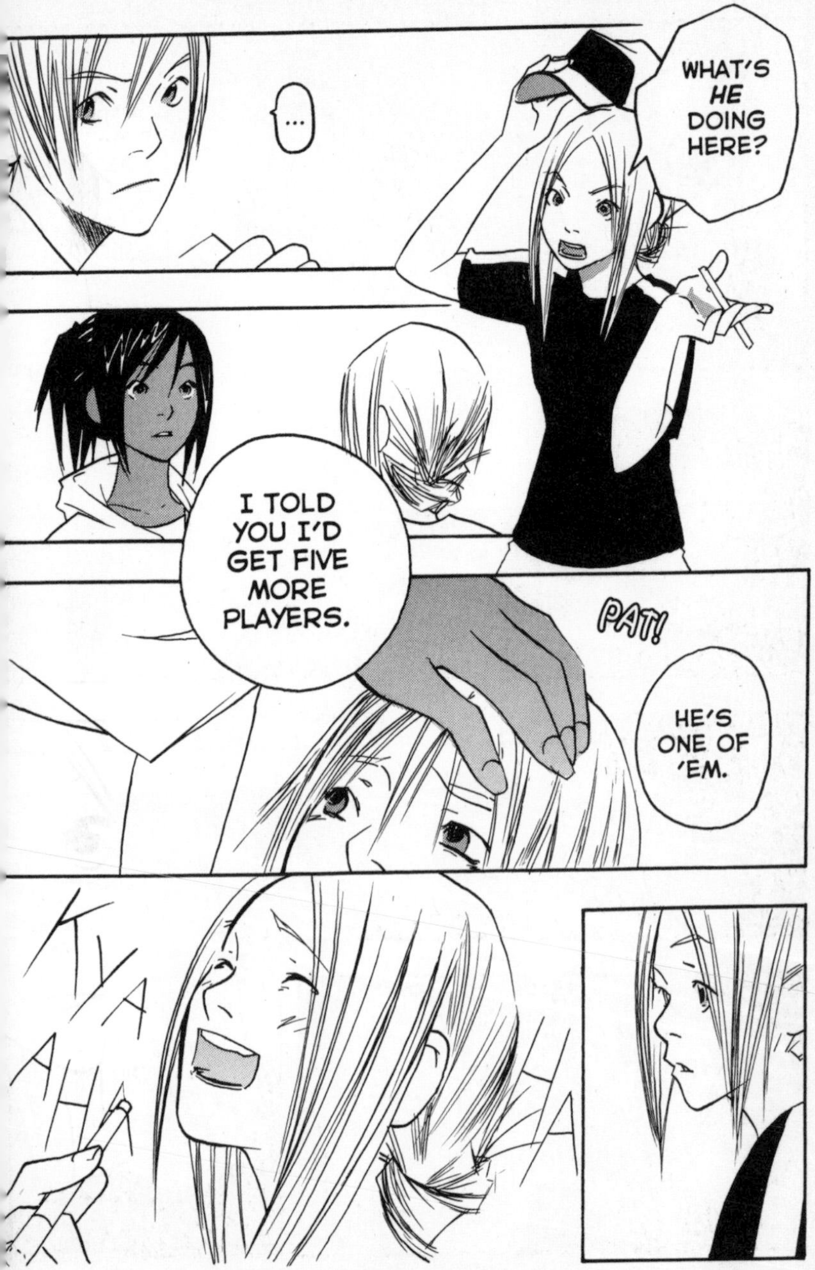
WHAT'S *HE* DOING HERE?
...
I TOLD YOU I'D GET FIVE MORE PLAYERS.
PAT!
HE'S ONE OF 'EM.
KYAHAHA HA

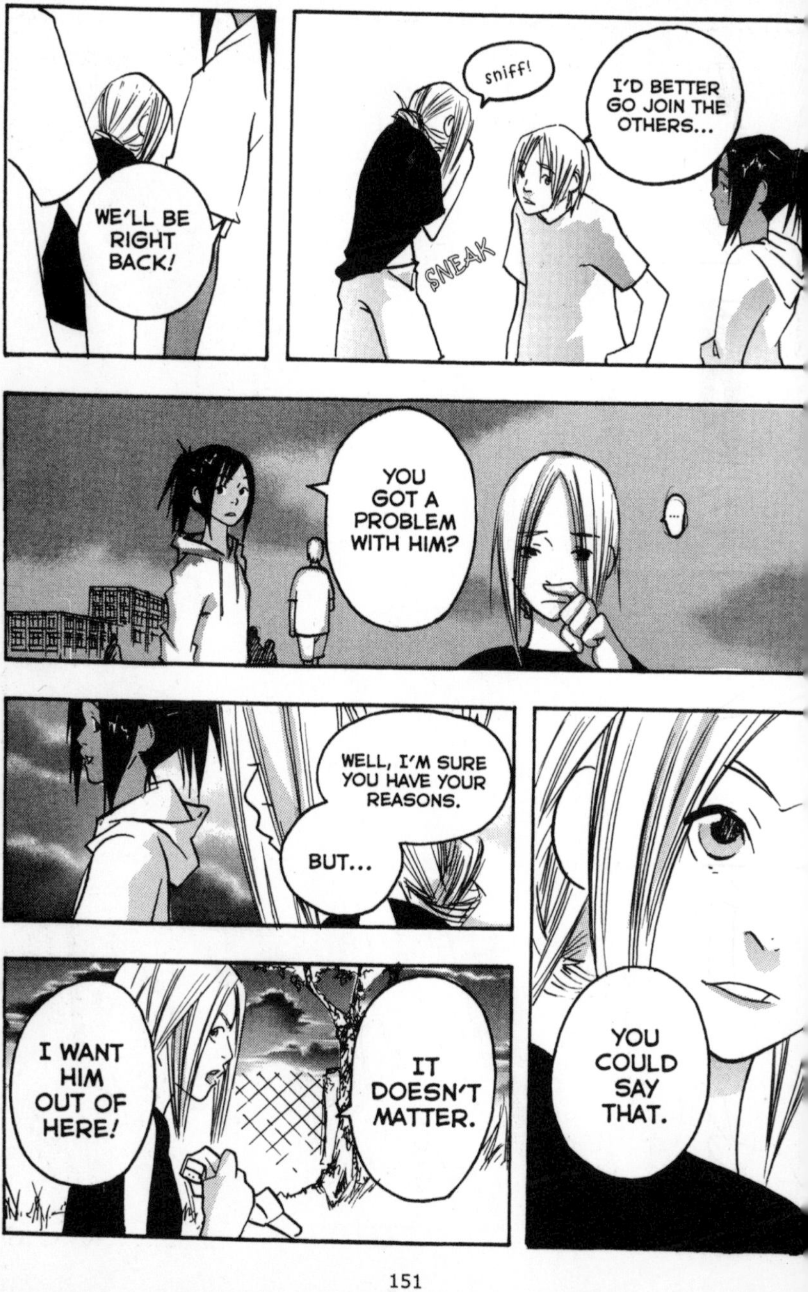
I'D BETTER GO JOIN THE OTHERS...
sniff!
SNEAK
WE'LL BE RIGHT BACK!
YOU GOT A PROBLEM WITH HIM?
...
YOU COULD SAY THAT.
WELL, I'M SURE YOU HAVE YOUR REASONS.
BUT...
IT DOESN'T MATTER.
I WANT HIM OUT OF HERE!

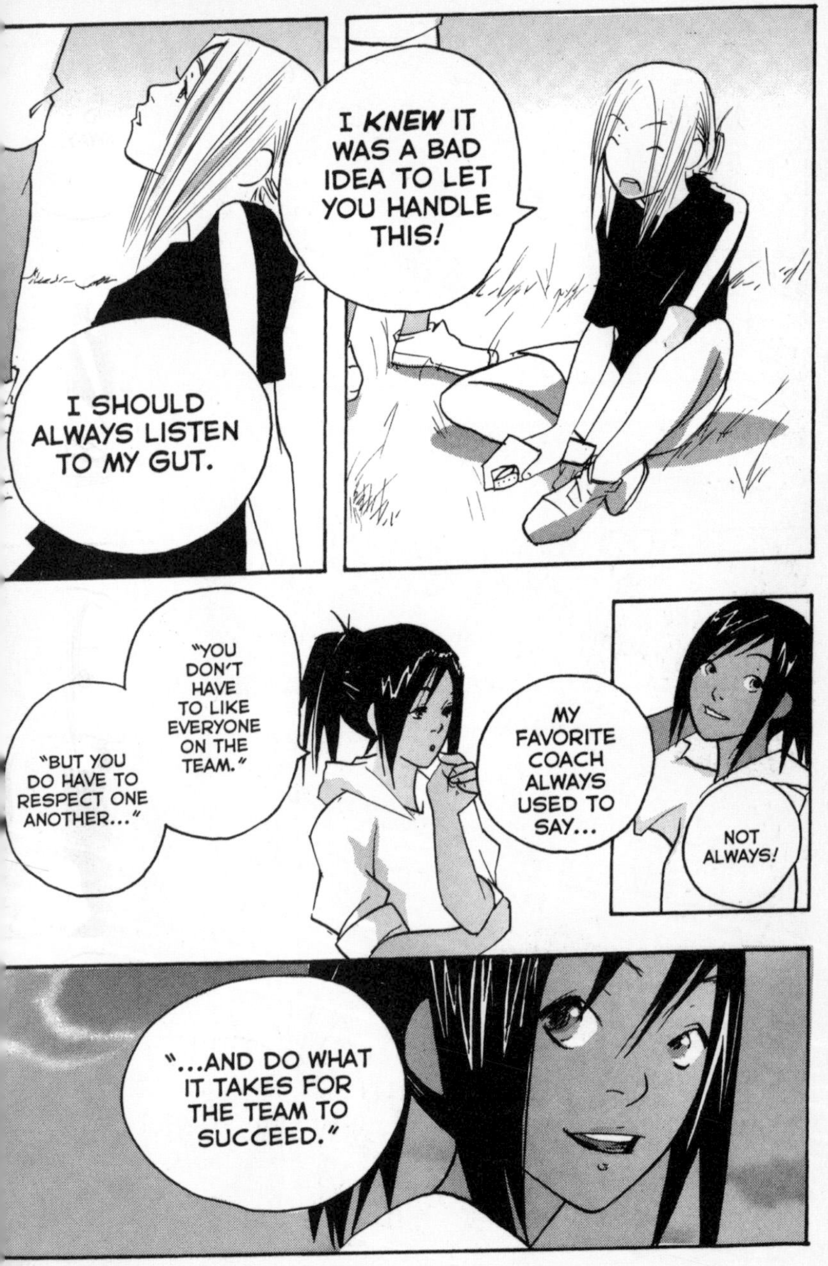
I *KNEW* IT WAS A BAD IDEA TO LET YOU HANDLE THIS!
I SHOULD ALWAYS LISTEN TO MY GUT.
NOT ALWAYS!
MY FAVORITE COACH ALWAYS USED TO SAY...
"YOU DON'T HAVE TO LIKE EVERYONE ON THE TEAM."
"BUT YOU DO HAVE TO RESPECT ONE ANOTHER..."
"...AND DO WHAT IT TAKES FOR THE TEAM TO SUCCEED."

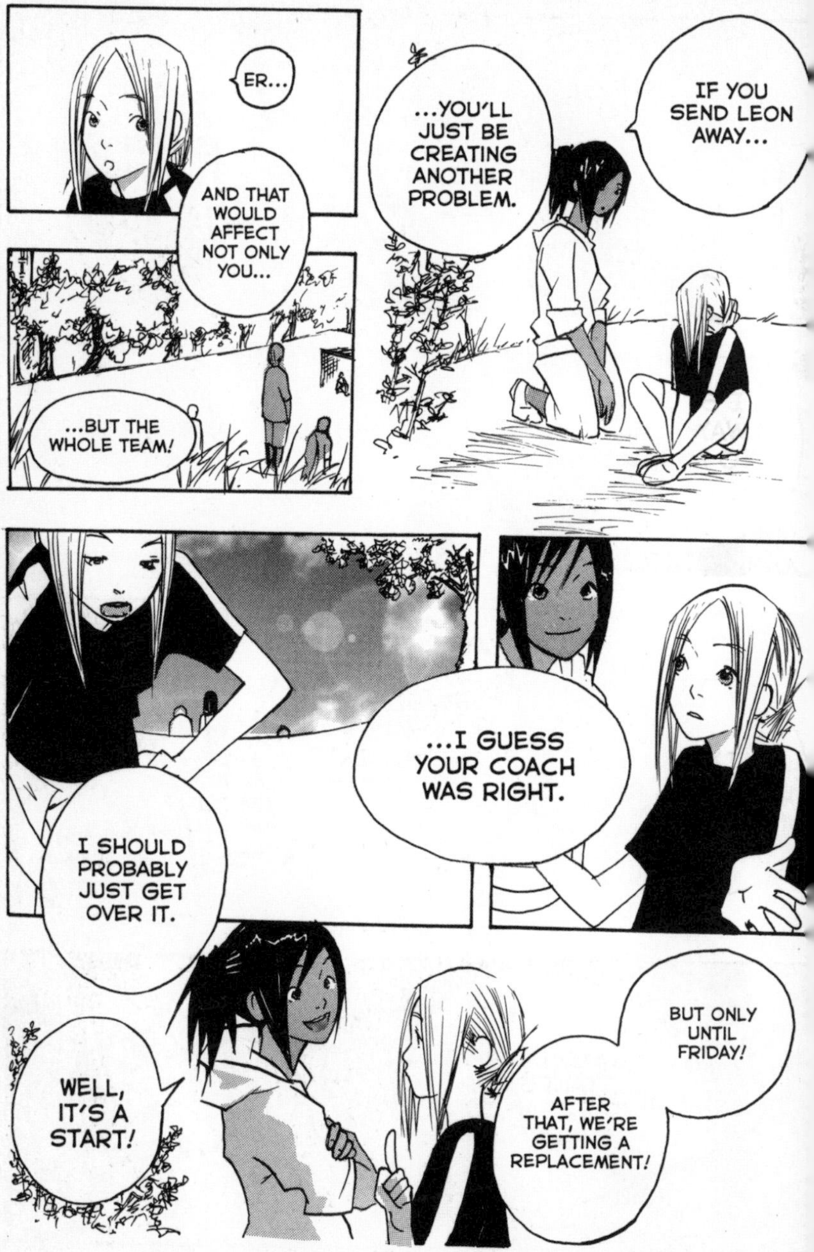
IF YOU SEND LEON AWAY...
...YOU'LL JUST BE CREATING ANOTHER PROBLEM.
ER...
AND THAT WOULD AFFECT NOT ONLY YOU...
...BUT THE WHOLE TEAM!
...I GUESS YOUR COACH WAS RIGHT.
I SHOULD PROBABLY JUST GET OVER IT.
WELL, IT'S A START!
BUT ONLY UNTIL FRIDAY!
AFTER THAT, WE'RE GETTING A REPLACEMENT!

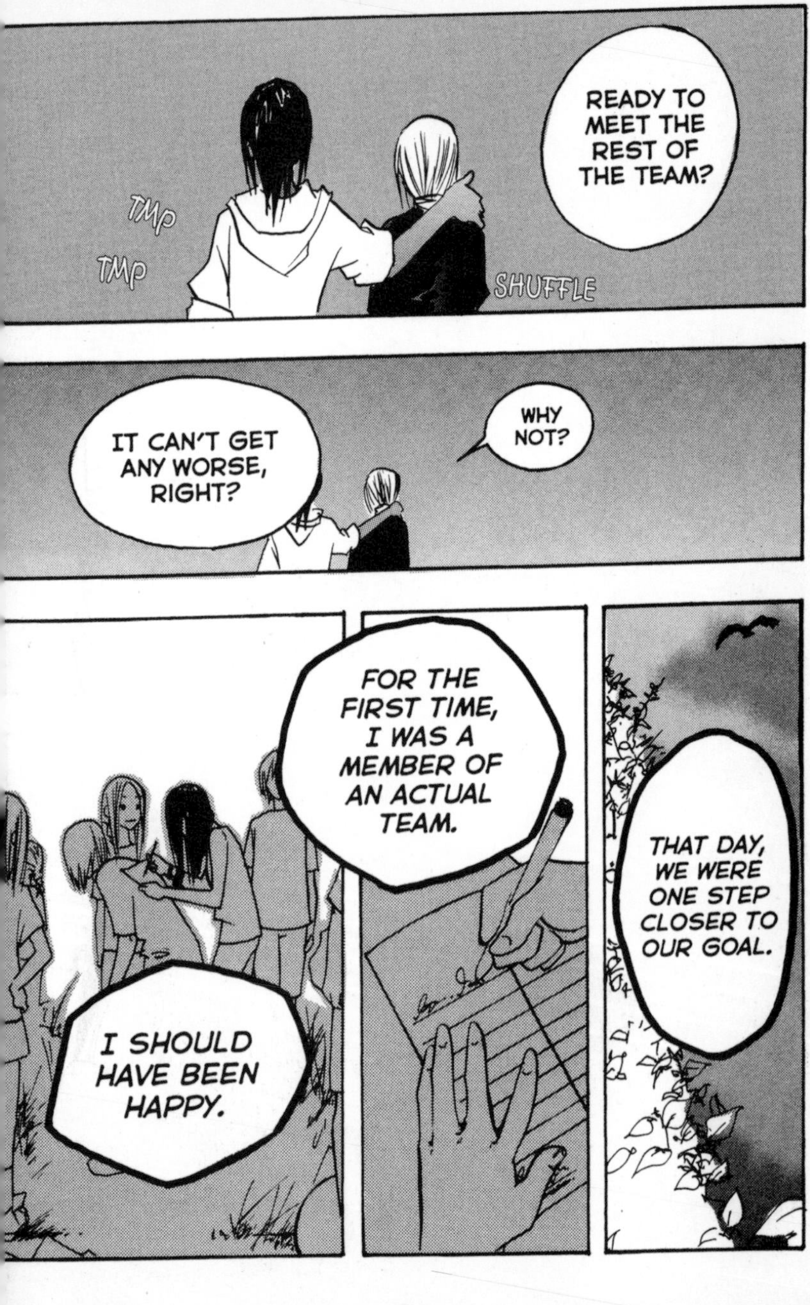
READY TO MEET THE REST OF THE TEAM?
TMP
TMP
SHUFFLE
WHY NOT?
IT CAN'T GET ANY WORSE, RIGHT?
THAT DAY, WE WERE ONE STEP CLOSER TO OUR GOAL.
FOR THE FIRST TIME, I WAS A MEMBER OF AN ACTUAL TEAM.
I SHOULD HAVE BEEN HAPPY.

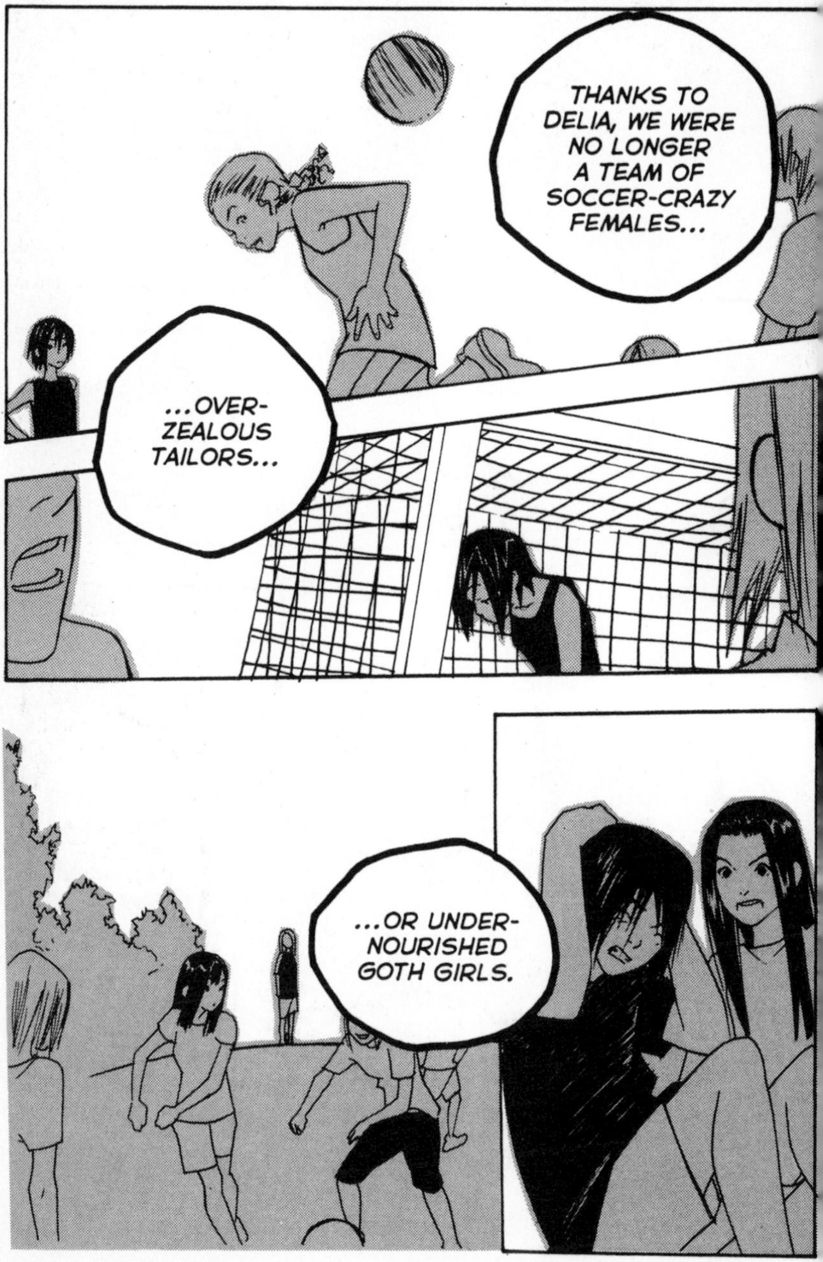
THANKS TO DELIA, WE WERE NO LONGER A TEAM OF SOCCER-CRAZY FEMALES...
...OVER-ZEALOUS TAILORS...
...OR UNDER-NOURISHED GOTH GIRLS.

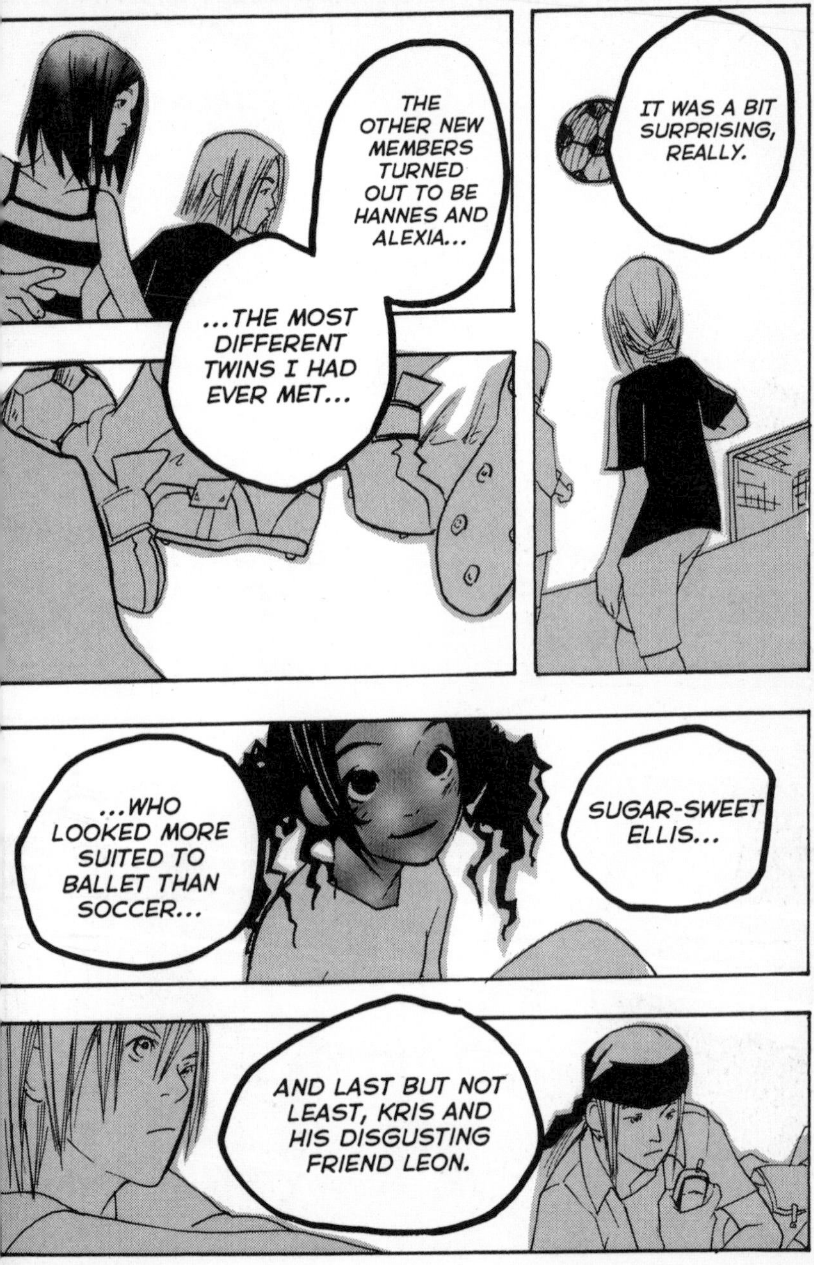
IT WAS A BIT SURPRISING, REALLY.
THE OTHER NEW MEMBERS TURNED OUT TO BE HANNES AND ALEXIA...
...THE MOST DIFFERENT TWINS I HAD EVER MET...
SUGAR-SWEET ELLIS...
...WHO LOOKED MORE SUITED TO BALLET THAN SOCCER...
AND LAST BUT NOT LEAST, KRIS AND HIS DISGUSTING FRIEND LEON.

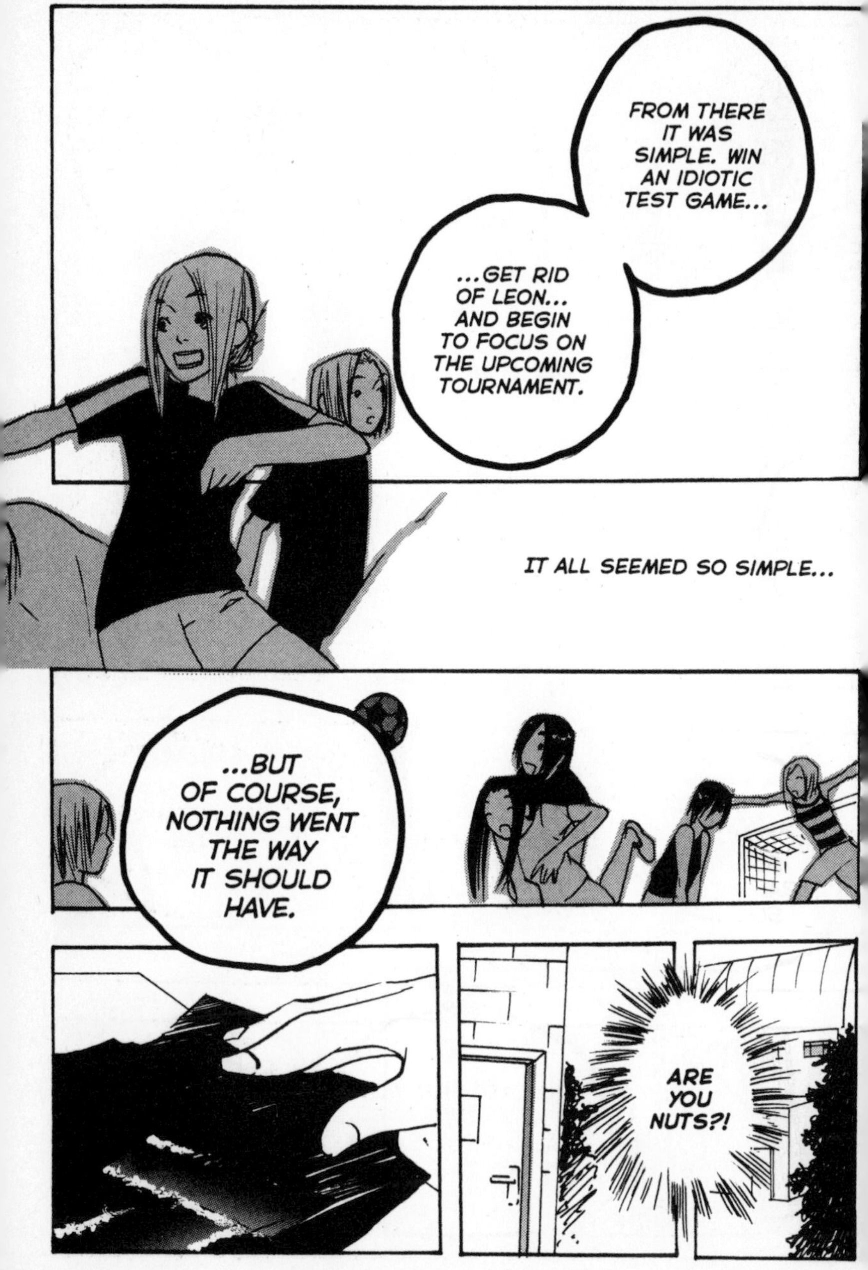
FROM THERE IT WAS SIMPLE. WIN AN IDIOTIC TEST GAME...
...GET RID OF LEON... AND BEGIN TO FOCUS ON THE UPCOMING TOURNAMENT.
IT ALL SEEMED SO SIMPLE...
...BUT OF COURSE, NOTHING WENT THE WAY IT SHOULD HAVE.
ARE YOU NUTS?!

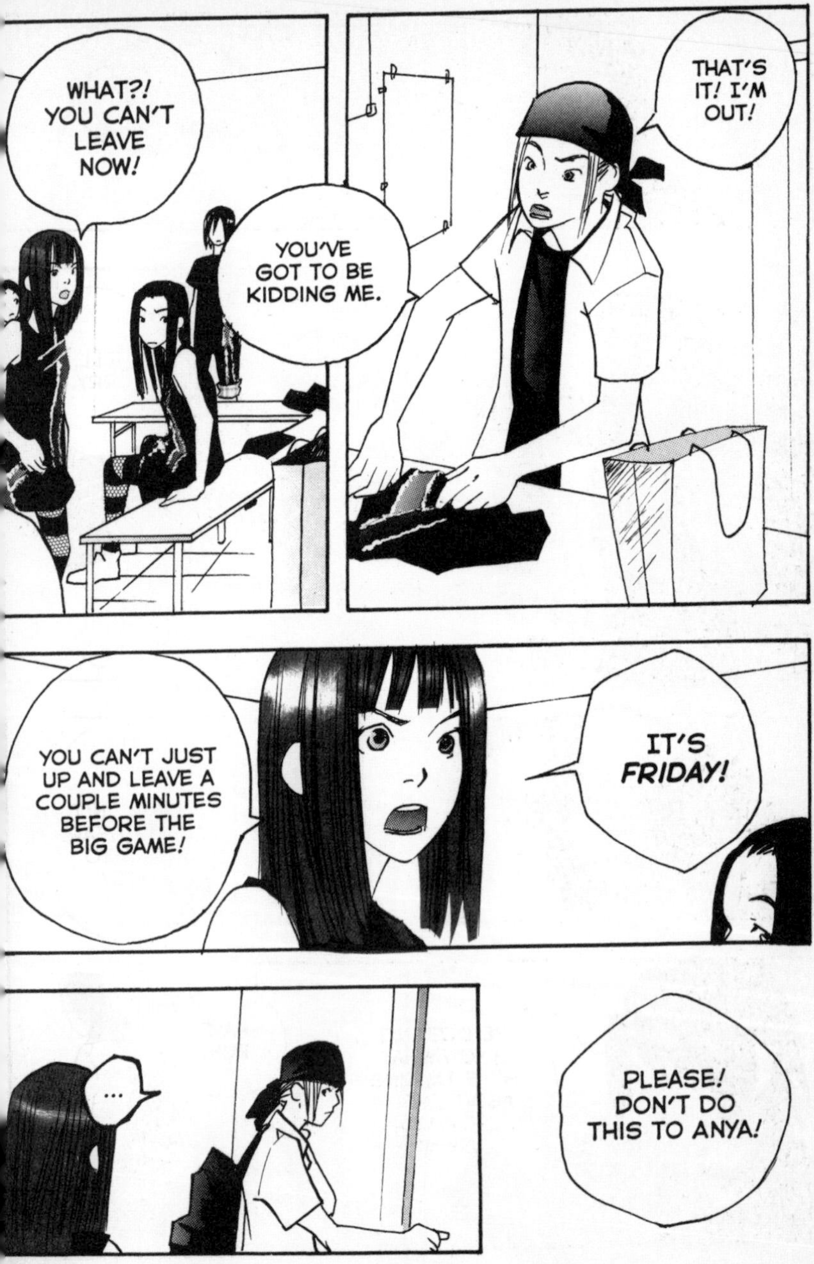
THAT'S IT! I'M OUT!
WHAT?! YOU CAN'T LEAVE NOW!
YOU'VE GOT TO BE KIDDING ME.
IT'S *FRIDAY!*
YOU CAN'T JUST UP AND LEAVE A COUPLE MINUTES BEFORE THE BIG GAME!
PLEASE! DON'T DO THIS TO ANYA!
...

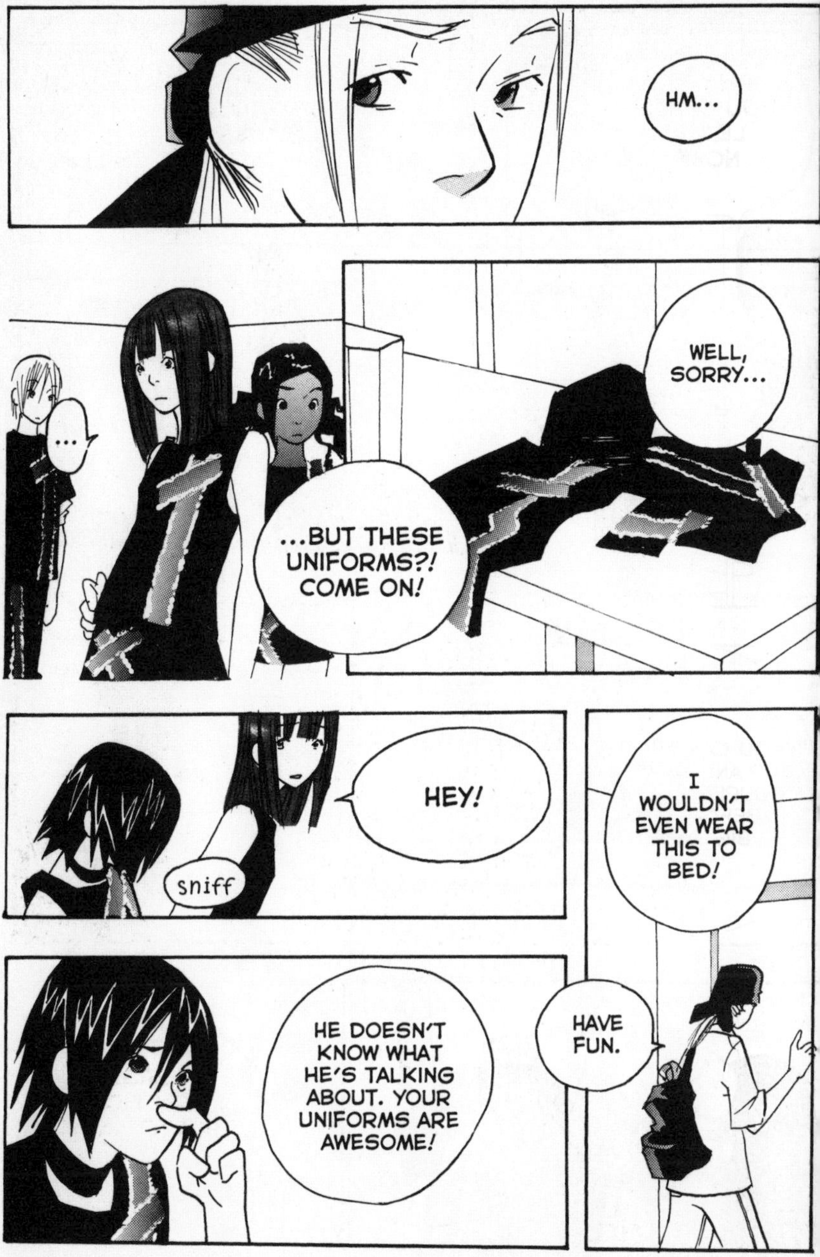
HM...
WELL, SORRY...
...
...BUT THESE UNIFORMS?! COME ON!
I WOULDN'T EVEN WEAR THIS TO BED!
HAVE FUN.
HEY!
sniff
HE DOESN'T KNOW WHAT HE'S TALKING ABOUT. YOUR UNIFORMS ARE AWESOME!

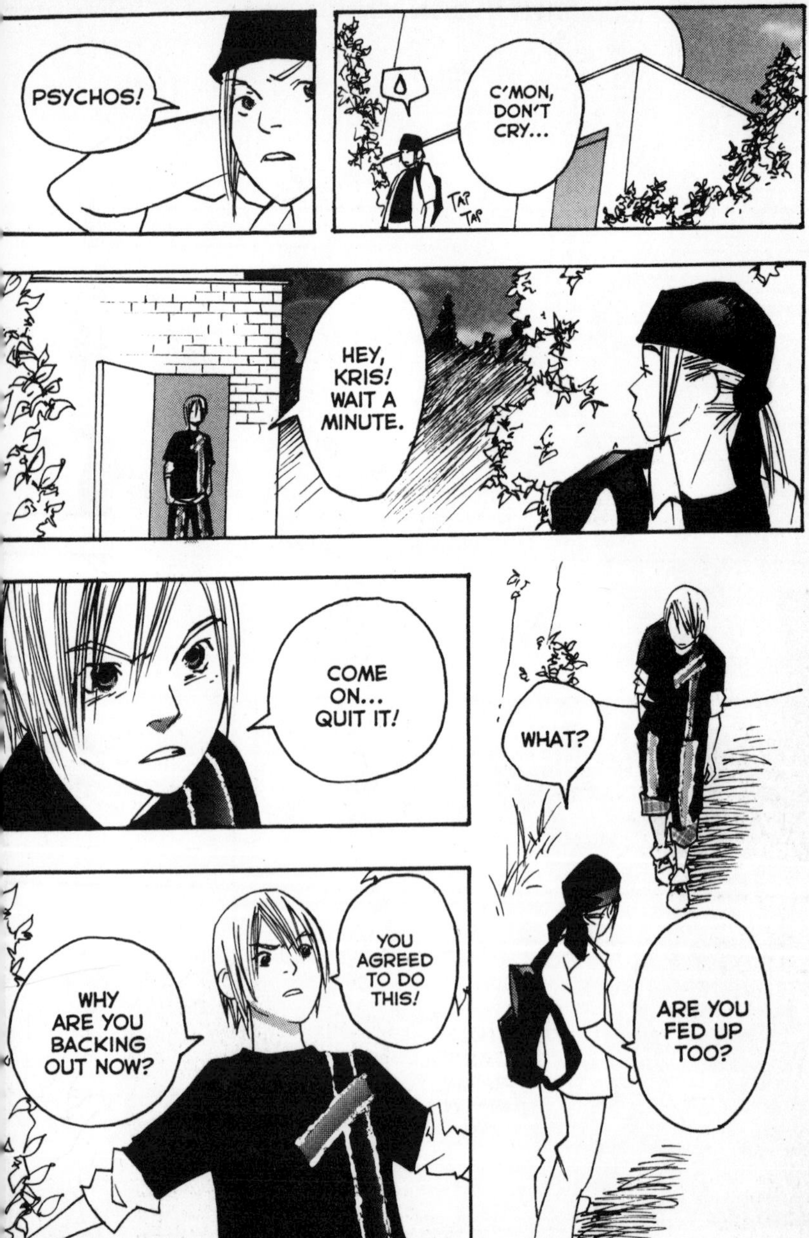
C'MON, DON'T CRY...
TAP TAP
PSYCHOS!
HEY, KRIS! WAIT A MINUTE.
WHAT?
ARE YOU FED UP TOO?
COME ON... QUIT IT!
YOU AGREED TO DO THIS!
WHY ARE YOU BACKING OUT NOW?

NO WORRIES.

HERE'S YOUR MONEY BACK.

I'M NOT GOING TO MAKE A FOOL OF MYSELF IN FRONT OF THE ENTIRE SCHOOL.

YOU CAN'T PAY ME ENOUGH FOR THAT!

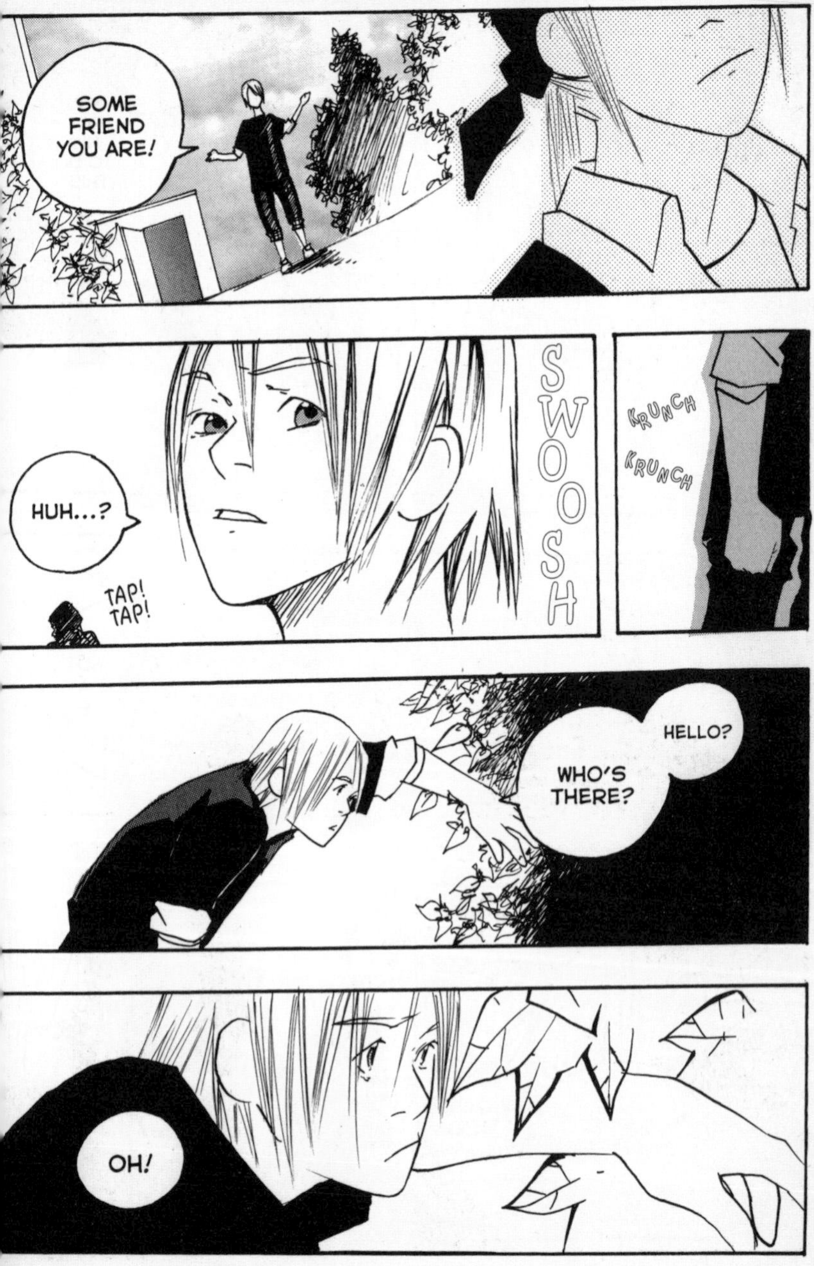
SOME FRIEND YOU ARE!
KRUNCH
KRUNCH
SWOOSH
HUH...?
TAP! TAP!
HELLO?
WHO'S THERE?
OH!

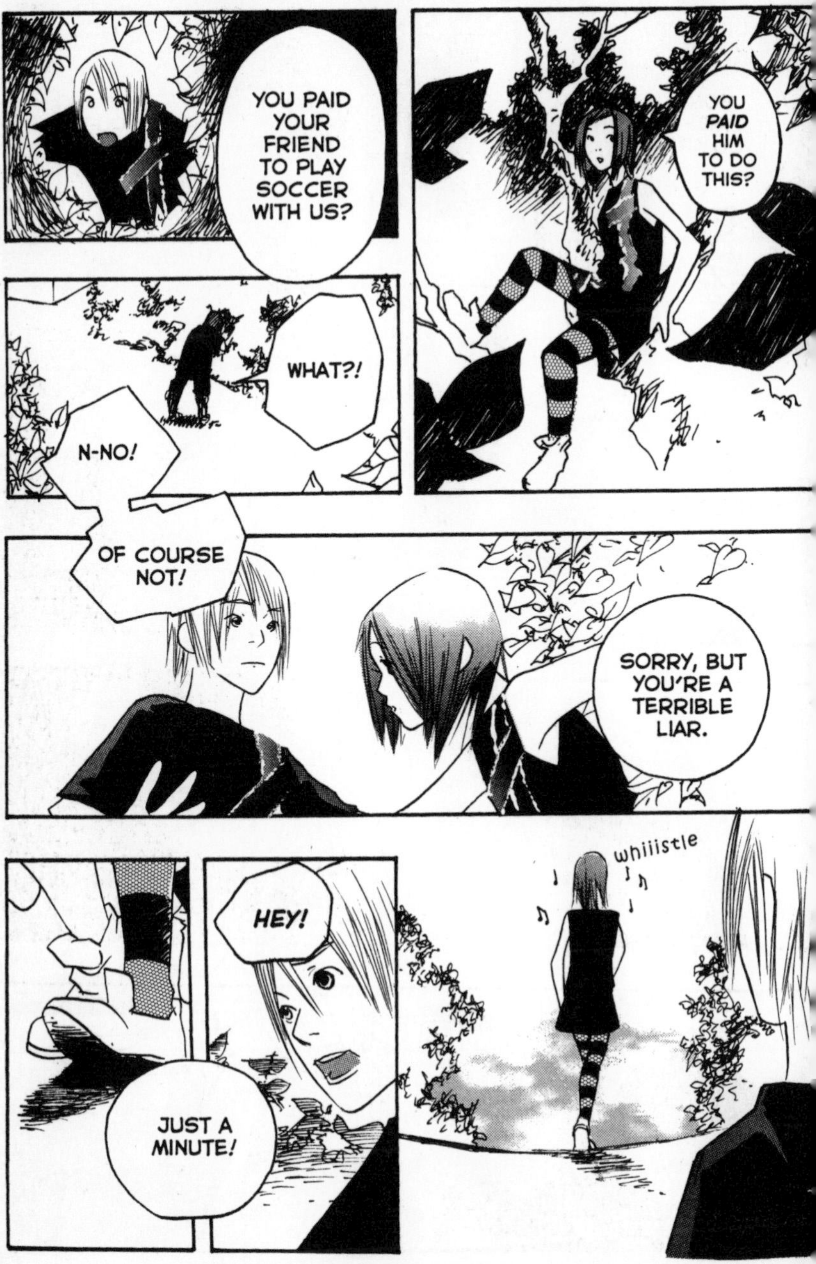
YOU PAID HIM TO DO THIS?
YOU PAID YOUR FRIEND TO PLAY SOCCER WITH US?
WHAT?!
N-NO!
OF COURSE NOT!
SORRY, BUT YOU'RE A TERRIBLE LIAR.
whiiistle
HEY!
JUST A MINUTE!

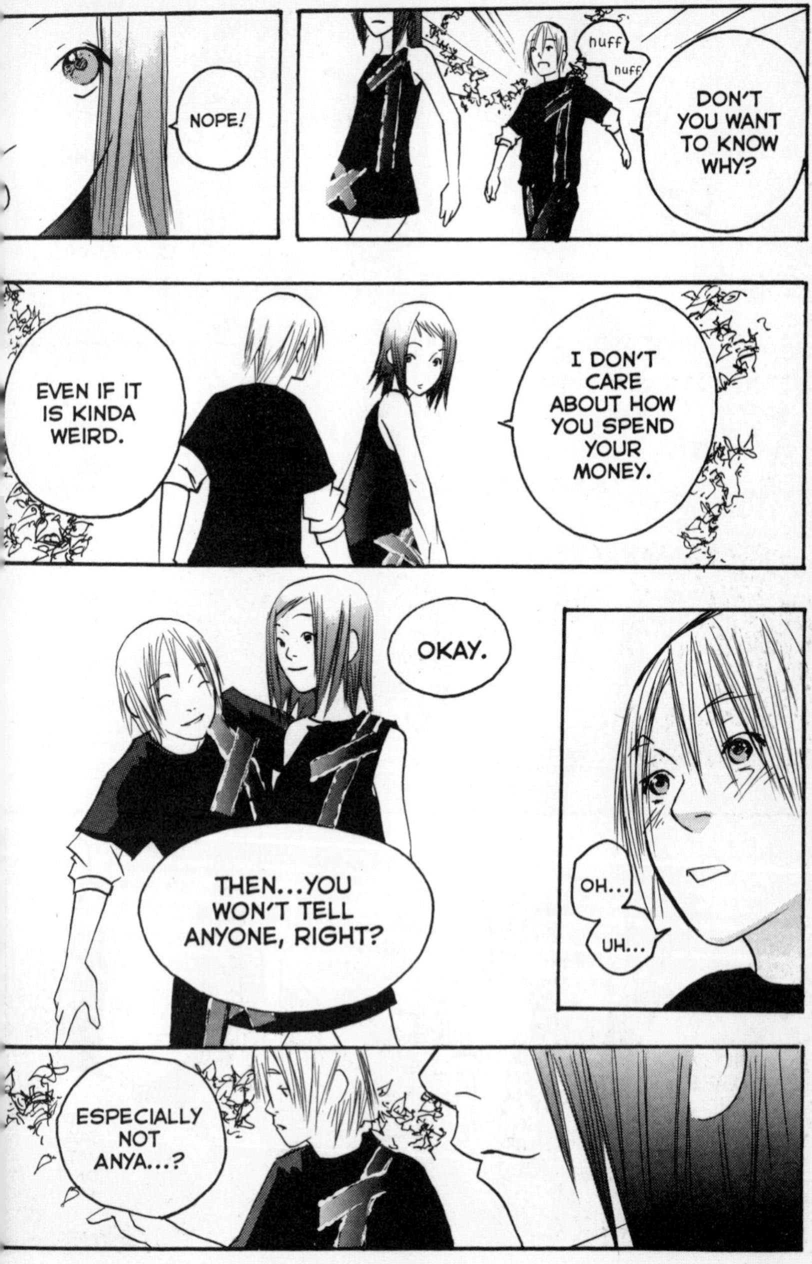
huff
huff
DON'T YOU WANT TO KNOW WHY?
NOPE!
I DON'T CARE ABOUT HOW YOU SPEND YOUR MONEY.
EVEN IF IT IS KINDA WEIRD.
OH...
UH...
OKAY.
THEN...YOU WON'T TELL ANYONE, RIGHT?
ESPECIALLY NOT ANYA...?

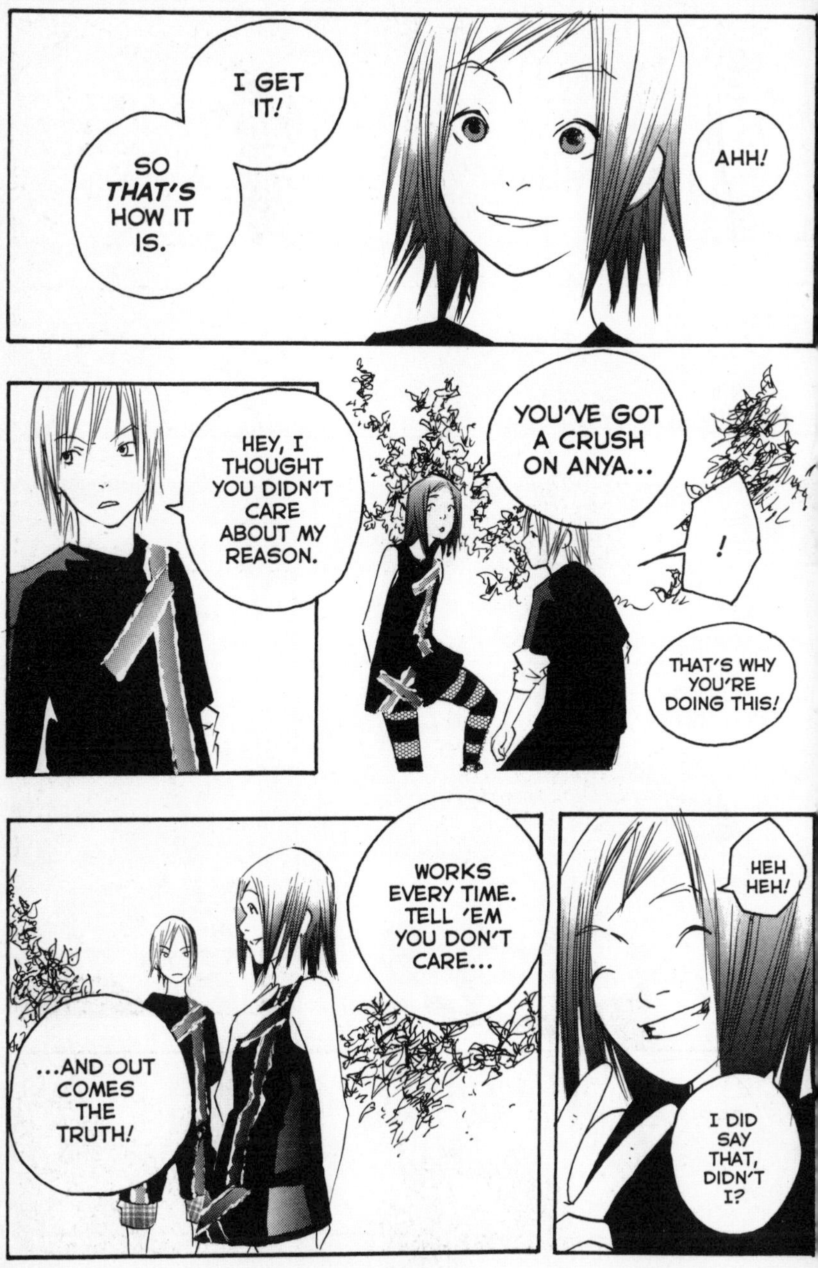
AHH!
I GET IT!
SO THAT'S HOW IT IS.
YOU'VE GOT A CRUSH ON ANYA...
!
THAT'S WHY YOU'RE DOING THIS!
HEY, I THOUGHT YOU DIDN'T CARE ABOUT MY REASON.
HEH HEH!
I DID SAY THAT, DIDN'T I?
WORKS EVERY TIME. TELL 'EM YOU DON'T CARE...
...AND OUT COMES THE TRUTH!

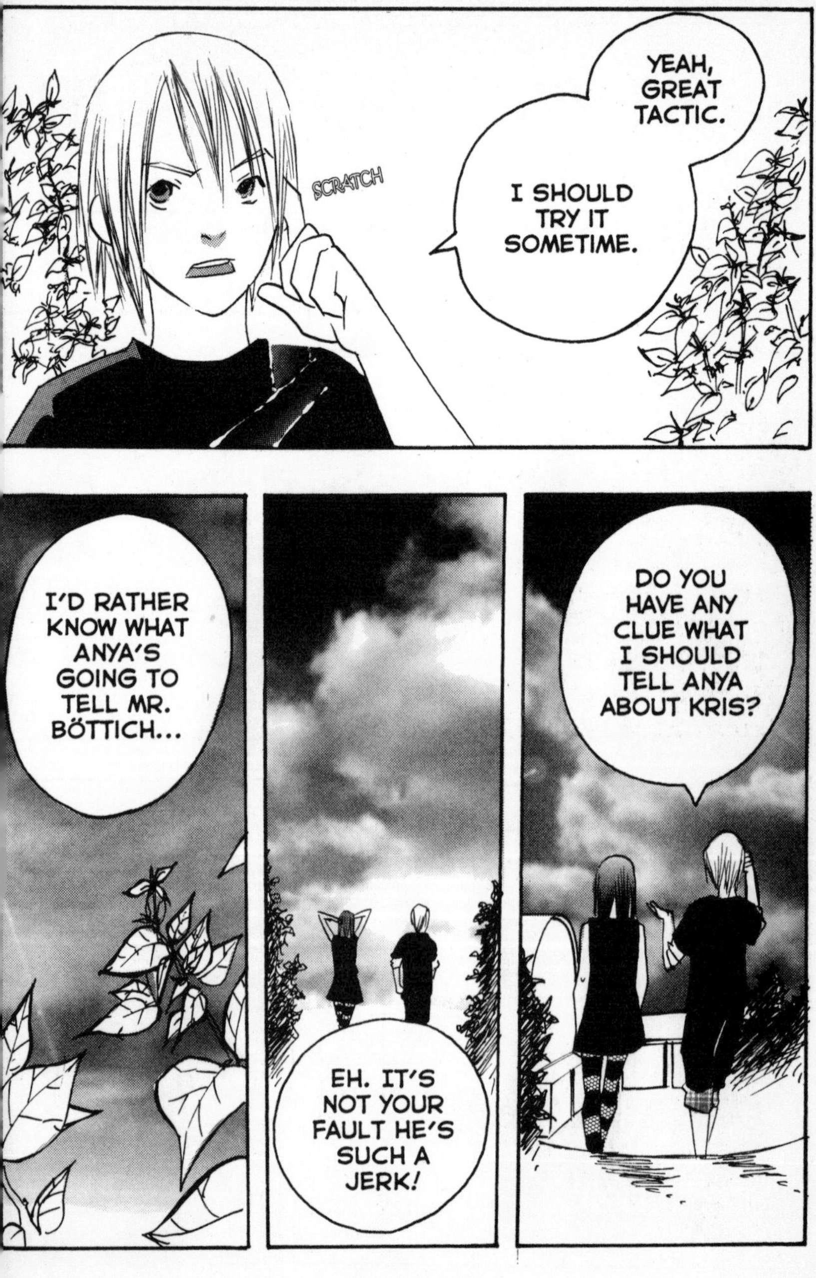
SCRATCH
YEAH, GREAT TACTIC.
I SHOULD TRY IT SOMETIME.
DO YOU HAVE ANY CLUE WHAT I SHOULD TELL ANYA ABOUT KRIS?
EH. IT'S NOT YOUR FAULT HE'S SUCH A JERK!
I'D RATHER KNOW WHAT ANYA'S GOING TO TELL MR. BÖTTICH...

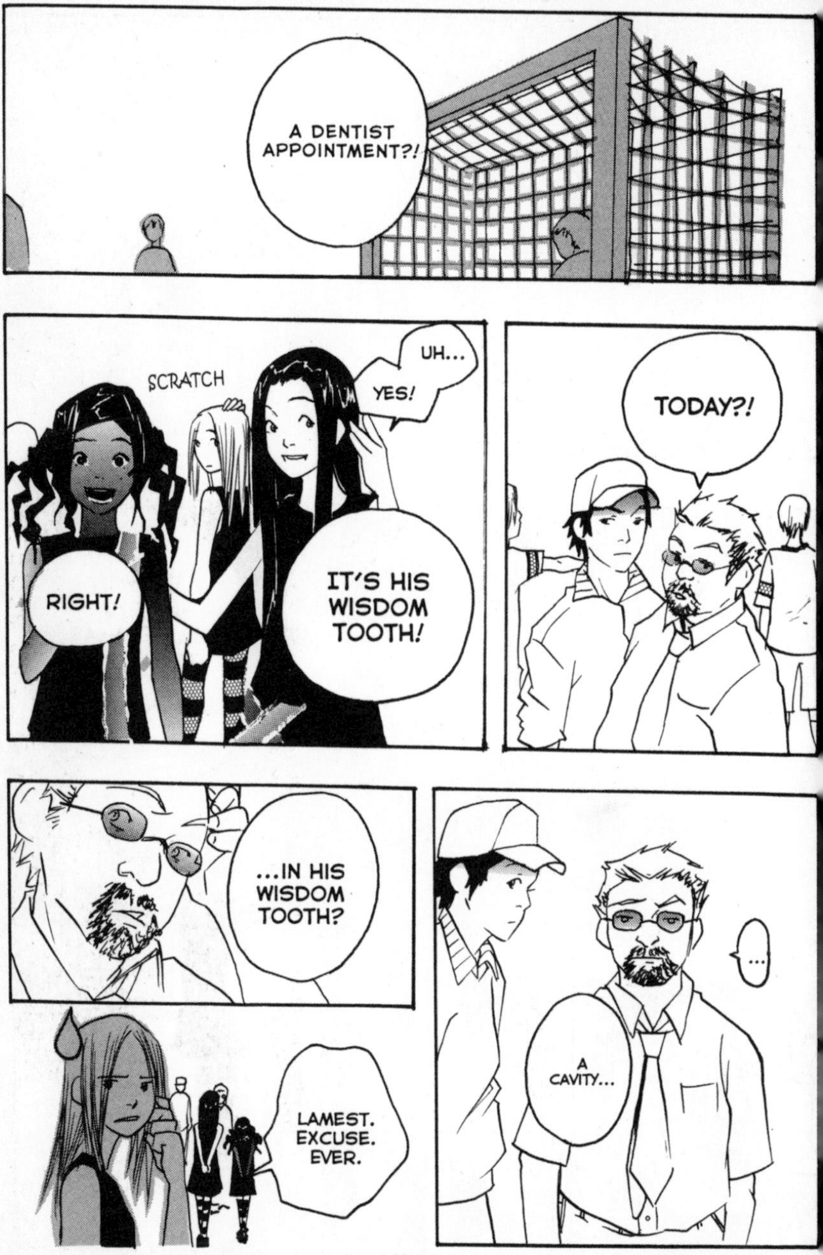
A DENTIST APPOINTMENT?!
TODAY?!
UH... YES!
SCRATCH
IT'S HIS WISDOM TOOTH!
RIGHT!
...
A CAVITY...
...IN HIS WISDOM TOOTH?
LAMEST. EXCUSE. EVER.

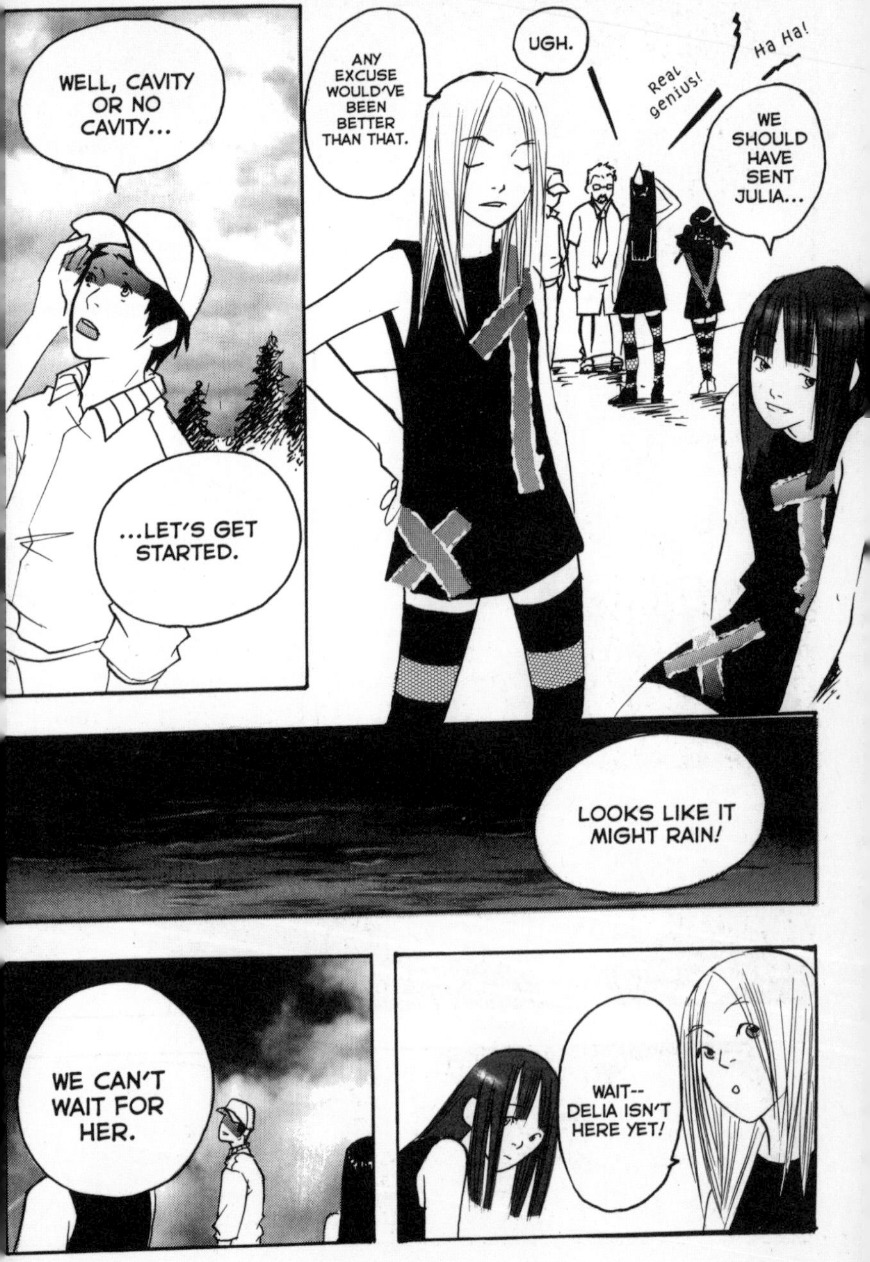
Ha Ha!
Real genius!
WE SHOULD HAVE SENT JULIA...
UGH.
ANY EXCUSE WOULD'VE BEEN BETTER THAN THAT.
WELL, CAVITY OR NO CAVITY...
...LET'S GET STARTED.
LOOKS LIKE IT MIGHT RAIN!
WAIT-- DELIA ISN'T HERE YET!
WE CAN'T WAIT FOR HER.

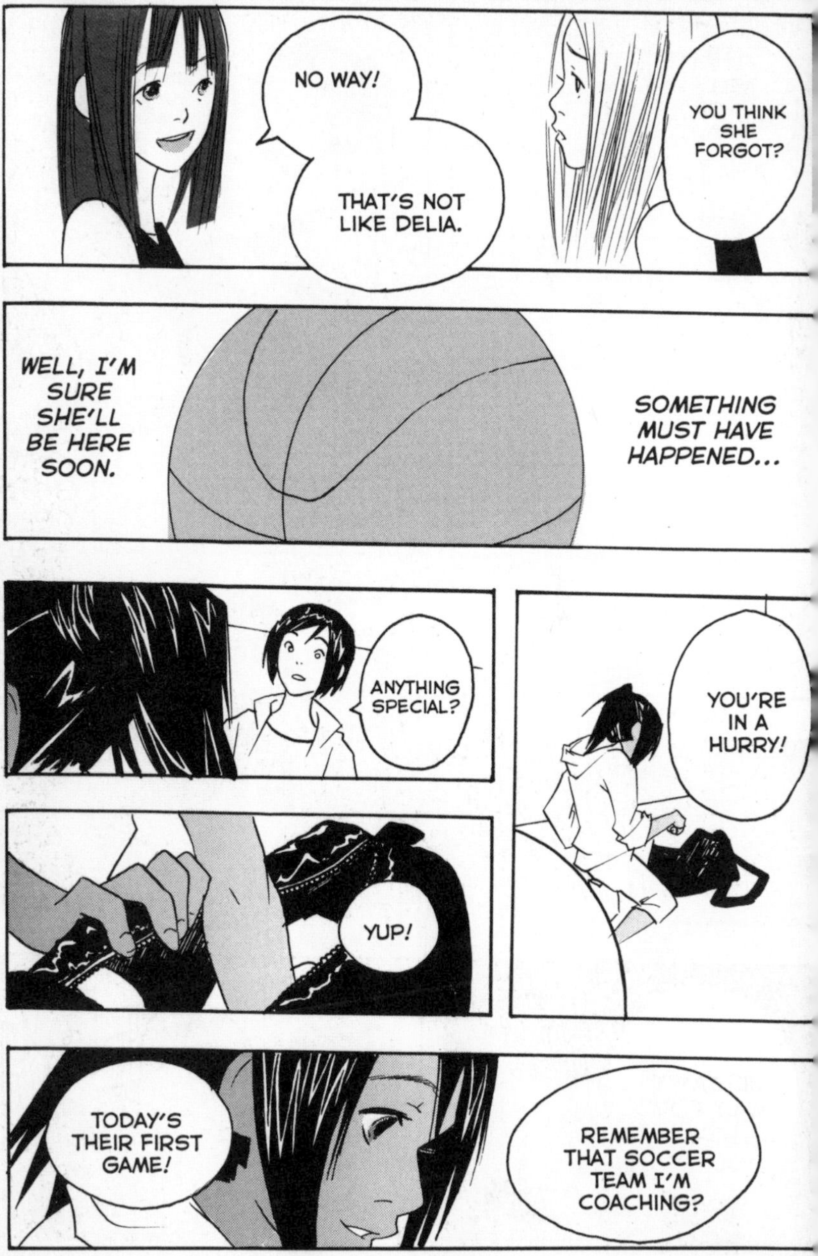
YOU THINK SHE FORGOT?
NO WAY!
THAT'S NOT LIKE DELIA.
SOMETHING MUST HAVE HAPPENED...
WELL, I'M SURE SHE'LL BE HERE SOON.
YOU'RE IN A HURRY!
ANYTHING SPECIAL?
YUP!
REMEMBER THAT SOCCER TEAM I'M COACHING?
TODAY'S THEIR FIRST GAME!

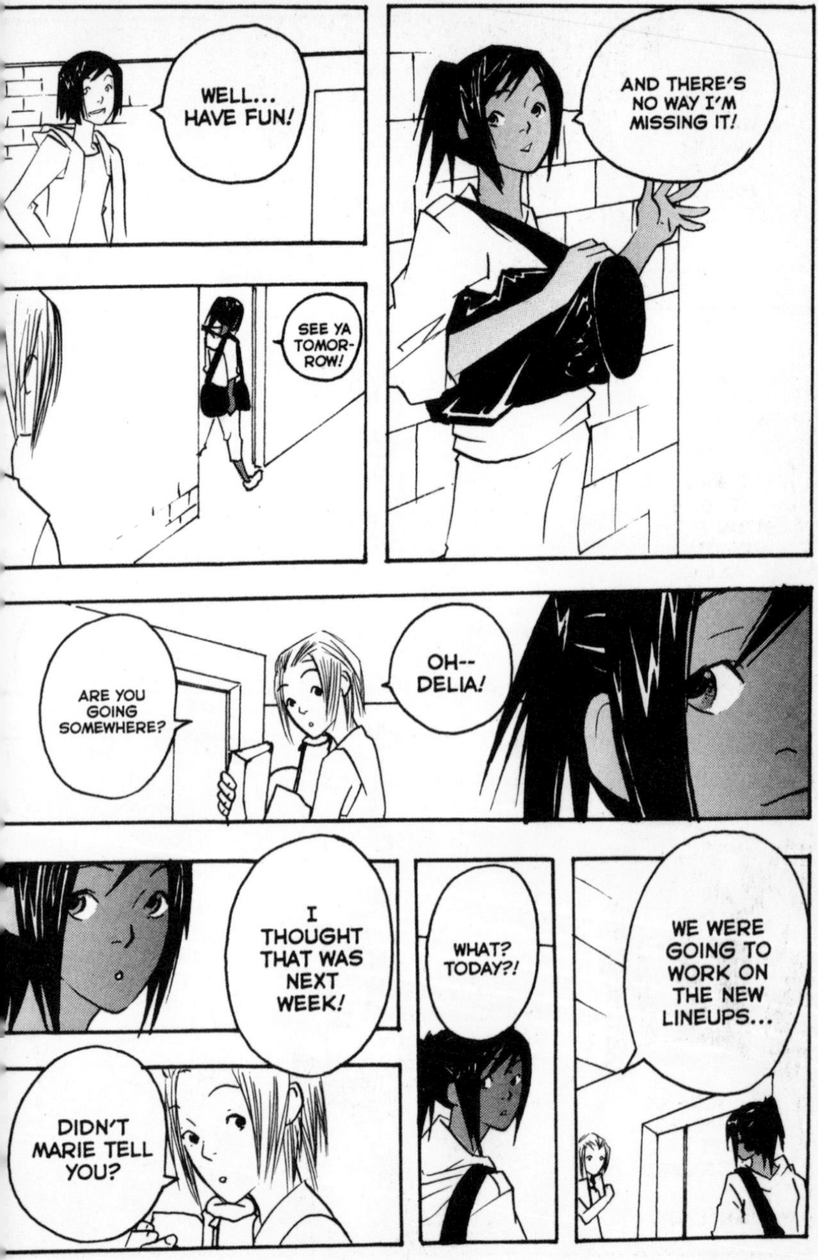
AND THERE'S NO WAY I'M MISSING IT!
WELL... HAVE FUN!
SEE YA TOMOR-ROW!
OH-- DELIA!
ARE YOU GOING SOMEWHERE?
WE WERE GOING TO WORK ON THE NEW LINEUPS...
WHAT? TODAY?!
I THOUGHT THAT WAS NEXT WEEK!
DIDN'T MARIE TELL YOU?

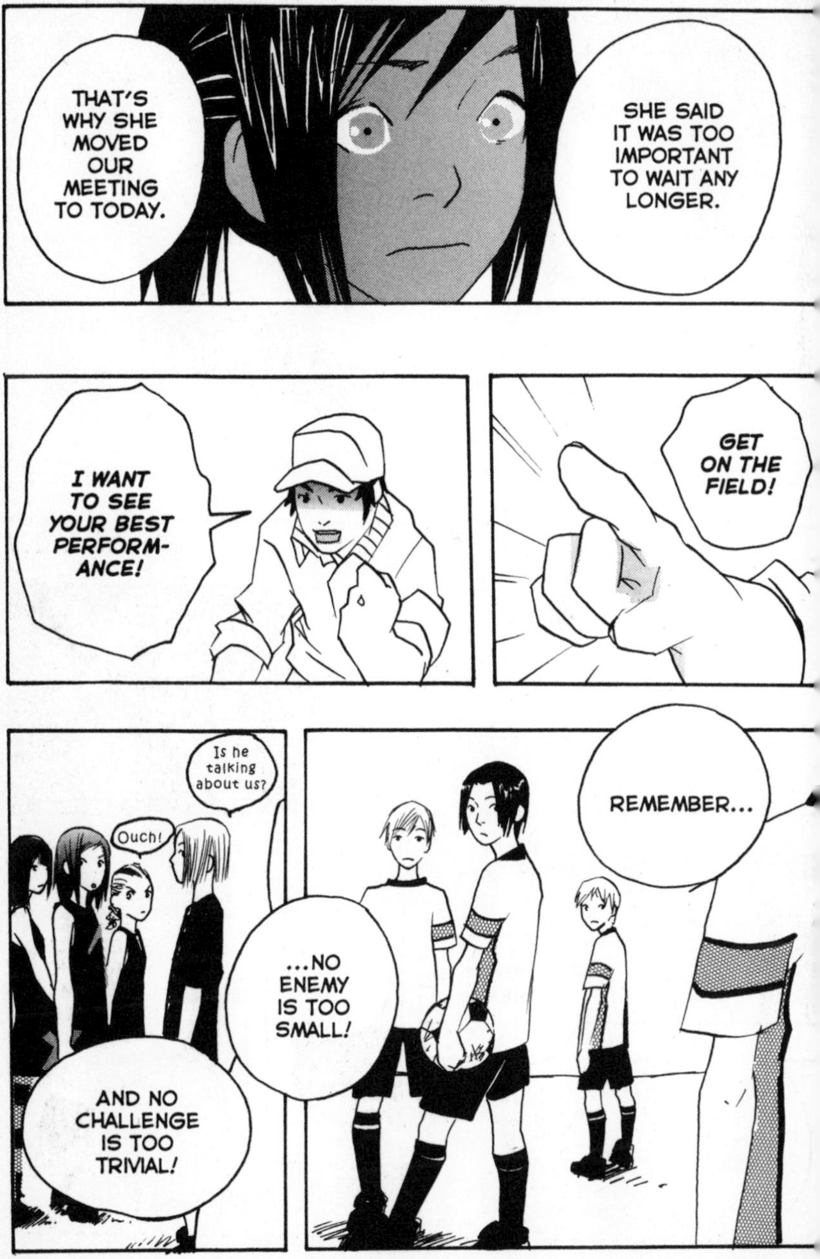
SHE SAID IT WAS TOO IMPORTANT TO WAIT ANY LONGER.
THAT'S WHY SHE MOVED OUR MEETING TO TODAY.
GET ON THE FIELD!
I WANT TO SEE YOUR BEST PERFORM-ANCE!
REMEMBER...
...NO ENEMY IS TOO SMALL!
AND NO CHALLENGE IS TOO TRIVIAL!
Is he talking about us?
Ouch!

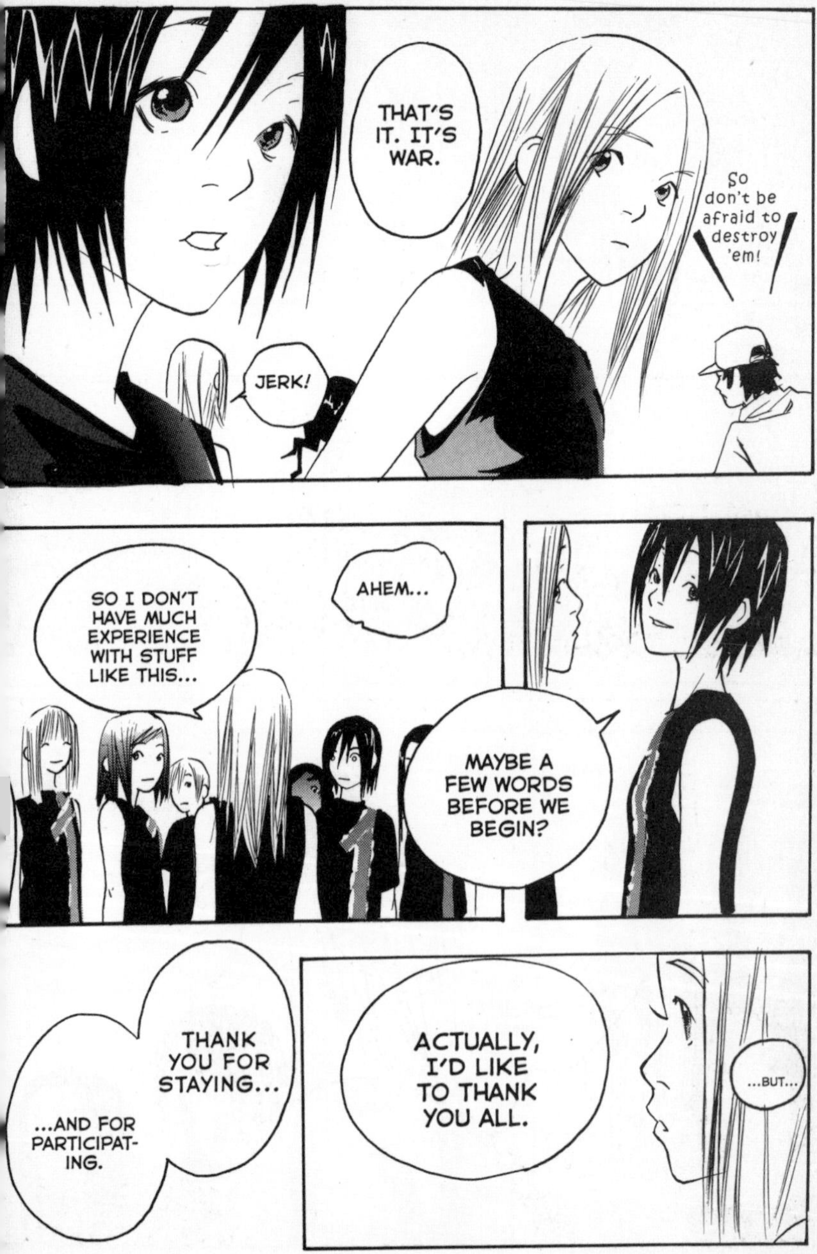
So don't be afraid to destroy 'em!
THAT'S IT. IT'S WAR.
JERK!
MAYBE A FEW WORDS BEFORE WE BEGIN?
AHEM...
SO I DON'T HAVE MUCH EXPERIENCE WITH STUFF LIKE THIS...
...BUT...
ACTUALLY, I'D LIKE TO THANK YOU ALL.
THANK YOU FOR STAYING...
...AND FOR PARTICIPAT-ING.

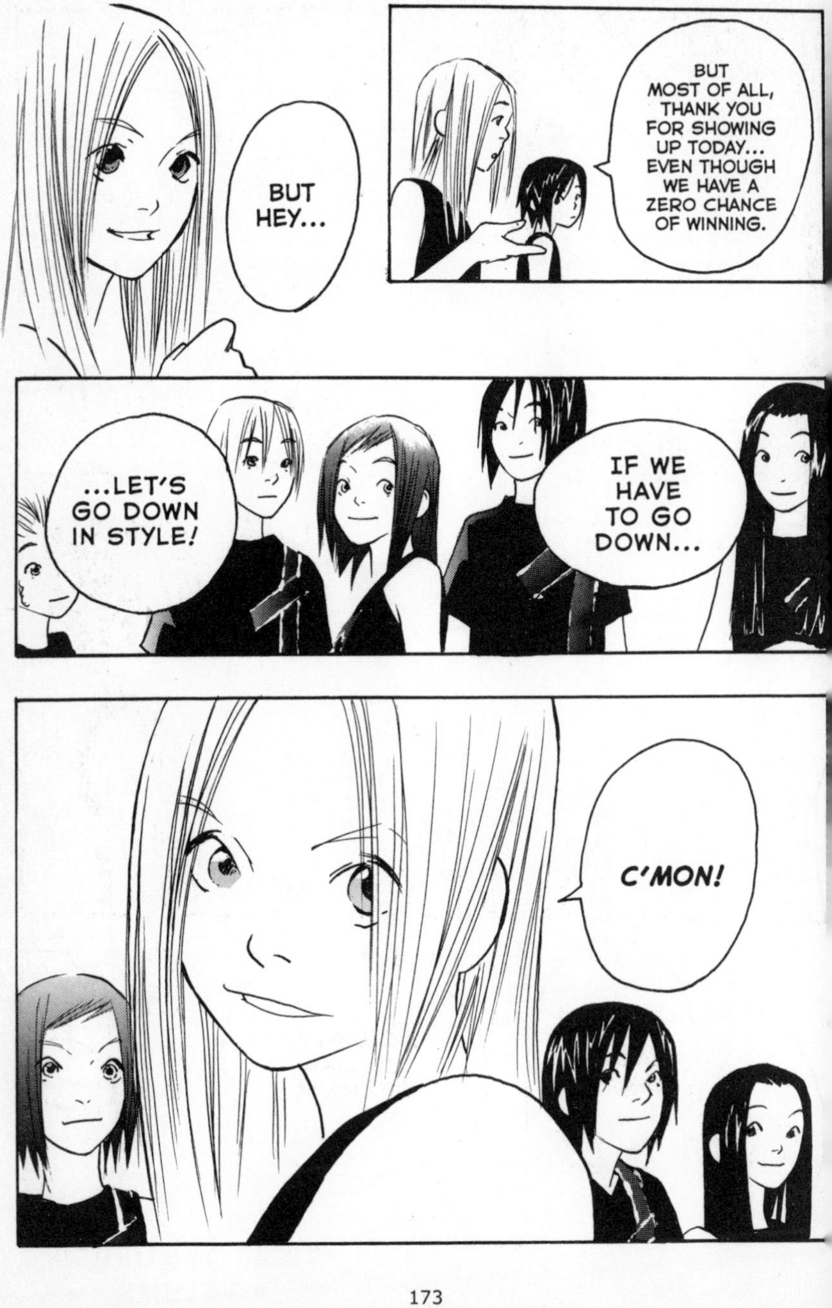
BUT MOST OF ALL, THANK YOU FOR SHOWING UP TODAY... EVEN THOUGH WE HAVE A ZERO CHANCE OF WINNING.
BUT HEY...
IF WE HAVE TO GO DOWN...
...LET'S GO DOWN IN STYLE!
C'MON!

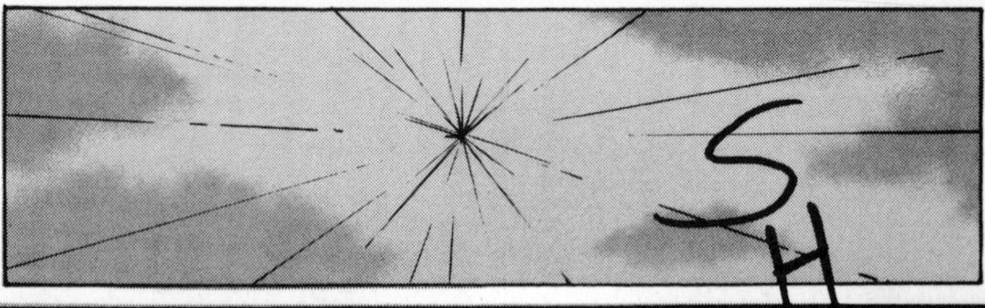
SH

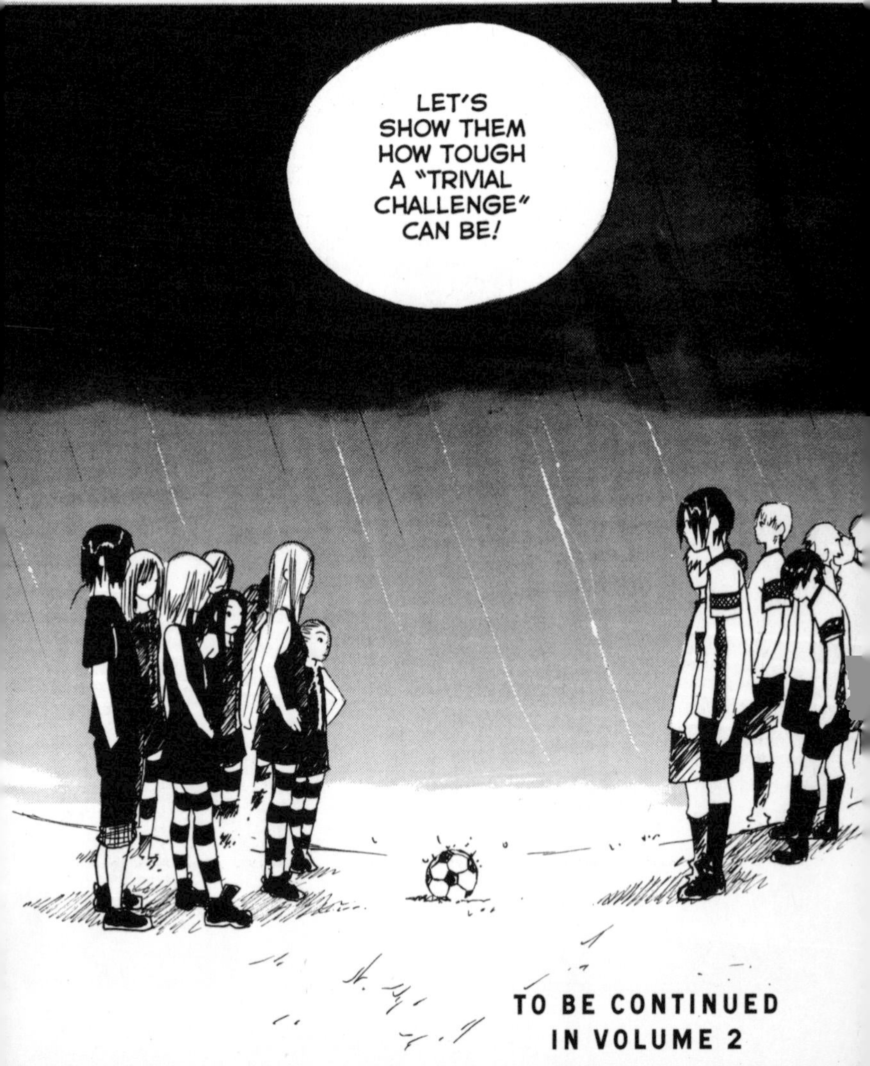
LET'S SHOW THEM HOW TOUGH A "TRIVIAL CHALLENGE" CAN BE!
TO BE CONTINUED IN VOLUME 2

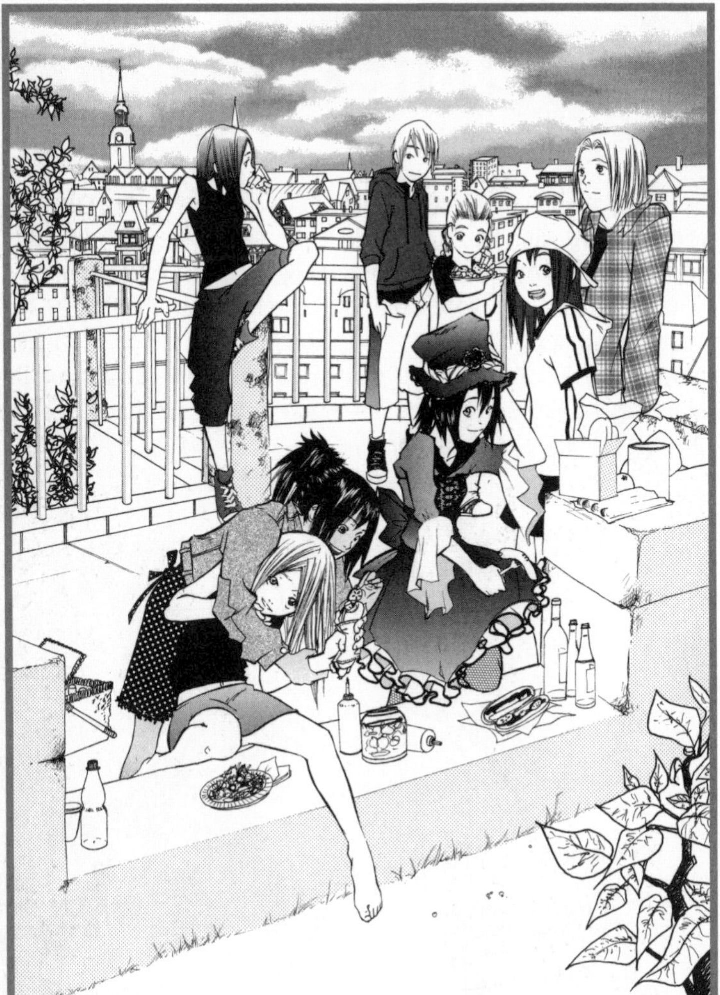

NEXT TIME IN

GothicSports

Our team had a rough start, but they've finally gotten their act together. Now they just have to win the game that will determine their entire future! But does this ragtag team of misfits even stand a chance against the more experienced team? And will they be able to stop fighting amongst themselves long enough to win? Will Delia escape Marie's clutches? And what's the deal with Anya's horrible memories of Leon? Find out the answers to these questions and more in Volume 2 of *Gothic Sports!*

WE INTERRUPT THE MANGA TO BRING YOU THIS VERY IMPORTANT ANNOUNCEMENT:

pause

READ RIGHT-TO-LEFT

If you've been enjoying the unforgettable left-to-right reading experience, we invite you to jump to the front for more cutting-edge manga!

READ LEFT-TO-RIGHT

If you've just soaked up the hottest manga, you need to turn to the back of the book for more of TOKYOPOP's originally created manga!

Of course, if you're blown away by what you've been reading, then e-mail your friends, call your loved ones, and write the president—tell them all about the Manga Revolution!

And make sure you log on to
www.TOKYOPOP.com
for more manga!

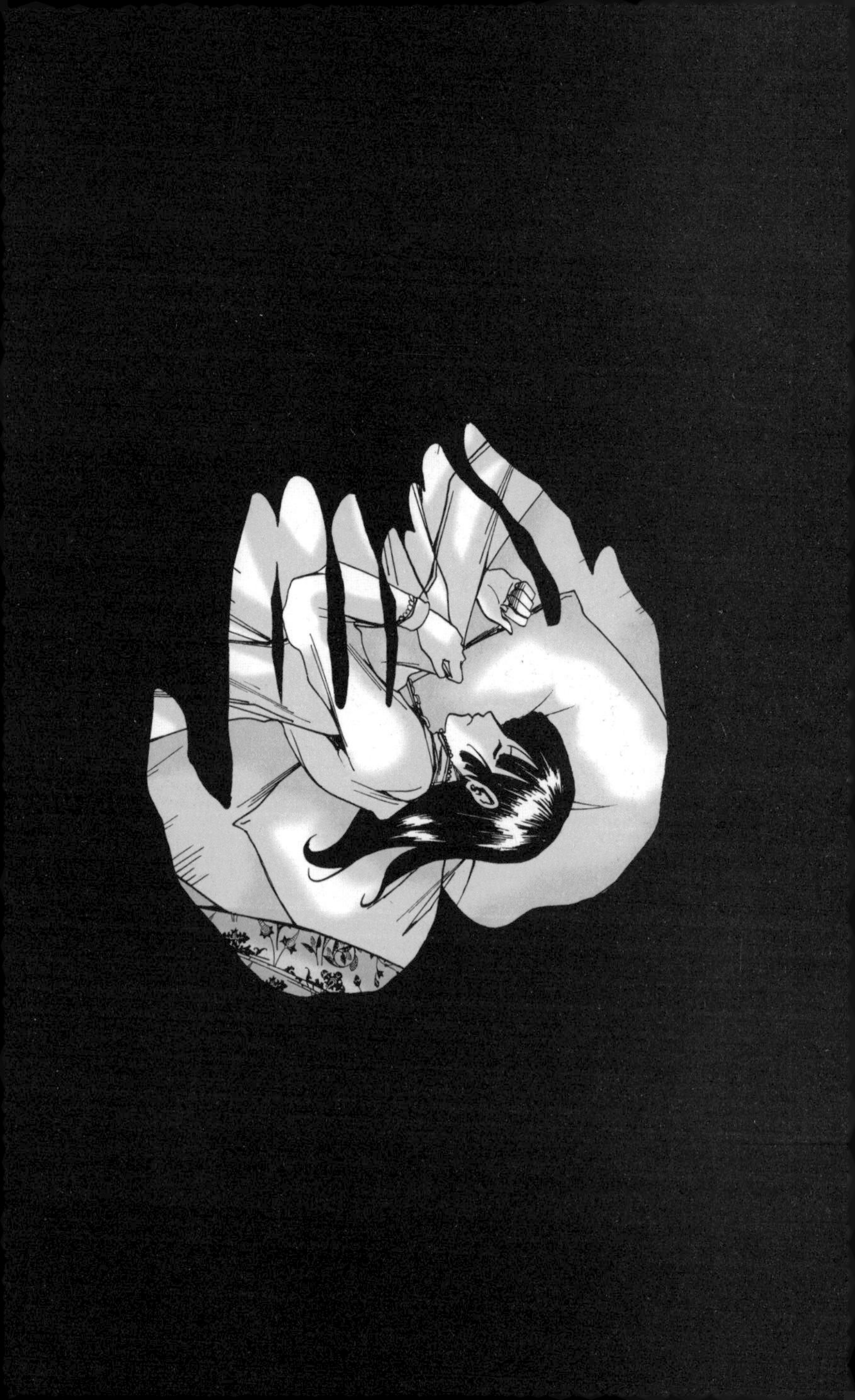

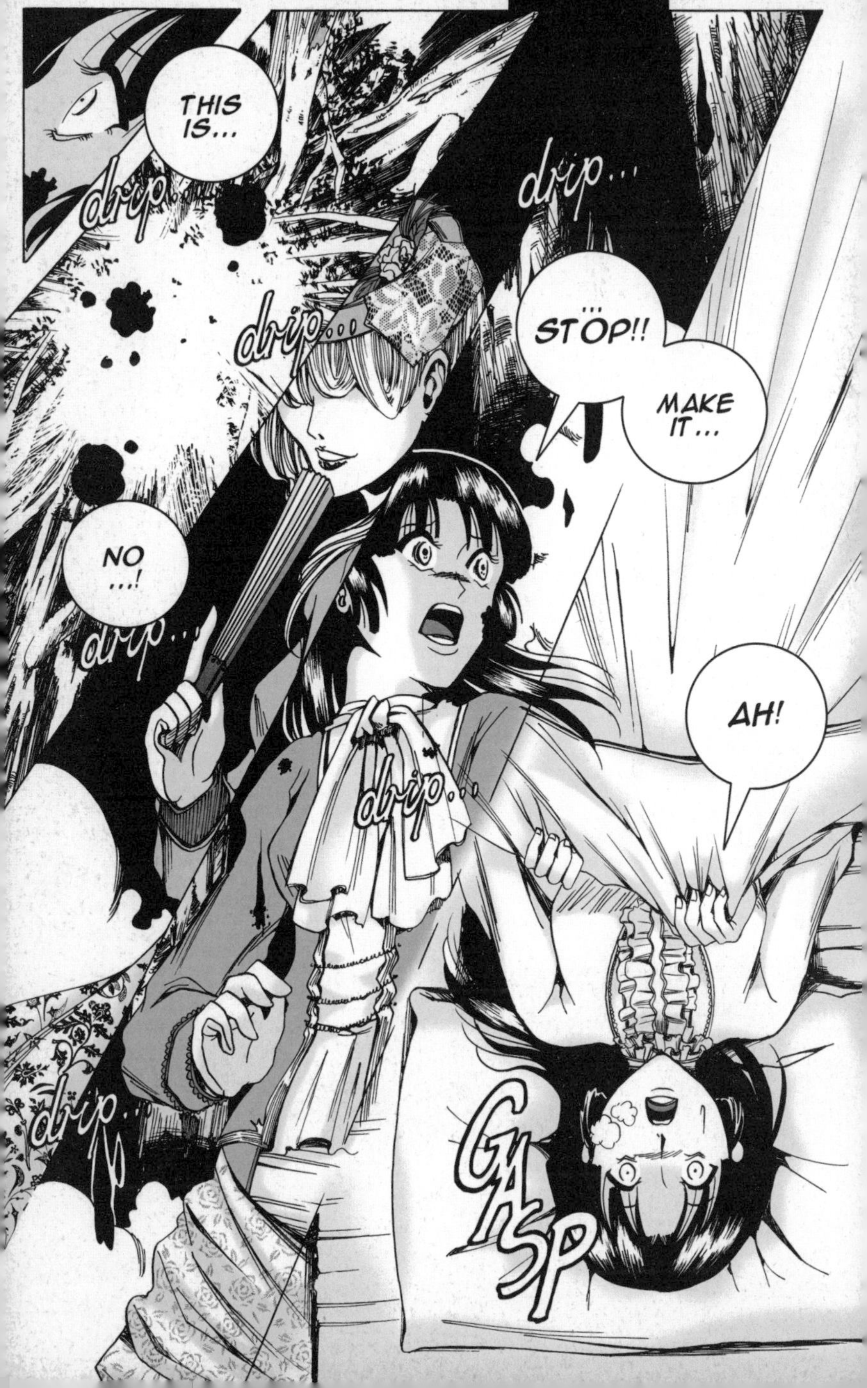

drip...
THIS IS...
drip...
drip...
...STOP!!
MAKE IT...
NO ...!
drip...
AH!
drip...
GASP
drip...

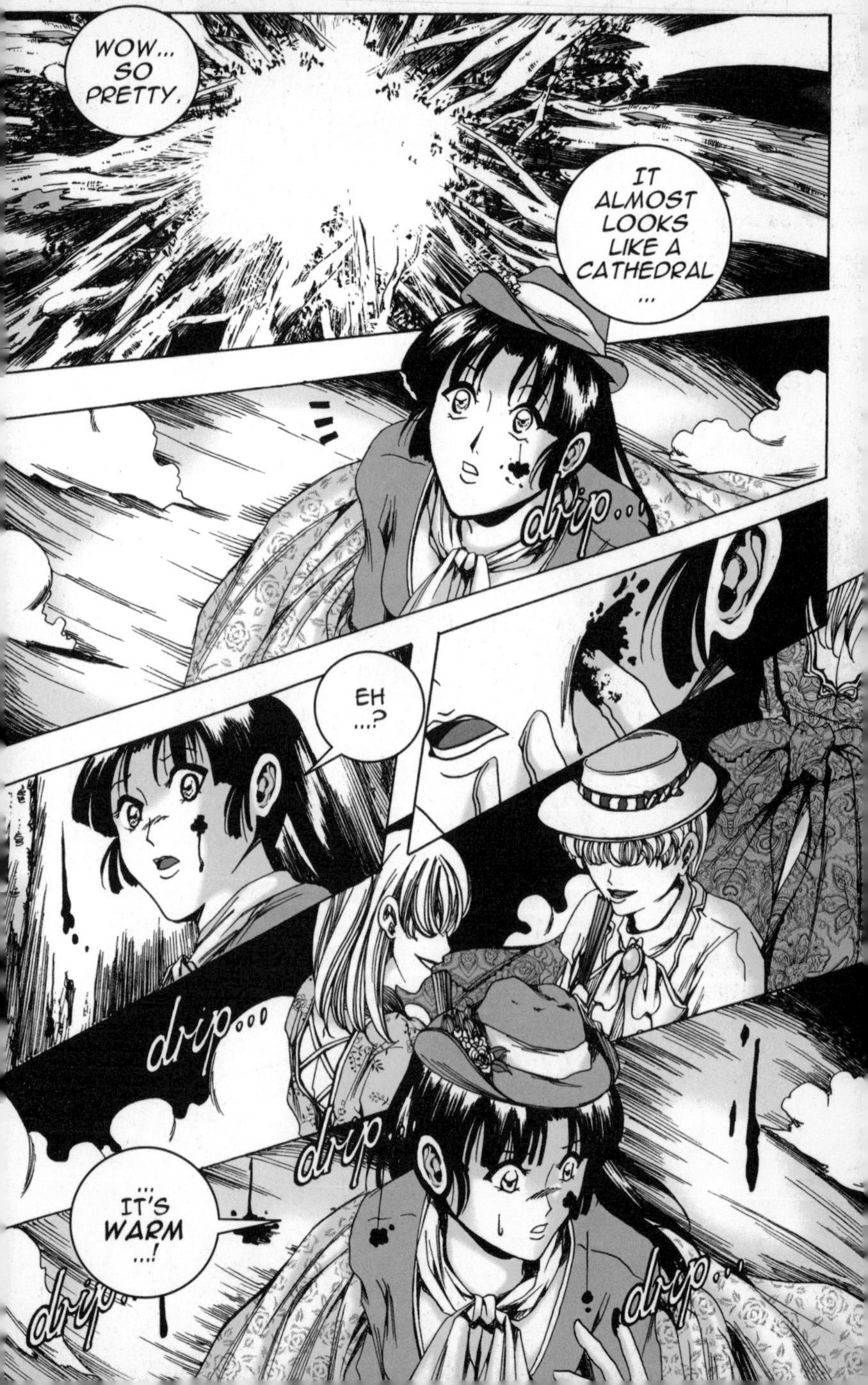
IT ALMOST LOOKS LIKE A CATHEDRAL ...
WOW... SO PRETTY.
drip...
EH ...?
drip...
drip...
... IT'S WARM ...!
drip...
drip...

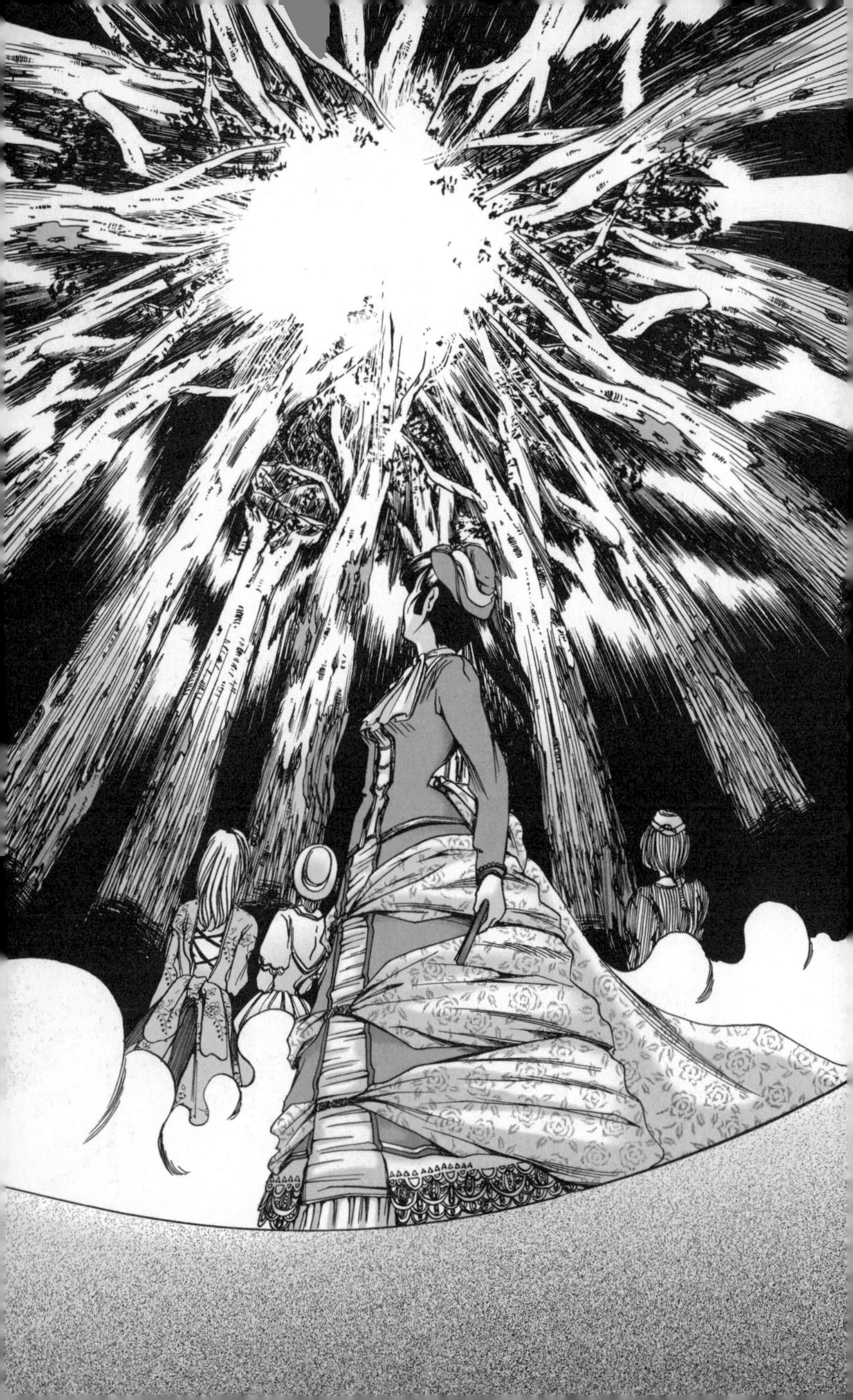

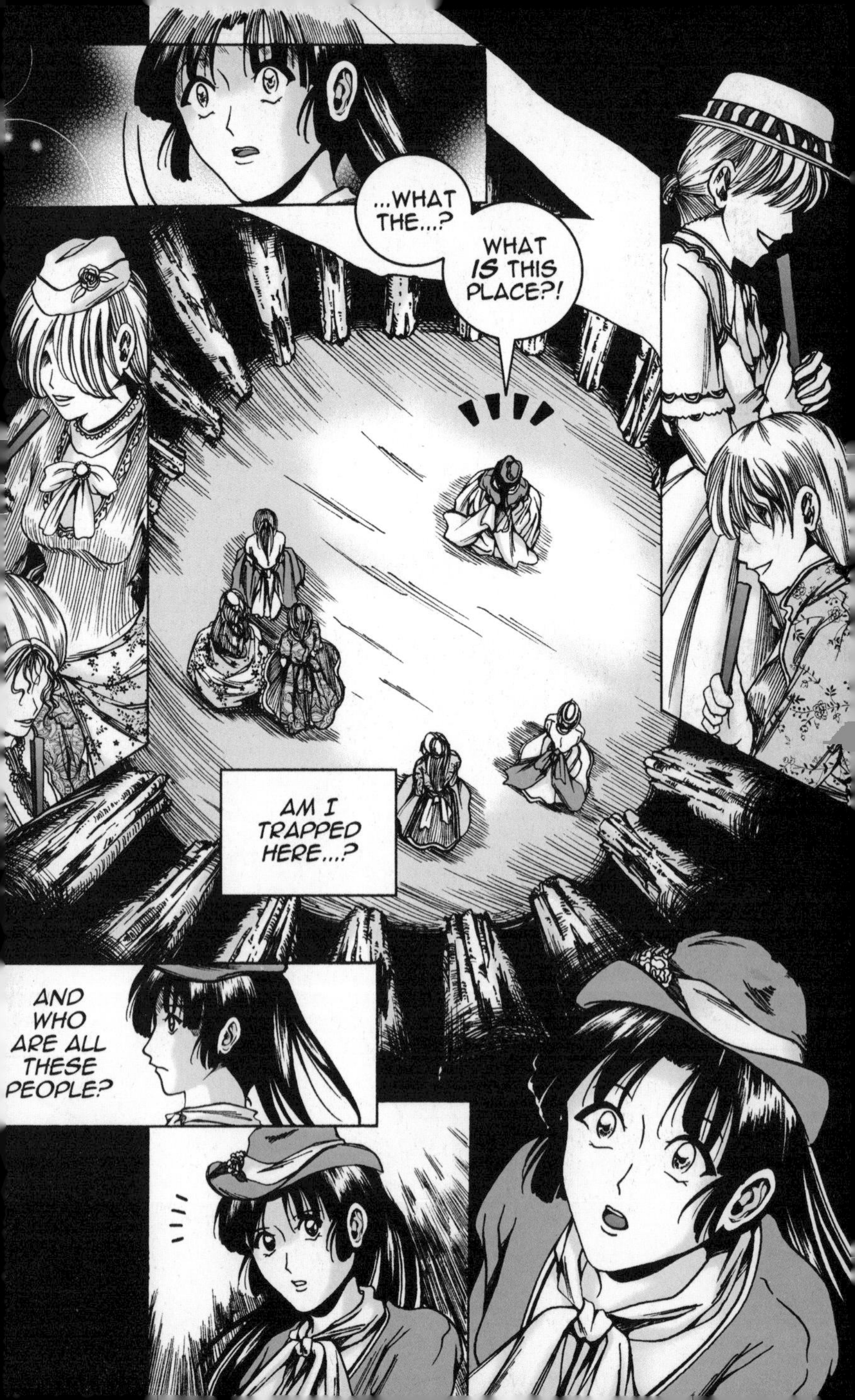
...WHAT THE...?
WHAT IS THIS PLACE?!
AM I TRAPPED HERE...?
AND WHO ARE ALL THESE PEOPLE?

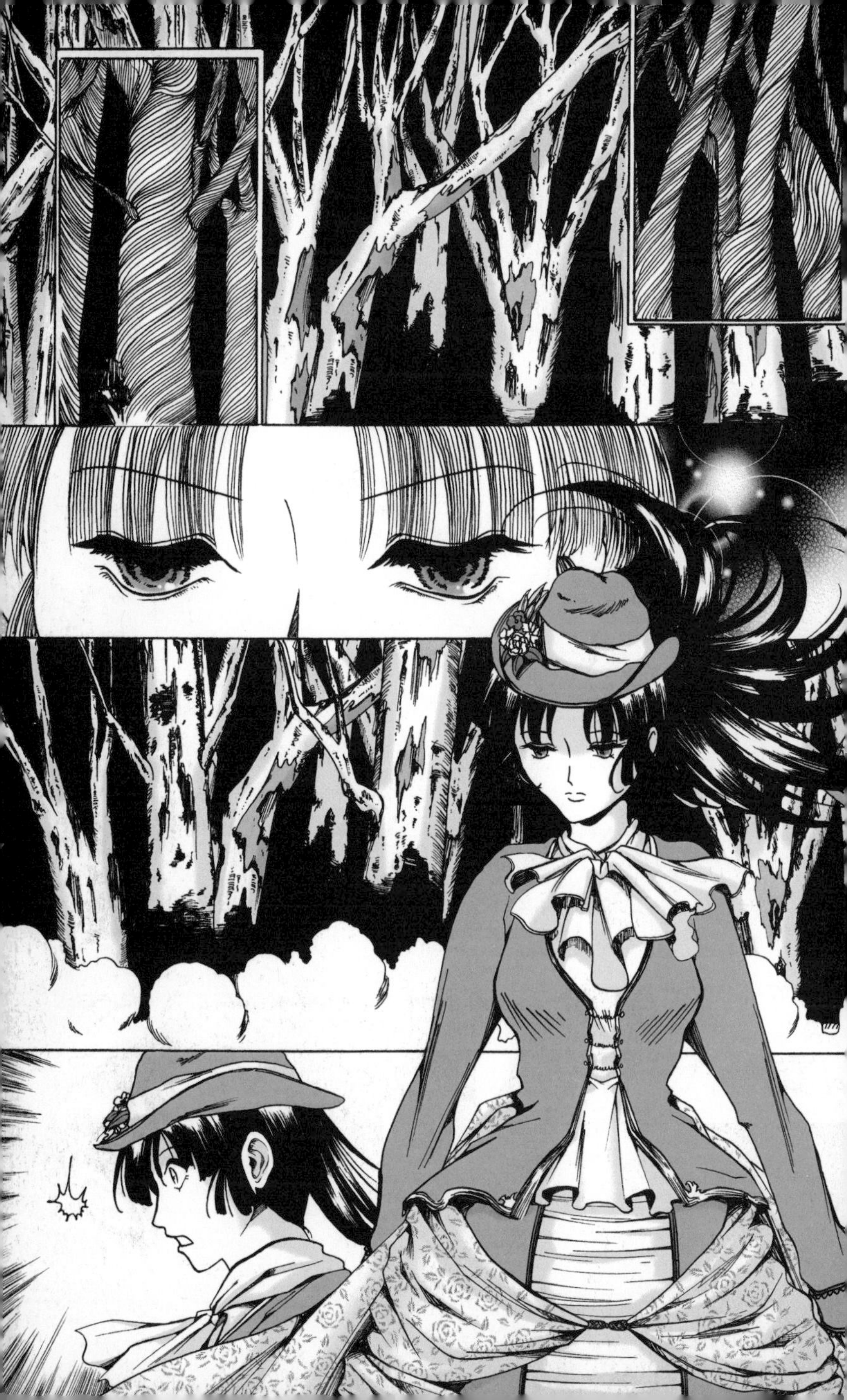

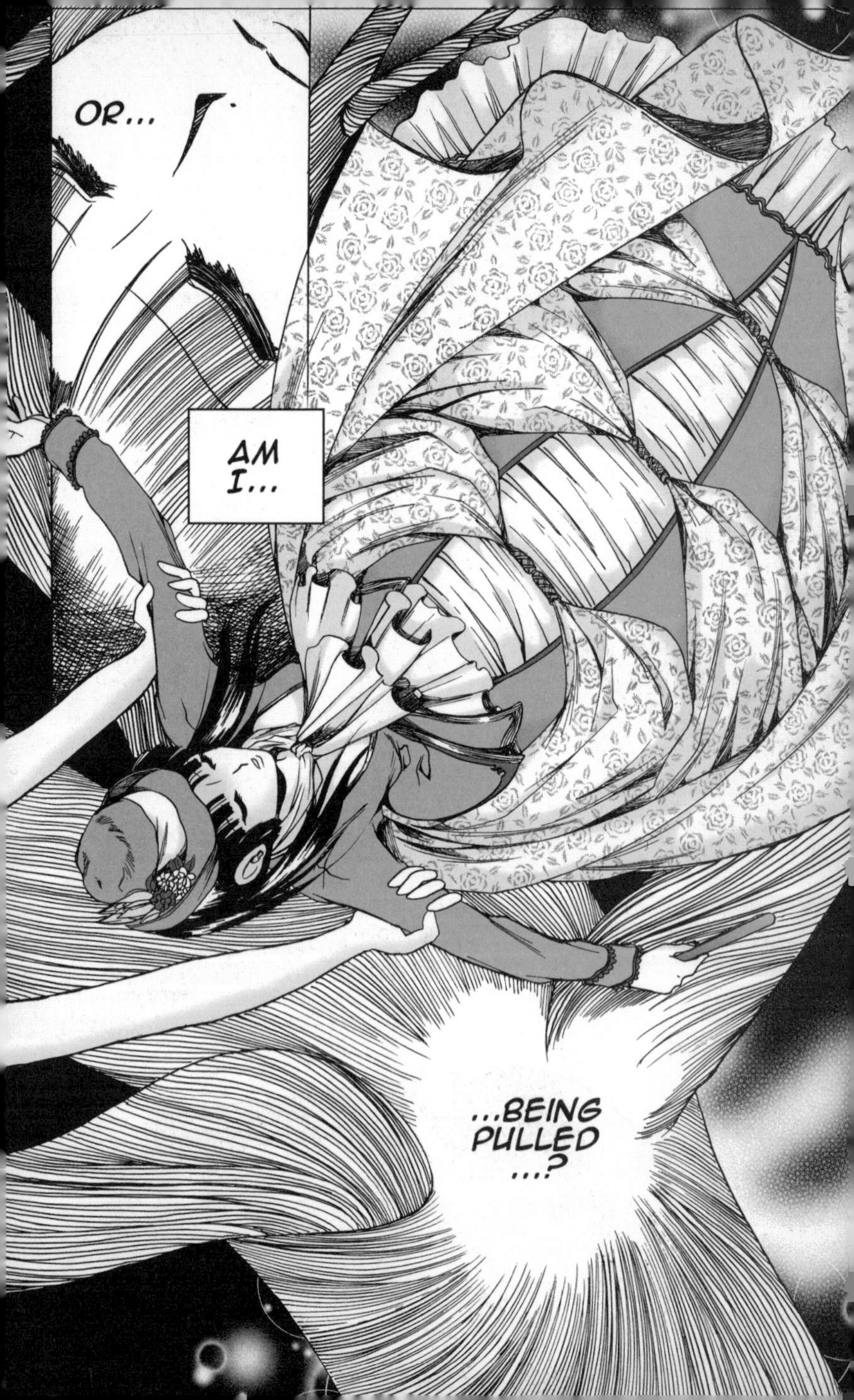
OR...
AM I...
...BEING PULLED ...?

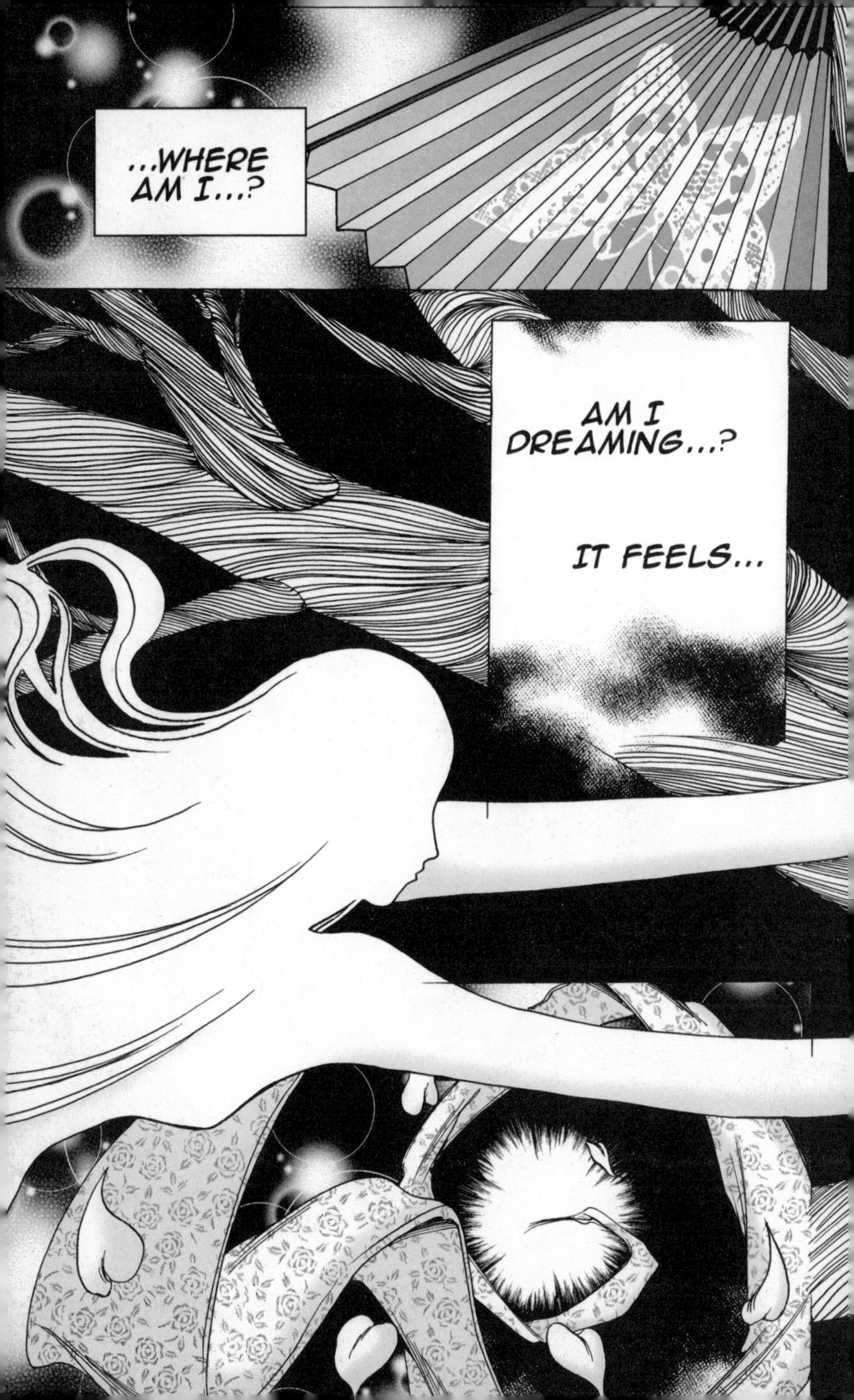
...WHERE AM I...?
AM I DREAMING...?
IT FEELS...

Chapter 3
The Dreaming

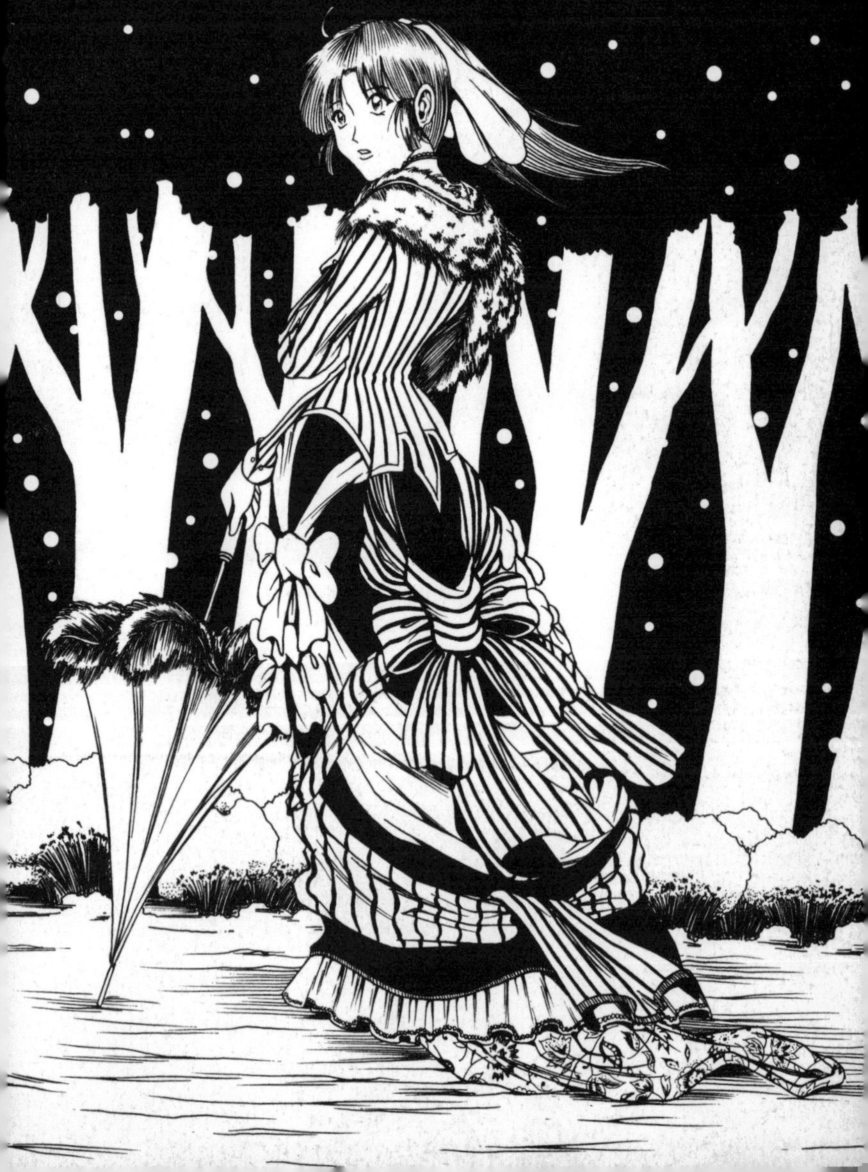

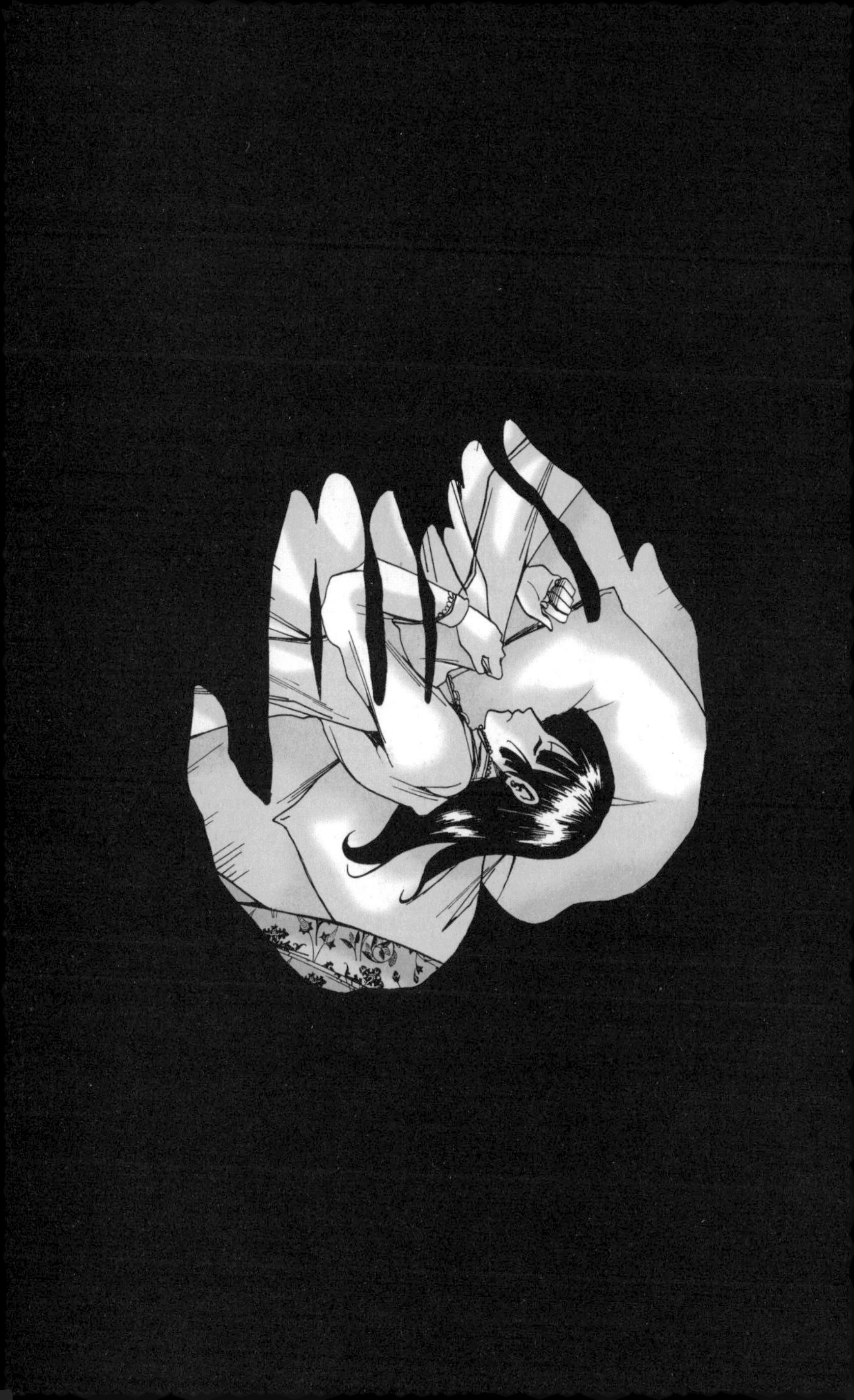

TOKYOPOP® · PRESENTS ·

A PREVIEW OF

the dreaming

ENJOY!

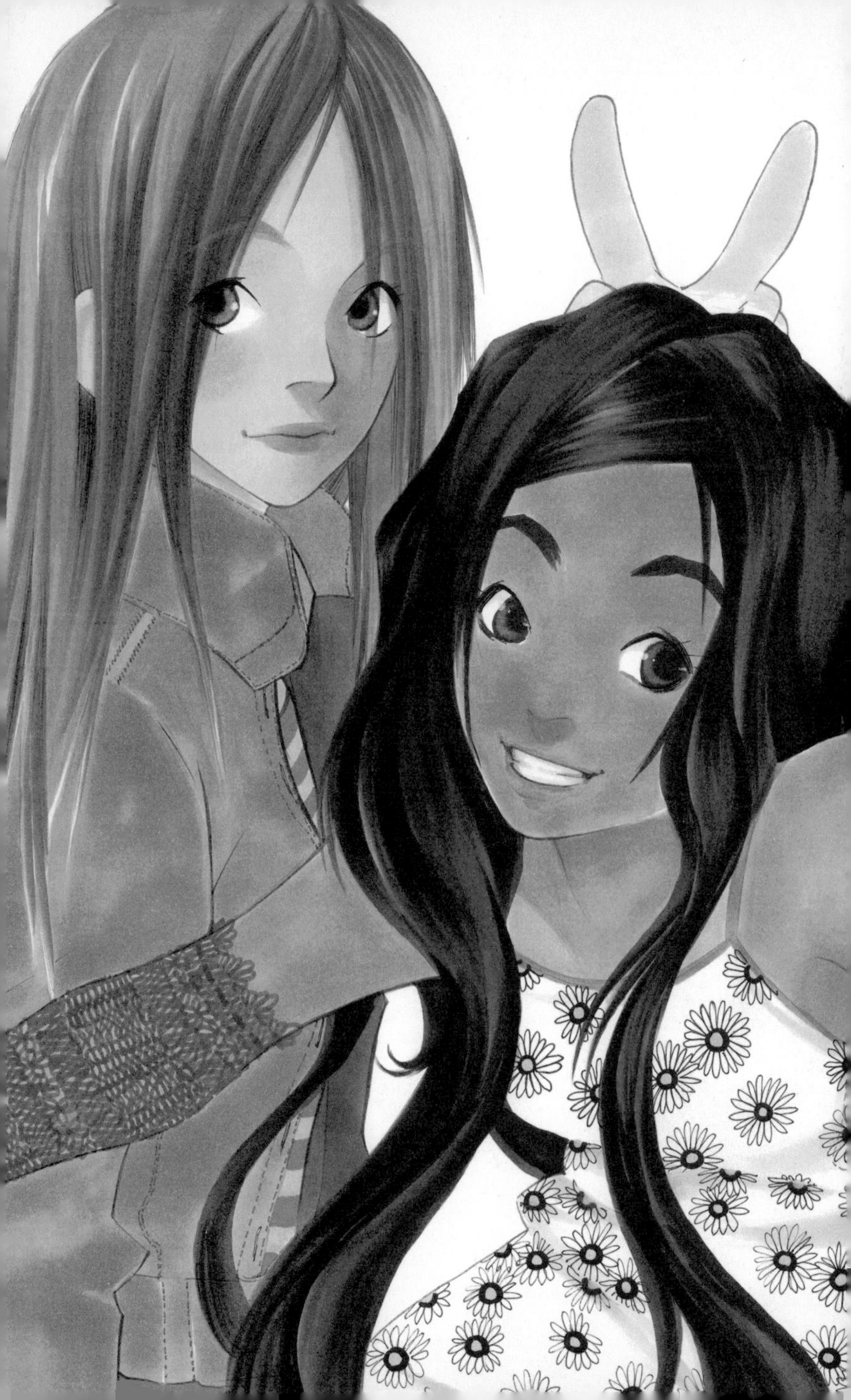

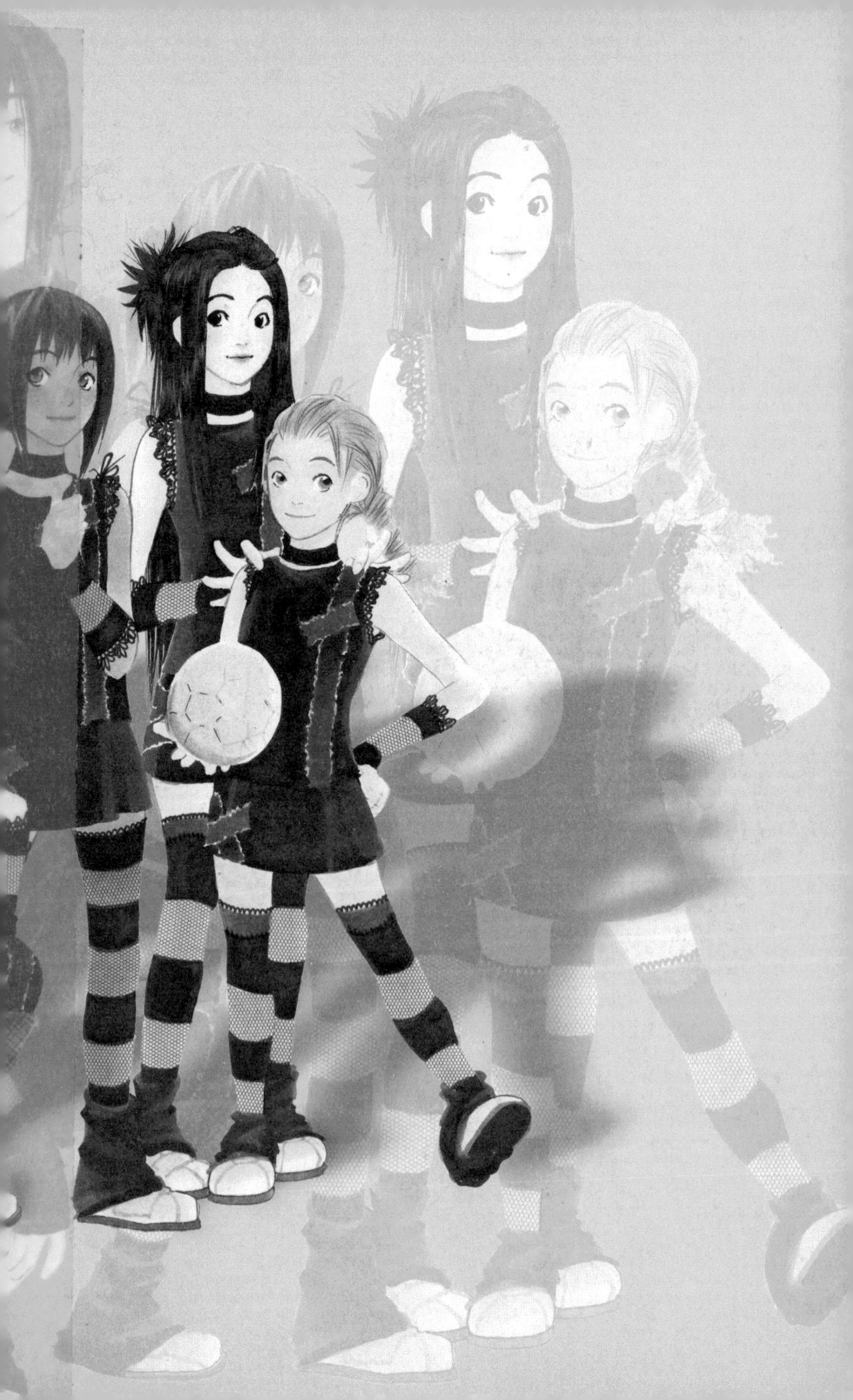

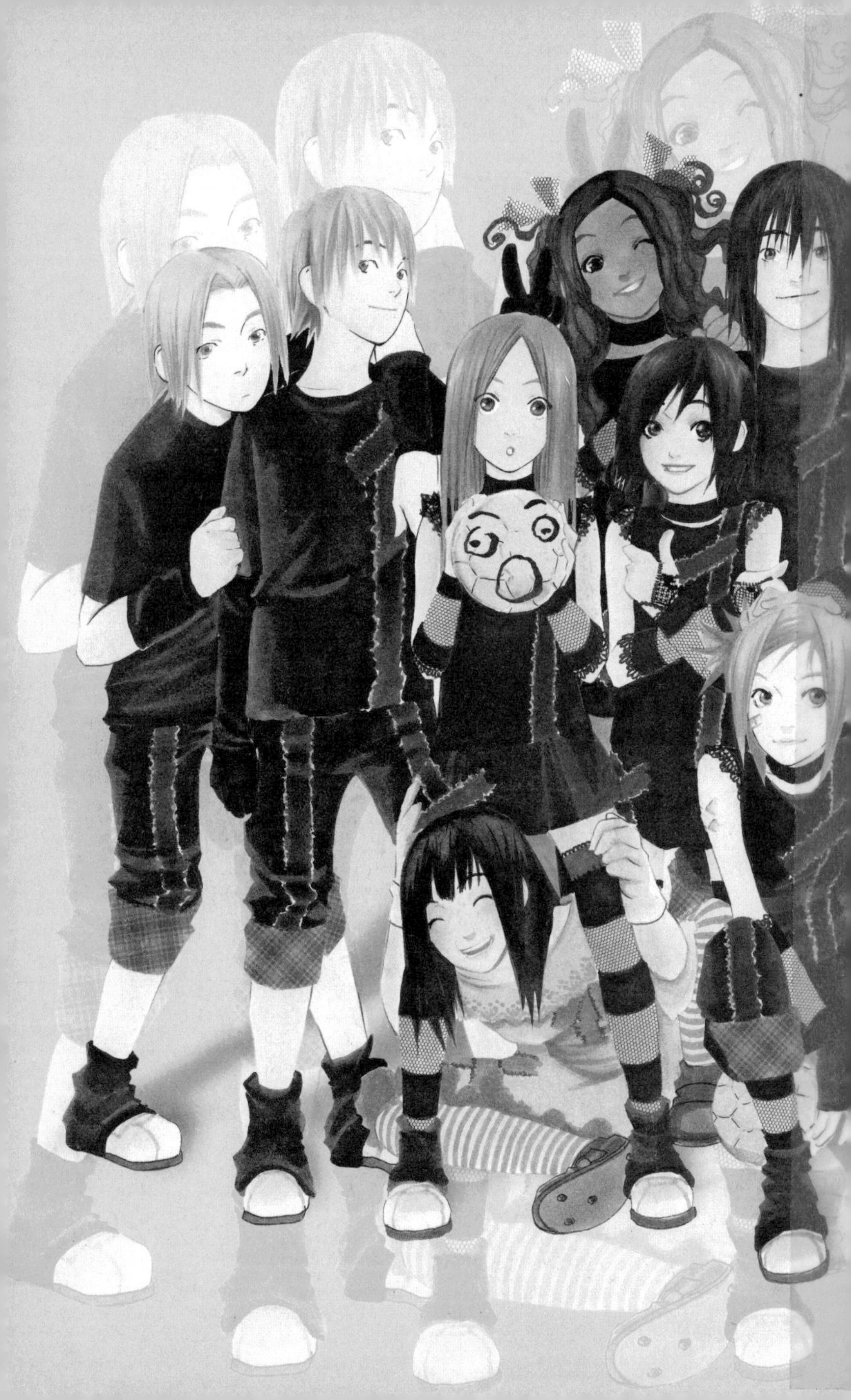

STOP!

This is the back of the book.
You wouldn't want to spoil a great ending!

This book is printed "manga-style," in the authentic Japanese right-to-left format. Since none of the artwork has been flipped or altered, readers get to experience the story just as the creator intended. You've been asking for it, so TOKYOPOP® delivered: authentic, hot-off-the-press, and far more fun!

DIRECTIONS

If this is your first time reading manga-style, here's a quick guide to help you understand how it works.

It's easy... just start in the top right panel and follow the numbers. Have fun, and look for more 100% authentic manga from TOKYOPOP®!